BUSINESS STUDIES now! FOR GCSE

Second edition

BUSINESS STUDIES now! FOR GCSE

Second edition

KAREN BORRINGTON

PETER STIMPSON

HODDER
EDUCATION
PART OF HACHETTE LIVRE UK

© Karen Borrington and Peter Stimpson 1999, 2002

First edition published in 1999
by John Murray (Publishers) Ltd,
338 Euston Road
London NW1 3BH

This second edition published 2002 by Hodder Education

Reprinted 2003, 2004, 2005, 2006, 2008

Layouts by Wearset Ltd
Illustrations by Tom Cross, Philip Ford, Mike Flanagan, Wearset Ltd
Cover design by John Townson/Creation
Cover photo: www.pictor.com
Typeset in 11/13 Galliard by Wearset Ltd, Boldon, Tyne and Wear
Printed and Bound in Dubai

A CIP record for this book is available from the British Library.

ISBN : 978 0 719 57266 1

Contents

Acknowledgements

The authors would like to thank Carolyn Burch and Jenny Francis at John Murray for their guidance and determination to keep us to schedule, and Jackie, Emma, Kimberley and Zoe for their unfailing patience and support.

Karen Borrington (*Ecclesbourne School, Derbyshire*)
Peter Stimpson (*Hurtwood House School, Surrey*)

There is a *Business Studies Now! CD-ROM* available to support your preparation for GCSE.
  The CD-ROM contains:

- A **Summary grid** showing how the book and the CD-ROM map on to the content of your course
- **Multiple-choice tests** and **gap-filler tests** to help you to check that you have understood and remembered key points from every unit
- **Class activities** to demonstrate how key business principles operate in practice
- **Worksheets**
- A **Revision case study** covering all aspects of the subject in a systematic sequence
- **Answers** to all of the above, where relevant
- A **Practice case study** modelled on the requirements of your examining body
- A **Glossary** with explanations of all key terms.

Business Studies Now! CD-ROM (ISBN 0 7195 7267 3) is available from Hodder Murray Publishers, 338 Euston Road, London, NW1 3BH.
Tel: 020 7873 6000

Introduction and guidance for students

What this book can offer you

This book has been planned with *all* GCSE Business Studies students in mind. Whether you are:

- studying the subject through a school or college for the first time and need a comprehensive textbook
- revising the subject before your examinations and need a helpful study guide
- learning on your own through distance or open learning and need a complete programme of supportive activities

this book should offer you the guidance and detail you are looking for. To make your studying easier, each unit:

- starts with a list of the key issues to be covered and a checklist of what you should know by the end of the unit
- is closely linked to the core content of the syllabus
- includes numerous activities to support and check your progress and to extend your learning beyond the contents of the unit itself
- provides *revision summaries* in the form of spider diagrams containing important ideas in an easy-to-remember style
- includes definitions of key terms – these can also be found in alphabetical order in the glossary on pages 402–408
- ends with revision questions for you to test your understanding of the concepts covered in the unit.

At the back of the book, as well as the Glossary and the Index, there are suggested answers to the unit activities and revision questions.

How to use the book to help your learning

How you use this book will depend much on your learning situation. If you are being taught Business Studies at school or college, your teacher may well suggest the ways in which the book will be used in class. If you are not at a school or college, you are encouraged to take each unit and each section within the units as a complete unit of work. Test your understanding of each of these units by using the activities and questions provided – only check the suggested answers when *you* have attempted each question!

This topic-by-topic approach works well for most students, but do try to remember one very important point – Business Studies is not made up of a series of separate and unconnected topics. The subject attempts to identify and analyse the key issues that managers must consider in running a business. Each of these issues, although they may seem to be only marketing- or finance-based, has an impact on the business in many other areas. If, by the end of this book, you have been made more aware of the way in which Business Studies brings together and integrates many different subject areas, then the book will have achieved one of its aims.

Exam preparation and technique

You should be able to perform to the best of your ability if you:

- revise thoroughly before the examinations – allow plenty of time for this and avoid leaving it until the last minute
- test yourself with the activities and questions in this book.

You can also help yourself greatly if you take the following steps.

- Obtain a copy of your syllabus. You may also be able to obtain past examination papers and mark schemes. It is very important that you check the progress of your learning and revision against the syllabus content. The book contains all the information you will need for the 'core' content of all GCSE Business Studies syllabuses.
- Make sure you know the *number* and *length* of each of the examination papers you will have to sit. The style of questions may vary from paper to paper so you must be quite clear about the type of question likely to appear on each paper. For example, will it contain short answer questions? Will it be based around a case study?

In the examination

- Make sure you check the instructions on the question paper, which will tell you the length of the paper and the number of questions you have to answer. In most cases you will have to answer every question as there will be no choice.
- Allocate your time sensibly between each question. Every year, good students let themselves down by spending too long on some questions and too little time (or no time at all) on others. You will be expected to spend much longer writing an answer to a question worth nine marks than you would when writing an answer worth three marks. Examiners often find that a three-mark question receives more attention than a nine-mark question, which obviously won't lead to the best possible results!
- Remember what the most common 'key' examination words mean. These are the prompt words in every question, such as 'list' or 'discuss'. The following guide should help you.

Key examination words you need to know

State or give

As in 'State three factors which might influence the price of a product.' These two key words mean 'write down without explaining or expanding upon' three factors which might influence the price of a product.

List

As in 'List four reasons why one firm may merge with another.' This is similar to 'state'. Write down, without discussing or expanding upon them, four reasons why firms may merge. You could number your list 1–4. Too often candidates write far too much to both 'state' and 'list' questions.

Explain

As in 'Explain your answer.' Here, the examiner is asking you to give more detail than just listing or stating points.

A common example of a question would ask you to 'State and explain three advantages to a business of developing a new product.' Here you are expected to list the three factors that you consider to be advantages and then go on to explain *why* you think they are advantages to the business. One of the three advantages you give in your answer might be: 'New products will take the place of older products in the market'. Your explanation could be: 'If a business develops new products then these goods can take over from older products, the sales of which may be falling due to loss of consumer interest.' You will then need to think of the two other advantages and to list and explain those in the same way.

Analyse

As in 'Analyse the impact of a new competitor opening a shop close to a business which sells fresh flowers.' This also requires an explained answer. You will have to examine or explain how a new competitor will affect an existing business.

A possible answer could be: 'As the new competitor is trying to get established, it may offer fresh flowers at very low prices to start with. This could force the existing business to lower prices too. Sales could increase but the profit on each sale will be less than before.'

Evaluate

As in 'Evaluate the arguments for and against the business locating its factory in the north east of the country.' This is asking you to show advanced skills. You should firstly list and explain/analyse the advantages and disadvantages. You should then 'weigh them up' or compare them and come to a final recommendation.

For example, the final sentences might read: 'On the one hand, there are advantages to building in the north east, such as cheap land. On the other, there are disadvantages, such as distance from consumers. However, on balance I believe that the factory should be built in the north east. The factory requires a large site so the cost of the land is very important. The finished product can be easily transported to consumers who are in several different parts of the country.'

Write a letter

This is a common request in Business Studies examinations. The question often asks you to write a letter in support of or against a particular issue, for example, building a new shopping centre. As well as showing skills of analysis and evaluation, you should remember the basic rules of letter writing.

■ Put your *address* at the top of the letter, usually on the right-hand side.
■ *Date* the letter.
■ The *name*, *position* (for example, managing director) and *address* of the person you are sending the letter to should also be given – usually on the left-hand side at the top.
■ Start the letter with a *greeting*, such as 'Dear Sir or Madam' or use the name of the person you are sending the letter to, if you know it.
■ At the end of the letter use 'Yours sincerely' or 'Yours faithfully' and then sign the letter. 'Yours sincerely' should be used if you have used the name of the person you are sending the letter to in your greeting.

Write a report

In the examinations for some syllabuses, this is a common request from examiners. Reports are frequently used in business. They contain a great deal of data and discussion on important issues. They should follow the format below, or a very similar one. If you do not use such a format in the examination then you may lose marks.

1 *Heading or title* of the report.
2 *Name of report writer.*
3 *Name of person to whom it is being sent.*
4 *Introduction* Explain the purpose or the terms of reference of the report.
5 *Findings* This is the main part of the report. It should contain the main evidence and arguments of the report. The sources of data used and methods of data collection should be stated.
6 *Conclusions* You should bring together the findings of the report and form a clear conclusion.
7 *Recommendation* The report should end with a clear final recommendation which is based on analysis of the findings.
8 *Date* the report.

Do not use 'Yours faithfully/sincerely' – it is *not* a letter!

Coursework guidelines

Most Business Studies courses have coursework as one of the components of the examination. It will usually carry a weighting of 25 per cent of the total marks. The specific requirements for the coursework vary from course to course and you will need to look at your course details to clarify what is needed. The following is intended as general guidance for carrying out investigations and writing up coursework.

Some courses have the coursework title(s) given to candidates with no choice, whilst other courses will allow the candidates to choose their own investigations. The length of the work and the number of different pieces of work will also vary and will need to be checked. The final written work will often be required to be in report format.

Coursework usually consists of the candidate choosing or being given a business problem/situation to investigate. A title for the assignment will be decided and it should take the form of a question. Research, both primary and secondary, will usually be undertaken and the data collected will form the basis of the written piece of coursework. The written work should contain the data gathered from the research, presented in appropriate formats. The findings should be analysed and discussed, and finally a conclusion, which answers the question posed in the title and evaluates the information collected, is required.

Nature of the tasks

The coursework will usually take the form of a response to a clearly formulated *question*. The assignment should relate to a realistic business problem/situation. This can come from any part of the syllabus, but some areas tend to provide more opportunities for investigation than others and therefore are more suitable. It usually concentrates on more than one aspect of the syllabus or can be taken from optional modules.

The coursework should include a variety of forms of investigation where appropriate, for example, questionnaires, interviews, library research, pedestrian and traffic counts, personal observation, mapping, visit to government offices, visit to planning regulations offices, visit to factory or offices, magazine or newspaper articles.

Candidates will usually be given credit for tables of statistics, maps, graphs, illustrations, photographs, etc., provided they are pertinent to the question being answered and clearly support some part of the text. They should not be included merely to make the coursework look more attractive. Quotations must be clearly indicated and their sources stated.

While the information can be gathered collectively by students working in groups, the writing up of the assignment must be done individually.

Your assignment should have:

- a title which poses a question
- a table of contents
- sub-headings (coursework is not an essay)
- the opportunity for different types of research (a wide variety of primary and secondary research) to be conducted, and a variety of presentation methods (graphs, charts, diagrams, tables, etc.) to display the data collected
- a conclusion which
  – evaluates the information you have collected
  – answers the question posed in the title
- an identification of where materials/resources have come from. This could be put at the end of the work as a list of where you went, how you carried out your research, what other sources you used – a bibliography or a list of sources of information. (Include appendices as and where appropriate.)

Criteria for assessment

Assignments will usually be assessed on the following:

- knowledge/use of information
- collection/selection/organisation/interpretation of data
- application/analysis and interpretation of the topic
- evaluation of the topic/reasoned judgements.

For the highest marks to be awarded, the information gathered must be clearly linked to the topic set and an appropriate and varied range of research methods should be used. The data gathered should be clearly presented with the data converted into different and appropriate forms of communication. A wide range of presentation skills should be used. The work needs to have been planned in a logical manner with evidence of original and clear analysis of the topic. There should also be relevant and accurate use of business ideas applied to the topic. Finally, the coursework ought to end with a detailed, reasoned and justified conclusion based on the evidence collected and it must be a clear answer to the question posed in the title.

Now that you have read this guide, you are ready to use the book. Do not forget to return to the guide for reinforcement of these important points, especially as the examinations approach. Good luck!

The purpose of business activity

1

The economic problem: needs and wants

Activity 1.1

Make lists of:

a) your needs – those things you think are necessary for living
b) your wants – things you would like to be able to buy and own.

For example, on your needs list you will probably include clean water, and on your wants list you may include a luxury house.

To limit the time spent on this activity you should put *no more than 25 items* on your wants list!

Definitions to learn:

A NEED is a good or service essential for living.

A WANT is a good or service which people would like to have, but which is not essential for living. People's wants are unlimited.

What do you notice about your lists? You will probably find that the really important items are on the NEEDS list – water, clothing for warmth and protection, food and some form of housing or shelter. And on your WANTS list? That will be up to you and your interests and tastes, but you could probably have written a very long list indeed.

Do you already own all of the items on your wants list – if you do then you must be very lucky and very rich! Most people in the world cannot afford to buy everything they want because our wants are unlimited. In many countries, some people cannot afford to buy the things they need and they are likely to be very poor.

Why are there so many wants and needs that we cannot satisfy? Why are millions of people living in poverty in many countries around the world? Most people will answer these questions by saying, 'Because there is not enough money'.

Is this the real ECONOMIC PROBLEM – shortage of money? An example may help to show you why more money is *not* the answer to the problems of being unable to satisfy all people's wants and needs.

Definition to learn:

The ECONOMIC PROBLEM results from there being unlimited wants but limited resources to produce the goods and services to satisfy those wants. This creates scarcity.

▥ *Case study example*

The government of a small country is worried about the large numbers of people who cannot afford enough of the basic needs of life. Even those citizens with more money are always complaining that the country is not producing enough of the luxuries that they want to buy. The government decides to print more bank notes and to double all of the incomes of everybody in the country.

Has the government solved the economic problem of the country? Are there now more goods for the people to buy? Are there more houses for them to live in? Are there more schools for their children's education? Will the standard of living of the population increase?

The answer to all of these questions is 'No'. Printing more money does not produce more goods and services or satisfy more wants or needs, because prices will rise. What is the point of having more money to spend, if the prices of everything you want to buy have gone up by the same amount?

The real cause of the economic problem

Definitions to learn:

FACTORS OF PRODUCTION are those resources needed to produce goods or services. There are four factors of production and they are in limited supply.

SCARCITY is the lack of sufficient products to fulfil the total wants of the population.

The real cause of the shortage of goods and services in a country is not having too little money. It is too few FACTORS OF PRODUCTION (also called *resources of production*). There are four factors of production.

■ *Land* This term is used to cover all of the natural resources provided by nature and includes fields and forests, oil, gas, metals and other mineral resources.
■ *Labour* This is the efforts of people needed to make products.
■ *Capital* This is the finance, machinery and equipment needed for the manufacture of goods.
■ *Enterprise* This is the skill and risk-taking ability of the person who brings the other resources together to produce a good or service. For example, the owner of a business. These people are called *entrepreneurs*.

In any one country, and in the world as a whole, these factors of production are *limited in supply*. As there is never enough land, labour, capital or enterprise to produce all of the needs and unlimited wants of a whole population, there is an economic problem of SCARCITY.

The real cause of the economic problem

Limited resources: the need to choose

We make choices every day. We have to because, as we have seen, not all of our wants can be met. Therefore we have to decide which wants we will satisfy and which we will not.

Should I take a bus to college or use the money to buy some more paper for my Business Studies notes? Do I buy a new coat or spend the money on a new radio? All choices involve giving something up.

This problem exists for governments and businesses as well as for individuals. Should the government build another hospital, or a new road into the city? Should the owner of a business purchase a computer or use the resources to pay for a new advertising campaign? All of these choices involve giving up something too. If the resources or the factors of production were not scarce, there would be no need to choose. We could all have everything we wanted!

In making any choice, we need to consider what we are giving up, to make sure it is not worth more to us than the option we are choosing. This is called considering the OPPORTUNITY COST of a decision – the lost opportunity resulting from the choice of something else. Some examples are shown below.

▥ **Definition to learn:**
OPPORTUNITY COST is the next best alternative given up by choosing another item.

HOLIDAY OR CAR?

MACHINE A OR MACHINE B?

ROAD OR SCHOOL?

The individual chooses the holiday – the car is the opportunity cost

The company chooses Machine A – Machine B is the opportunity cost

The government chooses to build the road – the school is the opportunity cost

Some examples of opportunity cost

Revision summary: the economic problem

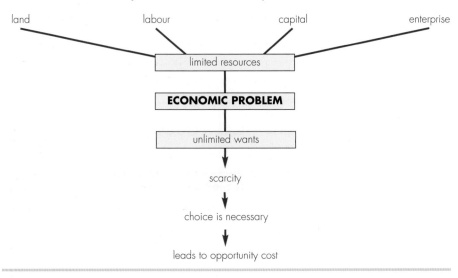

Making the best use of limited resources: specialisation

Factors of production – the resources we need to make goods and provide services – are in limited supply. When we choose to use them in a particular way, that choice involves a lost opportunity. It is therefore important to use these resources in the most efficient ways possible. The ways in which these resources are used has changed greatly in the last 200 years for two reasons.

- Machinery is now more widely used and this is often specialised to perform one task.
- Larger firms are now more common than they used to be and these often employ workers skilled in particular tasks.

▦ *Case study example*

This is how Joe Sharma, a carpenter, went about making a table 200 years ago:

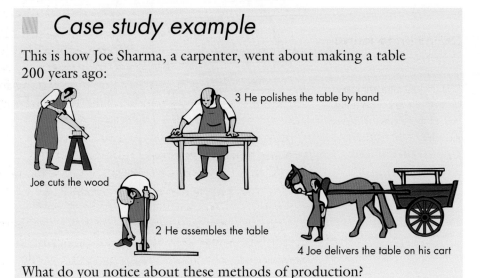

Joe cuts the wood

3 He polishes the table by hand

2 He assembles the table

4 Joe delivers the table on his cart

What do you notice about these methods of production?

- Joe did everything himself – including the cutting of the timber and the sale and delivery of the finished table.
- Production was very low – only one table per week.

Compare this with typical modern production methods. Two hundred years later, Jack Sharma owns the family business. This is how production is organised:

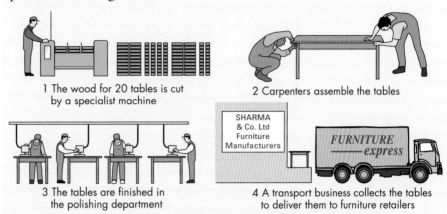

1 The wood for 20 tables is cut by a specialist machine

2 Carpenters assemble the tables

3 The tables are finished in the polishing department

4 A transport business collects the tables to deliver them to furniture retailers

What are the main features of this production method?

- Jack does not do everything himself – specialist workers are employed for each stage of production.
- He uses the services of specialist firms to supply him with materials and to sell his finished products.
- Output is much higher – 20 tables per week. This is an average of four tables per worker.
- The use of machines is more common – each machine needing a specialised worker to operate it.

Specialisation and the division of labour

Definition to learn:

DIVISION OF LABOUR is when the production process is split up into different tasks and each worker performs one of these tasks. It is also known as SPECIALISATION.

Jack Sharma is using the principles of SPECIALISATION and DIVISION OF LABOUR. By dividing up the different jobs and making each worker a specialist in one of these, output is increased. By concentrating on what each worker is best at and avoiding time wasting from moving people from one stage of production to another, total output and productivity (output per worker) are increased.

Also, Jack is using specialisation *between firms* by using timber firms to provide him with materials, and transport and retail firms to sell and distribute the goods to the customers. A chain of production has now been created using several firms to supply the product from its natural state (timber) to the final consumer.

Specialisation does have great benefits, but there could be drawbacks too. Workers may become bored by concentrating on only one stage of production. The firm is now relying on outside suppliers and retailers and these could prove to be unreliable.

Activity 1.2

a) Using another product, for example bread or clay pots, explain, with simple illustrations, how division of labour or specialisation could be used to make the product.

b) Explain the possible advantages and disadvantages of specialisation in the business you have chosen.

Why is business activity needed?

We have identified the following issues.

- People have unlimited wants.
- The four factors of production – the resources needed to make goods – are in limited supply.
- Scarcity results from limited resources and unlimited wants.
- Choice is necessary when resources are scarce. This leads to opportunity cost.
- Specialisation improves the efficiency with which resources are used.

So far, we have hardly mentioned *businesses* and yet this is the purpose of the book! Where does business activity fit into the ideas we have already looked at?

The aim of all business is to combine the factors of production to make products which will satisfy people's wants. These products can either be goods – physical items such as cars and shoes which we can touch and see – or they can be services, such as insurance, tourism or banking.

Businesses can be small – just one person, for example – or large. Some businesses employ thousands of people with operations in many different countries. Businesses can be privately owned or owned by the state. They can be owned by one person or thousands of shareholders. Whatever their size and whoever owns them, all businesses have one thing in common – *they combine factors of production to make products which satisfy people's wants.*

Businesses combine factors of production to make products which satisfy people's wants

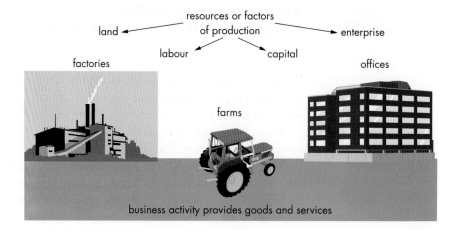

resources or factors of production

land ← → enterprise

labour ↓ ↓ capital

factories   farms   offices

business activity provides goods and services

What would life be like without business activity? In simple, undeveloped societies, businesses do not exist. Everybody attempts to do everything for themselves – they are self-sufficient. With their own plot of land and by their own efforts, such as hunting, they attempt to survive and produce enough for their own needs. This is a very basic existence. By a gradual process of specialisation, people began to concentrate on what they were best at. They then traded those goods for others made by people who had skills in other areas. In this way, businesses began to be formed, and trade and exchange of goods expanded. In today's world, most people work in one job for a weekly wage. With this money, they are able to purchase a wide range of goods and services produced by many different businesses. Business activity therefore:

- combines scarce factors of production in order to produce goods and services
- produces those goods and services which are needed to satisfy the needs and wants of the population
- employs people as workers and pays them wages to allow them to consume products made by other people.

Business objectives

An objective is an aim or a target to work towards. All businesses have objectives. These objectives are often different for different businesses. Businesses are started by people, and sometimes by governments, for many different reasons. A business may have been formed to provide employment for the owner or his/her family. It could have been started to make as big a profit as possible for the owner. On the other hand, the business might have a more charitable aim in mind – many of the leading world charities are very large businesses indeed. The most common business objectives are:

- to make a profit
- to increase added value
- to expand the business
- to achieve business survival
- to provide a service.

Profit

When a business is owned by private individuals, rather than the government, it is usually the case that the business is run to make profits. The owners will each take a share of these profits.

Will a business try to make as much profit as possible? It is often assumed that this will be the case. But there are dangers to this aim. Suppose a firm put up its prices to raise profits. It could find that consumers stop buying their goods. Other people will be encouraged to set up in competition, which will reduce profits in the long term for the original business.

It is often said that the owners of a business will aim for a *satisfactory* level of profits which will save them having to work too many hours or paying too much in tax to the government. Profits are needed to pay a return to the owners of the business. Without any profit at all, the owners are likely to close the business.

Added value

ADDED VALUE is not the same as profit. It is the difference between the selling price of a completed item and the value of the inputs or bought in materials and components. For example:

■ the selling price of a newly built house is €100,000
■ the value of the bought in bricks, cement, wood and other materials was €15,000
■ the value added by the builder is €85,000, but this is not the builder's profit as so many other costs and expenses have to be taken into account too.

Value is added to materials and components by working on them and turning them into much more expensive finished articles. So, a leather company could make leather jackets rather than just selling raw animal hides. A chocolate maker could wrap chocolates in more expensive looking boxes in order to sell them at a higher price. In these two examples the firm will have extra costs to pay, but they should be able to increase prices by more than costs. What is the point of increasing 'added value'? Higher added value means that the value of the firm's output rises, it sells goods in a more expensive market and it has the chance to earn higher profits – as long as it increases prices by more than costs.

selling price of product   LESS   material and bought in costs   =   value added by the business

Diagram showing added value

How can businesses increase added value?

■ A retailer such as a jeweller could present items in attractive displays, create a luxury feel to the shop and offer a gift-wrapping service. These could make consumers more willing to pay higher prices – they might think that the products are of a higher quality.
■ A manufacturer could add features to a product. For example, a camera maker could add a zoom lens and panoramic options. A higher price could then be charged. Any change that adds more to price than to costs of materials will add value.

Growth

The owners and managers of a business may aim for growth in the size of the business for a number of reasons:

■ to make jobs more secure if the business is larger
■ to increase the salaries and status of managers as the business expands
■ to open up new possibilities and help to spread the risks of the business by moving into new products and new markets
■ to obtain a higher market share from growth in sales
■ to obtain cost advantages, called *economies of scale*, from business expansion. These are considered in more detail in Unit 5.

Survival

When a firm has recently been set up, or when the economy is moving into recession, a business could be more concerned with survival than anything else. New competitors can also make a firm feel less secure. The managers of a business threatened in this way could decide to lower prices in order to survive, even though this would lower the profit on each item sold.

Providing a service

In some countries, important businesses are owned by the government. The main aim of these businesses could be to provide an essential service to the public, such as water or electricity supply, rather than making as much profit as possible.

■ *Activity 1.3*

Here are brief details of four businesses:

■ a small firm of builders which has noticed new businesses being created in the building industry
■ a recently established business in the rapidly expanding computer industry, which is owned by two young and ambitious entrepreneurs
■ a large book publishers which dominates the market in textbooks in your country
■ a government-owned postal company which delivers to all parts of the country.

a) Explain what is likely to be the main objective of the managers of each of these businesses.
b) What decisions could be taken to help the businesses to achieve these objectives?

Conflict of business objectives

In the section above we assumed that businesses could set one objective and aim for that. Life is not that simple and most businesses are trying to satisfy the objectives of more than one group as the diagram below shows.

▓ *Case study example*

A large oil company is operating in your country. The following groups are interested in the work of this company:

- *Owners of the company* They are likely to want the business to work towards as much *profit* as possible.
- *Directors* (senior managers of the company appointed by the owners) They will be interested in *growth* of the business as their salaries are likely to depend on this.
- *Workers* They will want as many *jobs* as possible with security of employment.
- *Local community* They will be concerned about jobs too, but they will be worried about *pollution* from the oil refinery.
- *Consumers* They will want reasonably priced products of appropriate *quality* – or they may buy goods from competitors.

In practice, these objectives could conflict with each other. For example:

- it could be that a cheap method of production increases *profits* but causes more *pollution*
- a decision to *expand* the plant could lead to a dirtier, noisier local environment
- a profitable decision to introduce new machines could reduce the *jobs* at the refinery
- a decision to expand could be expensive and this could reduce short-term *profits*.

Managers therefore have to compromise when they come to decide on the best objectives for the business they are running. They would be unwise to ignore the real worries or aims of other groups with an interest in the operation of the business. Managers will also have to be prepared to change the objectives over time. Growth could be the best option during a period of expansion in the economy, but survival by cost cutting might be better if the economy is in recession.

Revision summary: business objectives

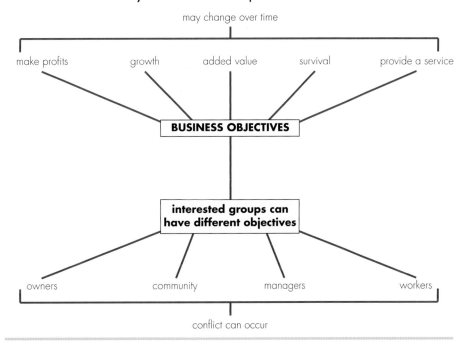

Which groups are involved in business activity?

All business activity involves people. The following groups of people are involved in business activity in one way or another or are affected by it:

- owners
- workers
- managers
- consumers
- government
- the community as a whole.

These groups are sometimes called the *stakeholders* of the business as they have an interest in how the business is run.

Why are these groups of people important to business? How are they affected by business activity?

Owners

Owners put money into the business to set it up. Without this capital, no business activity can begin. The owners will take a share of the profits if the business is successful. They may have to pay for any losses made. All owners are taking risks. Putting money into a business will not guarantee success. If the business makes the wrong type of product or does not attract enough consumers, the owners may lose their money. Owners are therefore *risk-takers*.

Workers

Workers are employed in the business. They are also called *employees*. They have to follow instructions given to them by the owners or managers. They may have part-time or full-time contracts. These are legal documents which give details of the hours of work and other conditions of employment. Workers earn money for the work they do and this is usually a weekly wage or monthly salary. Often workers need training to do their work well. If there is not enough work for all workers in a business, some may be made redundant (retrenchment), that is, they may be asked to leave the business. This could be of great concern to the workers involved.

Managers

Managers are employed by the business to control the work done by other workers. They give instructions to other workers, organise the resources of the firm and take important decisions. These decisions might include where to locate the business, what to produce and what price to sell products for. If these decisions are successful, the business does well. If managers make poor decisions, the business could fail. Good and successful managers often earn very large salaries.

Consumers

Consumers are important to every business. They are the customers who buy the product or service that a business makes. Without consumers buying enough products, a business will make losses and eventually fail. Businesses need to find out what products consumers are prepared to buy. This is called *market research* (see Unit 17). Consumers must then be attracted to the product by advertising and other forms of promotion.

Government

The government decides on laws which will affect business activity. These are explained in detail in Unit 4. The government wants businesses to be successful in its country. Successful businesses will employ more workers and reduce the numbers unemployed. When successful businesses make profits, a tax must be paid to the government. This money can be used to pay for the services which the government provides for the benefit of the population.

The whole community

Business activity affects the whole community. Land and resources are used up during business activity. Sometimes businesses produce goods which can be dangerous and might harm members of the community – such as cigarettes and cars. Factories can produce harmful pollution. Some products are very beneficial to the community, such as medicines or buses for public transport. In addition, business activity provides jobs for workers and managers and incomes are paid to these groups. This raises the community's standard of living. The whole community can therefore be affected by business activity in both positive and negative ways.

Revision summary: business stakeholders

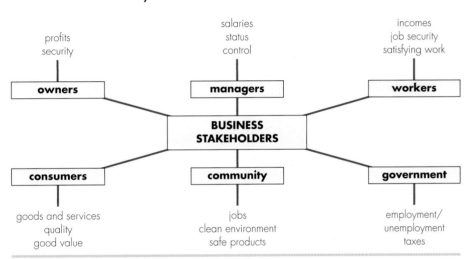

Revision questions

1 a) From the following list, decide which items are human needs and which are wants:
   • luxury house
   • shelter
   • *Coca-Cola*
   • car
   • clean water
   • designer jeans
   • clothing. [3]
   b) Explain briefly the reasons for your decisions in **a**). [3]

2 Define what is meant by *scarcity* when referring to the economic problem. [3]

3 List the *four* factors of production and explain briefly why each is necessary for production to take place. [4]

4 Explain, with the aid of an example, what the term *opportunity cost* means to a consumer. [4]

5 Give *two* other examples of opportunity cost that would affect groups other than consumers. [2]

6 Explain what is meant by *division of labour*. [2]

7 Why is a business likely to increase output if it adopts division of labour? [3]

8 List *four* tasks involved in the making of cakes that could be given to different workers through division of labour. [2]

9 State *three* benefits to society of business activity. [3]

10 What is meant by *business objectives*? [2]

11 Give *three* examples of the kind of objectives that a business owned by private individuals could establish. [3]

12 Define *added value*. [2]

13 How might a retailer of clothes *add value* to their products? (Hint: the answer is *not* to buy more expensive clothes for the shop as this will not necessarily add value.) [5]

14 Explain *two* reasons why business managers might set *growth* as a business objective. [4]

15 List *three* examples of the stakeholders in a business. [3]

16 Using examples, explain *two* reasons why conflict might occur between the objectives of these stakeholder groups. [4]

17 Purbeck plc owns and manages a major leisure complex. The directors of the company are considering demolishing the complex and building a new shopping centre. The directors have different opinions about this plan.
   • The Human Resources manager says that too many groups of people would suffer from the plan. He thinks that the plan should be dropped.
   • The Chief Executive says that his main responsibility is to the owners of the business and that profits should come first.
   a) How would the workers in the leisure centre be affected by the decision? [3]
   b) Do you agree with the Chief Executive that profits should be the main aim of the business? Explain your answer. [5]

The CD-ROM (see details on page x) provides further tests, activities and Case study work on the topics covered in this unit.

2 Types of business activity

This unit will explain:

- [?] the differences between primary, secondary and tertiary production
- [?] how public and private sectors of industry are organised
- [?] how business can expand by merger and take-over
- [?] how to measure and compare the size of businesses.

By the end of the unit you should be able to:

- [✓] understand how to classify firms into the primary, secondary and tertiary sectors
- [✓] explain the main features of the public and private sectors of industry
- [✓] understand the different forms of merger and take-over
- [✓] compare the different methods of measuring the size of businesses.

Levels of economic activity

As you read this book you are probably sitting at a desk. Most desks are still made of wood. How many different types of businesses might have been involved in converting the wood into a finished desk ready to be sold to a final consumer? What stages of production has the wood passed through to arrive at the finished desk?

The diagram below shows the most likely stages in the production and sale of a wooden desk.

The stages involved in making and selling a wooden desk

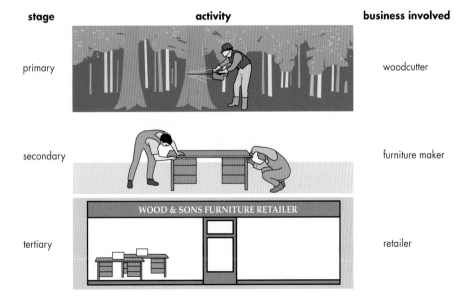

stage	activity	business involved
primary		woodcutter
secondary		furniture maker
tertiary	WOOD & SONS FURNITURE RETAILER	retailer

You will notice that there are *three* main stages between the cutting down of the timber and the sale of the completed desk. These stages are typical of nearly all production and they are called the levels of business activity.

■ **Definitions to learn:**
The PRIMARY SECTOR of industry extracts and uses the natural resources of the earth.

The SECONDARY SECTOR of industry manufactures goods using the raw materials provided by the primary sector.

The TERTIARY SECTOR of industry provides services to consumers and the other sectors of industry.

■ Stage 1 is called the *primary* stage of production. This stage involves the earth's natural resources. Activities in the PRIMARY SECTOR of industry include farming, fishing, forestry and the extraction of natural materials, such as oil and copper ore.

■ Stage 2 is called the *secondary* stage of production. This stage involves taking the materials and resources provided by the primary sector and converting them into manufactured or processed goods. Activities in the SECONDARY SECTOR of industry include building and construction, aircraft making, computer assembly, and baking.

■ Stage 3 is called the *tertiary* stage of production. This stage involves providing services to both consumers and other businesses. Activities in the TERTIARY SECTOR of industry include transport, banking, insurance, hotels and hairdressing.

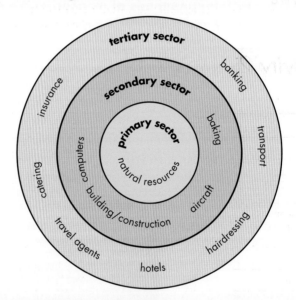

Which sector of industry is most important in your country? This depends on what is meant by 'important'. Usually the three sectors of industry are compared by:

■ the numbers of workers employed in each sector

or

■ the value of output of goods and services.

When these comparisons are made, some interesting differences often arise between countries. In some countries, primary industries such as farming and fishing employ many more people than manufacturing or service industries. These tend to be countries – often called *developing countries* – where manufacturing industry has only recently been established. As most people still live in the country areas with low incomes, there is little demand for services such as transport, hotels and insurance. The levels of both employment and output in the primary sector in these countries are likely to be higher than the other two sectors.

In countries which started up manufacturing industries many years ago, the secondary and tertiary sectors are likely to employ many more workers than the primary sector. The level of output in the primary sector is often small compared to the other two sectors. In very wealthy countries, it is now common to find that many manufactured goods are bought in from other nations. Most of the workers will be employed in the service sector. The output of the tertiary sector is often higher than the other two sectors combined. These are often called the *most developed countries.*

In the UK, there has been a decline in manufacturing industry – or the secondary sector – for over 30 years. Over 60 per cent of all workers are now employed in the tertiary sector of industry. This has been a major change in the structure of industry. Many workers who lost jobs as factories closed have found it difficult to obtain work in the service industries. The decline in the manufacturing or secondary sector of industry is called DE-INDUSTRIALISATION.

Definition to learn:

DE-INDUSTRIALISATION occurs when there is a decline in the importance of the secondary, manufacturing sector of industry in a country.

■ *Activity 2.1*

Copy this table. Indicate with a tick which sector of industry each business is in.

Business	Primary	Secondary	Tertiary
Insurance			
Forestry			
Coal mining			
Computer assembly			
Travel agent			
Brewery			
Car showroom			

Public and private sectors of industry

In Unit 1 we identified the problem of scarce resources. All countries have this problem, but they approach it in different ways. There are three different types of economic system which are used by countries to manage their resources as efficiently as possible. These are:

■ free market economy
■ command or planned economy
■ mixed economy.

Free market economy

In a free market economy all resources are owned *privately*. There is no government control over land, capital and labour. Businesses produce goods to make a profit. They make more of the more profitable goods – those most demanded by consumers. They make fewer of the less profitable goods – those least demanded by the consumers. Prices of goods are influenced by the demand for and supply of those goods.

Certain advantages and disadvantages are claimed for this type of economic system.

Advantages of a free market economy

☑ Consumers are free to choose what they want to buy.

☑ Workers are encouraged to work hard as they can keep most or all of their incomes because of low or non-existent taxes.

☑ Businesses compete with each other and this could keep prices low.

☑ New businesses are encouraged to set up in order to make profits.

Disadvantages of a free market economy

☒ There are no government-provided goods or services, such as health and education services, available to everybody. Only those who can afford to buy these important services will benefit from them.

☒ There is no government planning or control over the economy so there could be many uncontrolled booms or recessions in the economy.

☒ Businesses might be encouraged to create MONOPOLIES in order to increase prices. Consumers would have limited choice.

In fact, there is no country in the world with a completely free market system. In all countries, governments are involved in important economic decisions, to a greater or lesser degree. The United States is the country with an economy most like a free market system. But even there, the United States government has a lot of control over the economy.

Command or planned economy

In a command or planned economy, the government or the state plans and controls the use of resources. There might be no private property at all. The government decides what is to be produced and in what quantities. Consumers have little choice and workers could be told where to work and what work to perform. This system also has advantages and disadvantages.

Advantages of a command or planned economy

☑ Government control should eliminate any waste resulting from competition between firms.

☑ There should be work for everybody.

☑ The needs of the population are met, but there is little production of luxury goods for the wealthy.

Disadvantages of a command or planned economy

☒ There is less incentive to work as the government fixes wages and private property is not allowed.

☒ The government may not produce goods which people want to buy.

☒ The lack of a profit motive for firms leads to low efficiency.

■ **Definition to learn:**
A MONOPOLY is a business which controls all of the market for a product.

The clearest examples of command economies are the communist systems which exist in China and did exist in Eastern European countries before 1989. Even China is now introducing economic changes which involve less state control. There is now much more freedom of choice than before and some private property and trading are allowed.

Mixed economy

A mixed economy combines some features of both a free market economy and a command economy. Nearly every country in the world has a mixed economy with a:

■ *private sector* (like the free market economy) made up of businesses not owned by the government. These businesses will make their own decisions about what to produce, how it should be produced and what price should be charged for it. Most businesses in the private sector will aim to run profitably. Even so, there are likely to be some government controls over these decisions and these are explained in Unit 4.

■ *public sector* (like the command economy) made up of government- or state-owned and controlled businesses and organisations. The government, or other public authority, makes decisions about what to produce and how much to charge consumers. Some goods and services are provided free of charge to the consumer – such as state health and education services. The money for these comes not from the user but from the taxpayers. Profit is not always an aim of businesses in the public sector. Service to the community can be an alternative aim.

What are the most common areas of government ownership?

In many countries the government controls the following important industries or organisations:

■ health
■ education
■ defence

■ public transport
■ water supply
■ electricity supply.

■ *Activity 2.2*

For each of the examples of government-owned organisations listed above, suggest three possible reasons why the government of a country might decide to own and control that industry or service.

■ *Activity 2.3*

Find out whether, in your own country, the government owns and controls the following businesses:

a) railway system
b) local bus services
c) water supply

d) electricity supply
e) TV and radio stations
f) hospitals.

Revision summary: economic systems

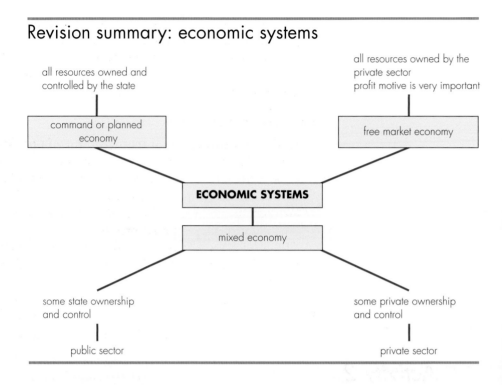

all resources owned and controlled by the state

all resources owned by the private sector
profit motive is very important

command or planned economy

free market economy

ECONOMIC SYSTEMS

mixed economy

some state ownership and control

some private ownership and control

public sector

private sector

Privatisation
Should the government own and control less than it does?

You may find in some countries that there is a mixture of government and private ownership. For example, it is common to have privately owned and managed hospitals as well as government-run hospitals. In many parts of the world, there has been a very important change in the balance between the public and private sectors in recent years. Many governments have sold off businesses they previously owned to new owners in the private sector. This is called *privatisation*. In many European countries the electricity supply, water supply and public transport systems have been privatised. Why is this and is the policy successful?

Arguments in favour of privatisation

☑ The new owners operate the business with profit as a main aim. This encourages them to run the business efficiently.

☑ Competition may now be encouraged if the business is sold off to several different private owners. This helps to increase efficiency and to keep prices low.

☑ Governments are often short of money. New owners may have additional CAPITAL to invest in improving the service offered by the business.

☑ Important business decisions will be made for business reasons – not by governments with politics in mind. For example, the government could decide to build a new power station in an area of high

■ **Definition to learn:**
CAPITAL is the money invested into a business by the owners.

unemployment to create jobs. This could make the members of the government more popular. Private owners would aim to build the power station in the cheapest and therefore most profitable location.

☑ The sale of the business to private owners raises money for the government.

Arguments against privatisation

☒ As the new owners are interested mainly in profits, some services making losses may be closed. These might be very important for some people or areas, for example, closing a country bus route or not delivering letters to isolated districts.

☒ Workers' jobs could be lost as the new owners attempt to increase efficiency in order to raise profits.

☒ The business might be sold off to one owner who would still be able to run it as a monopoly. This could lead to higher prices for the customers.

☒ Only a few people – the new owners – will benefit from owning the business, whereas before privatisation the whole country could benefit from any profits made as it was owned by the government.

■ *Activity 2.4*

Your government is considering the privatisation of your country's postal services. You decide to write to the government minister in charge explaining your views on this matter and stating your opinion. Your letter should contain:

■ an explanation of what privatisation is
■ the possible benefits of this privatisation suggestion
■ the possible disadvantages of this proposal
■ your recommendation to the minister on whether the postal services should be privatised.

Revision summary: sectors of industry

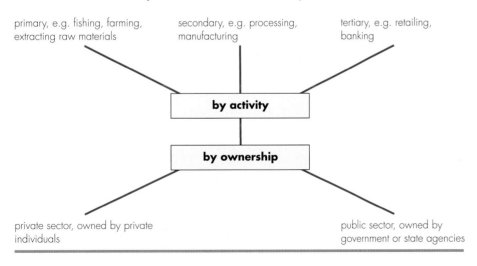

primary, e.g. fishing, farming, extracting raw materials

secondary, e.g. processing, manufacturing

tertiary, e.g. retailing, banking

by activity

by ownership

private sector, owned by private individuals

public sector, owned by government or state agencies

Comparing the size of businesses

Businesses can vary greatly in terms of size. On the one hand, firms can be owned and run by a single individual. At the other extreme, some businesses employ hundreds of thousands of workers all over the world. Some firms produce output worth hundreds of pounds a year, whilst the biggest businesses sell goods valued at billions of pounds each year.

Who would find it useful to compare the size of businesses?

■ Investors – before deciding which business to put their savings into.
■ Governments – often there are different tax rates for small and large businesses.
■ Competitors – to compare their size and importance with other firms.
■ Workers – to have some idea of how many people they might be working with.
■ Banks – to see how important a loan to the business is compared to its overall size.

Business size can be measured in a number of ways. The most common are:

■ by number of employees
■ by value of output and sales
■ by profit
■ by capital employed.

They all have advantages and disadvantages.

Comparing business size by number of employees

This method is easy to understand. However, some firms use production methods which employ very few people but which produce high output levels. This is true for *automated factories* which use the latest computer-controlled equipment. These firms are called *capital intensive firms* – they use a great deal of capital (high cost) equipment to produce their output. Therefore, a company with high output levels could employ fewer people than a business which produced less output.

Comparing business size by value of output and sales

This is a common way of comparing businesses in the same industry because it shows which one is most important in that industry. However, a high sales level does not mean that a business is large when using the other methods of measurement. A firm employing few people might sell several very expensive computers each year. This might give higher sales figures than a firm selling cheaper products but employing more workers.

Comparing business size by profit

This is one of the least accurate ways of comparing the size of firms. Profit depends on more than just the size of a firm. It depends on efficiency and the skills of the managers as well. Some very large businesses can make very low profits if they are badly managed.

Comparing business size by capital employed

This means the total amount of capital invested into the business. The same problem applies as before. A company employing many workers may use *labour-intensive* methods of production. These give low output levels and use little capital equipment.

There is no perfect way of comparing the size of businesses. It is quite common to use more than one method and to compare the results obtained.

■ *Activity 2.5: case study task*

You are employed by Company A, which makes motorcycles. You have been asked to write a brief report (following a report format) to the Managing Director comparing the size of your company with three others in the same industry. Use the following information in your report. State the advantages and disadvantages of each of the ways of comparing business size.

	Workers employed	**Capital employed (£ million)**	**Profit (£ million)**	**Sales (£ million)**
Company A	20,000	50	10	100
Company B	5,000	150	5	200
Company C	3,000	60	20	150
Company D	15,000	180	15	150

Revision summary: comparing business size

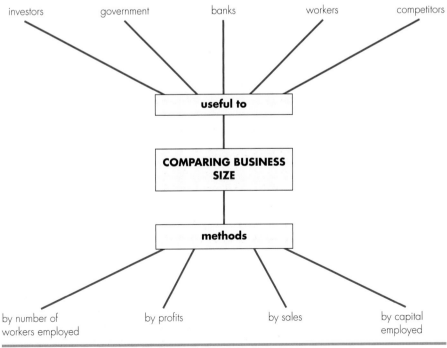

How can businesses grow?

The owners of businesses often want their firm to expand. What advantages will a business and its owners gain from expansion? Here are some likely benefits:

- ☑ the possibility of higher profits for the owners
- ☑ more status and prestige for the owners and managers – higher salaries are often paid to managers who control the bigger firms
- ☑ lower average costs (this is explained in Unit 6, page 92, *Economies of scale*)
- ☑ growth of a business often means that it controls a larger share of its market – the proportion of total market sales it makes is greater. This gives a business more influence when dealing with suppliers and distributors and consumers are often attracted to the 'big names' in an industry.

Businesses can expand in two main ways:

- by INTERNAL GROWTH, for example, a restaurant owner could open other restaurants in other towns – this growth is often paid for by profits from the existing business
- by EXTERNAL GROWTH, involving a TAKE-OVER or MERGER with another business.

Three examples of mergers are shown below. They all involve two firms coming together to form one business. However, they are all rather different in their impact.

- Horizontal merger (or HORIZONTAL INTEGRATION) – when one firm merges with or takes over another one in the same industry at the same stage of production.

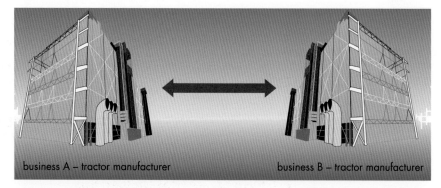

business A – tractor manufacturer   business B – tractor manufacturer

- Vertical merger (or VERTICAL INTEGRATION) – when one firm merges with or takes over another one in the same industry but at a different stage of production. Vertical integration can be *forward* – when a firm integrates with another firm which is at a later stage of production, i.e. closer to the consumer, or *backward* – when a firm integrates with another firm at an earlier stage of production, i.e. closer to the raw material supplies, in the case of a manufacturing firm.

▧ **Definitions to learn:**

INTERNAL GROWTH occurs when a business expands its existing operations.

EXTERNAL GROWTH is when a business takes over or merges with another business. It is often called INTEGRATION as one firm is integrated into another one.

A MERGER is when the owners of two businesses agree to join their firms together to make one business.

A TAKE-OVER or ACQUISITION is when one business buys out the owners of another business which then becomes part of the 'predator' business (i.e. the firm which has taken it over).

HORIZONTAL INTEGRATION is when one firm merges with or takes over another one in the same industry at the same stage of production.

VERTICAL INTEGRATION is when one firm merges with or takes over another one in the same industry but at a different stage of production. Vertical integration can be *forward* or *backward*.

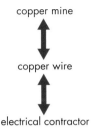

copper mine

↕

copper wire

↕

electrical contractor

a copper wire maker merges with a copper mine (backward integration) and with an electrical contractor (forward integration)

■ Conglomerate merger (or CONGLOMERATE INTEGRATION) – when one firm merges with or takes over a firm in a completely different industry. This is also known as DIVERSIFICATION.

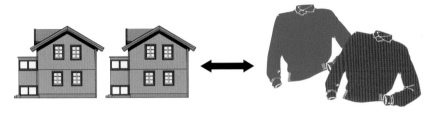

a business building houses merges with a business making clothes

You should notice that all three examples of integration are very different even though they all involve two businesses joining together.

The likely benefits of integration

Horizontal integration

☑ The merger reduces the number of competitors in the industry.
☑ There are opportunities for economies of scale.
☑ The combined business will have a bigger share of the total market than either firm before the integration.

Forward vertical integration

For example, a car manufacturer takes over a car retailing business.

☑ The merger gives an assured outlet for their product.
☑ The profit margin made by the retailer is absorbed by the expanded business.
☑ The retailer could be prevented from selling competing makes of car.
☑ Information about consumer needs and preferences can now be obtained directly by the manufacturer.

Backward vertical integration

For example, a car manufacturer takes over a firm supplying car body panels.

☑ The merger gives an assured supply of important components.
☑ The profit margin of the supplier is absorbed by the expanded business.
☑ The supplier could be prevented from supplying other manufacturers.
☑ Costs of components and supplies for the manufacturer could be controlled.

Conglomerate integration

☑ The business now has activities in more than one industry. This means that the business has diversified its activities and this will spread the risks taken by the business. For example, suppose that a newspaper business took over a computer manufacturer. If sales of newspapers fell due to changing consumer demand, sales of computers could be rising at the same time due to increased interest in home computing.

☑ There might be a transfer of ideas between the different sections of the business even though they operate in different industries. For example, an insurance firm buying an advertising agency could benefit from better promotion of its insurance activities as a result of the agency's new ideas.

▦ *Activity 2.6*

Identify the form of business growth which is used in each of these situations.

a) A garage agrees to merge with another garage.
b) A bicycle retailer expands by buying a shop in another town.
c) A fruit juice firm buys a fruit farm.
d) A business making electrical goods agrees to join with a business with retail shops specialising in electrical goods.
e) A mining firm takes over a firm supplying mining equipment.
f) A construction company buys a holiday company.

Revision summary: how businesses grow

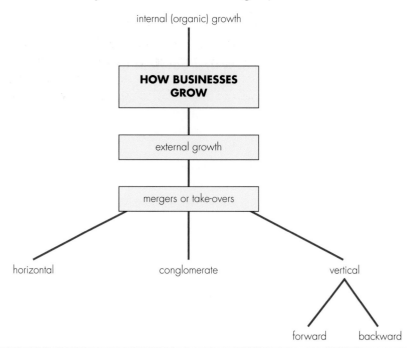

Why do some businesses stay small?

Not all businesses grow. Some stay small – in other words, they continue to employ few people and use relatively little capital. Why is this? There are several reasons why some businesses remain small:

- the type of industry the business operates in
- the market size
- the owners' objectives.

The type of industry the business operates in

Here are some examples of industries where most firms remain small: hairdressing, car repairs, window cleaning, convenience stores, plumbers, catering. Firms in these industries offer personal services or specialised products. If they were to grow too large, they would find it difficult to offer the close and personal service demanded by consumers.

In these industries, it is often very easy for new firms to be set up and this creates new competition. This helps to keep existing firms relatively small.

Market size

If the market – that is, the total number of consumers – is small, the businesses are likely to remain small. This is true for firms, such as shops, which operate in country areas far away from cities. It is also why firms which produce goods or services of a specialised kind, which appeal only to a limited number of consumers, such as very luxurious cars or expensive fashion clothing, remain small.

Owners' objectives

Some business owners prefer to keep their firm small. They could be more interested in keeping control of a small business, knowing all of their staff and customers, than running a much larger business. Owners sometimes wish to avoid the stress and worry of running a large firm.

■ *Revision questions*

1 Explain the difference between the primary, secondary and tertiary sectors of industry. [3]

2 Which sector of industry is often the most important in the *most developed economies*? State one reason for this. [2]

3 State *three* features of a market economy. [3]

4 Outline the benefits of free market economies to:
   a) owners of firms
   b) consumers. [6]

5 Explain the major difference between command economies and mixed economies. [3]

6 State *three* possible disadvantages of the privatisation of industries such as electricity and gas supplies. [3]

7 List *three* groups that are interested in comparing the size of businesses and explain why they want to do this. [6]

8 Two business owners cannot agree on which of them owns the larger business. One owner, who runs a printing firm using the latest expensive equipment, considers his firm to be larger. The other owner, who has a fruit farm that uses only manual labour to pick the fruit, considers her business to be larger.
   a) Which forms of measuring business size does each owner seem to be using? [2]

   b) Which method of measuring business size would you advise the two owners to use, and why? [4]

9 What is the difference between a take-over and a merger? [2]

10 Explain the difference between the internal and external growth of business. [3]

11 Give *two* examples of horizontal integration of businesses. [2]

12 Give *two* examples of forward vertical integration of businesses. [2]

13 Explain the benefits to a business of vertically integrating (forwards) with another business. [4]

14 Give *two* examples of backward vertical integration of businesses. [2]

15 The owner of a small hairdressing business asks for your advice. She is planning to expand the business. New branches will be opened and many more staff will be employed. She asks you to make a list of all of the possible advantages and disadvantages of this decision.
   a) Is this an example of internal or external growth? Explain your answer. [3]
   b) Make the list asked for by the owner. [6]

16 Explain *two* reasons why some businesses remain small. [4]

The CD-ROM (see details on page x) provides further tests, activities and Case study work on the topics covered in this unit.

3 | Forms of business organisation

This unit will explain:

[?] the main forms of business organisation in the private and public sectors
[?] the advantages and disadvantages of each of these forms of business organisation
[?] the appropriateness of each of these forms in different circumstances.

By the end of the unit you should be able to:

☑ understand the main legal and other differences between the forms of business organisation in the private and public sectors
☑ identify the main benefits and drawbacks of each of these forms of organisation
☑ recommend suitable forms of business organisation to owners and managers of firms in particular circumstances.

Business organisations: the private sector

There are five main forms of business organisation in the private sector. These are:

- sole traders
- partnerships
- private limited companies
- public limited companies
- co-operatives.

In addition, this unit will also consider close corporations (which are allowed in South Africa and some other countries), joint ventures and franchising.

Sole traders

This is the most common form of business organisation. It is a business owned and operated by just one person – although the sole trader can employ others, the owner is the *sole proprietor*. One of the reasons it is such a common form of organisation is because there are so few legal requirements to set it up. The only legal regulations which must be followed are that:

- the owner must register with, and send annual accounts to, the Inland Revenue or Tax Office
- the name of the business is significant. In some countries the name must be registered with the Registrar of Business Names. In other countries, such as the UK, it is sufficient for the owner to put the business name on all of the firm's documents and to put a notice in the main office stating who owns the business
- in some industries, the sole trader must observe certain laws which apply to all firms in that industry. These include health and safety laws and obtaining a licence, for example, to sell alcohol or operate a taxi.

Why do people set up a business on their own? What are the benefits and disadvantages to sole traders of running their own business rather than having other people join in with them? If you wanted to set up your own business, why might you choose to create a sole trader organisation? We can answer these questions by looking at the following example.

■ *Case study example*

Mike decided to run his own taxi business. Initially, he set up the business as a sole trader. There are advantages to being a sole trader – Mike had the following benefits.

Advantages of a sole trader

☑ There were *few legal regulations* for him to worry about when he set up the business.

☑ He was his own boss. He had complete *control* over his business and there was no need to consult with or ask others before making decisions.

☑ He had the *freedom* to choose his own holidays, hours of work, prices to be charged and whom to employ (if he found that he could not do all the work by himself).

☑ Mike had close *contact* with his own customers, the personal satisfaction of knowing his regular customers and the ability to respond quickly to their needs and demands.

☑ Mike had an incentive to work hard as he was able to keep all of the *profits*, after he had paid tax. He did not have to share these profits.

☑ He did not have to give information about his business to anyone else – other than the Tax Office. He enjoyed complete *secrecy* in business matters.

Mike was convinced by these advantages, so he had decided to set up his taxi business as a sole trader.

After operating the business for several months, Mike realised that there are also some disadvantages to being a sole trader. He made a list of these drawbacks.

Disadvantages of a sole trader

✖ I have no one to *discuss* business matters with as I am the sole owner.

✖ I do *not* have the benefit of LIMITED LIABILITY. The business accounts cannot be separated from my own accounts. The business is not a separate legal unit. I am therefore fully responsible for any debts that the business may have. *Unlimited liability* means that if my business cannot pay its debts then the people I owe money to (my creditors) can force me to sell all of my own possessions in order to pay them.

■ **Definition to learn:**
LIMITED LIABILITY means that the owners of a company – the shareholders – cannot be held responsible for the debts of the company they own. Their liability is limited to the investment they made by buying the shares.

Case study example continued

⊠ I want to expand the business by buying other taxis. However, I do not have enough money to do this. The sources of *finance* for a sole trader are *limited* to the owner's savings, profits made by the business and small bank loans. There are, by definition, no other owners who can put capital into the business. Banks are often reluctant to lend businesses like mine large sums of money.

⊠ I spend many hours trying to repair my taxi when it breaks down and much of my spare time is spent keeping the accounts of the business. Because my business is so small I cannot afford *specialists* to do these and other jobs for me. I therefore have to do many jobs that I am not skilled at.

⊠ My business is likely to remain *small* because capital for expansion is so restricted. My business is unlikely, therefore, to benefit from economies of scale. The size of the business is one of the reasons why I find it difficult to recruit good workers. I cannot offer much training or opportunities for their future careers.

⊠ I now realise that if I am ill there is no one who will take control of the business for me. I cannot pass on the business to my sons – when I die the business will legally not exist any longer. This is because there is no continuity of the business after the death of the owner.

The disadvantages of a sole trader that Mike experienced are typical of all businesses organised in this way. Did Mike take the correct decision to set up a sole trader business? He still thought so. He would recommend a sole trader organisation to people who:

■ are setting up a new business
■ do not need much capital to get the business going
■ will be dealing mainly with the public, for example retailing or services like hairdressing. Personal and direct contact between the customer and the owner is often very important for the success of these businesses.

But, as his business began to expand Mike wondered if another form of business organisation would now be more suitable.

As a sole trader, Mike has several advantages and disadvantages in running his business

independence
keeps all profits
but
unlimited liability
takes all the risks

Partnerships

A partnership is a group or association of between two and 20 people who agree to own and run a business together. The partners will contribute to the capital of the business, will usually have a say in the running of the business and will share any profits made.

Partnerships can be set up very easily. Indeed, Mike could just ask someone he knew to become his partner in the taxi business. This would be called a *verbal agreement*. Mike would be advised to create a *written agreement* with a partner called a PARTNERSHIP AGREEMENT or Deed of Partnership. Without this document, partners may disagree on who put most capital into the business or who is entitled to more of the profits. A written agreement will settle all of these matters.

■ **Definition to learn:**

A PARTNERSHIP AGREEMENT is the written and legal agreement between business partners. It is not essential for partners to have such an agreement but it is always recommended.

■ *Case study example*

Mike offered his friend, Gita, the chance to become a partner in the taxi business. They prepared a written Partnership Agreement which contained the following points:

- the amount of capital invested in the business by both partners
- the tasks to be undertaken by each partner
- the way in which the profits would be shared out
- how long the partnership would last
- arrangements for absences, retirements and how new partners could be admitted.

After the two partners had signed the agreement and the partnership had been operating for some time, it became clear to Mike that this form of business organisation had several advantages over a sole trader.

Advantages of a partnership

☑ *More capital* could now be invested into the business from Gita's savings and this would allow expansion of the business. Additional taxis could now be purchased.

☑ The *responsibilities* of running the business were now *shared*. Gita specialised in the accounts and administration of the business and Mike concentrated on marketing the services of the taxi firm and on driving. Absences and holidays did not lead to major problems as one of the partners was always available.

☑ Both partners were *motivated* to work hard because they would both benefit from the profits made. In addition, any *losses* made by the business would now be *shared* by the partners.

The taxi firm continued to be successful. The number of customers increased, but so did the expenses and bills of running the business.

Case study example continued

Although profits were being made, Gita became worried about what would happen if the business failed, perhaps because so many new competitors were entering the market. Gita explained to Mike that although their partnership was working well, this form of business organisation still had a number of disadvantages.

Disadvantages of a partnership

⊠ The partners *did not have limited liability*. If the business failed then creditors could still force the partners to sell their own property to pay business debts.

⊠ The business *did not have a separate legal identity*. If one of the partners died then the partnership would end. (Both sole traders and partnerships are said to be UNINCORPORATED BUSINESSES because they do not have a separate legal identity from the owners.)

⊠ Partners can *disagree* on important business decisions and consulting all partners takes time.

⊠ If one of the partners is very *inefficient* or actually *dishonest* then the other partners could suffer by losing money in the business.

⊠ Most countries *limit* the number of partners to *20* and this means that business growth would be limited by the amount of capital 20 people could invest.

Mike and Gita discussed these points with their solicitor. She explained that partnerships were very suitable in certain situations:

■ where people wished to form a business with others but wanted to avoid legal complications
■ where the professional body, such as medicine and the law, only allowed professional people to form a partnership, not a company
■ where the partners are well known to each other, possibly in the same family, and want a simple means of involving several of them in the running of the business.

Gita and Mike made it clear that they wanted to expand the business further but wanted to protect their own possessions from business creditors in the event of failure.

As partners, Mike and Gita often discuss important business issues together. They share their ideas on how to run the business

The solicitor advised them to consider forming a private limited company. She explained that this type of business organisation would be very different from a partnership and would have its own benefits and drawbacks.

■ **Definition to learn:**
An UNINCORPORATED BUSINESS is one that does not have a separate legal identity. Sole traders and partnerships are unincorporated businesses.

■ *Activity 3.1: case study task*

Your friend, Amin, is an expert computer engineer. He currently works for a large computer manufacturer. He thinks that he could run his own successful business. He has no experience of running a business. He has very few savings to invest into a business.

Amin has a rich uncle who knows nothing about computers! He is a retired businessman. He is friendly but rather bossy as he always thinks he knows best.

Amin asks for your advice about whether he should set up his own business and what form of organisation he should choose. He asks for your help on three questions that are worrying him.

a) What would be the advantages and disadvantages of running his own business rather than working for the computer manufacturer?

b) Should he set up a sole trader business?

c) His uncle would like to become his partner in the business if Amin decides to go ahead. What would be the advantages and disadvantages of forming a partnership with his uncle?

Write detailed notes to Amin giving your advice on all three points which are worrying him.

Limited partnerships

In some countries, such as the UK after 2000, it is possible to create a Limited Liability Partnership. The abbreviation for this new form of legal structure is LLP. It offers partners *limited liability* (see *Case study example* opposite) but shares in such businesses cannot be bought and sold. This type of partnership is a separate legal unit, unlike ordinary partnerships that end with the death of one of the partners.

Revision summary: sole traders and partnerships

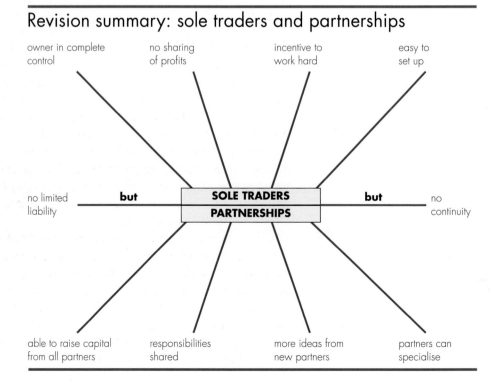

owner in complete control

no sharing of profits

incentive to work hard

easy to set up

no limited liability **but** **SOLE TRADERS / PARTNERSHIPS** **but** no continuity

able to raise capital from all partners

responsibilities shared

more ideas from new partners

partners can specialise

■ **Definition to learn:**

SHAREHOLDERS are the owners of a limited company. They buy shares which represent part ownership of a company.

Private limited company

There is one essential difference between a company and an unincorporated business, such as a sole trader or partnership. A company is a separate legal unit from its owners. This means that:

■ a company exists separately from the owners and will continue to exist if one of the owners should die

■ a company can make contracts or legal agreements

■ company accounts are kept separate from the accounts of the owners.

Companies are *jointly* owned by the people who have invested in the business. These people buy *shares* in the company and they are therefore called SHAREHOLDERS. These shareholders appoint directors to run the business. In a private limited company, the directors are usually the most important or majority shareholders. This is usually not the case in a public limited company, as we shall see in the next section.

■ *Case study example*

Mike and Gita asked their solicitor to list the benefits of forming a private limited company for their taxi firm.

Advantages of a private limited company

☑ *Shares* can be sold to a large number of people. These would be likely to be friends or relatives of Mike and Gita – they could not advertise the shares as being for sale to the general public. The sale of shares could lead to much *larger sums of capital* to invest in the business than the two original partners could manage to raise themselves. The business could therefore expand more rapidly.

☑ All shareholders have *limited liability*. This is a very important advantage. It means that if the company failed with debts owing to creditors, the shareholders could not be forced to sell their possessions to settle the debts. The shareholders could only lose their original investment in the shares – their liability is limited to that original investment. This is a major benefit compared to the position sole traders and partners can find themselves in if their business fails. Limited liability encourages people to buy shares knowing that the amount they pay is the maximum they could lose if the business is unsuccessful.

It is important that the people and other businesses that deal with companies know that they are not sole traders or partnerships. Creditors, for example, need to be aware that if the business did fail then they could not take the owners to court to demand payment from their savings. For this reason all private limited company names must end with 'Limited', or 'Ltd' as an abbreviation. In some countries, although not the UK, this title is amended to 'Proprietary Limited' or '(Pty) Ltd'.

☑ The people who started the company – Mike and Gita in our example – are able to keep control of it as long as they do not sell too many shares to other people.

The solicitor was keen for Mike and Gita to know exactly what they would be committed to if they formed a company. She also listed the disadvantages.

Disadvantages of a private limited company

☒ There are significant legal matters which have to be dealt with before a company can be formed. In particular, two important forms or documents have to be sent to the Registrar of Companies.
– *The Articles of Association* This contains the rules under which the company will be managed. It states the rights and duties of all of the directors, the rules concerning the election of directors and the holding of official meetings, and the procedure to be followed for the issuing of shares.
– *The Memorandum of Association* This contains very important information about the company and the directors. The official name and the address of the registered offices of the company must be stated. The objectives of the company must be given and also the amount of share capital that the directors intend to raise. The number of shares to be bought by each of the directors must also be made clear.
    Both of these documents are intended to make sure that companies are correctly run and to reassure shareholders about the purpose and structure of the company.
    Once these documents have been received by the Registrar of Companies then a *Certificate of Incorporation* will be issued to allow the company to start trading.

☒ The shares in a private limited company cannot be sold or transferred to anyone else without the agreement of the other shareholders. This rule can make some people reluctant to invest in such a company because they may not be able to sell their shares quickly if they require their investment back.

☒ The accounts of a company are much less secret than for either a sole trader or a partnership. Each year the latest accounts must be sent to the Registrar of Companies and members of the public can inspect them. Mike and Gita would have to be prepared to allow more information about their business to be known to other people.

☒ Most importantly for rapidly expanding businesses, the company cannot offer its shares to the general public. Therefore it will not be possible to raise really large sums of capital to invest back into the business.

Mike and Gita were impressed by the benefits of a private limited company form of organisation. The solicitor told them it was a very common form of organisation for family businesses or partnerships when the owners wished to expand them further. Firms, excluding the largest ones, will often find that the capital they can raise as a private limited company is sufficient. The solicitor offered to help Mike and Gita fill out the necessary legal forms to turn their business into a private limited company.

As directors of the private limited company, both Mike and Gita had very important roles

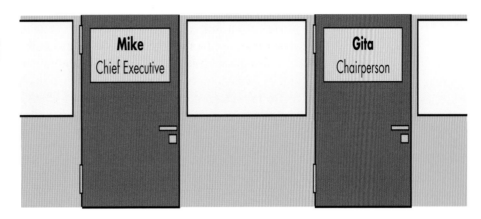

Revision summary: private limited companies

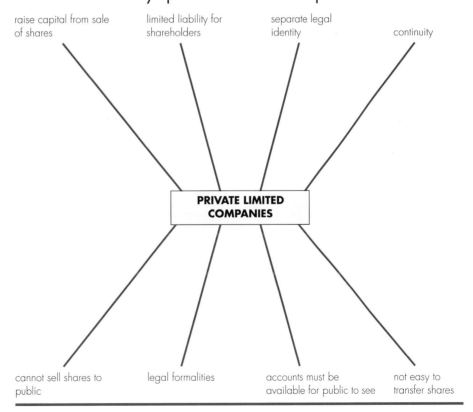

raise capital from sale of shares

limited liability for shareholders

separate legal identity

continuity

PRIVATE LIMITED COMPANIES

cannot sell shares to public

legal formalities

accounts must be available for public to see

not easy to transfer shares

Public limited companies

This form of business organisation is most suitable for very large businesses. Most of the businesses which are well known to the public because they own large chains of shops or many factories are public limited companies.

Students commonly make two mistakes about public limited companies.

■ It is often assumed that public limited companies are in the public sector of industry. This is not true. They are not owned by the government but by *private individuals* or *private businesses* and as a result they are in the *private sector* of industry.
■ The title given to public limited companies can cause confusion. This is why.
   – In the UK, public limited companies are given the title 'plc' after the business name, for example J Sainsbury plc.
   – In other countries, the title 'Limited' is used. This must not be confused with the UK use of 'Limited' which refers only to private limited companies.

The table below might help.

Private sector companies

	Private limited companies	**Public limited companies**
UK	Limited or Ltd	plc
South Africa and some other countries	Proprietary Limited or (Pty) Ltd	Limited

■ *Case study example*

Express Taxis Ltd had been operating and expanding for many years. The two directors, Mike and Gita, still owned most of the shares. The company owned 150 taxis and had diversified into bus services. It owned 35 buses. The government had recently announced the privatisation of all bus services in the country. Both Mike and Gita were determined to expand the business further by buying many of these bus routes from the government. Many new buses would be needed. A huge investment of around £90 million would be needed. Although profitable, the private limited company could not afford this sum of money.

Mike and Gita went to see a specialist business financial consultant at a large bank. The consultant was impressed by the directors' plans and advised them to convert their company into a public limited company. He explained the procedure for doing this and the benefits and drawbacks of this change in business organisation.

Procedure for converting a private to a public limited company

1 A statement must now be made in the Memorandum of Association that it is now a public limited company.
2 A certain minimum value of shares must be issued (£50,000 in the UK).
3 Accounts must be laid out in a certain way and made available to members of the public.
4 Usually, the company will apply to the Stock Exchange for a 'listing', which means that it will be easy for shareholders to buy and sell shares. The Stock Exchange will look carefully at the accounts and the trading record of the company to ensure that it is not a poorly operated company.

When these stages have been completed the company will issue a PROSPECTUS. This is an invitation to the public to buy shares in the company. It is a very detailed document giving details of the company's past record and its plans for the future. The reasons for raising more capital and how it will be spent will be fully explained.

A public limited company has certain advantages and disadvantages.

Advantages of a public limited company

☑ This form of business organisation still offers limited liability to shareholders.
☑ It is an incorporated business and is a separate legal unit. Its accounts are kept separately from those of the owners and there is continuity should one of the shareholders die.
☑ There is now the opportunity to raise *very large capital* sums to invest in the business. There is no limit to the number of shareholders a public limited company can have.
☑ There is no restriction on the buying, selling or transfer of shares.
☑ A business trading as a public limited company usually has *high status* and, if properly managed, will find it easier to attract suppliers prepared to sell goods on credit and banks willing to lend to it than other types of businesses.

Disadvantages of a public limited company

✪ The *legal formalities* of forming such a company are quite complicated and time consuming.
✪ There are many more *regulations and controls* over public limited companies in order to try to protect the interests of the shareholders. This includes the publication of accounts which anyone can ask to see. Some public limited companies grow so large that they become *difficult to control and manage*.
✪ Selling shares to the public is *expensive*. The directors will often ask a specialist bank, a merchant bank, to help them in this process and they will charge high commission for their services. Also, the publication and printing of thousands of copies of the prospectus is an additional cost.

■ **Definition to learn:**
A PROSPECTUS is a detailed document issued by the directors of a company when they are converting it to public limited company status. It is an invitation to the general public to buy shares in the newly formed plc.

❌ There is a very real danger that although the original owners of the business might become rich by selling shares in their business they may *lose control* over it when it 'goes public'. This is an important point which we will investigate further.

Control and ownership in a public limited company

In all sole trader businesses and partnerships the owners have control over how their business is run. They take all the decisions and they will try to make the business achieve the aims that they have set.

This is also the case in most private limited companies, most of which have relatively few shareholders. The directors are often the *majority* shareholders which means that they can ensure that their decisions are passed at all meetings.

With a public limited company the situation is very different. There are often thousands of shareholders – even millions in the case of the largest companies. It would be impossible for all these people to be involved in taking decisions – although they are all invited to attend the ANNUAL GENERAL MEETING (AGM). The only decision that shareholders can have a real impact on at this meeting is the election of *company directors*. These professional managers may not be major shareholders. They are given the responsibility of running the business and taking decisions. They will only meet with the other shareholders once a year at the AGM. The directors cannot possibly run the business by themselves so they appoint managers, who may not be shareholders at all, to take day-to-day decisions. The diagram below explains this situation.

> ■ **Definition to learn:**
> ANNUAL GENERAL MEETING is a legal requirement for all companies. All shareholders may attend. They vote on who they want to be on the Board of Directors for the coming year.

Control and ownership in a public limited company

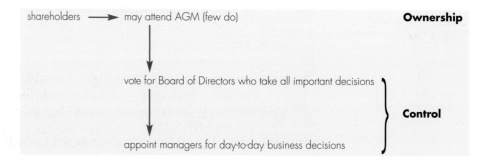

So, the *shareholders own*, but the *directors* and *managers control.* Sometimes, this is called the *divorce between ownership and control.*

Does this matter? It might be important for the shareholders, who after all, actually own the company and have risked their own money to buy shares. It means that the directors and managers may run the business to meet their own *objectives*. These could be increased status, growth of the business to justify higher management salaries, or reducing DIVIDENDS to shareholders to pay for expansion plans. The shareholders are not able to influence these decisions – other than by replacing the directors at the next AGM. This could give the company very bad publicity and cause the business to be unstable as the new directors may be inexperienced.

> ■ **Definition to learn:**
> DIVIDENDS are payments made to shareholders from the profits of a company after it has paid corporation tax (see page 56). They are the return to shareholders for investing in the company.

■ *Case study example*

Mike and Gita had decided to convert the company into a public one – Express Taxi and Bus plc. By selling shares in their company, they had not only raised the capital they needed but they had also become very rich. They were elected as directors at the first AGM for the new plc. The expansion into buying the privatised bus companies was successful – at first. Profits rose and management salaries did too. However, new bus competitors were forcing bus fares down. Profits started to fall. The accounts published last year showed the lowest profits for three years. Mike and Gita were voted off the Board of Directors. They no longer had a majority of the shares – when it was a private limited company they owned 50 per cent of the shares each. Since 'going public', they owned only 20 per cent of the total shares issued. They had lost control of what had been their business. The new directors owned few shares. They cut dividends to shareholders and announced a new expansion programme to increase profits.

Mike and Gita were rich but no longer controlled the business that had once belonged just to them. Mike missed being in control. He was thinking of setting up his own business by buying a luxury hotel. He planned to operate as a sole trader!

Mike and Gita now had to explain the performance of the company to a large number of shareholders at the AGM

Express Taxi & Bus plc Annual General Meeting

Revision summary: public limited companies

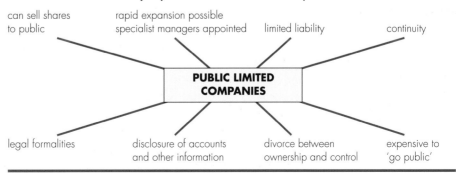

can sell shares to public

rapid expansion possible
specialist managers appointed

limited liability

continuity

PUBLIC LIMITED COMPANIES

legal formalities

disclosure of accounts and other information

divorce between ownership and control

expensive to 'go public'

■ *Activity 3.2*

a) How does the existence of limited liability benefit an individual shareholder?

b) Does limited liability make it easier or more difficult for companies to attract new shareholders? Explain your answer.

c) Explain why a sole trader might *not* want to convert the business into a partnership.

d) It is possible to convert a public limited company back into a private limited company. This is done by individuals buying up a majority of the shares. Richard Branson did this several years ago with the Virgin Group. Why might Mike and Gita have wanted to do this with the Express Taxi and Bus plc?

Co-operatives

Co-operatives are groups of people who agree to work together and pool their resources. They can take several different forms, but co-operatives all have certain common features.

■ All members have one vote, no matter how many shares they have bought.

■ All members help in the running of the business. The workload and decision-making are shared. In larger co-operatives it is common to find that a manager is appointed to manage the day-to-day matters of the business.

■ The profits are shared equally amongst members.

In the UK, the two most common forms are:

■ *producer co-operatives* which are groups of workers who design and produce products in just the same way as other manufacturing businesses

■ *retail co-operatives* which have the aim of providing their members with good quality consumer goods and services at reasonable prices.

In other countries the main type of co-operative exists in the agricultural industry. The members arrange for the purchase of materials in bulk in order to benefit from economies of scale. The co-operative also often arranges to sell the output of all of its members at attractive prices to big customers. Farmers owning small farms would be unable to gain from either of these features if they traded on their own.

Other business organisations in the private sector

We have looked at the main forms of business organisation in the private sector. Three other types of business organisation exist and these also merit some attention.

Close corporations

This type of business does not exist in the UK, but it is actively encouraged in other countries, such as South Africa. This type of business organisation is similar to a private limited company but is quicker to set up. There are fewer rules and regulations about its formation and management.

The key features of close corporations are as follows.

■ They are limited to a maximum of ten people.
■ A simple founding statement, sent to the Registrar of Companies, is all that is needed to set up the organisation.
■ The members are also the managers (no separation between ownership and control).
■ They are separate legal units offering both limited liability and continuity.

There are two criticisms of close corporations.

■ As membership is limited to ten people, it is not a suitable form of organisation for large businesses.
■ As in a partnership, members may disagree over decision-making.

Joint ventures

Many businesses now use joint ventures, especially for new projects. A joint venture is when two or more businesses agree to start a new project together. This could be setting up a factory to supply components and spare parts to two manufacturers. When research and development into new products, such as aircraft, is likely to be very expensive, two firms might agree to share costs. When production starts they will probably share manufacture and profits as well. Joint ventures, therefore, spread risks and reduce costs for any one business. However, they can lead to disagreements and disputes over policy and management of the new venture.

Franchising

This is now an extremely widespread form of business operation. The *franchisor* is a business with a product or service idea that it does not want to sell to consumers directly. Instead, it appoints *franchisees* to use the idea or product and to sell it to consumers. Two of the best known international examples are McDonalds restaurants and The Body Shop.

Advantages to the franchisor

☑ Expansion is paid for by the franchisee who pays for the shop and has to purchase the licence to use the product name.

☑ Expansion is much faster than if the franchisor had to finance new outlets from its own capital.

☑ The sale of the licences to use the brand name and products is a major source of profits.

☑ The franchisor does not operate the retail units – the management problems belong to the franchisee.

Advantages to the franchisee

☑ The chances of the business failing are much reduced because a well-known brand and product are being sold.

☑ The advertising is paid for, usually, by the franchisor.

☑ All supplies are obtained from a single source – the franchisor.

☑ Many decisions have already been made by the franchisor and cannot be changed, for example the layout and decor of the store and the prices to be charged. There are fewer decisions to worry about.

☑ Training for staff and management is provided by the franchisor.

☑ Banks are often prepared to lend to franchisees when they might refuse the loan application of a business operating without the support and advice of a huge franchisor organisation.

Franchised businesses give benefits to both the franchisor and the franchisee – but they must both contribute too

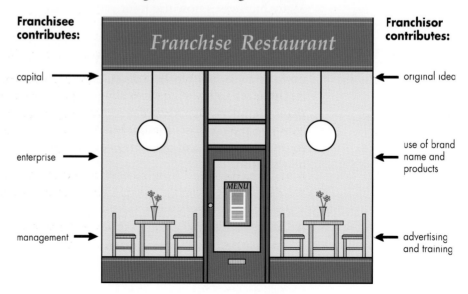

Business organisations: the public sector

The public sector is a very important part of the economy of all countries. The term 'public sector' includes all businesses owned by the state and local government, public services, such as hospitals, schools and the fire services, and government departments. This section is concerned with the business organisations owned by the state and local government.

There are two main types of business organisations in the public sector:

■ public corporations
■ municipal enterprises.

Public corporations

These are wholly owned by the state or central government. They are usually businesses which have been *nationalised*. This means that they were once owned by private individuals, but were purchased by the government. Examples of these in many countries include water supply and rail services – but, as we saw in Unit 2, even these businesses are now being *privatised* in many countries.

Public corporations are owned by the government but the government does not directly operate the businesses. Government ministers appoint a Board of Directors who will be given the responsibility of managing the business. The government will, however, make clear what the objectives of the business should be. The directors are expected to run the corporation according to these objectives.

Objectives of public corporations

These objectives have, in most countries, changed in recent years. Public corporations, or *parastatals* as they are referred to sometimes, used to be given certain *social objectives*. These may have included:

■ to keep prices low so that everybody can afford the service
■ to keep people in jobs so that unemployment does not rise
■ to offer a service to the public in all areas of the country.

To keep to these objectives often costs a great deal of money. Public corporations often made huge losses. These were paid for by *subsidies from the government* out of taxes. Most governments realised that they could not continue to pay for these subsidies. So public corporations have, in general, been given other objectives:

■ to reduce costs, if necessary, by reducing the number of workers
■ to increase efficiency and operate more like a company in the private sector
■ to close loss-making services, even if this means that some consumers are no longer provided with the service.

This policy of reducing subsidies and operating more like a private sector business is sometimes called *corporatisation* – the public corporations are being made ready for full privatisation. The arguments for and against privatisation were considered in Unit 2, but it is useful to remind ourselves of the claimed advantages and disadvantages of operating a business as a public corporation.

Advantages of public corporations

☑ Some industries are considered to be so important – strategically necessary – that government ownership is thought to be essential. In many countries the state airline is still in the public sector and electricity generation is rarely in the private sector.

☑ If industries are controlled by monopolies because it would be wasteful to have competitors – two sets of railway lines to a certain town, for example – then these *natural monopolies* are often owned by the government. It is argued that this will ensure that consumers are not taken advantage of by privately owned monopolists.

☑ If an important business is failing and likely to collapse the government can step in to nationalise it. This will keep the business open and secure jobs. If the business becomes profitable again the government has the option of privatising it.

☑ Important public services, such as TV and radio broadcasting, are often in the public sector. The BBC is a good example of a public corporation in this industry. Non-profitable but important programmes can still be made available to the public.

Disadvantages of public corporations

☒ There are no private shareholders to insist on high profits and efficiency. The profit motive might not be as powerful as in private sector industries.

☒ Subsidies can lead to inefficiency as managers will always think that the government will help them if the business makes a loss. It is also considered unfair if the public corporation receives a subsidy but private firms in the same industry do not.

☒ Often there is no close competition to the public corporations. There is therefore a lack of incentive to increase consumer choice and increase efficiency.

☒ Governments can use these businesses for political reasons, for example just before an election they could create more jobs. This prevents the public corporations being operated like other profit-making businesses.

Municipal enterprises

Local government authorities or municipalities usually operate some trading activities. Some of these services are free to the user and paid for out of local taxes, such as street lighting and schools. Other services are charged for and expected to break even at least (see Unit 6). These might include street markets, swimming pools and theatres. If they do not cover their costs, a local government subsidy is usually provided. In order to cut costs and reduce the burden on local taxpayers, an increasing range of services are now being privatised, so reducing the role of local government in providing goods and services.

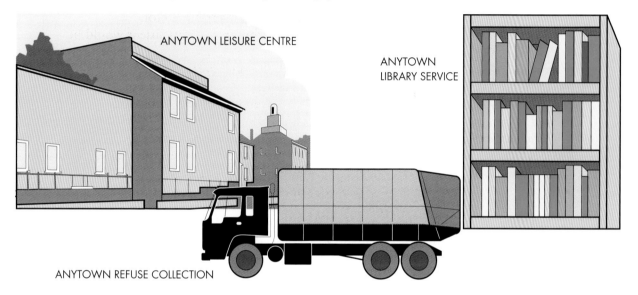

ANYTOWN LEISURE CENTRE

ANYTOWN LIBRARY SERVICE

ANYTOWN REFUSE COLLECTION

■ *Revision questions*

1 Which form of business organisation do you think is most suitable for each of the following businesses? Explain your answer fully.
   a) A group of workers have been made redundant (lost their jobs) following a business failure. They agree to put some of their savings together to buy an old factory. They plan to make bicycles for export. They want everybody to have equal rights in running the business.   [3]
   b) A business with many hotels is planning to expand abroad. A substantial sum of money will be needed to finance this expansion. Expert managers will be needed to run the business.   [3]
   c) A young student is planning to offer his services to neighbours as a gardener. He will purchase only cheap tools to start with.   [3]
   d) A TV and radio broadcasting business aims to provide services to the whole population regardless of their ability to pay.   [3]
   e) A small group of lawyers wish to set up in business together. Their professional association does not allow lawyers to have limited liability.   [3]
   f) The Managing Director of a small garage business is planning to retire. He hopes that his son will be able to take over the business at this time.   [3]

2 Explain *two* disadvantages of a partnership.   [4]

3 Explain *two* benefits to a sole trader of converting to private limited company status.   [4]

4 State *three* possible drawbacks to converting a private limited company into a public limited company.   [3]

5 Explain the difference between the *public sector of industry* and *public limited companies*.   [3]

6 State *two* reasons why two businesses might decide to set up a joint venture.   [2]

7 'Sometimes there is a conflict between the management of a public limited company and its owners over how the profits should be used.' Explain what is meant by this statement.   [2]

8 Explain why the *conflict* referred to in Question 7 can occur.   [3]

9 Explain what is meant by a *franchise*.   [2]

10 Tom Shah has just gained a qualification in catering. He wants to run a small fast food outlet. He is not sure whether to run it as an independent sole trader or as a franchise.
   a) Explain one advantage and one disadvantage for Tom if he decides to run the business as a sole trader.   [4]
   b) Explain one advantage for Tom if he decides to run the business as a franchise and one advantage for the franchisor.   [4]

11 Explain *two* possible benefits to society of having the main TV service operated as a public corporation.   [4]

The CD-ROM (see details on page x) provides further tests, activities and Case study work on the topics covered in this unit.

Government and economic influences on business

This unit will explain:

- ☑ the effect that uncontrolled business activity can have on society
- ☑ why governments control business activity
- ☑ why governments help business, in particular small firms
- ☑ the economic objectives of governments
- ☑ the measures governments can take to control the economy.

At the end of this unit you should be able to:

- ☑ analyse why governments control business activity and how this is done
- ☑ explain why governments assist some businesses and how this is done
- ☑ understand the aims of government policy
- ☑ explain the ways in which businesses are affected by government economic decisions.

The impact of business activity on society

The following table outlines some of the *benefits* of business activity as well as some of the possible *undesirable effects*. This will help us to understand why governments usually take steps to control business activity in important ways.

Possible benefits to society of business activity	Possible undesirable effects of business activity
■ Production of useful goods and services which people wish to buy ■ Creation of jobs and incomes. These increase workers' living standards ■ Introduction of new products and processes that widen product range and reduce costs of production ■ Tax payments made by business to governments help to finance essential public services ■ By producing goods for export, businesses earn foreign currency that the country can spend on imports	■ Profit motive of business can lead to decisions to locate in cheap but attractive and unspoilt areas ■ Managers aiming to lower costs might offer very low wages with poor and unsafe working conditions ■ Some production methods lead to serious pollution problems ■ Certain goods made by industry are dangerous or can add to the pollution problem, e.g. fast cars ■ Profit motive can lead firms to merge and this can lead to monopoly control with less consumer choice ■ Advertising is very powerful and can be used to give a misleading image or incorrect information to persuade consumers to buy

■ **Definition to learn:**
STAKEHOLDERS are those groups in society that have a direct interest in the performance and activities of business.

The great problem for all governments is this: how can the *benefits* of business activity be encouraged whilst controlling or outlawing the *undesirable effects?* The answer to this problem is often for governments to use changes in the law to control *undesirable* business activity whilst giving support to firms engaging in *desirable* activity.

Look again at the list of undesirable effects – for all of these reasons governments in most countries have decided to control business decision-making. This control is thought to be for the good of consumers, workers, local residents and the whole community – the STAKEHOLDERS in the business.

Governments and the economy

From Unit 2 you will remember the different types of economic system which can exist in a country. No perfect example of a market system exists. Therefore, in all countries of the world the government has some power in the economy. This power can have a great effect on businesses. What economic power do most governments have and what are they trying to achieve with this power? We will look, firstly, at the economic aims of government – then we will consider the economic decisions that they can make.

Government economic objectives

Most governments consider that the following objectives are desirable:

■ **Definitions to learn:**
INFLATION is the increase in the average price level of goods and services over time.

UNEMPLOYMENT exists when people who are willing and able to work cannot find a job.

ECONOMIC GROWTH is when a country's Gross Domestic Product increases – more goods and services are produced than in the previous year.

The BALANCE OF PAYMENTS records the difference between a country's exports and imports.

REAL INCOME is the value of income in the context of current price levels.

- low price INFLATION
- low levels of UNEMPLOYMENT
- ECONOMIC GROWTH
- BALANCE OF PAYMENTS (equality between exports and imports).

Low price inflation

Inflation occurs when prices rise. Low inflation is a very important aim. When prices rise rapidly it can be very serious for the whole country. These are the problems Country A will have if there is rapid inflation.

- Workers' wages will not buy as many goods as before. This means that people's REAL INCOMES will fall. Real income is the value, in terms of what can be bought, of an income – if a worker receives a 6 per cent wage increase but prices rise by 10 per cent in the same year, then the worker's real income has fallen by 4 per cent. Workers may demand higher wages so that their real incomes increase.
- Prices of the goods produced in the country will be higher than those in other countries. People may buy foreign goods instead. Jobs in Country A will be lost.
- Businesses will be unlikely to want to expand and create more jobs in the future. The living standards in Country A are likely to fall.

Therefore low inflation tends to encourage businesses to expand and it makes it easier for a country to sell its goods and services abroad.

High rates of inflation
reduce real incomes

Low levels of unemployment

When people want to work but cannot find a job then they are
unemployed. Country B has a very high level of unemployment. These
are the problems which this causes.

■ Unemployed people do not produce any goods or services. The total
level of output in the country will be lower than it could be.
■ The government of Country B pays unemployment benefit to those
without jobs. A high level of unemployment will cost the government a
great deal of money. This cannot be spent on other things such as
schools and hospitals.

Therefore, low unemployment will help to increase the output of a
country and improve workers' living standards.

High unemployment
reduces output and can
reduce living standards

■ **Definition to learn:**
GROSS DOMESTIC PRODUCT
(GDP) is the total value of
output of goods and
services in a country in
one year.

Economic growth

An economy is said to grow when the total level of output of goods and
services in a country increases. The value of goods and services produced
in a country in one year is called GROSS DOMESTIC PRODUCT (GDP).
When a country is experiencing economic growth, the *standard of living*
of the population is likely to increase.

When Country C's GDP is falling, it has no economic growth. These are the problems this causes.

■ As the country's output is falling, fewer workers are needed and unemployment will occur.
■ The average standard of living of people in the country – the number of goods and services they can afford to buy in one year – will decline. In effect, most people will become poorer.
■ Business owners will not expand their firms as people will have less money to spend on the products they make.

Economic growth, however, makes a country richer and allows living standards to rise.

Economic growth will make a country richer and will allow living standards to rise

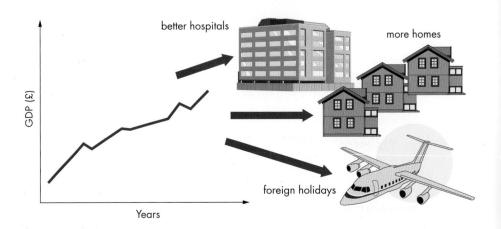

Economic growth and the trade cycle

Economic growth is not achieved every year – there are often years when the economy does not grow at all or when the value of GDP actually falls. This pattern is shown below on the *trade cycle* diagram:

A trade cycle diagram

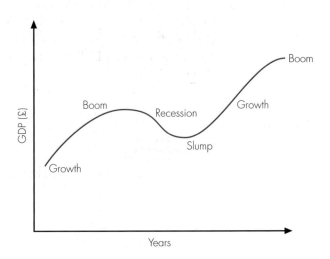

The trade cycle (sometimes known as the business cycle) has four main stages, as shown on the diagram.

- *Growth*   This is when GDP is rising, unemployment is generally falling and the country is enjoying higher living standards. Most businesses will do well at this time.
- *Boom*   This is caused by too much spending. Prices start to rise quickly and there will be shortages of skilled workers. Business costs will be rising and firms will become uncertain about the future.
- *Recession*   Often caused by too little spending. This is a period when GDP actually falls. Most businesses will experience falling demand and profits. Workers may lose their jobs.
- *Slump*   A serious and long-drawn-out recession. Unemployment will reach very high levels and prices may fall. Many businesses will fail to survive this period.

Clearly, governments will try to avoid the economy moving towards a recession or a slump, but will also want to reduce the chances of a boom. A boom with rapid inflation and higher business costs can often lead to the conditions that result in a recession.

■ **Definitions to learn:**

EXPORTS are goods and services sold from one country to other countries.

IMPORTS are goods and services bought in by one country from other countries.

EXCHANGE RATES are the price of one currency in terms of another, for example £1:$1.5.

EXCHANGE RATE DEPRECIATION is the fall in the value of a currency compared with other currencies.

Balance of payments

EXPORTS are goods and services sold by one country to people and businesses in another country. These bring money (foreign currency) into a country. IMPORTS are goods bought in from other countries. These must be purchased with foreign currency so these lead to money flowing out of a country. Governments will aim to achieve equality or balance between these over a period of time. The difference between a country's exports and imports is called the balance of payments.

Country D imports more than it exports – it has a balance of payments deficit. These are the problems that could result:

- The country could 'run out' of other countries' currencies (foreign currencies) and it may have to borrow from abroad.
- The price of Country D's currency against other currencies – the EXCHANGE RATE – will be likely to fall. This is called EXCHANGE RATE DEPRECIATION. Country D's currency will now buy less abroad than it did before depreciation. Exchange rates are explained further in Unit 25.

A balance of payments deficit can lead to major problems for a country

■ Activity 4.1

a) The GDP of Country E was £500 million in 1991. The population was 1 million. The average income per person was therefore £500. By 2001, as a result of economic growth, GDP was £1,500 million. The population had also risen to 2 million. What was the average income in 2001?

b) Joe earned £20,000 in 2000. He had a pay rise of 10 per cent in 2001. Inflation was 15 per cent in 2001.
  i) How much did Joe earn in 2001?
  ii) Did his real income rise or fall in 2001? Explain your answer.

c) For Country F, identify which of the following are imports or exports:
  i) washing machines purchased from Country D
  ii) cars made in Country F's factories and sold to a garage in Country E
  iii) machines sold to Country A
  iv) tourists from Country B who spend two weeks on holiday in a hotel in Country F.

Revision summary: economic objectives of government

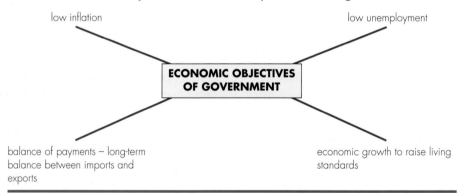

low inflation

low unemployment

ECONOMIC OBJECTIVES OF GOVERNMENT

balance of payments – long-term balance between imports and exports

economic growth to raise living standards

Government economic policies

Governments have a great deal of economic power. They raise taxes and spend this money on a wide range of services and state benefits. It is not unusual for governments to have control over 40–50 per cent of a country's GDP through the taxes they raise. Governments can also pass laws which can have an impact on the economy, such as a law to introduce a minimum wage. Governments use this power to try to achieve the objectives we have just looked at. The decisions made by government can have a great effect on all businesses in a country. Business managers need to know how their firm could be affected by government economic decisions. The main ways in which governments can influence the economy – sometimes called *economic policies* – are:

■ taxes and government spending – fiscal policy
■ interest rates – monetary policy
■ supply side policies.

Taxes and government spending

All governments spend money. They spend it on schools, hospitals, roads, defence, and so on. This expenditure is very important to some businesses. For example:

- construction firms will benefit from a new road building scheme
- defence industries will gain if the government re-equips the army
- bus manufacturers will benefit from government spending on public transport.

Where do governments raise this money from? Largely from taxes on individuals and businesses.

What are the main types of taxes? DIRECT TAXES on the income of businesses and individuals and INDIRECT TAXES on spending.

How do these taxes affect business activity? In a number of different ways. We will look at these by studying the effects of four common taxes:

- income tax
- profits tax or corporation tax
- indirect taxes, for example Value Added Tax (VAT)
- import duties and tariffs.

Income tax

This is a tax used by most governments. It is a tax on people's incomes. Usually, the higher a person's income the greater will be the amount of tax they have to pay to the government. Income tax is set at a certain percentage of income, for example 25 per cent of income. In many countries, income tax is *progressive*. This means that the rich pay tax at a higher rate than the poor.

How would businesses be affected by an increase in the rate of income tax? Individual taxpayers would have a lower disposable income. They would have less money to spend and save. Businesses would be likely to see a fall in sales. Managers may decide to produce fewer goods as sales are lower. Some workers could lose their jobs.

Which businesses are likely to be most affected by the increase in income tax rates? Businesses which produce luxury goods which consumers do not have to buy are likely to be the most affected. Businesses producing essential goods and services will be less affected. Consumers will still have to buy these products.

■ Case study example

The government of Country A has set the following rate of income tax:

Income level	Tax rate paid to government
€1–€5,000 per year	20%
More than €5,000 per year	30%

How much tax would John, earning €10,000 per year, pay to the government? The answer is €2,500. This is worked out as follows:

20 per cent of the first €5,000 = €1,000
30 per cent of the next €5,000 = €1,500

How much income has John left to spend or save after tax? The answer is €7,500. This is called the taxpayer's DISPOSABLE INCOME. John can now 'dispose' of it, i.e. spend it or save it, as he chooses.

■ **Definition to learn:**
DISPOSABLE INCOME is the level of income a taxpayer has after paying income tax.

■ Activity 4.2

Here are eight products:

bread   petrol   TVs   foreign holidays
cooking oil   jewellery   salt   home computers

The sales of four of these products are likely to fall following an increase in income tax rates. Sales of the other four will not be much affected. Identify the four products likely to be most affected.

Profits tax or corporation tax

This is a tax on the profits made by businesses – usually companies.
How would an increase in the rate of corporation tax affect businesses? There would be two main effects.

■ These businesses would have lower profits after tax. Managers will therefore have less money or finance to put back into the business. The business will find it more difficult to expand. New projects, such as additional factories or shops, may have to be cancelled.
■ Lower profits after tax is also bad news for the owners of the business. There will be less money to pay back to the owners who originally invested in the business. Fewer people will want to start their own business if they consider that the government will take a large share of any profits made.

Indirect taxes

Indirect taxes, such as Value Added Tax (VAT), are added to the prices of the products we all buy. They obviously make goods and services more expensive for consumers. Governments often avoid putting these taxes on really essential items, such as food, because this would be considered unfair, especially to poorer consumers.

How would businesses be affected by an increase in an expenditure tax? Again, there would be two main effects.

■ Prices of goods in the shops would rise. Consumers may buy fewer items as a result. This will reduce the demand for products made by businesses. Not all businesses will be affected in the same way, however. If consumers need to buy a product such as a new battery for their alarm clock, then the price increase is unlikely to stop them from doing so. However, they could buy fewer ice creams as their prices have risen and they are hardly essential to anyone!

■ As prices rise so the workers employed by a firm notice that their wages buy less in the shops. It is said that their *real incomes* have declined. Businesses may be under pressure to raise wages, which will force up the costs of making products.

Import duties and tariffs

Many governments try to reduce the imports of products from other countries by putting special taxes on them. These are called *duties* or *tariffs* and they raise money for the government. As we will see, many international organisations are trying to reduce the number of governments which do this.

How would business in a country be affected if the government put tariffs on imports into the country? There are three possible effects.

■ Firms will benefit if they are *competing with imported goods*. These will now become more expensive, leading to an increase in sales of home-produced goods.

■ Businesses will suffer *higher costs* if they have to import raw materials or components for their own factories. These will now be more expensive.

■ Other countries may now take the same action and put on import tariffs too. This is called *retaliation*. A business trying to export to these countries will probably sell fewer goods than before.

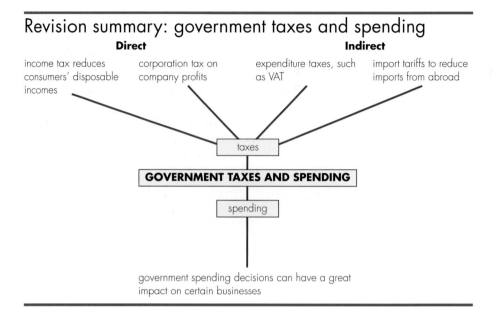

Revision summary: government taxes and spending

Direct

income tax reduces consumers' disposable incomes

corporation tax on company profits

Indirect

expenditure taxes, such as VAT

import tariffs to reduce imports from abroad

taxes

GOVERNMENT TAXES AND SPENDING

spending

government spending decisions can have a great impact on certain businesses

Interest rates

An *interest rate* is the cost of borrowing money. In most countries, the level of interest rates is fixed by the government or the central bank. In some societies, the charging and the payment of interest is against the customs and traditions of the population. In most countries, however, businesses and individuals can borrow money, from a bank for example, and they will have to pay interest on the loan.

What impact would higher interest rates, imposed by the government, have on businesses in that country? The following are likely to be the main effects.

■ Firms with existing loans will have to pay *more in interest* to the banks. This will reduce their profits. Lower profits mean less is available to distribute to the owners and less is retained for business expansion.
■ Managers thinking about borrowing money to expand their business may delay their decision. *New investment* in business activity will be reduced. Fewer new factories and offices will be built. People hoping to start a new business may not now be able to afford to borrow the capital needed.
■ If consumers have taken out loans such as *mortgages* to buy their houses, then the higher interest payments will reduce their *disposable incomes*. Demand for all goods and services could fall as consumers have less money to spend.
■ In addition to the point above, if the business makes expensive consumer items like cars or if they build houses then they will notice that *consumer demand will fall* for another reason. Consumers will be unwilling to borrow money to buy these expensive items if interest rates are higher. These businesses may have to reduce output and make workers redundant.

■ **Definition to learn:**

EXCHANGE RATE APPRECIATION is the rise in the value of a currency compared to other currencies.

■ Higher interest rates in one country will encourage foreign banks and individuals to deposit their capital in that country. They will be able to earn higher rates of interest on their capital. By switching their money into this country's currency they are increasing the demand for it. The exchange rate will rise – this is called EXCHANGE RATE APPRECIATION. This will have the effect of making imported goods appear cheaper and exports will now be more expensive. Firms will notice the demand for their products falling for this reason. (The opposite effect, if the exchange rate of a currency declines, is called an *exchange rate depreciation*.)

Revision summary: interest rates

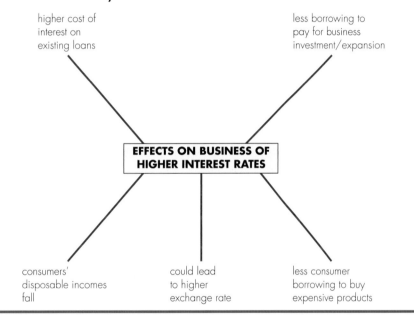

higher cost of interest on existing loans

less borrowing to pay for business investment/expansion

EFFECTS ON BUSINESS OF HIGHER INTEREST RATES

consumers' disposable incomes fall

could lead to higher exchange rate

less consumer borrowing to buy expensive products

Supply side policies

In recent years many governments have tried to make the economy of their country more efficient. They aim to increase the competitiveness of their industries against those from other countries. Governments want the businesses in their country to expand, produce more and employ more workers. Some of the policies which have been used to achieve these aims are listed below – they are called *supply side policies* because they are trying to improve the efficient supply of goods and services.

■ *Privatisation* As we saw in Unit 2, privatisation is now very common. The aim is to use the profit motive to improve business efficiency.
■ *Improve training and education* Governments plan to improve the skills of the country's workers. This is particularly important in those industries such as computer software which are often very short of skilled staff.
■ *Increase competition in all industries* This may be done by reducing government controls over industry or by acting against monopolies.

■ *Activity 4.3: case study task*

You are the Managing Director of the largest computer manufacturing company in your country. Your business sells products at home and in foreign markets. Materials are imported from abroad. You employ hundreds of skilled workers to develop, assemble and test the computers. Your business is planning a major expansion programme.

The government of your country has recently announced the following policies. Explain the likely impact of *each* of these policies on your business:

a) an increase in income tax rates on high income earners
b) lower corporation tax rates
c) higher import tariffs on all imports
d) higher interest rates
e) lower expenditure taxes on luxury goods
f) new training colleges to increase the supply of qualified workers
g) strict controls on monopoly businesses to encourage new businesses to be formed.

Revision summary: government economic policies

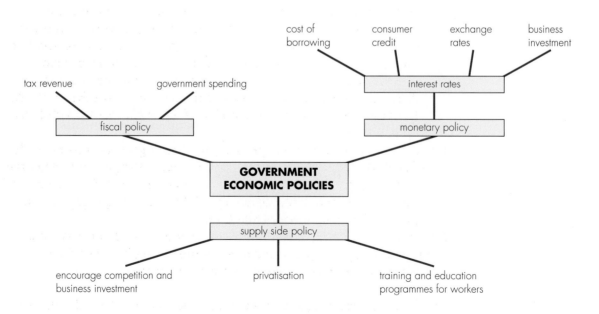

Government controls over business activity

You should now understand the impact governments can have on businesses by changing economic policies. These policies are not the only influence governments have on business. Business activity is also controlled more directly by government. These are some of the main areas of business activity which are often directly controlled by government action:

■ production decisions – what firms can and cannot produce
■ responsibilities to employees, including working conditions
■ responsibilities to consumers
■ responsibilities to the natural environment
■ location decisions (see also Unit 24).

Why is government control of business sometimes seen as desirable? Business activity produces goods and services which people wish to buy. It creates jobs and incomes for workers. Government receives a great deal of its tax income from businesses. Why, then, is it desirable to control business activity? Several points will help to make this clearer.

■ Businesses are usually operated with the aim of making a profit. The profit objective can lead to managers sometimes taking decisions which may be harmful to others. For example:
  – The most profitable site for a new factory might be in a beautiful country area. Building the factory there would damage the natural environment.
  – Some products are considered dangerous and their production or use of them could lead to death or injury. Explosives or dangerous drugs are good examples. Businesses might still make these goods if they could make a profit, unless the government stopped them.
  – The production of some goods leads to pollution, for example, dangerous waste products such as chemicals or radioactive materials. Businesses might continue to pollute if it was cheaper than cleaning up the waste.
■ Some businesses are very large. They might not give consumers much choice if they control the market for a product. Also, workers may have no chance of gaining a job with any other business and the managers of a large business could take advantage of this. They might pay very low wages or offer poor working conditions.
■ With TV and cinema advertising so common, it would be easy for a business to give people an incorrect or misleading image of their products in order to encourage more to buy them.

For all of these reasons, governments in most countries have decided to control some business activities. This control is thought to be for the good of the consumers, workers, local residents and the community.

How do governments control business activity?

Control is usually achieved by passing laws which make certain business activities illegal. The following are some of the main examples of business activities controlled by the law.

Production of certain goods

Some products are so dangerous that it would be unwise for a society to allow them to be made available to consumers. Guns, explosives and dangerous drugs are illegal in many countries. The production and sale of alcohol is also against the law in some countries. The government of each country will decide which goods and services it believes should not be sold to its people. The production and sale of these will then either be strictly controlled or made illegal.

Goods which harm the natural environment can also be banned. In certain countries it is now not possible to generate electricity by nuclear power – the pollution danger is thought to be too great. In cases like these, the government is restricting business activity for the sake of the natural environment.

Governments can use controls to stop or limit certain business activities

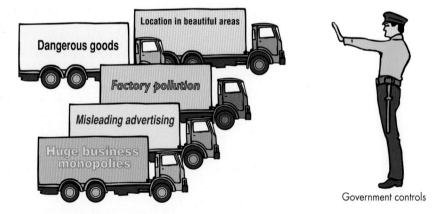

Government controls

Consumer protection

Consumers can be easily misled. It is quite easy to sell to many consumers goods that are either unsuitable for the purpose intended or that fail to perform as the manufacturer claimed. This is not because consumers are stupid! It is because products are now so complicated and technical that it is very difficult for a consumer to know how good they are or how they are likely to work. Also modern advertising can be so persuasive that nearly all of us could be sold products, even if they were later discovered to be of poor quality or not as good as the advert claimed. Consumers need protection against businesses which could, unfortunately, take advantage of the consumers' lack of knowledge and lack of accurate product information.

In the UK, the laws on consumer protection are typical of those existing in most countries. The most important laws – called Acts of Parliament – which protect the consumer are:

■ *1951 Weights and Measures Act* Retailers and producers commit an offence if they sell under-weight goods or if the weighing equipment they use is inaccurate.

■ *1968 Trade Descriptions Act* This makes it illegal to give the consumer a deliberately misleading impression about a product. For example, it is illegal to state that a pair of trousers is made of wool, when they are made of cotton. Advertisements must therefore be truthful.

■ *1974 Consumer Credit Act* Many consumers can be encouraged to buy goods on credit when they do not have enough cash. This Act makes it illegal not to give consumers a copy of the credit agreement – they must be able to check how long they have borrowed money for and at what rate of interest.

■ *1979 Sale of Goods Act* This is a most important law. It states that it is illegal to sell:
  – products which have serious flaws or problems with them, i.e. they are not of a satisfactory quality
  – products which are not fit for the purpose intended by the consumer, for example if the consumer asks for a drill to make holes in walls and is sold one which is only suitable for wood
  – products which do not perform as described on the label or by the retailer, for example, if the label states 'These shoes are completely waterproof' and they leak the first time they are used!

■ *1987 Consumer Protection Act* This brought UK consumer protection law up to date with that in the European Union (EU). It makes illegal misleading pricing claims such as '£40 off for this week only', when the product was also being sold for the same price the previous week. Most importantly, the law makes retailers and manufacturers liable – that is, responsible – for any damage which their faulty goods might cause. Anyone injured by faulty goods can take the supplier to court and ask for compensation.

It is illegal in the UK to sell items that do not live up to the claims made for them

These shoes are completely waterproof!

■ Activity 4.4

Here are five situations in which consumers might need some protection.

a) 'These shoes are made of the finest leather.' In fact they are made of plastic.
b) A consumer buys 1 kg of potatoes and re-weighs them at home. In fact, she has only 800 g.
c) A motorist asks for a tow rope 'strong enough for my trailer'. It breaks the first time he tries to use it.
d) '£5 below the manufacturer's recommended price.' In fact the product is being sold at the recommended price.
e) A consumer agrees to buy a car on credit. He signed the agreement but is told that all the copies must be sent to head office.

Do you think the consumer needs some legal protection in these cases? For each example, identify which UK law has been broken by the business selling the goods.

Is all consumer protection a good idea? Most people would say that the consumer needs to be protected as much as possible. They believe that goods should be as safe and as suitable for the purpose intended as possible. However, some business managers believe that these laws add to the costs of making and selling products and this increases the prices in the shops. What is your view?

Control of monopolies

A monopoly is when one firm controls or dominates the market for a good or service. Such firms may have eliminated their competitors by mergers or take-overs. They may have invented a product and then prevented other firms from making it. In other cases monopolies arise because it would be so expensive for other firms to set up in competition. For example, if the supply of electricity is controlled by one business, it would cost another firm a huge sum of money to build power stations to compete with it. Whatever the reason for monopolies existing, they can lead to important disadvantages.

Disadvantages of monopolies

- They can fix high prices to make high profits as they have no direct competitors.
- They can prevent new firms from setting up to compete with them. They might do this by charging very low prices for a short period, thus forcing the new firm out of business.
- As there are no competitors, the monopoly is not encouraged to become more efficient or to introduce new products.

Most governments attempt to control monopoly power in one way or another. In some countries monopolies are illegal and they must be broken up into a series of smaller firms. In other countries, such as the UK, monopoly businesses can be investigated by a committee set up by the government. In the UK, this is called the Competition Commission. This Commission reports to the government on two main types of problems:

- decisions taken by monopolists which are thought to be against consumer interests – such as trying to eliminate competitors or refusing to supply retailers which charge lower prices or sell competing products
- proposed mergers or take-overs that will create a monopoly.

The government can act upon the Commission's findings and prevent these business decisions from going ahead.

Protecting employees

Employees are workers in a business. This section also covers the legal rights of those who wish to become employees and who apply for jobs.
   Employees need protection in the following areas:

- against unfair discrimination at work and when applying for jobs
- health and safety at work
- employment protection
- wage protection.

Protection against unfair discrimination

Discrimination means to make a choice. The discrimination we are concerned with is when it is based on *unfair reasons.* For example, some employers discriminate unfairly against workers or people applying for jobs because they are:

- of a different race or colour
- belong to a different religion
- are of the opposite sex
- considered too old/young for the job
- disabled in some way.

In most countries many of these forms of discrimination are illegal. If they were not illegal, many sections of society would find it very difficult to gain jobs or to achieve promotion at work. Businesses can also lose out by practising unfair discrimination. They could fail to select a very good worker just because they used one of the reasons above not to select the person.
   In the UK, the Acts of Parliament which make unfair discrimination illegal are:

- *1975 Sex Discrimination Act* This makes it illegal to discriminate against people because of their sex or because they are married. Employers must not advertise for people of a certain sex or show discrimination in training, promotion or dismissal because of a worker's sex. The law tries to ensure that there is equal opportunity for people of both sexes in all work situations.

- *1976 Race Relations Act* This makes it clear that it is illegal to advertise for people of a certain race or to show discrimination in training, promotion or dismissal because of a worker's race.
- *1944 Disabled Persons (Employment) Act* Firms over a certain size are required to ensure that registered disabled people make up at least 3 per cent of the workforce. This Act is designed to give those who may be left out of the job market an opportunity to gain employment.

At present, there is no law in the UK to make discrimination on the basis of age illegal.

In addition to these laws, many employers have an *equal opportunities policy*. Employees who consider that they have been unfairly discriminated against can appeal to an equal opportunities committee.

Health and safety at work

Many years ago, most employers cared little for the safety of their workers. Machines did not have safety cages. Protective clothing was not issued. Conditions were often very hot or cold, noisy and unpleasant. The arguments often used by employers to explain such conditions were that: it would cost too much to make workplaces safe; if the existing workers did not like the conditions then they could leave as there were many unemployed who would do their work!

In our modern world such attitudes are no longer acceptable. Most employers now care for their workers' safety. One reason for this is that many laws have been passed that have forced them to improve health and safety at work. In most countries there are now laws which make sure that all employers:

- protect workers from dangerous machinery
- provide safety equipment and clothing
- maintain reasonable workplace temperatures
- provide hygienic conditions and washing facilities
- do not insist on excessively long shifts and provide breaks in the work timetable.

■ **Definition to learn:**
An ETHICAL DECISION is a decision taken by a manager because of the moral code observed in that firm. This can include improving working conditions for staff beyond legal requirements, or not producing dangerous or polluting goods – even if these activities are not illegal.

Are health and safety laws and controls over business a good idea? Most managers think so. Workers cost a great deal to recruit and train. It is worthwhile keeping them safe and healthy. Such workers are likely to be better motivated, work more efficiently and stay with the firm for a longer period of time.

For these reasons, some employers in countries where there are weak health and safety laws will still provide working conditions of a very high safety standard. The managers of these firms have taken an ETHICAL DECISION. That means that they have a set of standards or a set of moral rules that prevent them from acting in an unfair or dangerous way towards their workers. Do these managers make better employers? Most workers would think so, and would be better motivated to work harder and stay with the business because of this.

Unfortunately, in some countries there are employers who still take advantage of workers. There may be no protection on the length of shifts and many millions of children can still be seen working in industries that offer little protection from danger and ill health. In these countries workers are exploited and often paid low wages. Business costs are therefore very low. Should the rest of the world continue to buy products from these countries? What is your view?

Employment protection

Once in work, employees need protection from being dismissed unfairly. Obviously if the worker has stolen from the employer or is always late for work, dismissal would be reasonable. The following examples of dismissal are unfair:

- for joining a trade union
- for being pregnant
- when no warnings are given before dismissal.

In the UK if a worker feels that they have been dismissed unfairly then they can take their case to an INDUSTRIAL TRIBUNAL. This will hear both sides of the argument and may give the worker compensation if it believes that dismissal was unfair. Industrial tribunals are similar to courts of law and they can also be used to hear disputes between workers and employers on sex and race discrimination and redundancy.

Wage protection

Workers have a right to be paid for work they do for employers. There should be a written agreement between worker and employer – the CONTRACT OF EMPLOYMENT – which will contain details not only of hours of work and nature of the job but also of:

- the wage rate to be paid
- how frequently wages will be paid
- what deductions will be made from wages, for example, income tax.

In some countries employers can pay whatever wage rate they like. If there is high unemployment or if unemployment benefits are low, workers may be offered very low wages. Workers could find it very difficult to live on these wages. Increasingly, governments are taking action against employers who pay low wages. This action often takes the form of a legal *minimum wage*. A minimum wage exists in the UK and in other European countries and the USA. A minimum wage makes it illegal for an employer to pay an hourly rate below the minimum set. A legal minimum wage has a number of claimed advantages and disadvantages.

■ Definitions to learn:

An INDUSTRIAL TRIBUNAL is a legal meeting which considers workers' complaints of unfair dismissal or discrimination at work.

A CONTRACT OF EMPLOYMENT is a legal agreement between employer and employee listing the rights and responsibilities of workers.

Advantages of a legal minimum wage

☑ It should prevent strong employers from exploiting unskilled workers who could not easily find other work.

☑ As many unskilled workers are receiving higher wages, it might encourage employers to train them to make sure that they are more productive.

☑ It will encourage more people to seek work. There should be fewer shortages of workers.

☑ Low-paid workers will earn more and will be able to afford to spend more.

Disadvantages of a legal minimum wage

☒ It increases business costs which will force them to increase prices.

☒ Some employers will not be able to afford these wage rates. They may make workers redundant instead. Unemployment may rise.

☒ Other workers receiving just above the minimum level may ask for higher wages to keep the same *differential* between themselves and lower paid workers. Business costs will again increase.

■ *Activity 4.5: case study task*

Consider the way in which Gowri Kumaran was treated by her employer.

She applied for a job as machine operator in a radio assembly factory. The employer offered her the job and said that her contract of employment would be sent to her after one month's trial. After one month, Gowri received her wages but was surprised to see that her wage rate was much less than expected. She was also earning much less than other workers doing the same work. There had been several deductions from her wages which she did not understand. She did not receive a contract of employment as had been promised.

Gowri had complained to her supervisor that there were some loose electrical wires on her machine but no action had been taken. She worked 10-hour shifts with only one break. Gowri decided to join a trade union but when the manager heard about this he called her into his office. He told her that her work was unsatisfactory and she was no longer required. Gowri was very upset about the way she had been treated. She asked for your advice, as her legal adviser, on what she should do.

a) Do you think that Gowri has been badly treated by her employer? Give reasons for your answer.

b) As Gowri's legal adviser write a letter to the manager of the factory where she used to work. Explain to the manager all of the points of law which you think the manager has broken.

c) What might be the advantages to employers from treating their staff well?

Location of industry

The decisions by firms about where to locate their business can have a very important effect on the firm's profitability. Managers will want to locate their businesses in the best possible area, taking into account factors such as: cost of land, proximity to transport links and customers, availability of workers, and so on. These factors are looked at in much more detail in Unit 24. Why do governments try to influence these location decisions? Usually for two main reasons:

■ to encourage businesses to set up and expand in areas of high unemployment – often called development areas
■ to discourage firms from locating in overcrowded areas or on sites which are noted for their natural beauty.

Two types of measures are often used by government to influence where firms locate.

■ *Planning controls* will legally restrict the business activities that can be undertaken in certain areas. For example, a business planning to open a factory in an area of residential housing might be refused PLANNING PERMISSION. It would then be against the law for the firm to build the factory on this site. In certain parts of many countries, especially in particularly beautiful areas, it is not possible to establish any kind of business other than farming.
■ Many governments provide *regional assistance* to businesses to encourage them to locate in undeveloped parts of the country. This assistance could be in the form of financial grants or low rental factories. These DEVELOPMENT AREAS usually have a very high unemployment rate and there is a great need for new jobs.

Definitions to learn:

PLANNING PERMISSION is given by a government body to allow a business to build a factory or office in a particular location. This permission can be refused if the site is not suitable.

A DEVELOPMENT AREA is a region of a country where businesses will receive financial support to establish there. High unemployment is often a problem in these areas.

■ *Activity 4.6*

DEF Chemicals announce plans to build a new factory

Workers' leaders were delighted to hear today of plans by DEF Chemicals to build a huge new paint and chemicals plant in the Southern province. Many of these products will be sold abroad. The factory will create 1000 new jobs in an area badly affected by other factory closures. The new plant will require materials, components and supplies from many local firms. It is claimed that the Government is planning to offer substantial grants to DEF for locating in this area of high unemployment.

However, it has insisted that it should not be too close to housing estates and schools. The grants being offered have angered other firms in the industry as being unfair competition for them.

Local residents have mixed feelings about the plans. One elderly resident claimed: 'It will only bring more road traffic and risk of pollution. Don't forget that one DEF plant in the North was destroyed by an explosion several years ago, killing several workers.' However, other local people welcomed the news as it will bring more businesses and wealth to the area.

a) Make a list of the stakeholders likely to be affected by DEF's plan to build a new chemical factory.
b) For each of the groups that you have identified in a), explain why they are likely to be in support of, or are likely to oppose, these new plans.
c) Explain three reasons why, in your opinion, the Government ought to be involved in this decision.

Revision summary: government controls on business activities

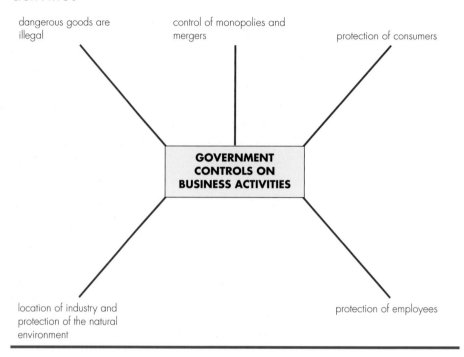

dangerous goods are illegal

control of monopolies and mergers

protection of consumers

GOVERNMENT CONTROLS ON BUSINESS ACTIVITIES

location of industry and protection of the natural environment

protection of employees

Governments can help businesses too

As well as controlling business activities, government can positively encourage businesses too. This is often done for three main reasons:

■ to encourage business development in poorer areas of the country – called regional assistance
■ to encourage enterprise by assisting small firms to set up and survive
■ to encourage firms to export.

Regional assistance

Serious social and economic problems can result from a country having some very rich areas and some very poor ones.

■ It is common for governments to try to make economic development more evenly spread throughout the country. As we saw in the previous section this can be done by imposing controls on businesses wishing to set up in wealthy areas.
■ In addition, financial grants and subsidies can be used to attract new firms to areas of high unemployment or to persuade existing firms to relocate there.

Small firms

Small businesses have important advantages for an economy.

Advantages of small businesses for an economy

☑ They provide jobs to many workers. They tend to be labour intensive as they often cannot afford expensive machinery.

☑ Many small firms operate in rural areas where unemployment would otherwise be very high.

☑ They can sometimes grow into very important businesses employing thousands of workers and producing output worth many millions of pounds.

☑ Small firms provide choice and variety for consumers. This acts as competition for larger firms.

☑ They are often managed in a very flexible way. The owner is often in close contact with consumers and can quickly adapt goods and services to meet consumers' needs.

Governments can provide assistance to entrepreneurs running their own small business or planning to set one up by:

■ setting lower rates of profits tax so that more finance can be used back in the business

■ giving grants or cheap loans to people setting up in business

■ providing advice and information centres for owners of small firms

■ providing college courses and other training programmes for those interested in establishing a new business.

Exporting of goods and services

Governments are very keen to encourage businesses in their country to export for the following reasons.

■ Exports earn a country foreign exchange. This can be used to pay for imports or to pay off foreign loans.

■ The more goods and services exported, the more people have to be employed to produce them. These employed people will have more money to spend and this will lead to even more goods being produced.

■ Successful exporters will make profits and this will increase the money the government earns from profits tax.

Governments can support exporters by:

■ encouraging banks to lend to exporters at lower interest rates

■ offering subsidies or tax reductions to exporters. However, other countries may offer exactly the same help to their firms so there could be no overall advantage

■ trying to keep the exchange rate of the currency as stable as possible so that exporters know how much they can earn from selling goods abroad

■ organising trade fairs abroad to encourage foreign businesses to buy a country's exports

■ offering credit facilities to exporters so that if a foreign customer should refuse to pay for goods the government will guarantee payment.

Business in the economic and legal environment

This unit has shown how businesses can be very greatly affected by government actions. Government decisions on economic issues and legal controls on business create the environment in which businesses must operate. No business can ignore this environment – although as we will see in later units, multinational firms will locate in countries where the economic and legal environment is most suitable for them. However, most businesses do not have the option to move abroad. The managers of these businesses must therefore adapt their business to meet economic and legal changes.

The environment created by legal and economic controls is one of the *constraints* or limitations on managers when they take decisions for their business.

■ *Revision questions*

1 State *two* possible effects on society if business activity was not controlled by government. [2]

2 List *three* economic objectives of governments. [3]

3 List *two* disadvantages to a country's economy arising from rapid inflation. [2]

4 Why might a government want to achieve a lower rate of unemployment in a country? [3]

5 Define economic growth. [2]

6 Define Gross Domestic Product. [2]

7 Draw a labelled diagram of the trade cycle and explain the boom and recession stages. [5]

8 What is a balance of payments deficit? [3]

9 Explain the difference between direct and indirect taxes. [3]

10 Explain *two* possible effects on a luxury hotel of an increase in interest rates. [4]

11 How would a government decision to lower interest rates be likely to affect the demand for luxury foreign holidays? [4]

12 Two managers are comparing details about their businesses.
 • Firm A produces DVD players. Many of these are exported. The business has expanded recently and has borrowed large sums of money from banks.
 • Firm B produces flour for bakeries. It buys its wheat from other countries.

Both managers are discussing these recent changes in government economic policy:
 • Increased interest rates
 • Higher tariffs on all imports
 • Raised income tax rates.

Which business do you think will be more affected by these changes? Explain your answer. [6]

13 Give *two* examples of how consumers are protected by laws in your country. [2]

14 What is a *monopoly*? [2]

15 Why might a monopoly be bad for consumers? [3]

16 What is *unfair discrimination* at work? [3]

17 List *three* ways in which Health and Safety Laws could force a firm to change the way it runs a factory. [3]

18 State *two* advantages of a minimum wage law. [2]

19 Why do governments often provide assistance to small firms? [4]

20 Give *two* examples of assistance that your government could offer to an exporting business. [2]

The CD-ROM (see details on page x) provides further tests, activities and Case study work on the topics covered in this unit.

5 Other external influences on business

This unit will explain:

[?] that business activity is limited or constrained by factors other than the law and the economy
[?] how technological changes force most firms to adapt in important ways
[?] that the growing concern for the environment is influencing business decisions
[?] how cost-benefit analysis can be used to assess the overall impact of a business decision.

By the end of this unit you should be able to:

[✓] explain what is meant by technological change and how it affects business decisions
[✓] understand the impact that business decisions can have on the environment and how pressure groups influence business activity
[✓] apply simple cost-benefit analysis to business investment decisions.

External constraints on business activity

A *constraint* is something that limits or controls actions. The last unit explained how governments' economic policies and legal controls impose constraints on business activity. This unit now looks at other constraints on how businesses behave and the decisions they take.

Technological change

The products we buy and the ways in which these products are made are constantly changing. A consumer of 40 years ago could only dream of personal computers, the internet, mobile phones, cheap air flights, air-conditioned cars, and so on. Similarly, workers of 40 years ago could not even dream of robots or automated equipment, computer graphics and computer assisted design or e-mails.

The pace of development of new products means that a new computer model or mobile phone can be out of date within months, and the latest electronic games machine will be unsellable by the end of the year. In factories, the speed of change is just as fast. In Europe in 2001 a new microchip factory was declared as being too old fashioned in its manufacturing techniques before it was even completed. There is a constant development and change in the role of information technology in business; office computers have an increasingly wide range of software and applications.

What would happen if businesses refused to adopt such changes? What problems does introducing new technology cause businesses? Let's consider these questions.

Do firms have to accept technological change?

The short answer to this question is no – business managers could completely ignore technological change if they wished to. Consider the effects of this, though. The products being made would become more and more outdated. Newer models with new features or completely different products altogether would be introduced by competitors. Methods of making goods would also remain unchanged. While rival firms became quicker at producing goods, firms ignoring such changes would find their costs becoming much higher compared to the other businesses.

So, what kind of businesses could actually afford to ignore these technological changes? Perhaps firms with a unique product whose major selling point is the fact that it is *'made in the old-fashioned way just like our grandfathers knew'*. Some specialist car makers claim this and so do some skilled tailors who still cut and sew material in traditional ways. Such market segments are likely to be quite small, however. Most firms compete in the mass market where new features and cheaper prices are important selling points. For this reason, most businesses *have* to accept technological changes sooner or later, or else they will face lost sales and eventual failure.

Failure to introduce information technology will leave firms with old-fashioned methods of letter typing, record keeping and communication with suppliers and customers, and with manual methods of stock control. All of these factors will make them less efficient and less competitive.

Problems of introducing new technology

There are two possible problems areas.

Costs of new technology

There will be three main costs:

- costs of researching into new products and methods
- costs of buying the new machinery and equipment
- costs of training staff.

Some businesses will find it very difficult to pay for these costs – smaller firms in particular may have real problems in raising the necessary finance. This is one reason why there are very few successful small firms in advanced technology industries such as chemicals or car production.

Resistance to changes

Some people are likely to be against technological change, will oppose it and may try to prevent it. Workers who may lose their jobs owing to new automated equipment may go on strike to express their opposition. Staff who need to be completely retrained may be very worried about not being able to handle the new machines and production methods. Older workers in particular may be afraid of not being able to learn the new skills and of losing out to younger staff. Even managers may be against change. If the new, so-called 'technology experts' know much more than they do then managers might be made to feel inferior or less useful to the business.

How to introduce technological change

The most successful firms try to involve the workers in the changes rather than just telling them of how their working lives will be different. People are much more likely to accept and look forward to change if they are told why it is necessary and how they will be affected. They might even be able to make useful suggestions about how the new technology could help to make their work more efficient. There is also a positive side that can be explained. New technology creates new job opportunities for skilled staff and it opens up new markets, so jobs might not be lost at all.

Revision summary: new technology

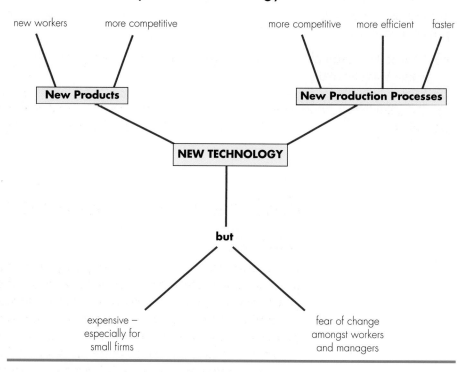

■ *Activity 5.1: case study task*

Ranjit's dilemma

Ranjit was disappointed with the latest company profit figures. The small watchmaking firm was losing market share to rivals that had invested in the latest automated machinery and office technology. The costs of producing each unit were lower for these firms than for Ranjit Watchmakers. This meant that they could charge lower prices. They were also able to make the latest styles of watches with the newest types of electronic movements. Ranjit was unsure of how to react. Should he borrow the money to invest in this new technology too? Or could he continue to manufacture watches and clocks with his skilled craftworkers and market them as 'traditional products for the modern age'? He wondered how large the market was for watches that were still mostly hand-assembled.

If he invested in new styles and new automated machinery the costs would be high to start with. Many of his craftworkers had been with the company for many years – how would they take to this change? New IT (Information Technology) equipment would also revolutionise the work of the office staff and allow modern forms of communication and record keeping.

Ranjit decided to look into the cost of some of the latest machinery. He wanted to find out how many newly trained people would be needed to operate it. He was anxious about making changes like this as he had little experience of new technology himself. He did not tell his workers about his possible new plans.

a) Outline two examples of new technology that could change the production or office methods at Ranjit Watchmakers.

b) Explain why there might be resistance within the firm to the introduction of new technology.

c) Was Ranjit right to keep his plans secret from the workers? Explain your answer.

d) Advise Ranjit on how he should proceed with the issue of new technology.

Environmental constraints on business activity

By the environment we mean the quality of the air we breathe and the water we drink, the appearance of our towns and countryside, the risk of global warming and other aspects of the world around us.

Should business be concerned about the environment? Some people believe no – the task of business is to produce goods and services, usually for a profit, and it cannot therefore be worried about the environment too. The argument continues: if business had to protect the environment by using *clean* methods of production and by producing expensive recyclable products then costs would rise and so would prices. Both businesses and consumers would lose out.

It is now quite rare for people to hold these views. It is quite widely believed that business has a *responsibility* to protect the environment as much as possible by producing more environmentally friendly products, using less-polluting methods.

The reasons for this view are:

■ Problems such as global warming, pollution and overuse of scarce natural resources will affect the whole world. All consumers and producers have some responsibility to help overcome them.
■ The whole of society has to pay to clean up pollution and to dispose of waste products. It would be better if these problems were reduced by producing less-polluting products in less-polluting ways in the first instance.
■ By using scarce resources such as rainforest timber or metals that cannot be replaced, industry is creating future problems of shortages and cost increases.
■ Consumers are now increasingly looking for environmentally friendly goods. It might even be more profitable to make goods that are less damaging even if they cost more to produce.
■ Powerful world PRESSURE GROUPS, such as Greenpeace, publicise the damaging activities of some companies and this gives them a bad press. This can lead to consumer boycotts and loss of contracts from people concerned about the environment.

Ways to make business more environmentally friendly

How can society make business give the environment a higher priority? There are three main ways.

Legislation

Governments pass laws that restrict business development in environmentally sensitive areas, such as nature reserves. The dumping of waste products by industry, e.g. into rivers or lakes, is illegal, but it is sometimes difficult to find out which firm was responsible for a leak of chemicals into a river, for example. The EU is planning to make all car manufacturers legally responsible for paying for the scrapping of their old models. This should stop people from dumping their old cars. The manufacturers complain about the cost of this, but it is making them produce cars with many more easily recycled parts and materials.

■ **Definition to learn:**

PRESSURE GROUPS are formed by people who share a common interest and who will take action to achieve the changes they are seeking.

It is often difficult for governments to find out which firms are responsible for dumping chemical waste

Permits

These are *licences to pollute*. Governments can sell a permit to a factory that produces a lot of pollution. If it exceeds the limit of pollution stated on the permit then it will be heavily fined. If it produces *less* pollution than stated on the permit then it will pay less for the permit. This encourages firms to produce goods in less polluting ways.

Consumer action and pressure groups

Firms want to sell goods profitably. If consumers stop buying a good because it is considered too harmful to the environment then the firm will quickly have to change its products and methods. Pressure groups often take action to stop unpopular or damaging business activity.

Bad publicity is bad news! If a firm is reported as destroying an important natural site or dumping waste in the sea then consumers will react against the firm and its products. Some pressure groups are very effective. They elect to use direct action – trying to block up firms' waste pipes, for example – as well as organising consumer boycotts and publicity campaigns. They may pay for advertisements which publicise the firm's activity and the damage it is causing. These campaigns do not always work. Sometimes firms will resist pressure from these groups. They will refuse to introduce the changes being asked for. The reasons why some firms do not give in to pressure include:

■ what they are doing may be unpopular but it is still legal, e.g. drug testing on animals
■ the cost of changing production methods may be too great
■ the firm does not sell directly to the public but to other firms (then public pressure is unlikely to be effective).

Revision summary: environmental constraints

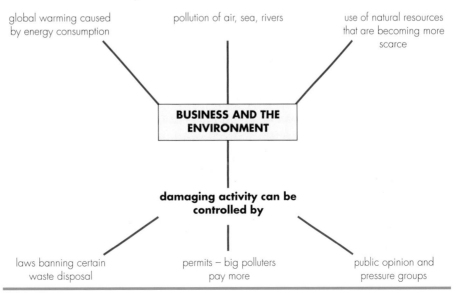

■ *Activity 5.2: case study task*

For years Acme Oil Co. had been dumping waste products in the sea off the east coast of the country. The Government did not try to stop them because it was afraid that the company might decide to pull out of the country altogether. This would lose the country jobs, investment and exports. The company argued that the dumping was far out at sea and harmed no one. It was the cheapest method of getting rid of the waste. Low costs helped the firm to keep down prices to consumers.

Environmental pressure groups had taken some action but it was ineffective. Then, one day, thousands of dead fish and sea birds started to be washed up on the east coast. After examination it was found that they contained dangerous levels of oil-based poisons. Acme Oil denied all responsibility and blamed a recent oil spill from a rival's tanker. Environmental groups started to blockade Acme's petrol filling stations. They gained great support from the public. Acme's sales fell but they refused to change their policy. Foreign news reporters were following the story closely. The Chief Executive was then suddenly replaced and a press conference was announced for the following week. Perhaps the company was about to change its environmental policy after all?

a) Was the Government right not to intervene in the dumping of these waste products? Explain your answer.
b) Why was Acme Oil so reluctant to change its dumping policy after the fish and birds were washed ashore?
c) Define the term *pressure group*.
d) Would you advise Acme Oil to announce a change in its dumping policy at the press conference? Give reasons for your answer.

■ **Definitions to learn:**

COST–BENEFIT ANALYSIS is the valuation by a government agency of all social and private costs and benefits resulting from a business decision.

SOCIAL COSTS are the costs paid by the rest of society, other than the business, as a result of a business decision. They are also known as EXTERNAL COSTS.

SOCIAL BENEFITS are the gains to society resulting from a business decision. These are also known as EXTERNAL BENEFITS.

Environmental factors and cost-benefit analysis

In recent years governments have become very concerned about the social and environmental effects of business activities. Increasingly governments are using a relatively new form of analysis to investigate important business, or even government, proposals. This is called COST-BENEFIT ANALYSIS. It takes into account *all* of the costs of a particular decision, not just the obvious financial ones.

For example, a firm might be planning to open a new airport. Being concerned only with profits, it might consider only the financial costs and revenues from the scheme. Governments now say this is not enough. The wider effects on society and the environment must also be *valued*, or taken into account – and this is called cost-benefit analysis.

Cost-benefit analysis requires an awareness of SOCIAL COSTS and SOCIAL BENEFITS. An example will help to make the points more clearly.

■ **Definitions to learn:**
PRIVATE COSTS are the costs of a business decision actually paid for by the business.

PRIVATE BENEFITS are the financial gains made by a business as a result of a business decision.

■ *Case study example*

A chemical firm wishes to open a new chemical plant. It has chosen a site which it believes is the most profitable one. In coming to this decision, the managers considered only the costs and benefits to the firm itself. These are called the PRIVATE COSTS and PRIVATE BENEFITS. These are likely to be:

Private costs	Private benefits
Cost of land	The money made from the sale of the chemical products
Cost of construction	
Labour cost	
Costs of running the plant when it has been built	
Transport costs of materials and completed products	

Unfortunately, the site chosen is near a housing estate. It is currently part of a park used by local residents. Waste products from the plant will be tipped into local rivers or quarries. The plant will create a lot of noise and fumes. The area is one with a high level of unemployment – people's incomes are below the national average.

Before deciding whether or not to grant planning permission the government also considers the social costs and social benefits – that is, the impact on the rest of society other than the business itself.

Social (external) costs	Social (external) benefits
Waste products will cause pollution	Jobs will be created
Smoke and fumes may damage the health of residents	Other firms may move into the area to give services to the chemical firm
Parkland cannot now be used by local residents	Important chemicals will be produced to benefit society

The government will try to give a value to all of these costs and benefits – hence *cost-benefit analysis*. This is not easy to do. For example, what is the cost of losing parkland for children to play on? Estimates are made and then the total costs and benefits of the decision are added up:

■ private costs, added to social (external) costs, give a *total social cost*
■ private benefits, added to social (external) benefits, give a *total social benefit* figure.

If the total social benefit is greater than the total social cost, the scheme is likely to be accepted. If, however, the total social cost is greater than the total social benefit, the government will probably refuse permission.

■ *Activity 5.3*

Here is a recent newspaper article:

'The government has just announced that many new motorways are to be built around major cities. The idea is to reduce traffic in city centre areas. This should reduce people's journey times. Businesses will be encouraged to build new factories near these new roads as it will be easy to deliver supplies. People living in the country districts will both gain and lose out from these new roads.'

a) Where could the government get the money from to build these new roads?
b) List as many social costs and benefits as you can which could result from these new roads.
c) Explain how *one* of these social costs and *one* of these social benefits might be valued.

■ *Revision questions*

1 What is meant by a *constraint* on business activity? [3]

2 Give *two* examples of products that did not exist 50 years ago. [2]

3 Give *two* examples of technological changes that have affected industrial processes (the way goods are produced). [2]

4 A clothing manufacturer decides not to purchase new machinery for his factory. He wants to maintain the traditional ways of working. Do you think that his business will continue to be successful? Explain your answer. [4]

5 A car manufacturer decides not to invest in new models but to promote them as 'traditional cars with traditional values'. Do you think that his business could still be successful? Explain your answer. [4]

6 Why might *workers* be reluctant to accept technological changes at work? [3]

7 Why might *managers* be reluctant to accept technological changes at work? [3]

8 A business is planning major technological improvements to its factory and office systems. Explain how managers could keep worker resistance to these changes as low as possible. [4]

9 State *two* examples of pollution produced by business. [2]

10 Why is it often cheaper to pollute than to use other *cleaner* forms of production? [2]

11 What is a pressure group? [2]

12 Explain how a pressure group might take action against an oil company that allowed oil to leak from one of its tankers. [4]

13 Why do businesses often respond to pressure from groups such as Greenpeace? [3]

14 Why might a firm *not* respond to pressure group activity? [3]

15 'Businesses often take into account the financial (private) costs of a decision and ignore the social costs.' Using an example, explain what is meant by this statement. [4]

16 Define cost-benefit analysis. [3]

17 Many business activities result in social costs and benefits. Imagine that a new 24-hour fast food restaurant is set up in your town.
   a) What would be the possible social benefits of the new restaurant? Give reasons for your answer. [4]
   b) What would be the possible social costs of the new restaurant? Give reasons for your answer. [4]

18 Explain *two* measures that a government might take to reduce the environmental effects of business activity. [4]

The CD-ROM (see details on page x) provides further tests, activities and Case study work on the topics covered in this unit.

6 Business costs and revenue

This unit will explain:

- [?] why businesses need to know the costs of running their activities and the revenue gained by selling their products
- [?] the different types of cost involved in running a business
- [?] how break-even analysis helps managers make decisions
- [?] the purpose of budgets and financial forecasts.

By the end of this unit you should be able to:

- [✓] distinguish between different kinds of cost
- [✓] explain the purposes of budgets
- [✓] prepare examples of budgets to show their purpose
- [✓] explain the purpose of forecasts
- [✓] prepare examples of forecasts to show their purpose
- [✓] draw a break-even chart based on given data about a business.

Business costs

All business activities involve costs of some sort. These costs cannot be ignored. For example, why does the owner or manager of a business, about to open a new factory making sports shoes, need to think about costs? Below are some of the reasons.

- So that the costs of operating the factory can be compared with the revenue from the sale of the sports shoes to calculate whether or not the business will make a profit or loss. This calculation is one of the most important made in any business.
- To compare the costs of two different locations for the new factory. This would help the owner make the best decision.
- To help the manager decide what price should be charged for a pair of sports shoes.

■ Activity 6.1

These are some of the costs involved in opening and running a new factory making sports shoes:

- rent of the factory
- insurance of the factory and stock
- bank charges
- raw materials used
- management salaries.

Add to this list six other costs that the owner would have to pay.

Accurate cost information is therefore very important to business managers.

In calculating the costs of the business it is important to understand the difference between different types of costs. The main types of costs are FIXED and VARIABLE costs.

Revision summary: business costs

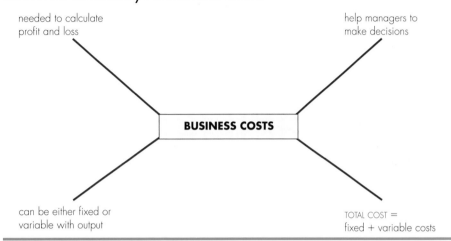

needed to calculate profit and loss

help managers to make decisions

BUSINESS COSTS

can be either fixed or variable with output

TOTAL COST = *fixed + variable costs*

■ *Activity 6.2*

Separate the costs you listed in Activity 6.1 into fixed and variable costs. Explain your answer.

Break-even charts: comparing costs with revenue

Drawing a break-even chart

In order to draw a BREAK-EVEN CHART we need information about the fixed costs, variable costs and REVENUE of a business. For example, in the sports shoe business:

- fixed costs are £5,000 per year
- the variable costs of the business are £3 per unit of output (a pair of sports shoes)
- each pair of shoes is sold at £8
- the factory can produce a maximum output of 2,000 pairs of shoes per year.

To draw a break-even chart it will help if a table, such as the one on page 86, is completed. Take note of variable costs and revenue when no output is being produced. Clearly, there will be no variable costs as no shoes are being made and, as no shoes are being sold, there will be no revenue.

	Sales (£) = 0	**Sales (£) = 500**	**Sales (£) = 2000 units**
Fixed costs	5,000	5,000	5,000
Variable costs	0	1,500	6,000
Total costs	5,000	6,500	11,000
Revenue	0	4,000	16,000

When output is 2,000 units, variable costs will be: 2,000 × £3 = £6,000. Assuming all output is sold, total revenue will be: 2,000 × £8 = £16,000.

Make sure you understand how the other figures were arrived at before moving on to the graph.

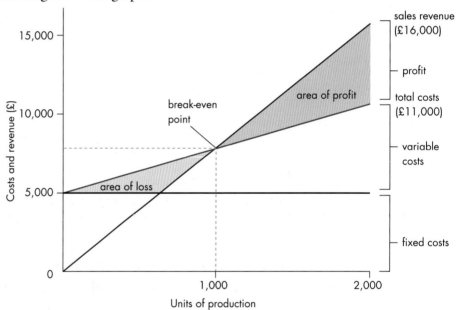

Now we can plot the information on the graph. Note the following points:

■ The 'y' axis (the vertical axis) measures money amounts.
■ The 'x' axis (the horizontal axis) shows the number of units produced and sold.
■ The fixed costs do not change at any level of output.
■ The total cost line is the addition of variable and fixed costs.

■ **Definition to learn:**
BREAK-EVEN POINT is the level of sales at which Total costs = Total revenue.

What does the graph show?

The BREAK-EVEN POINT of production is where total costs and total revenue cross. The business must therefore sell 1,000 pairs of shoes in order to avoid making a loss.

At production below the break-even point, the business is making a loss. At production above this point, the firm makes a profit. Maximum profit is made when maximum output is reached and this is a profit level of £5,000.

■ *Activity 6.3: case study task*

Namib Tyres Ltd produce motorcycle tyres. The following information about the business has been obtained.

- Fixed costs are £30,000 per year.
- Variable costs are £5 per unit.
- Each tyre is sold for £10.
- Maximum output is 10,000 tyres per year.

a) Fill in the missing figures in this table.

	Output = 0	**Output = 10,000**
Fixed costs	x	£30,000
Variable costs	0	a
Total costs	y	b
Revenue	z	£100,000

b) Draw a break-even chart from the information in the table.
c) From your break-even chart identify:
   i) the break-even level of production   ii) the level of profit at maximum output.

Uses of break-even charts

Apart from the use we have already made of these graphs – identifying the break-even point of production and calculating maximum profit – there are other benefits of this form of chart.

Advantages of break-even charts

☑ Managers are able to read off from the graph the expected profit or loss to be made at any level of output.

☑ The impact on profit or loss of certain business decisions can also be shown by re-drawing the graph. Consider again the sports shoe business. What would happen to the break-even point and the maximum output level if the manager decided to increase the selling price to £9 per pair? This new situation can be shown on another break-even chart.

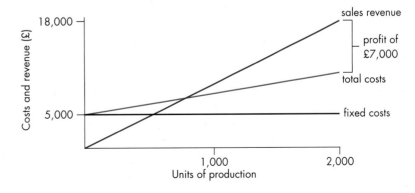

☑ Maximum revenue now rises to £18,000. The break-even point of production falls to 833 units and maximum profit rises to £7,000. Seems like a wise decision! However, the manager needs to consider competitors' prices too and he may not be able to sell all 2,000 pairs at £9 each. This point is explained below.

☑ The break-even chart can also be used to show the *safety margin* – the amount by which sales exceed the break-even point. In the graph on page 87, if the firm is producing 1,000 units, the safety margin is 167 units.

Drawbacks of break-even charts

The break-even chart is therefore useful to managers, but the technique does have some limitations, as listed below. These must be remembered by managers whenever they use these charts to help them take decisions.

✖ They are constructed assuming that all goods produced by the firm are actually sold – the graph does not show the possibility that stocks may build up if not all goods are sold.

✖ Fixed costs only remain constant if the scale of production does not change. For example, a decision to double output is almost certainly going to increase fixed costs. In the case of the sports shoe business, an increase in output above 2,000 will need a larger factory and more machinery.

✖ Break-even charts concentrate on the break-even level of production and there are many other aspects of the operations of a business which need to be analysed by managers, for example how to reduce wastage or how to increase sales.

✖ The simple charts used in this section have assumed that costs and revenues can be drawn with straight lines. This will not often be the case, for example, increasing output to the capacity of a factory may involve paying overtime wage rates to production workers. This will make the variable cost line slope more steeply upwards as output expands. Also, in order to increase sales a business may need to offer discounts for large orders and this will cause the slope of the revenue line to be less steep.

Revision summary: uses and limitations of break-even charts

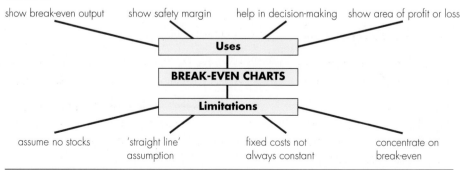

Break-even point: the calculation method

It is not always necessary to draw a break-even chart in order to show the break-even level of production. It is possible to calculate this. Study the following example.

■ *Case study example*

Cape Designs Ltd make wooden desks. They are able to sell all output. The selling price of each desk is €50. The variable costs of materials and production labour are €20. The weekly fixed costs are €6,000.

How many desks must be made and sold for Cape Designs Ltd to break even? It is necessary to calculate the CONTRIBUTION of each desk. This is the selling price less the variable cost. For example, if a product sells for €15 and the variable cost of production is €8, then it *contributes* €7 per unit to the fixed costs and profit of the business.

The calculation for the contribution of each desk is:

$$\text{Selling price} - \text{Variable cost} = \text{Contribution}$$
$$€50 - €20 = €30$$

Each desk gives a contribution of €30. This contributes towards the fixed costs of the business. In order to break-even each week, the business must make sufficient desks, contributing €30 each, to cover the fixed costs of €6,000.

The following formula should be used:

$$\text{Break-even level of production} = \frac{\text{Total fixed costs}}{\text{Contribution per unit}}$$

$$= \frac{€6,000}{€30}$$

$$= 200 \text{ units per week}$$

■ **Definition to learn:**

The CONTRIBUTION of a product is selling price less variable cost.

■ *Activity 6.4: case study task*

A fast food restaurant sells meals for £6 each. The variable costs of preparing and serving each meal are £2. The monthly fixed costs of the restaurant amount to £3,600.

a) How many meals must be sold each month for the restaurant to break even?
b) If the restaurant sold 1,500 meals in one month, what was the profit made in that month?
c) If the cost of the food ingredients rose by £1 per meal, what would be the new break-even level of production?

Business costs: other definitions

In some situations it is important for managers to be able to analyse costs in ways other than just splitting them up into fixed and variable costs.

■ **Definitions to learn:**

DIRECT COSTS are those that can be directly related to or identified with a particular product or department.

MARGINAL COSTS are the extra costs a business will incur by producing one more unit of output.

INDIRECT COSTS are those costs which cannot be directly related to a particular product. They are often termed OVERHEADS or OVERHEAD COSTS.

■ *Case study example*

The Olympus Computer Co. manufactures three different types of computer, A, B and C, in one factory. The three computer models all use different parts and components. They are assembled on separate production lines. The Managing Director wants to know:

■ how much on average each computer costs to manufacture
and
■ whether it would be profitable to increase the production of any of these computers.

The Managing Director asks the Production Manager to calculate:

■ the DIRECT COST of each product – those costs that can be directly related to or identified with a particular product or department. For example, the direct costs of making sports shoes will be the raw materials and production labour needed to make them. It is clear that these costs can be related directly to the sports shoes. They are usually variable costs, for example the materials used to make a product, but they could be fixed. An example of a fixed direct cost would be a special machine needed for only one of the computer designs made by Olympus Computers

■ the MARGINAL COST of each product – the extra costs a business will incur by producing one more unit of output. These would be the extra direct costs of making an additional unit. For example, the marginal cost of one additional computer would be the cost of components and labour cost of assembling it

■ the total INDIRECT COSTS of production – those costs which cannot be directly related to a particular product. They are often termed OVERHEADS or OVERHEAD COSTS. They are usually fixed costs, for example the rent of the factory, but they could be variable. An example of variable indirect costs would be the maintenance cost of machinery. This would increase with the number of units produced, but could not be directly related to any one unit of output made.

To be able to calculate the total cost of each computer type, these indirect costs have to be allocated or spread in some way between the three products. Different techniques exist to enable managers to do this, but one of the easiest is to calculate the proportion of factory floor space used by the production line for each product and to allocate the indirect costs on this basis.

■ **Definition to learn:**

AVERAGE COST PER UNIT is the total cost of production divided by total output.

An AVERAGE COST PER UNIT can then be calculated. This is the total cost of production divided by total output. For Computer A this would be calculated as follows:

Total costs of Computer A = Total direct costs of Computer A + A proportion of total indirect costs

If the total cost of producing Computer A in one year was £350,000 and 700 units were made, the *average cost per unit* will be:

$$\frac{\text{Total cost}}{\text{Output}} = \frac{£350,000}{700} = £500 \text{ per computer}$$

■ *Activity 6.5: case study task*

A car manufacturer produces three types of vehicle, X, Y and Z. It has calculated the costs of these three products to be:

	X	**Y**	**Z**	**(all £000)**
Direct material costs	5,000	10,000	8,000	
Direct labour costs	10,000	14,000	6,000	
Special machinery costs	3,000	0	0	
Proportion of indirect costs	6,000	12,000	6,000	
Annual output of vehicles	4,000	12,000	5,000	

The total cost of manufacturing X = £24,000,000

$$\text{The average cost per unit of X} = \frac{£24,000,000}{4,000 \text{ units}} = £6,000 \text{ per vehicle}$$

a) Calculate the total cost of manufacturing vehicle types Y and Z.
b) Calculate the average cost of manufacturing Y and Z.
c) Calculate the average direct cost of manufacturing Z.
d) What is likely to be the marginal cost of making an additional Z vehicle?

We can now add to the revision summary of business costs on page 85.

Revision summary: business costs

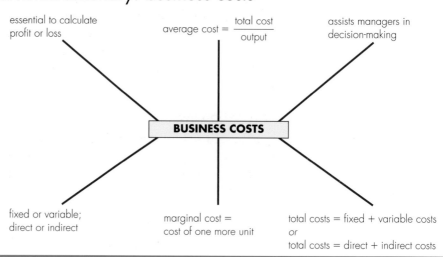

essential to calculate profit or loss

$$\text{average cost} = \frac{\text{total cost}}{\text{output}}$$

assists managers in decision-making

BUSINESS COSTS

fixed or variable; direct or indirect

marginal cost = cost of one more unit

total costs = fixed + variable costs
or
total costs = direct + indirect costs

Economies and diseconomies of scale

Look again at the definition of average costs on page 91. It is the cost of producing one unit of output. Would you expect all businesses in the same industry to have the same average costs? This would be rather unlikely.

■ *Case study example*

Consider the average cost and total output of the following two businesses, which both make bricks:

	Brick Co. A	Brick Co. B
Total output per year	10 million	1 million
Average cost per brick	50 pence	75 pence

The bigger company has much lower average costs than the smaller one. This cost advantage results from the economies of being a large business. These are called the ECONOMIES OF SCALE.

Economies of scale

There are five economies of scale.

Purchasing economies

When businesses buy large numbers of components, for example materials or spare parts, they are able to gain discounts for buying in bulk. This reduces the unit cost of each item bought and gives the firm an advantage over smaller businesses which buy in small quantities.

■ Definition to learn:
ECONOMIES OF SCALE are the factors that lead to a reduction in average costs as a business increases in size.

Marketing economies

There are several advantages for a large business when marketing its products. It might be able to afford to purchase its own vehicles to distribute goods rather than depend on other firms. Advertising rates in papers and on television do not go up in the same proportion as the size of an advertisement ordered by the business. The business will not need twice as many sales staff to sell ten product lines as a smaller firm needs to sell five.

Financial economies

Larger businesses are often able to raise capital more cheaply than smaller ones. Bank managers often consider that lending to large organisations is less risky than lending to small ones. A lower rate of interest is therefore often charged.

Managerial economies

Small businesses cannot usually afford to pay for specialist managers, for example marketing managers and qualified accountants. This tends to reduce their efficiency. Larger companies can afford specialists and this increases their efficiency and helps to reduce their average costs.

Technical economies

There are many of these, but a few examples will help to show how important they can be. Large manufacturing firms often use flow production methods. These apply the principle of the division of labour (see Unit 1). Specialist machines are used to produce items in a continuous flow with workers responsible for just one stage of production. Small businesses cannot usually afford this expensive equipment. It could also be that they sell their products in small quantities and flow production could not be justified. The use of flow production and the latest equipment will reduce the average costs of the large manufacturing businesses.

In addition, some machinery is only made with a certain high output capacity. For example, an automatic welding machine can do 100 welds a minute. A small firm, if it bought such a machine, could not keep it working all day and the average cost of using it would be high. This is because the machinery is not 'divisible' into smaller capacity machines.

Diseconomies of scale

Is it possible for a business to become so large that it becomes less and less efficient? Is there a limit to economies of scale? Some research suggests that very large businesses may become *less* efficient than the smaller ones and this could lead to higher average costs for big firms.

How is this possible? It could occur because of certain DISECONOMIES OF SCALE.

Poor communication

The larger the organisation the more difficult it becomes to send and receive accurate messages. It often takes longer for decisions made by managers to reach all groups of workers and this could mean that it will take a long time for workers to respond and act upon managers' decisions. Also, the top managers will be so busy directing the affairs of the business that they may have no contact at all with the customers of the firm and they could become too removed from the products and markets the firm operates in.

Low morale

Large businesses can employ thousands of workers. It is possible that one worker will never see the top managers of the business. Workers may feel that they are unimportant and not valued by the management. In small firms it is possible to establish close relationships between workers and top managers. The lack of these relationships in a big firm can lead to low morale and low efficiency amongst the workers. This will tend to push up average costs.

It is very difficult to 'prove' that these diseconomies exist in practice. However, many very large businesses are now breaking themselves up into smaller units which can control themselves. This trend is aimed at preventing the diseconomies of scale from reducing efficiency and raising average costs.

Revision summary: economies and diseconomies of scale

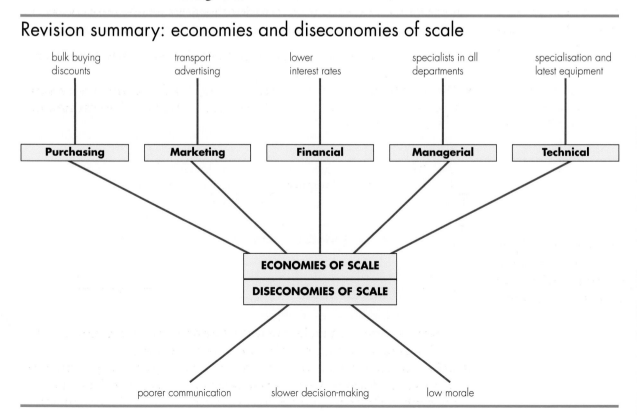

Budgets and forecasts: looking ahead

Are you the sort of person who makes plans for the future? Do you ever think about what might happen to you in the future and try to plan to take advantage of these developments? Some people, and businesses, fail to consider the future at all and make no plans. They are therefore unprepared for unforeseen events and often fail to benefit from those events.

All businesses should plan for the future. Those managers who concentrate only on the present problems of a business often fail to see future opportunities and threats. Managers often try to predict what is likely to happen in the future and how changes will affect their business. For example, managers may attempt to predict:

■ sales or consumer demand
■ exchange rates of the currency
■ wage increases.

These predictions are called FORECASTS and there are many specialist firms claiming to be able to predict changes in market or economic conditions who sell their reports to other businesses for large amounts of money. These forecasts are trying to reduce one of managers' biggest problems – that is, uncertainty about what will happen in the future.

Forecasting methods

There are several methods of forecasting. For example, the most common methods of forecasting future sales figures include the following.

■ Past sales figures could be used to calculate the TREND, which can then be extended into the future.
■ Past sales figures could be plotted on a graph (called a *scatter diagram*) to draw a LINE OF BEST FIT which can then be extended into the future. Here is an example:

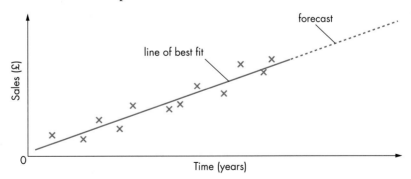

Scatter diagram of past sales with a line of best fit. This shows how sales could rise in the future

■ A panel of experts could be asked for their opinions on the most likely level of sales in the future. This is called *panel consensus*.
■ Market research surveys (covered in Unit 17) are particularly useful for forecasting sales of products which have not yet been launched onto the market. Obviously, no previous sales data exists for these products.

■ **Definitions to learn:**

FORECASTS are predictions of the future, for example, likely future changes in the size of the market.

A TREND is an underlying movement or direction of data over time, for example, the trend of sales data may be increasing.

A LINE OF BEST FIT is a line drawn through a series of points, for example, sales data, which best shows the trend of that data. It can be used to forecast results in the future.

Budgets

However useful, a forecast does not tell a business *how* to react to the future. Managers must still decide how to direct their business in the months and years to come. To help them in this important process they use a method of planning and control known as BUDGETS.

The essential features of budgets are that they contain *targets* for the *future* expressed in *numerical* or *financial* terms. For example, the sales department for a business may have a budget to 'increase sales by 15 per cent in export markets in the next financial year'.

Well-managed businesses will set budgets for revenue, costs, production levels, raw materials required, labour hours needed and cash flow. Once these budgets have been set for all departments in the organisation, an overall or *master budget* can be established. This will show the planned revenue, costs and profit or loss for the business over the next period of time, usually one year.

The advantages of budgets

☑ They provide targets for departments and managers to work towards. This helps to give focus to the work people do and helps to motivate them.

☑ They can be used to control how the business is performing by comparing budgets with actual results. This form of budgetary control is called *variance analysis*, because the difference between a *budgeted* figure and the *actual* figure is called the *variance*.

☑ The setting of budgets can involve all workers and supervisors as well as managers. Budgets are likely to be more accurate if the people who have to put them into effect are asked to help set the original targets. This participation can lead to greater motivation and more realistic budgets. Workers may be more likely to work hard to achieve a target if they have had a say in setting it.

☑ Budgets help to control the whole business. They control the amount of money allocated to each department and in this way resources should be efficiently allocated within the business.

A particularly important use of budgets is in *cash flow planning* and the construction and use of these will be covered in Unit 8.

Budgeting is useful for:

reviewing *past* activities –
←————————————————
comparing actual with budgeted figures

controlling *current* business activity – keeping to targets

planning for the *future* –
————————————————→
setting goals to be achieved

■ *Activity 6.6: case study task*

Here is a part of the cost budget, for last year, produced by College Books Ltd. The manager is comparing the original budget figures with the actual costs for last year.

College Books Ltd Budget for last year

Cost area	Budget (£)	Actual (£)	Variance (£)
Staffing	14,000	17,000	(3,000)
Paper	5,200	4,800	400
Equipment	6,500	7,500	(1,000)
Electricity and telephone	4,000	5,000	x
Rent	3,000	3,000	–
Total	32,700	37,300	y

a) Calculate the x and y variances.
b) Should the manager be satisfied with the cost levels of this firm? Explain your answer.
c) If the manager wanted to reduce costs to the budgeted levels, which costs do you think he should pay most attention to?

Revision summary: budgets

provide financial targets   aid motivation   aid planning

BUDGETS

give focus and sense of direction to managers   aid control and review of business performance   variance = budget – actual

■ *Revision questions*

1 Explain *two* reasons why it is important for a business manager to know the costs of the business. [4]

2 State *one* example of a fixed cost for a carpet manufacturer. Explain why you consider it to be a fixed cost. [3]

3 Explain why the cost of wool would be a variable cost for a carpet manufacturer. [3]

4 Draw this sketch of a break-even chart and label each of the lines and axes marked with a question mark: [4]

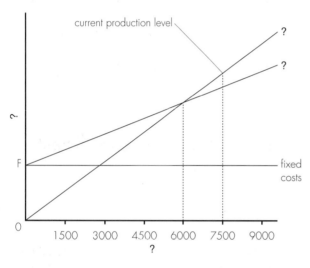

5 Identify from the break-even chart:
   a) the break-even level of production
   b) the safety margin. [2]

6 Calculate the break-even level of production for Malawi Bricks Ltd from the following data:
   Fixed costs £40,000 per year
   Variable costs £5 per 100 bricks
   Selling price £13 per 100 bricks. [3]

7 How might this firm try to reduce its break-even level of output? [3]

8 What would be the advantage to the business of reducing the level of output at which it breaks even? [2]

9 Explain *two* possible uses of break-even charts. [4]

10 Explain *two* possible drawbacks to break-even charts. [4]

11 What is the difference between a direct cost and an indirect cost? [4]

12 What is meant by the term *total cost*? [2]

13 What is meant by the term *average cost*? [2]

14 Define *economies of scale*. [2]

15 Give *three* examples of economies of scale that a supermarket might gain as it expands by opening new stores. [3]

16 Explain *two* possible diseconomies of scale for this supermarket as it expands. [4]

17 What is meant by a *sales forecast*? [2]

18 Define the term *budget*. [2]

19 Explain *two* benefits to a firm from setting budgets. [4]

20 What is meant by a *variance from budget*? [3]

The CD-ROM (see details on page x) provides further tests, activities and Case study work on the topics covered in this unit.

Business accounting

What are accounts and why are they necessary?

Case study example

Shazad Nidal has been in business for ten months. He is a tailor making expensive suits. He operates as a sole trader.

Imagine what could happen to his business if he failed to keep a written record of all financial transactions, such as purchases and sales.

- He could sell goods on credit to customers without keeping a record of the sale. He could, therefore, overlook the fact that customers still owed him money.
- He might order too many raw materials because no record was kept of previous orders.
- He might pay all of the business costs, for example electricity, raw materials and wages, on the same day and then find out that there was no money in the bank.
- The profits or losses of the business could not be calculated.
- The government tax collector would not be able to check how much tax Shazad owed – a heavy fine could be charged if the tax is not paid.

Obviously, without written financial records, the business would soon be in deep trouble.

▓ **Definitions to learn:**
ACCOUNTS are the financial records of a firm's transactions.

ACCOUNTANTS are the professionally qualified people who have responsibility for keeping accurate accounts and for producing the final accounts.

FINAL ACCOUNTS are produced at the end of the financial year and give details of the profit or loss made over the year and the worth of the business.

The financial records of a business are called its ACCOUNTS. They should be kept up to date and with great accuracy – this is the responsibility of the ACCOUNTANTS.

At the end of each financial year, the accountant will produce the FINAL ACCOUNTS of the business. These will record the main financial results over the year and the current worth or value of the business.

Limited companies are required by law to publish their final accounts and these are much more detailed than those required from non-company businesses, such as sole traders and partnerships.

Financial documents involved in buying and selling

The *final* accounts of a business are prepared at the end of each financial year. During the year a very large number of financial documents will be created as the business buys and sells goods and services. These documents will be used by accountants to:

- keep records of what has been bought and from which supplier
- keep records of what has been sold and to which customers
- provide the data needed to create the final accounts.

▓ *Case study example*

The main financial documents used in a small retail business such as Abdul's Sweet Shop will be the following (required for the purchasing and selling of goods):

- *Purchase orders* – these are requests for goods or materials sent to suppliers. A typical example is shown below. Notice the essential information that it contains.

PURCHASE ORDER		
Abdul Sweets Ltd To: Sweet Wholesalers Ltd Manor Road Newtown Please supply:–		15 Old Road Newtown Tel: 0381 865 4121 Fax: 0381 865 4022 Date 18/9/03 Order No. 02/136
QUANTITY	DESCRIPTION	PRICE
3 Boxes @ £80 2 Boxes @ £50 1 Box @ £50	Belgian Chocolates Crunch Nuts Juicy Fruits	£240 £100 £ 50
Deliver ASAP to above address		TOTAL £390

- *Delivery notes* – these are used by the supplier to confirm that the goods have been received by Abdul. He must sign these when the goods are delivered.
- *Invoices* – these are sent by the supplier to the customer as a request for payment for the goods delivered. Abdul would be advised to check each invoice carefully to make sure that the goods being charged for have actually been received and were charged at the correct amount.
- *Credit notes* – these are only issued if a mistake has been made. If the sweet supplier sends the wrong sweets to Abdul then the supplier will give him a credit note for the value of the goods incorrectly supplied. Also an error could have been made on the invoice, for example the correct goods were delivered but were charged at the wrong price on the invoice.
- *Statements of account* – each month the supplier will send his customers, such as Abdul, a statement. This will record the total value of deliveries made each month, the value of any credit notes issued and any payments made by the customer. These statements from the sweet supplier remind Abdul of how much he owes. E.g.:

STATEMENT OF ACCOUNT

Sweet Wholesalers Ltd
Manor Road
Newtown
Tel: 0381 862 3002
Fax: 0381 862 3220

Account date: 26/9/03   Account: Abdul Sweets Ltd
Abdul Sweets Ltd
15 Old Road
Newtown

Date	Invoice No.	Reference	£ value	Outstanding
8/9/03	360	275X	240	240
13/9/03	421	273Z	100	100
21/9/03	560	2715A	390	390
				Total £630

- *Remittance advice slips* – these are usually sent with the statement of account. When Abdul makes a payment to the supplier he will indicate on this slip which invoices he is paying. This allows the supplier to make sure that Abdul is credited with this amount and does not get charged again for this amount.
- *Receipts* – when the customer pays an invoice a receipt should be issued by the supplier. If Abdul paid off all of his September statement then the sweets supplier will send a receipt, keeping a copy of it. This confirms to Abdul that he has paid and it ensures that the supplier does not charge him for this amount again.

Methods of making payment

Payments for goods and services can be made in several ways.

Cash

The traditional method of payment is still widely used for most small amounts. For security reasons many firms are reluctant to use cash to make payments, other than for small amounts such as buying stamps. When a business makes a cash payment a *petty cash voucher* is written out by the person in charge of the firm's cash. This person signs the voucher to authorise payment and the person making the purchase with cash also signs it to show that they have received the money.

Cheque

Cheques are not money, they are instructions to a bank to transfer a specified sum in the form of a bank balance to a named person. With less of a security risk than cash, cheques are a very common form of payment between businesses. Many retail customers also pay by cheque. The supplier of the goods runs the risk of the customer not having a big enough bank balance to cover the amount. The bank will then return the cheque unpaid unless it is supported by a *cheque guarantee card*.

Credit card

This allows the consumer to obtain goods and services now but to pay for them in the future. Effectively it is the same as taking out a brief loan. If the repayments are not made within the agreed period of time (usually a month) then the card user has to pay interest on the money owed on the card. Credit card payments can be made over the counter (the card is 'swiped' and the amount added to the cardholder's card bill) or simply by the credit card details being given to the seller over the phone or internet.

Debit card

These are used in the same way as credit cards but, instead of a 'credit' bill being acccumulated on the cardholder's card account, the money is simply transferred directly from the cardholder's bank account to that of the seller. No credit is involved. If there is insufficient money in the cardholder's account, the transaction is cancelled.

Recording accounting transactions

In most businesses, there are so many transactions each year that it would be very time-consuming to record them all by hand in accounting books. This is one reason why such a large number of organisations now use computers. Computer files store records of all the sales, purchases and other financial transactions made by a firm and the information can be retrieved or printed out when required.

Who uses the final accounts of a business?

As it is only the accounts of limited companies that have to be published, we shall concentrate on the uses of these. The following groups have an interest in a limited company's accounting records.

■ *Shareholders* As you learned in Unit 3, limited companies are owned by shareholders. They will clearly have an interest in knowing how big a profit or loss the company makes. They will want to know if the business is worth more at the end of the year than at the beginning.
■ *Creditors* These are other businesses including banks which have lent money to the company or have supplied goods without yet receiving payment. They will want to study the accounts to see if the company can afford to pay them back.
■ *Government* The government and the tax office will want to check on the profits tax paid by the company. If the company is making a loss, this might be bad news for the whole economy, especially if it means that workers' jobs may be lost.
■ *Other companies* The managers of other companies may be considering a bid to take over the company or they may just wish to compare the performance of the business with that of their own.

Revision summary: business accounts

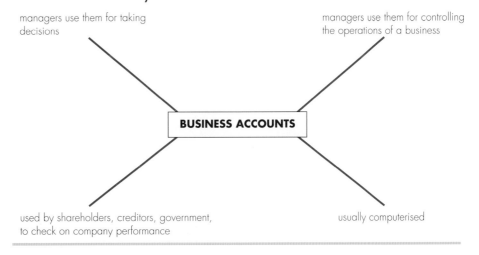

managers use them for taking decisions

managers use them for controlling the operations of a business

BUSINESS ACCOUNTS

used by shareholders, creditors, government, to check on company performance

usually computerised

What do final accounts contain?

The trading account

The TRADING ACCOUNT shows the difference between the COST OF GOODS SOLD and what they were sold for, the SALES REVENUE. This difference is called the GROSS PROFIT of the business.

For example, if a shop bought €50,000 worth of goods during the year and sold them for €75,000, the gross profit would be €25,000.

$$\text{Gross profit} = \text{Sales revenue} - \text{Cost of goods sold}$$

Clearly, if the cost of goods bought was greater than the revenue they were sold for, the firm would have made a loss.

It is important to note the following.

- Gross profit does not make any allowance for overhead costs or expenses.
- Cost of goods sold is not necessarily the same as the total value of goods bought by the business. Look at the example below.

▥ *Case study example*

The City Cafe Co. buys cans of drink from a wholesaler for £1 each. It sells them for £2 each.

City Cafe Co. started the year with 200 cans in stock (opening stocks). It bought in 1,500 cans. At the end of the year it had 300 left (closing stocks).

1 How many cans did the business sell during the year?
2 What was the cost to the business of the goods sold?
3 What was the gross profit?

The answers to these questions are as follows.

1 Add together the opening stock and the cans bought during the year: 200 + 1,500 = 1,700 cans.

The business could have sold 1,700 cans during the year. We know that it did not sell this many. How? Because there were closing stocks of 300. Therefore, the business must have sold 1,400 cans.

Goods sold = Opening stocks + Purchases − Closing stocks

2 As the goods were all bought by the business for £1 each, the cost of goods sold was £1,400.

3 Remember:

Gross profit = Sales revenue − Cost of goods sold

In this example, sales revenue = £2 × 1,400 cans sold

$$= £2,800$$

$$\text{Gross profit} = £2,800 - £1,400$$

$$= £1,400$$

▥ *Activity 7.1*

Complete the following table (all figures in £).

	Sales revenue	Cost of goods sold	Gross profit
a)	3,000	1,500	????
b)	25,000	16,000	????
c)	80,000	?????	20,000
d)	?????	25,000	50,000

▥ *Activity 7.2*

Complete this table.

	Cost per unit	Opening stocks	Purchases of goods	Closing stocks	Cost of goods sold
a)	£3	500	3,000	200	£9,900
b)	£2	1,000	5,000	500	?????
c)	£5	100	400	300	????
d)	£1	2,000	60,000	2,000	?????

▥ *Case study example*

This is an example of a typical trading account.

Newtown Garden Nursery
Trading Account for year ending 31/3/2005

Sales revenue	£55,000
Opening stock	£10,000
Purchases	£25,000
Total stock available	£35,000
Less closing stock	£12,000
Cost of goods sold	£23,000
Gross profit	£32,000

It is important to note that in a *manufacturing* business, rather than a retailing one, the direct labour cost and direct production costs will also be deducted before arriving at the gross profit total.

The gross profit is not the final profit for the business because all of the other expenses have to be deducted. Costs such as salaries, lighting and rent of the buildings need to be subtracted from gross profit. This is shown in the profit and loss account of the business (see page 106).

Revision summary: trading account

sales revenue is the income from selling goods or services

cost of goods sold = opening stocks + purchases − closing stocks

TRADING ACCOUNT

gross profit = sales revenue − cost of goods sold

does *not* include overhead expenses

The profit and loss account

Could the owner of Newtown Garden Nursery take all of the gross profit as personal drawings from the business? The answer is definitely 'No', because not all of the costs of the business have been subtracted from sales revenue. Once this has been done, then NET PROFIT is arrived at.

The PROFIT AND LOSS ACCOUNT of a business shows how net profit is calculated.

■ The profit and loss account begins with the gross profit calculated from the trading account.

■ All other expenses and overheads of the business are subtracted. Any income from non-trading activities of the business is added on, such as rent from a flat above a shop. As this is income to the business which was not made from its normal activities, it is not included in the trading account.

▓ **Definitions to learn:**

NET PROFIT is the profit made by a business after all costs have been deducted from sales revenue. It is calculated by subtracting overhead costs from gross profits.

The PROFIT AND LOSS ACCOUNT shows how the net profit of a business and the retained profit of a company are calculated.

▓ *Case study example*

This is an example of a typical profit and loss account for a business which is not a limited company.

Newtown Garden Nursery
Profit and Loss Account for year ending 31/3/2005

Gross profit	£32,000
Non-trading income	£5,000
	£37,000
Less expenses:	
Wages and salaries	£12,000
Electricity	£6,000
Rent	£3,000
DEPRECIATION	£5,000
Selling and advertising expenses	£5,000
	£31,000
Net profit	£6,000

Definitions to learn:
DEPRECIATION is the fall in the value of a FIXED ASSET over time (see page 108).

An APPROPRIATION ACCOUNT is that part of the profit and loss account which shows how the profit after tax is distributed – either as dividends or kept in the company as retained profits.

Depreciation is the fall in the value of a FIXED ASSET over time. This is included as an annual expense of the business. For example, a new truck bought by a building firm will fall in value with age and use. Each year, this fall in value or depreciation is recorded as an expense on the profit and loss account.

Profit and loss accounts for limited companies

The final accounts for limited companies follow exactly the same principles as those shown above. The main differences are that:

- corporation tax paid on company profits will be shown
- the final section of the profit and loss account is called the APPROPRIATION ACCOUNT – it shows what the company has done with the profits made
- results from the previous year are also included.

■ *Case study example*

Here is a typical profit and loss account for a public limited company (plc).

Profit and Loss Account for Ace Engineering plc for the year ending 31/3/2005

	2005	**2004**
	(£000)	(£000)
Sales turnover	1,250	1,300
Cost of sales	900	900
Gross profit	350	400
Operating expenses	105	120
Operating profit	245	280
Interest payable	50	40
Profit before taxation (Net profit)	195	240
Corporation tax	35	40
Profit after tax	160	200
Dividends	120	130
Retained profit for the year	40	70

How retained profit is calculated

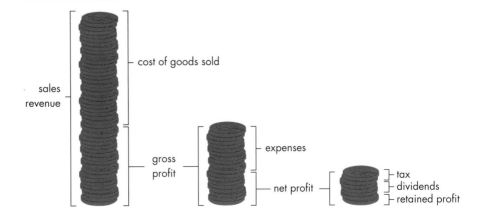

sales revenue — cost of goods sold — gross profit — expenses — net profit — tax / dividends / retained profit

▮ *Activity 7.3: Case study task*

Using the same pattern as the typical profit and loss account on page 107, calculate the retained profits of ABC plc for the year ending 31/3/2005 from the following data.

	(£000)
Sales revenue	280
Tax paid	40
Operating expenses	30
Cost of sales	100
Interest paid	15
Dividends	25

Revision summary: profit and loss accounts

takes gross profit from trading account

net profit = gross profit − expenses

PROFIT AND LOSS ACCOUNT

companies pay corporation tax on profits

appropriation account shows how profit after tax is distributed

Balance sheets

So far we have shown how a manager can calculate whether the business is making a profit or a loss. This is clearly of great importance. However, by itself, the profit and loss account does not tell us how much the business is worth in total. Business owners would be very interested to know how much their business was worth. This information, together with other details, is given on the BALANCE SHEET.

The balance sheet is very different from the profit and loss account. The profit and loss account records the *income* and *expenses* of a business, and the profit or loss it makes, over a period of time – usually one year. The balance sheet records the *value* or *worth* of a business at just one moment in time – at the end of the financial year.

The balance sheet lists and gives a value to all of the ASSETS and LIABILITIES of the business. It is important to understand these terms before the layout of the balance sheet is explained.

▮ **Definitions to learn:**
The BALANCE SHEET shows the value of a business's ASSETS and LIABILITIES at a particular time.

ASSETS are those items of value which are owned by the business. They may be long-term (FIXED) or short-term (CURRENT).

LIABILITIES are items owed by the business.

■ Assets are those items of value which are owned by the business.
 – Land, buildings, equipment and vehicles are examples of *fixed assets* which are likely to be kept by the business for more than one year. Most fixed assets, apart from land, *depreciate* over time so the value of these will fall on the balance sheet from one year to the next.
 – Cash, stocks and debtors (customers who owe money to the business) are only held for short periods of time and are called *current assets*.

- Liabilities are items owed by the business. Again, there are two main forms of these.
  - *Long-term liabilities* are long-term borrowings which do not have to be repaid within one year.
  - *Current liabilities* are amounts owed by the business which must be repaid within one year, for example, bank overdraft and creditors (suppliers owed money by the business).

What is the importance of these terms? Consider your own personal finances. If the value of your assets was greater than the value of your debts or liabilities, you would own *wealth*. In the case of a business, this wealth belongs to the *owners*, or in the case of companies to the *shareholders*. This is why the balance sheet is so important to the users of the accounts, i.e. the owners of the business. It shows how much *wealth* the owners have invested in the business. They would obviously like to see this increase year by year.

Total assets − Total liabilities = Owners' wealth (Shareholders' funds)

▮ *Case study example*

This is a typical balance sheet. The terms that have not yet been explained are looked at in more detail on page 110.

Ace Engineering plc
Balance Sheet as at 31/3/2005 (£000)

Year	2005	2004
Fixed assets		
Land and buildings	450	440
Machinery	700	600
	1,150	1,040
Current assets		
Stocks	80	50
Debtors	50	60
Cash	10	15
	140	125
Less		
Current liabilities		
Creditors	65	40
Bank overdraft	65	60
	130	100
Working capital (net current assets)	10	25
Net assets	**1,160**	**1,065**
Financed by:		
Shareholders' funds		
Share capital	500	500
Profit and Loss Account reserves	360	320
Long-term liabilities		
Long-term bank loan	300	245
Capital employed	**1,160**	**1,065**

Explanation of balance sheet terms

- Fixed and current assets, current and long-term liabilities – see pages 108–109.
- *Working capital* is a very important term on the balance sheet. It is also known as *net current assets*. It is calculated by the formula:

  Working capital = Current assets − Current liabilities

  No business can survive without working capital. It is used to pay short-term debts. If these debts cannot be paid because the business does not have enough working capital, the creditors could force the business to stop trading.
- *Net assets* is calculated by the following formula:

  Fixed assets + (Current assets − Current liabilities) *or*

  Fixed assets + Working capital

  This shows the users of the accounts the net value of all the assets owned by the business. These assets must be paid for, or financed, by money put into the business in two ways – *shareholders' funds* and *long-term liabilities.*
- *Shareholders' funds* is the total sum of money invested into the business by the owners of the company – the shareholders. This money is invested in two ways.
  - *Share capital* is the money put into the business when the shareholders bought newly issued shares.
  - *Reserves* arise for a number of reasons. *Profit and loss reserves* are retained profits from this and previous years. This profit is owned by the shareholders but has not been paid out to them in the form of dividends. It is kept in the business as part of the shareholders' funds.
- *Capital employed* is calculated by the following formula:

  Capital employed = Shareholders' funds + Long-term liabilities

  This is the total long-term and permanent capital of the business which has been used to pay for the net assets of the business. Therefore:

  Capital employed = Net assets.

■ Activity 7.4

Here is a list of questions managers frequently ask:

a) What was the gross profit of the business?
b) What dividends did we pay our shareholders?
c) What is the total value of current assets?
d) What expenses did the business incur last year?
e) What was the net profit of the business?
f) What is the capital employed of the business?

For each question, indicate where the answer can be found, choosing from one of the following:

- trading account
- profit and loss account
- appropriation account
- balance sheet

Activity 7.5

A Managing Director of a company is trying to write out the balance sheet for the business. The following items have been listed. You have been asked to help the Managing Director by putting them all under their correct heading. Copy out the table and tick the correct box.

	Current assets	Fixed assets	Current liabilities	Long-term liabilities	Share capital	Reserves
Company vehicles						
Cash in the till						
Ten-year bank loan						
Ordinary share capital						
Money owed by customers						
Unsold goods						
Factory						
Retained profit						
Amounts owed to suppliers						
Tax owed to government						

Revision summary: balance sheet

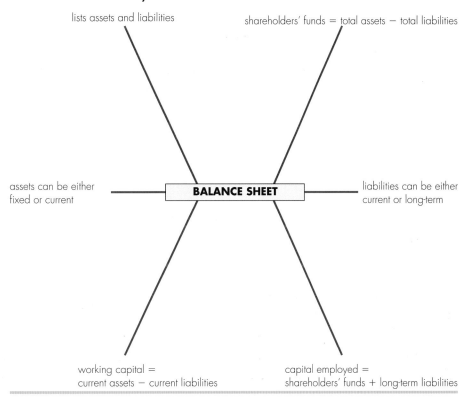

lists assets and liabilities

shareholders' funds = total assets − total liabilities

assets can be either fixed or current

BALANCE SHEET

liabilities can be either current or long-term

working capital = current assets − current liabilities

capital employed = shareholders' funds + long-term liabilities

Analysis of published accounts

The company accounts we have studied contain a great deal of information which is made available to all those interested in the performance of the business. You will recall which groups were interested in using the accounts of a company. We must now look at how these accounts can be used and analysed to give the information these groups need.

What do the published accounts tell us about:

- the performance of the company?
- the financial strength of the company?

Without further analysis, the answer is – not a great deal!

▚ *Case study example*

Consider these results for two food retailing companies:

	Freshfoods plc	**Foodstore plc**
Operating profit (2005)	£300,000	£30,000

What conclusions can be drawn from these figures?

- Is Freshfoods plc much more successful than Foodstore plc? You may think so just from these figures.
- Is the management of Freshfoods plc ten times more efficient than the management of Foodstore plc?
- Is Freshfoods plc making much better use of its assets than its competitor is?
- Is the profit margin made on each item sold much higher in one company than the other?

Definite answers to these questions cannot be given unless other information is considered. Take, for example, the *capital employed*:

	Freshfoods plc	**Foodstore plc**
Capital employed (2005)	£900,000	£60,000

Which company seems to have made more efficient use of the capital invested? We need to compare *profit* made with *capital employed* in each company.

Foodstore plc has made £30,000 profit from an investment of £60,000 and Freshfoods plc has made £300,000 profit from an investment of £900,000. By comparing *two* figures from the accounts, Foodstore plc appears to have achieved a better performance even though its overall level of profits is lower.

This example shows how important it is to use *more than one* figure from the accounts when trying to assess how a business is performing. Comparing *two* figures from the accounts in this way is called *ratio analysis*. This is a very important use of the published accounts.

Ratio analysis of accounts

▨ **Definition to learn:**
LIQUIDITY is the ability of a business to pay back its short-term debts.

There are many ratios which can be calculated from a set of accounts. This unit concentrates on five of the most commonly used. These ratios are used to measure and compare *performance* and LIQUIDITY of a business.

Performance ratios

Three common performance ratios are:

■ *Return on net assets* (sometimes known as *return on capital employed*)

This is calculated by the formula:

$$\text{Return on net assets (\%)} = \frac{\text{Operating profit}}{\text{Net assets}} \times 100$$

▨ *Case study example*

Refer back to the accounts of Ace Engineering plc on pages 107–109.

Ace Engineering plc had a return on net assets in 2004 of:

$$\frac{\text{Operating profit}}{\text{Net assets}} \times 100 = \frac{280}{1,065} \times 100 = 26.3\%$$

This means that in the financial year ending 31 March 2004, the company made a return on its assets (or return on the capital employed in the business) of 26.3 per cent. The higher this result, the more successful are the managers in earning gross profit from sales. If this percentage increases next year it would suggest that:

■ prices have been put up by more than costs have risen

or that

■ costs of goods bought in have been reduced. Possibly a new supplier is being used or managers have negotiated lower cost prices.

This result should now be compared with other years and other companies to see if the managers are running the business more efficiently or not.

- *Gross profit margin* This is calculated by the formula:

$$\text{Gross profit margin (\%)} = \frac{\text{Gross profit}}{\text{Sales turnover}} \times 100$$

▨ *Case study example*

Ace Engineering plc had a gross profit margin in 2004 of:

$$\text{Gross profit margin} = \frac{400}{1,300} \times 100 = 30.8\%$$

This means that on every £ worth of goods sold, the company made on average 30.8 pence gross profit. Do not forget that this is before other expenses have been deducted and is not the final profit of the company. Again, this result needs to be compared with other years and other companies.

- *Net profit margin* This is calculated by the formula:

$$\text{Net profit margin (\%)} = \frac{\text{Net profit before tax}}{\text{Sales turnover}} \times 100$$

▨ *Case study example*

Ace Engineering plc had a net profit margin in 2004 of:

$$\text{Net profit margin} = \frac{240}{1,300} \times 100 = 18.5\%$$

This is lower than the gross profit margin because all other expenses including interest have been deducted from gross profit to arrive at net profit before tax. The higher this result, the more successful the managers are in making net profit from sales. What could this result be compared with? Again, with other years and other companies.

▨ *Activity 7.6: case study task*

a) Using the 2005 accounts for Ace Engineering plc on pages 107–109, calculate:
   i) return on net assets
   ii) gross profit margin
   iii) net profit margin.
b) Do you feel that the company performed better in 2004 or 2005? Give reasons for your answer.

Liquidity ratios

Three common liquidity ratios are:

■ *Current ratio* This is calculated by the formula:

$$\text{Current ratio} = \frac{\text{Current assets}}{\text{Current liabilities}}$$

▓ *Case study example*

Ace Engineering plc had a current ratio in 2004 of:

$$\text{Current ratio} = \frac{125}{100} = 1.25$$

This result is rather low. It means that the business could only just pay off all of its short-term debts from current assets. A safer current ratio would be between 1.5 and 2. A result of less than 1 would mean that the business could have real cash flow problems. It could not pay off its short-term debts from current assets.

The current ratio is useful but it assumes that all current assets could be turned into cash quickly. This is not always the case. For example, it might be very difficult to sell all stocks in a short period of time. For this reason a second liquidity ratio is used.

■ *Acid test or liquid ratio* This is calculated by the formula:

$$\text{Acid test ratio} = \frac{\text{Current assets} - \text{stocks}}{\text{Current liabilities}}$$

▓ *Case study example*

Ace Engineering plc had an acid test ratio in 2004 of:

$$\text{Acid test ratio} = \frac{125 - 50}{100} = 0.75$$

Again, this is rather low. A result of 1 would mean that the company could just pay off its short-term debts from its most liquid assets. A result of 0.75 means that it cannot even do this. This would be worrying for the management and steps would have to be taken to improve the working capital of the business.

■ *Stock turnover ratio* This is an indication of how efficiently the working capital of the business is being managed. It measures the number of times in a financial year the business is able to turn stock into sales. The more often stock can be sold the more benefit there will be to the business.

$$\text{Stock turnover ratio} = \frac{\text{Cost of sales}}{\text{Stocks}}$$

▦ *Case study example*

Ace Engineering plc had a stock turnover in 2004 of:

$$\text{Stock turnover} = \frac{900}{50} = 18 \text{ times}$$

This figure needs to be compared with other years to see if the business is managing its stocks more or less efficiently. A result greater than 18 in 2005 would mean that the business is managing stocks more efficiently and turning stocks into sales more quickly.

▦ *Activity 7.7: case study task*

a) Using the accounts for Ace Engineering plc, calculate the following ratios for 2005:
i) current ratio   ii) acid test ratio   iii) stock turnover ratio.
b) Using your results, compare the liquidity of the company in 2005 with its liquidity in 2004. Also comment on the efficiency of the company in its management of stocks.

Ratios are very useful as a quick way of comparing a firm's performance and liquidity. Ratio results may be compared with:

- other years
- other businesses.

However the following disadvantages need to be remembered.

Disadvantages of ratio analysis

☒ Ratios are based on past results and may not indicate how a business will perform in future.

☒ Accounting results over time will be affected by inflation (rising prices) and comparisons between years may be misleading.

☒ Different companies may use slightly different accounting methods, for example, in valuing their stock. These different methods could lead to different ratio results, therefore making comparisons difficult.

Revision summary: ratio analysis

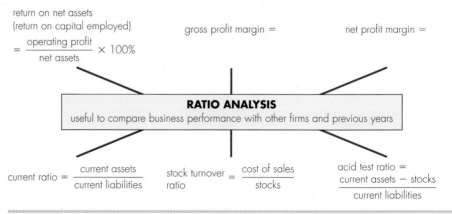

return on net assets (return on capital employed)

$$= \frac{\text{operating profit}}{\text{net assets}} \times 100\%$$

gross profit margin =

net profit margin =

RATIO ANALYSIS
useful to compare business performance with other firms and previous years

current ratio = $\dfrac{\text{current assets}}{\text{current liabilities}}$

stock turnover ratio = $\dfrac{\text{cost of sales}}{\text{stocks}}$

acid test ratio = $\dfrac{\text{current assets} - \text{stocks}}{\text{current liabilities}}$

Revision questions

1 State *two* reasons why managers need accounting information about their business. [2]

2 State *three* other groups that would be interested in the accounts of a business. [3]

3 Explain the difference between gross and net profit. [3]

4 What does an appropriation account show (on the profit and loss account)? [2]

5 Define *depreciation*. [2]

6 Explain what a balance sheet tells a manager about a business. [3]

7 Distinguish between business assets and liabilities. [3]

8 What is meant by *capital employed*? [2]

9 Explain why ratio analysis is more useful than just comparing individual figures from company accounts. [3]

10 What does a 'return on capital employed of 20 per cent' mean? [3]

11 Why would a current ratio of 0.75 be considered 'too low'? [3]

12 Use performance ratios to analyse these accounting results for P & K Ltd, a firm of builders:

	2004 (€000s)	2005
Gross profit	15	16
Expenses including interest	6	9
Capital employed	70	80
Sales turnover	100	120

Comment on your results. [8]

13 Explain *two* limitations of ratio analysis. [4]

14 Explain why someone thinking of buying shares in a company would find the published (final) accounts of a business useful. [4]

15 Rashid owns a farm that has some spare buildings. He thinks that the best idea is to turn them into holiday flats. 'I could convert the buildings into 6 holiday flats. I would need to spend £40,000 on building work, £8,000 on fittings and £12,000 on decoration. In the holiday season I could get £200 a week in revenue from each flat. I should be able to calculate the gross profit from the first year's operations.'

a) Explain what is meant by the term *gross profit*. [2]

b) Calculate the total cost of converting the barn into 6 flats. Show your working. [2]

c) List *three* variable costs to Rashid if he were to let the flats. [3]

d) Rashid succeeds in letting the flats for £180 per week each for 10 weeks. His variable costs total £6,000. Calculate the gross profit Rashid can expect to make. Show all workings. [4]

16 Calculate the acid test ratios for both years, for Company X:

	2004 (£000s)	2005
Current liabilities	15	18
Stocks	3	4
Debtors	12	8
Cash	5	4

Comment on your results. [4]

The CD-ROM (see details on page x) provides further tests, activities and Case study work on the topics covered in this unit.

8 Cash flow planning

This unit will explain:

- ❓ the importance of cash flow to business operations
- ❓ how firms can run short of cash and the likely consequences of this
- ❓ how a cash flow budget (forecast) is constructed.

By the end of this unit you should be able to:

- ☑ explain the difference between the profit made by a business and its cash flow
- ☑ understand why cash flow is of such importance to businesses and how cash flow might be improved
- ☑ construct and understand a simple cash flow forecast for a business based on expected future transactions.

What is meant by cash flow?

Cash is a liquid asset. This means that it is immediately available for spending on goods and services.

Do you ever run out of cash? Have you ever been unable to pay for goods which you need at one particular time because you did not have enough cash? Have you ever borrowed money or incurred bills which you cannot immediately settle? If you answered 'yes' to any of these questions, you have already experienced a CASH FLOW problem! In business terms, cash flow means the flow of money into and out of a business over a certain time period.

How can cash flow into a business (CASH INFLOW)? Here are five of the most common ways:

- by the sale of goods for cash
- through payments made by debtors – debtors are customers who have already purchased goods from the business but did not pay for them at the time
- by borrowing money from an external source – this will lead to cash flowing into the business (it will have to be repaid eventually!)
- through the sale of assets of the business, for example unwanted property
- from investors – shareholders in the case of companies – putting more money into the business.

How can cash flow out of a business (CASH OUTFLOW)? Here are five of the most common ways:

- by purchasing goods or materials for cash
- by the payment of wages, salaries and other expenses in cash
- by purchasing fixed assets
- by repaying loans
- by paying creditors of the business – other firms who had originally supplied items to the business but who were not paid immediately.

■ Definitions to learn:

The CASH FLOW of a business is the CASH INFLOWS and OUTFLOWS over a period of time.

CASH INFLOWS are the sums of money received by a business during a period of time.

CASH OUTFLOWS are the sums of money paid out by a business during a period of time.

■ *Activity 8.1: case study task*

For each of the following transactions, tick in the correct column to indicate whether they are cash inflows or cash outflows for Good Hope Enterprises Ltd.

Transaction	Cash inflow	Cash outflow
Purchase of new computer for cash		
Sale of goods to customers – no credit given		
Interest paid on bank loan		
Wages paid to staff		
Debtors pay their bills		
Additional shares are sold to shareholders		
Creditors are paid		
Bank overdraft is paid off		

Cash flow cycle

■ **Definition to learn:**

A CASH FLOW CYCLE shows the stages between paying out cash for labour, materials, etc. and receiving cash from the sale of goods.

The following diagram will help to explain the link between some of the inflows and outflows mentioned above – the CASH FLOW CYCLE. It explains why cash paid out is not returned immediately to the business.

The cash flow cycle

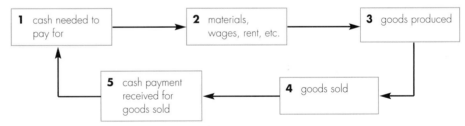

The diagram shows how (1) cash is needed to pay for essential materials (2) and other costs required to produce the product. Time is needed to produce the products (3) before they can be sold to customers (4). If these customers receive credit, they will not have to pay straightaway. When they do pay for the goods in cash (5), this money will be needed to pay for buying further materials, etc. and so the cycle continues.

The longer the time taken to complete these stages, the greater will be the firm's need for *working capital* (see Unit 7) and cash.

The diagram also helps us to understand the importance of *planning* for cash flows.

■ What would happen if the business did not have enough cash at stage 1? Not enough materials and other requirements could be purchased and so output and sales would fall.

■ What would happen if a business insisted on its customer paying cash at stage 4 because the business was short of money? It might lose the customer to a competitor who could offer credit.

■ What would happen if the business had insufficient cash to pay its bills such as rent and electricity? It would be in a *liquidity crisis* and it might be forced out of business by its creditors.

These three examples illustrate the need for managers to plan ahead for their cash needs so that the business is not put at risk in these ways.

What cash flow is not!

Cash flow is *not* the same as profit. This is an important distinction.

■ Case study example

Good Hope Enterprises Ltd records the following transactions over the month of June:

| Goods sold to customers | (50% cash, 50% on one month's credit) | £40,000 |
| Costs of goods sold | (paid for in cash) | £15,000 |

■ What was the gross profit in June?

Sales revenue − Cost of goods sold = £25,000

■ Assuming the business started the month with no cash, how much cash did it have at the end of June? (Ignore any other transactions.)

Cash inflow − Cash outflow

£20,000 (cash sales) − £15,000 = £5,000

■ Activity 8.2: case study task

A business records the following transactions for one month:

| Sales of goods | £45,000 (50% for cash; 50% on one month's credit) |
| Materials purchased and used | £12,000 (all paid in cash during the month) |

Assume no other transactions.

a) Calculate the gross profit made by the business in this month.
b) Calculate the cash held by the business at the end of this month (assume they had no cash at the start of the month).
c) Explain why the answers to a) and b) are different.

There is a clear difference between the profit made by Good Hope Enterprises Ltd and the cash flow over the same period. Why is the cash figure lower than the gross profit? Because, although all goods have been sold, cash payment has been received for only half of them. The customers buying the goods on credit will pay cash in later months.

This important example leads to further questions:

■ Can profitable businesses run out of cash? Yes – and this is a major reason for businesses failing. It is called *insolvency*.
■ How is this possible? In a number of ways:
  – by allowing customers too long a credit period, perhaps in order to encourage sales
  – by purchasing too many fixed assets at once
  – by purchasing or producing too high a level of stocks when expanding too quickly. This means that cash is used to pay for higher stock levels. This is often called *overtrading*.

Revision summary: cash flow

cash is needed to pay expenses

cash is received from customers, but also from bank loans and sale of assets

cash is the most liquid asset

CASH FLOW

cash flow is *not* the same as profit

cash flow problems can occur from overtrading or giving too much credit

lack of cash can cause a liquidity problem

Cash flow forecasts

We have seen how important cash is to any business. Without sufficient cash to pay bills and repay loans, a business may be forced to stop trading by its creditors and banks. It is therefore very important indeed for the manager of a business to know what cash will be available month by month. A CASH FLOW FORECAST can be used to tell the manager:

■ how much is available for paying bills, repaying loans or for buying fixed assets
■ how much the bank might need to lend in order to avoid insolvency
■ whether the business is holding *too much* cash which could be put to a more profitable use.

Managers use cash flow forecasts to help them find out the future cash position of their business.

Uses of cash flow forecasts

Cash flow forecasts are useful in the following situations:

■ starting up a business
■ keeping the bank manager informed
■ running an existing business
■ managing cash flow.

Case study example

Cash flow statement – Good Hope Enterprises Ltd
January to March 2005 (£). Figures in brackets are negative.

	January	February	March
OPENING BANK BALANCE (A)	10,000	15,000	(5,000)
Cash inflows (B)	35,000	45,000	50,000
Cash outflows (C)	30,000	65,000	40,000
NET CASH FLOW {D = (B − C)}	5,000	(20,000)	10,000
CLOSING BANK BALANCE (A + D)	15,000	(5,000)	5,000

Note the following points:

■ a positive net cash flow will increase the closing bank balance
■ a negative net cash flow (as in February) will reduce the bank balance
■ each closing bank balance becomes the opening bank balance for the next month
■ the bank account becomes *overdrawn* in February.

Starting up a business

When planning to start a business, the owner will need to know how much cash will be needed in the first few months of operation. This is a very expensive time for new businesses as premises have to be purchased or rented, machinery must be purchased or hired, stocks must be built up and advertising and promotion costs will be necessary to make consumers aware of the product. New businesses are often unsuccessful because the owner does not realise how much cash is needed in the first few crucial months. A cash flow forecast should avoid these problems from occurring.

Keeping the bank manager informed

Banks provide loans to businesses. However, before bank managers will lend any money, they need to see the firm's cash flow forecast. This is particularly true of a new business, but also for an existing one. The bank manager will need to see how big a loan or overdraft is needed, when it is needed, how long the finance is needed for and when it might be repaid.

It is very rare for a bank to lend to a business unless a cash flow forecast is produced which shows all of these things.

Running an existing business

As seen from earlier examples, it is not just newly formed businesses which need to forecast cash flows. Any business can run out of cash and require an overdraft, perhaps because of an expensive fixed asset being bought or a fall in sales. Borrowing money needs to be planned in advance so that the lowest rates of interest can be arranged. Telling the bank today that a loan is needed tomorrow could lead to the bank either refusing the loan – because of poor business planning – or charging high rates of interest. The bank will know that the business has little alternative but to pay these rates.

If the business exceeds the overdraft limit from the bank without informing the bank manager first, the bank could insist that the overdraft is repaid immediately and this could force the business to close.

■ Activity 8.3: case study task

Cash flow forecast for Sierra Promotions Co.
January to April 2005 (£). Figures in brackets are negative.

	January	February	March	April
Opening bank balance	3,000	5,000	7,000	4,000
Cash inflows:				
Cash sales	15,000	15,000	20,000	25,000
Payments from debtors	5,000	5,000	7,000	8,000
Total cash inflows	20,000	20,000	27,000	33,000
Cash outflows:				
Materials and wages	3,000	3,000	5,000	7,000
Rent and other expenses	15,000	15,000	25,000	15,000
Total cash outflows	18,000	18,000	30,000	z
Net cash flow	2,000	x	(3,000)	11,000
Closing bank balance	5,000	7,000	y	15,000

a) Calculate values for x, y and z.
b) Suggest one reason why 'rent and other expenses' were so much higher in March than in the other months.

■ Activity 8.4: case study task

The manager of Capri Motors Ltd is concerned about planning the cash flows of the business over the next four months. She asks for your help in making a cash flow forecast. She provides you with the following information.

■ Forecasted sales are: January £22,000; February £25,000; March £20,000; April £22,000.
■ Customers always pay cash.
■ Materials are purchased each month and are paid for in cash. The materials used each month are 50 per cent of sales revenue for that month.
■ Other cash expenses (wages, rent, insurance, etc.) are forecast to be: January £4,000; February £13,000; March £15,000; April £15,000.
■ The opening cash balance in January is £2,000.

a) Explain to the manager the importance of a cash flow forecast.
b) Using the same structure as in the examples above, draw up a cash flow forecast for this business over the four months from January to April.
c) What do you notice about the bank balance in April? What action could the manager take now that she is aware of this problem?

Managing cash flow

Too much cash held in the bank account of a business means that this capital could be better used in other areas of the business. If it seems that the business is likely to have a very high bank balance, the accountant could decide to pay off loans to help to reduce interest charges. Another option would be to pay creditors quickly to take advantage of possible discounts. These are examples of actively managing the cash flow of a business.

Revision summary: cash flow forecasts

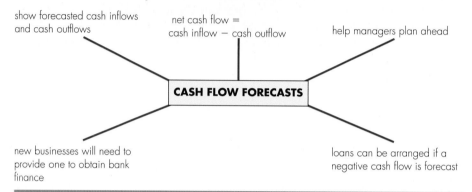

How can cash flow problems be solved?

Suppose that you have calculated that over the next few months you are likely to have your own cash flow problem, i.e. your cash expenses are likely to exceed your cash income. What steps could you take to solve this problem?

Here are four suggestions.

■ Arrange with your bank to borrow money over the time when you have a negative cash flow.
■ Reduce or delay some of your planned expenses.
■ Increase your forecasted cash income in some way, for example a part-time job.
■ Delay paying for some of your expenses until cash is available, i.e. ask for credit on your purchases.

Very similar solutions exist for businesses when they are short of cash – but there are even more options available.

The case study task on page 125 is typical of the standard of questions that you can expect at GCSE level on this important topic. You should now be able to understand why cash flow is so important to business survival and how forecasts can help managers plan the cash flows of their businesses carefully.

■ *Activity 8.5: case study task*

Manuel Guitano set up in business as a sole trader nine years ago. He called his business Gardener's Green. Manuel designs the gardens for hotels, offices and large private houses. He also maintains customers' gardens. The business is very busy in the spring, summer and autumn but not very busy in winter.

Manuel is a sole trader and therefore the owner of the business. He employs six full-time employees. These employees have been with him for the past four years. Experienced gardeners are not always easy to find.

Gardener's Green has a small amount of land with six greenhouses although there is space for more. Gardener's Green grows about 50 per cent of the plants that it supplies to customers.

The work is seasonal and so are the incomes to the business, but expenses occur every month. Look at the cash flow forecast below to see what is likely to happen in the next financial year. There is a cash flow problem. You have been asked by Manuel to consider this problem and make recommendations as to what he can do to solve it.

Cash flow forecast for Gardener's Green 1997/1998. All figures in brackets are negative.

	Aug. $	Sept. $	Oct. $	Nov. $	Dec. $	Jan. $	Feb. $	Mar. $	Apr. $	May $	Jun. $	Jul. $
Cash inflows												
Sales revenue	70,000	80,000	1,000	1,400	200	200	1,000	50,000	80,000	80,000	60,000	60,000
Cash outflows												
Wages	20,000	20,000	20,000	20,000	20,000	20,000	20,000	20,000	20,000	20,000	20,000	20,000
Plants & trees purchased	20,000	0	0	0	0	0	0	30,000	30,000	30,000	30,000	30,000
Seeds & compost	0	6,000	6,000	0	0	6,000	8,000	8,000	7,000	0	0	0
Heating & water	1,000	1,000	1,000	1,000	1,000	1,000	1,000	1,000	1,000	1,000	1,000	1,000
Bank interest	0	0	0	0	0	1,018	3,549	4,649	3,150	910	216	0
Business tax on land	100	100	100	100	100	100	100	100	100	100	100	100
Total cash outflow	41,100	27,100	27,100	21,100	21,100	28,118	32,649	63,749	61,250	52,010	51,316	51,100
Opening balance	100	29,000	81,900	55,800	36,100	15,200	(12,718)	(44,367)	(58,116)	(39,366)	(11,376)	(2,692)
Net cash flow	28,900	52,900	(26,100)	(19,700)	(20,900)	(27,918)	(31,649)	(13,749)	18,750	27,990	8,684	8,900
Bank balance (closing)	29,000	81,900	55,800	36,100	15,200	(12,718)	(44,367)	(58,116)	(39,366)	(11,376)	(2,692)	6,208

a) Why is cash flow forecasting important to managers such as Manuel?

b) Who else, apart from Manuel, is likely to be interested in a cash flow forecast for Gardener's Green? Give reasons for your answer.

c) Refer to the cash flow forecast.
   i) Why do some costs stay the same every month? Use an example to explain your answer.
   ii) Why do some costs vary in some months? Use an example to explain your answer.

d) Manuel has just been informed that his major supplier of plants and trees is about to raise prices. If these costs rise how will the cash flow forecast for Gardener's Green be affected?

e) What can be done to improve the cash flow of this business? Make three recommendations to Manuel, explaining their advantages and disadvantages, for improving the cash flow of Gardener's Green.

[Adapted from IGCSE Business Studies, June 1997, Paper 4]

■ *Revision questions*

1 What is meant by *cash inflow?* [2]

2 State *four* ways in which a business can receive cash inflows. [4]

3 What is meant by *cash outflow?* [2]

4 State *three* forms of cash outflow from a business. [3]

5 What is meant by a *cash flow cycle?* [3]

6 Explain the operation of the cash flow cycle shown below. [6]

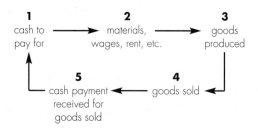

7 Refer to the cash flow cycle above. Explain why a business needs more cash and working capital when the time between stage 1 and stage 5 is very long. [4]

8 Fill in the missing values (a)–(d) on the following cash flow forecast for Curls Hairstyles Ltd. [8]

9 Sanjay runs a profitable and expanding computer training company. He is concerned to see that even though his business made a profit of £6,000 last year, the bank balance fell during the year. Explain to Sanjay the possible reasons for this situation. [8]

10 a) Construct a three month cash flow forecast (from April) for A & P Traders Ltd from the following forecasted data:
   ■ Sales are: March £15,000; April £14,000; May £16,000; June £14,000.
   ■ All sales are 50 per cent cash and 50 per cent on one month's credit.
   ■ Purchases are made in the month of sale and are all for cash. The value of purchases is 50 per cent of sales value.
   ■ Expenses are: April £6,000; May £8,000; June £12,000.
   ■ Opening cash balance in April is £1,000. [12]

   b) What action would you advise the manager of this business to take before the problem arises in June? [8]

	January (£)	February (£)	March (£)	April (£)
Cash inflows:				
Cash sales	1,000	1,000	3,000	3,000
Cash outflows:				
Purchases of stock	100	100	300	200
Rent	0	100	0	100
Wages and other expenses	600	600	**(c)**	1,500
Opening cash balance	500	**(b)**	1,000	2,500
Net cash flow	300	200	1,500	1,200
Closing cash balance	**(a)**	1,000	2,500	**(d)**

The CD-ROM (see details on page x) provides further tests, activities and Case study work on the topics covered in this unit.

9 Financing business activity

This unit will explain:

- ❓ **why businesses need finance**
- ❓ **the different sources of finance available to business**
- ❓ **how managers choose between different sources.**

By the end of the unit you should be able to:

- ☑ **recognise the different reasons why businesses need finance**
- ☑ **classify different sources of raising finance between internal and external and period of time**
- ☑ **analyse the advantages and disadvantages of different sources of finance**
- ☑ **analyse a firm's need for funds and make a choice between the available sources**
- ☑ **make decisions on whether finance should be made available to a business from the viewpoint of shareholders, banks and other institutions.**

Why do businesses need finance?

What is finance? Finance is money. We all need money to purchase the goods and services we require.

We need money to buy everyday goods, like food, but we also need money, or finance, to pay rent or to buy a house or other expensive things. Businesses need finance too. Without money they could not pay wages, buy materials or pay for assets. Here are three examples of why businesses need money.

Starting up a business

When an individual plans to start their own business, they should consider all of the assets they will need to buy in order to start trading. From studying Unit 7 you should now have a clear idea of what fixed assets are and why new businesses will need to purchase some of these. In addition, the owner of the firm will need to obtain finance to purchase current assets, for example stocks, before goods can be sold to the first customers.

The finance needed to launch a new business is often called START-UP CAPITAL.

■ **Definition to learn:**
START-UP CAPITAL is the finance needed by a new business to pay for essential fixed and current assets before it can begin trading.

Expanding an existing business

The owners of a successful business will often take a decision to expand it in order to increase profits.

Additional fixed assets could be purchased – such as buildings and machinery. Another business could be purchased through a take-over. In both cases, it will probably be necessary to increase the firm's working capital in order to finance additional stocks and debtors.

Other types of expansion include developing new products to reach new markets. This form of growth could require substantial amounts of finance for research and development.

A business in difficulties

Finance may also be needed by businesses that are not doing so well. For example, a loss-making business may need to purchase new machinery in order to become more efficient. In another case, a firm with negative cash flow may need finance to cover short-term expenses. It is often very difficult for either loss-making businesses or those with negative cash flow (see Unit 8) to raise essential finance.

■ Definitions to learn:

CAPITAL EXPENDITURE is money spent on fixed assets which will last for more than one year.

REVENUE EXPENDITURE is money spent on day-to-day expenses which do not involve the purchase of a long-term asset, for example wages and rent.

In all three cases above, businesses may need finance to pay for either CAPITAL EXPENDITURE or REVENUE EXPENDITURE. It is important to understand the difference.

■ Capital expenditure is money spent on fixed assets which will last for more than one year. These are needed at the start of a business and as it expands.
■ Revenue expenditure is money spent on day-to-day expenses which do not involve the purchase of a long-term asset, for example wages and rent.

Revision summary: financial needs of business

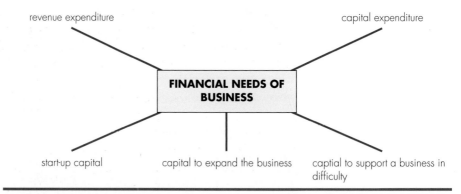

■ *Activity 9.1: case study task*

Look at the list below of expenses for a sports centre and tick whether you consider them to be either revenue expenditure or capital expenditure.

	Revenue expenditure	**Capital expenditure**
Purchase of building		
Water rates		
Staff wages		
Office computer		
Gym equipment		
Maintenance of equipment		

■ *Activity 9.2: case study task*

Wally Shah has decided to leave his job to set up his own taxi business.

a) Make a list of the likely set-up costs of this business for its first month of operation.
b) Indicate which of these costs are revenue expenditure and which are capital expenditure. Explain your answer.

Sources of finance

As there are so many different sources of finance, it is common to split them up, or classify them, into different groups. The two most common ways of doing this are to define whether the finance is:

■ internal or external
■ short-term, medium-term or long-term.

Internal finance

This is money which is obtained from within the business itself. The most common examples of internal finance are:

■ *Retained profit* Those profits kept in the business after the owners have taken their share of the profits. These are often called *ploughed back* profits, and have the following advantage and disadvantage.
  ☑ Retained profit does not have to be repaid unlike, for example, a loan.
  ☒ A new business will not yet have any retained profits and many firms could find that their profits are too low to finance the expansion needed.
■ *Sale of existing assets* Those assets which are no longer required by the business, for example, redundant buildings or surplus equipment.
  ☑ This makes better use of the capital tied up in the business.
  ☒ It may take some time to sell these assets and this source is not available for new businesses as they have no surplus assets to sell.
■ *Running down stocks to raise cash.*
  ☑ This reduces the opportunity cost and storage cost of high stock levels.
  ☒ It must be done carefully to avoid disappointing customers if not enough goods are kept in stock.
■ *Owners' savings* A sole trader or members of a partnership can put more of their savings into their unincorporated businesses. As we saw in Unit 3, the owners of these firms are not separate from their businesses and therefore such finance is called internal.
  ☑ It should be available to the firm quickly and no interest is paid.
  ☒ Savings may be too low and it increases the risk taken by the owners.

Revision summary: internal sources of finance

retained profits

sale of surplus assets

INTERNAL SOURCES OF FINANCE

selling stocks – reducing stock levels

sole trader or partnership – owners' savings

■ *Activity 9.3: case study task*

Wally Shah needs advice on sources of finance before going ahead with his plan (Activity 9.2). Explain to him why:

a) retained profits are not, to start with, a possible source of finance
b) his savings will be likely to be an important source of funds
c) selling off stocks is never likely to be an available source of finance to his taxi business.

External finance

This is money obtained from individuals or institutions outside of the business. The most common forms of external finance are:

■ *Issue of shares* (only possible for limited companies).
   ☑ This is a permanent source of capital which would not have to be repaid to shareholders. No interest has to be paid.
   ✖ Dividends will be expected by the shareholders and the ownership of the company could change hands.
■ *Bank loans.*
   ☑ Usually quick to arrange and can be for varying lengths of time. Large companies are often offered low rates of interest by banks if they borrow large sums.
   ✖ A bank loan will have to be repaid eventually and interest must be paid. Security or collateral is usually required. For example, a bank may insist that it has the right to sell some of the firm's property if it fails to pay interest or does not repay the loan. A sole trader may have to put his or her own house up as security on a bank loan.
■ *Selling debentures* These are long-term loan certificates issued by limited companies.
   ☑ Debentures can be used to raise very long-term finance, for example, 25 years.
   ✖ As with loans, these must be repaid and interest must be paid.
■ *Factoring of debts* Debt factors are specialist agencies that 'buy' the debts of firms for immediate cash. They may offer 90 per cent of an existing debt. The debtor will then pay the factor and the 10 per cent represents the factor's profit.

☑ Immediate cash is made available and the risk of collecting the debt becomes the factor's.

☒ The firm does not receive 100 per cent of the value of its debts.

■ *Grants and subsidies* from outside agencies, for example, the government.

☑ These usually do not have to be repaid.

☒ They are often given with 'strings attached', for example, the firm must locate in a particular area.

Revision summary: external sources of finance

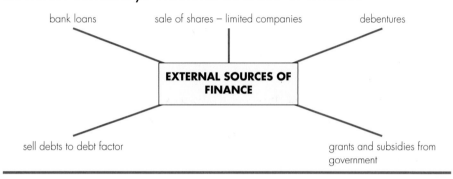

Activity 9.4: case study task

Wally Shah's taxi business has now been operating for two years. He wants to expand by buying another taxi and employing two drivers on a shift system.

a) Explain to Wally the benefits of using the business profits to buy the taxi rather than taking out a bank loan.

b) In what circumstances would you advise Wally to take out a bank loan to expand his business?

Short-, medium- and long-term finance

Short-term finance

This provides the working capital needed by businesses for day-to-day operations. It is finance which is needed for up to three years. Shortages of cash in the short-term can be overcome in three main ways:

■ *Overdrafts* These are arranged by a bank.

☑ The bank gives the business the right to 'overdraw' its bank account, i.e. spend more money from the account than is currently in it. The firm could use this finance to pay wages or suppliers but, obviously, it cannot do this indefinitely. The overdraft will vary each month with the needs of the business – it is said to be a 'flexible' form of borrowing. Interest will be paid only on the amount overdrawn. Overdrafts can turn out to be cheaper than loans.

■ Interest rates are variable, unlike most loans which have fixed rates. The bank can ask for the overdraft to be repaid at very short notice.
■ *Trade credit* This is when a business delays paying its suppliers, which leaves the business in a better cash position.
  ✓ It is almost an interest-free loan to the business for the length of time that payment is delayed for.
  ✗ The supplier may refuse to give discounts or even refuse to supply any more goods if payment is not made quickly.
■ *Factoring of debts* See page 130 under *External finance*.

Medium-term finance

This is finance which is available for between three and ten years. It is usually needed to purchase machinery and vehicles, which often have useful lives for this period.

The three most common sources of medium-term finance are:

■ *Bank loans* Payable over a fixed period of time. The advantages and disadvantages of these have already been considered under *External finance*.
■ *Hire purchase* This allows a business to buy a fixed asset over a long period of time with monthly payments which include an interest charge.
  ✓ The firm does not have to find a large cash sum to purchase the asset.
  ✗ A cash deposit is paid at the start of the period. Interest payments can be quite high.
■ *Leasing* Leasing an asset allows the firm to use an asset but it does not have to purchase it. Monthly leasing payments are made. The business could decide to purchase the asset at the end of the leasing period. Some businesses decide to sell off some fixed assets for cash and lease them back from a leasing company. This is called *sale and leaseback*.
  ✓ The firm does not have to find a large cash sum to purchase the asset to start with. The care and maintenance of the asset are carried out by the leasing company.
  ✗ The total cost of the leasing charges will be higher than purchasing the asset.

Long-term finance

This is finance which is available for more than ten years. Usually this money would be used to purchase long-term fixed assets to update or expand the business or to finance a take-over of another firm. The main sources of long-term finance are:

■ *Issue of shares* As we have seen already, this option is available only to limited companies. (See Unit 3 for details of how sole traders and partnerships can convert to limited company status.)

  Shares are often referred to as *equities* – therefore the sale of shares is sometimes called *equity finance*.

Private limited companies can raise more capital by selling shares privately to family, friends or business contacts. The more shares sold in this way, the weaker may be the control of the people who started the company, as all shareholders have the right to vote at AGMs.

Public limited companies have the ability to sell a large number of shares to the general public. These *new issues*, as they are called, can raise very large sums of money but can be expensive to organise and advertise. A *rights issue* of new shares is a very common way for plcs to raise additional capital. This gives existing shareholders the right to buy new shares in proportion to their current holding. This avoids the problem of new shareholders changing the balance of ownership.

☑ A share issue provides *permanent capital* which does not have to be repaid. There are no interest payments.

☒ Dividends are paid after tax whereas interest on loans is paid before tax is deducted. The balance of ownership can be affected by a large share issue.

■ *Long-term loans* or *debt finance* Loans differ from share capital in the following ways:
  – interest is paid before tax as an expense
  – interest must be paid every year but dividends do not have to be paid if, for example, the firm has made a loss
  – they must be repaid as they are not permanent capital
  – they are often 'secured' against particular assets.

The advantages and disadvantages of loans have already been mentioned under *External finance*.

■ *Debentures* See page 130 under *External finance*.

Revision summary: For how long is the finance required?

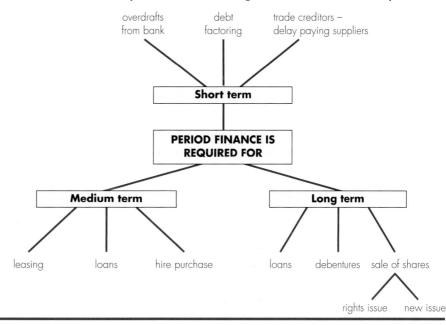

■ *Activity 9.5*

Consider all of the following sources of finance. Copy out the table and tick the relevant column for each source. Are these short-, medium- or long-term sources of finance?

Source of finance	Short-term	Medium-term	Long-term
Overdraft			
Debentures			
Issue of shares			
Three-year bank loan			
Trade credit			
Hire purchase			

■ *Activity 9.6*

Consider all of these different reasons for a private limited company needing finance. Copy out the table and fill in the gaps with:

a) what you consider could be the most suitable source of finance
b) the reason for your choice.

Need for finance	Most suitable source	Reason for choice
Planned take-over of another business		
Temporary increase in stocks over the summer		
Purchase of new car for the Chief Executive		
Research and development of new product – to come on the market in four years time		
Cost of building modern factory requiring much less land than the present one		

How the choice of finance is made in business

We now know the main types of finance available to firms. What factors do managers consider before deciding where to obtain finance from?

Purpose and time period

What is the finance to be spent on? Is it to be used to pay for fixed assets or is it needed to pay for a short-term cash flow crisis?

The general rule is to *match* the source of finance to the use that will be made of it.

- If the use is long term, for example the purchase of a fixed asset, the source should be long-term.
- If the use is short term, for example the purchase of additional stocks to cover a busy period, the source should be short-term.

Think about the disadvantages of buying additional stocks which will only be needed for a few months, with a long-term bank loan. Can you see why this would be unwise? What source of finance would be suitable for this?

Amount needed

Different sources will be used depending on the amount of money needed.

Status and size

Companies, especially public limited companies, have a greater choice of sources of finance. Issuing shares or debentures is not an option for sole traders and partnerships.

■ *Case study example*

If a company needs €5,000 to repair a van, a new issue of shares would be the wrong choice. This is because the issue of shares is complicated and would take a long time – the firm wants the van repaired now! Also, the cost of arranging a share issue would be much more than the €5,000 raised. What source of finance could this business use instead?

If the same company wanted to take over another company and offered €5 million, a new share issue would be much more likely – the cost of arranging for the new shares to be sold would be much less than the €5 million raised.

These businesses, if they wish to expand, may have to depend on the savings of their owners – personal capital. They also often have the disadvantage of having to pay higher interest rates to banks for loans than large and well established companies.

Control

Owners of businesses may lose control of that business if they ask other people to invest into their firm.

Risk and gearing

A further point about loan capital is that it will raise the *gearing* of the business – and this is a common measure of *risk* that the managers are taking. The gearing of a business measures the proportion of total capital raised from long-term loans. If this proportion is very high – say more than 50 per cent – the business is said to be *highly geared*. It is being financed more from loans than from shareholders. This is said to be a risky way of financing a business.

Why is this said to be risky? Because interest must be paid on the loans whether the business is making profits or not. When interest rates are high and company profits are low, the firm may not be able to pay all of the interest. The future of the business will be at risk. Therefore, banks are usually reluctant to lend to highly geared businesses. Such businesses may have to use sources of finance other than loans.

Revision summary: choosing sources of finance

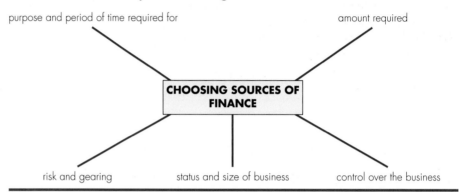

■ *Case study examples*

- A sole trader could take on a partner to bring in extra capital – but could that partner start to take important decisions without the original owner's permission?
- The directors of a private limited company could decide to 'go public'. This could raise very large sums of money for the business but would the new shareholders own a controlling interest in the business?
- An existing plc could arrange a new issue of shares, but could these be bought by just one or two other companies who may put in a take-over bid?

These problems would all be overcome by using loan finance instead – but you should, by now, also be aware of the other drawbacks of borrowing.

Sources of finance: will banks lend and will shareholders invest?

Activity 9.8 on pages 137–38 should help to show that banks and other lending institutions will make loans available to businesses only as long as:

- financial information is provided about the firm's trading record (if it is already operating) and forecasts about its future
- the forecasts show that the firm is likely to remain solvent, i.e. able to pay the interest on the loan and repay the loan when this is due.

■ *Activity 9.7: case study task*

Imagine you are the manager of a branch of a bank called Anybank plc. Two of your customers – Jack and Gowri Kumaran – come to see you about starting a cleaning business. They ask you for a bank loan to help them get started. They are unable to give you any financial details about their business plan – they did not realise that you would want to see some forecasts. You turn down their request for a bank loan until they are able to provide you with more information.

a) Write a letter to Jack and Gowri explaining why you cannot offer them a loan without more details about their new business idea.

b) Explain to them why you will need to see:
   i) a cash flow forecast
   ii) a forecast profit and loss account for their first year
   iii) a forecast balance sheet for the business at the end of their first year of trading.

■ *Activity 9.8: case study task*

Three weeks later, Jack and Gowri ask to see you again and present you with the following forecasts for the business.

Cash flow budget for 2005 (€000) Jack and Gowri Cleaning Services. Figures in brackets are negative.

	Jan.	Feb.	Mar.	Apr.	May	Jun.	Jul.	Aug.	Sept.	Oct.	Nov.	Dec.
Opening bank balance	0	5	(1)	(2)	(2)	(2)	(2)	(5)	(4)	(3)	(4)	(5)
Cash inflows												
Receipts from customers	–	–	5	6	8	8	8	10	10	7	7	7
Bank loan	10											
Owner's capital	5											
Total cash inflow	15		5	6	8	8	8	10	10	7	7	7
Cash outflows												
Wages	4	4	4	4	5	5	5	6	6	5	5	5
Cleaning materials	2	1	1	1	2	2	2	2	2	2	2	2
Rent	3						3					
Interest	0.1	0.1	0.1	0.1	0.1	0.1	0.1	0.1	0.1	0.1	0.1	0.1
Other expenses	0.9	0.9	0.9	0.9	0.9	0.9	0.9	0.9	0.9	0.9	0.9	0.9
Total cash outflow	10	6	6	6	8	8	11	9	9	8	8	8
Net cash flow	5	(6)	(1)	0	0	0	(3)	1	1	(1)	(1)	(1)
Closing balance	5	(1)	(2)	(2)	(2)	(2)	(5)	(4)	(3)	(4)	(5)	(6)

(continued)

Forecast profit and loss account for Jack and Gowri Cleaning Services Year ending 31/12/05

	(€000)
Sales revenue	87
Cost of sales	20
Gross profit	67
Wages and other expenses	80
Net profit/loss	(13)

The forecasted balance sheet was also provided and this showed not only the bank loan of €10,000 but an overdraft of €6,000. Capital employed was forecasted to be €40,000.

As their bank manager, now that you have the information you asked for, would you lend the original €10,000 to Jack and Gowri? Write a report to them, giving your decision and the reasons for it.

The bank will also consider the experience of the people in the business and how convincing they are as likely successful business people. Banks will not take unnecessary risks and will refuse to give loans to businesses that are in a risky situation.

Business plans

A bank will almost certainly ask for a business plan before agreeing to a loan or overdraft – particularly if it is a newly created firm. A business plan is a document containing the business objectives and important details about the operations and finance of the firm. By completing this form – and most banks are able to give business owners a ready-printed form that they fill out – the owners are forced to think ahead and plan carefully for the first few years. They will have to consider:

■ What products do we intend to make and which consumers are we 'aiming at'?
■ What will be our main costs and will enough products be sold to pay for them?
■ Where will the firm be located?
■ What machinery and how many people will be required in the business?

Without this detailed plan the bank will be reluctant to lend money to the business. This is because the owners of the business cannot show that they have thought seriously about the future of their business. Even *with* a detailed business plan, the bank might not offer a loan if the bank manager believes that the plan contains points of concern, e.g. poor forecasted cash flow.

An example of a business plan is shown opposite. It was completed by the owners of a business planning to open a take-away pizza restaurant.

■ *Case study example*

Business plan for Pizza Place Ltd.
(Outline only – other, more detailed information, would be given in an actual plan.)

Name of business	Pizza Place Ltd
Type of organisation	Private limited company
Business aim	To provide a high-class take-away pizza service including home delivery.
The product	High quality home-cooked pizzas
The price	Average price of £5 with £1 delivery charge
The market aimed for	Young people and families
The market research undertaken and the results	Research in the area conducted using questionnaires. Also, research into national trends in take-away sales and local competitors. (See results of all research in the appendix to this plan.)
Human Resources plan	Two staff (the business owners) to be the only staff to be employed initially.
Details of senior staff/ business owners	Peter Yang – chef of 15 years' experience Sabrina Hsui – deputy manager of restaurant for three years.
Production details and business costs	Main suppliers – P & P Wholesalers Fixed costs of business – £50,000 per year Variable costs – approximately £1 per unit sold
Location of business	Site in shopping street (Brunei Avenue) just away from the town centre. Leasehold site (10 years).
Main equipment required	Second-hand kitchen equipment – £4,000 Second-hand motorbike – £1,000
Forecast profit	(See financial appendix to this plan.) Summary: In the first year of operations the total costs are forecast to be £55,000 with revenue of £85,000. Predicted profit = £30,000. Break-even point – 12,500 units per year.
Cash flow	(See financial appendix to this plan.) Due to the high set-up and promotion costs there will be negative cash flow in the first year.
Finance	£10,000 invested by each of the owners. Request to bank for a further £10,000 plus an overdraft arrangement of £5,000 per month.

■ *Activity 9.9: case study task*

Joe Dagglio has £15,000 in savings. He wants to buy shares in public limited companies because he has heard that he could earn dividends and make a capital gain if the shares rise in price. He has received details of a plc that is arranging a new issue of shares. The company wishes to expand. He makes a note of the following information.

■ The current share price is £5 but it has been as high as £7.
■ The average value of shares on the Stock Exchange has risen over the last year.
■ The gearing ratio of the company is 55 per cent.
■ Interest rates are likely to rise in the next month or so.
■ The company is offering high dividends to its existing shareholders.

a) Considering all of the risks and possible gains, advise Joe whether he should buy these shares or not.
b) What other information would you find helpful in advising Joe?

This example helps to show that shareholders and those hoping to become shareholders have many factors to consider before buying shares in a company. Fortunes can be won or lost on the Stock Exchange and people like Joe will want to try to make sure that they do not turn out to be one of the losers!

Revision summary: finance from banks and shareholders

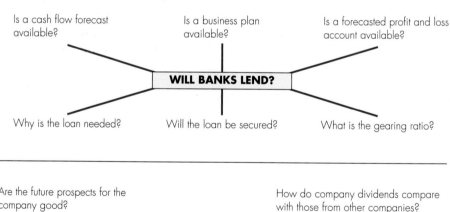

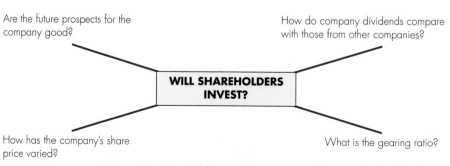

■ *Revision questions*

1 Explain *two* reasons why the owners of a new business will need finance to set it up. [4]

2 What is the difference between revenue and capital expenditure? [3]

3 What is the difference between internal and external business finance? [3]

4 State *two* methods of raising finance internally and list *one* advantage of each method. [4]

5 Explain the difference between short- and long-term sources of finance. [3]

6 State *two* methods of raising short-term finance externally and list *one* advantage of each method. [4]

7 Explain the advantages to a business of an overdraft as opposed to a bank loan. [4]

8 When a company issues more shares this is termed *permanent capital* – explain this term. [2]

9 Explain *three* advantages a bank loan may have over a share issue for a company. [6]

10 The directors of a company are planning to install a new computer system in the office. The computers are expected to last about three years. They will cost €60,000. Three methods of finance are being considered:
– leasing without purchasing at the end
– long-term bank loan
– new share issue.
Advise the directors on the most suitable method of finance. Give reasons for your answer. [6]

11 Explain how the sources of finance available for a limited company are different to those available for a sole trader. [5]

12 What is a business plan? [2]

13 Explain *two* benefits to a firm of preparing a business plan. [4]

14 Give *three* examples of information contained in a business plan. Explain, for each one, why a bank manager would consider this information important. [6]

15 Explain *two* factors that an investor would consider before deciding whether to invest in a company. [4]

The CD-ROM (see details on page x) provides further tests, activities and Case study work on the topics covered in this unit.

10 Organisational structure

This unit will explain:

- ❓ why organisations such as businesses need an internal structure and show how structure changes as businesses expand
- ❓ how organisational charts describe the internal structure of an organisation
- ❓ the ideas of hierarchical structure, chain of command, span of control, line and staff managers, delegation
- ❓ how businesses may be either centralised or decentralised and the different forms of decentralisation.

By the end of this unit you should be able to:

- ☑ draw and explain the significance of a simple organisation chart
- ☑ understand that the organisation of a business is likely to change as that business expands
- ☑ know the difference between span of control and levels of hierarchy; line and staff managers
- ☑ understand the importance of delegation
- ☑ analyse the difference between a centralised and decentralised organisation and explain different forms of decentralisation.

■ Definition to learn:
ORGANISATIONAL STRUCTURE refers to the levels of management and division of responsibilities within an organisation.

What is organisational structure?

ORGANISATIONAL STRUCTURE refers to the levels of management and division of responsibilities within an organisation. This structure is often presented in the form of an organisational chart.

■ Case study example

The Cosy Corner Convenience Store is owned and managed by Bill Murray. It is a sole trader business. Bill has no employees. He works a long day – 12 hours usually. As he works alone in the business he has to do all the jobs which are involved in running a busy convenience store. Here is a list of just six of his tasks:

- ordering new stock
- serving customers
- going to the bank to pay in cash – he does this on Wednesday afternoons when the shop is closed
- arranging shelf displays
- keeping all the paperwork up to date, for example, to make sure suppliers are paid on time
- contacting the local newspaper to arrange an advertisement for the shop.

■ Activity 10.1: case study task

List three other tasks that you think Bill has to do in order to run Cosy Corner efficiently.

In Bill's business there is no need for an organisational structure because he works alone. There is no need to lay out the responsibilities and duties of other employees or to indicate their links with other workers – because there aren't any! As he is the only manager, there can be no other management levels. This example shows the simplest form of business. What would happen to the organisation of Bill's business if it expanded?

Why does organisational structure change as a business expands?

■ *Case study example*

Bill was exhausted. It was the end of another long day. He had decided during the day that he could no longer do all of the work of running the store by himself. He was going to advertise for a shop assistant. He thought carefully about what work he would want the assistant to perform. Bill remembered from his previous job, working for a large retail chain, that it was important to make clear the tasks and responsibilities of employees. If this was not done then two people might end up doing the same work – and some work might not get done at all.

He decided to write out a JOB DESCRIPTION which he would give to all the people who applied for the job. This would make clear what the job would involve. Bill thought this would have two main advantages.

- People applying for the job could see if they were suitable for the work expected of them.
- Once in the job, the new employee would know exactly what their duties and responsibilities were. Their work should therefore help Bill, not just repeat what he was doing.

Bill wrote out the following job description.

Definition to learn:

A JOB DESCRIPTION outlines the responsibilities and duties to be carried out by someone employed to do a specific job.

Job Description

Shop Assistant

Main tasks
- To open the shop in the morning
- To be responsible for ordering all goods from suppliers
- To arrange all shelf displays
- To help serve customers
- To assist the manager in other ways directed by him

Working conditions
- Five days a week
- Eight hours a day
- Four weeks' holiday – by negotiation, but not at same time as the manager

■ *Activity 10.2: case study task*

a) Study the job description on page 143. Do you think Bill is looking to recruit an *experienced* shop assistant? What evidence is there to support your answer?

b) Make a list of the important tasks and responsibilities Bill still has to perform himself.

Bill's business now has a very simple organisational structure. There are now two people in the organisation and they are *specialising* in different jobs. (See Unit 1 for advantages of specialisation.)

Delegation

Even though Bill's business is still very small it is possible to see that a very important idea is already being used. This idea is called DELEGATION. This means giving a subordinate the authority to perform particular tasks. It is very important to remember that it is the *authority* to perform a task which is being delegated – *not* the final responsibility. If the job is done badly by the subordinate then it is the manager who has to accept the responsibility for this.

From the job description on page 143, it is clear that Bill is giving the authority or power to the new employee to be in charge of two areas of business operations – shelf arrangement and stock ordering. Why has he done this and what are the advantages of this?

Advantages of delegation for the manager

☑ Managers cannot do every job themselves. As we have seen, it was becoming very difficult for Bill to control all of the running of Cosy Corner by himself. By delegating jobs to the assistant, he is able to find more time to do the jobs that he considers should be left to him.

☑ Managers are less likely to make mistakes if some of the tasks are being performed by their subordinates (those to whom the tasks are being delegated). Bill can spend more time on ensuring the accounts of the business are kept accurately, for example.

☑ Managers can measure the success of their staff more easily. They can see how well they have done in performing the tasks delegated to them.

Advantages of delegation for the subordinate

☑ The work becomes more interesting and rewarding.

☑ The employee feels more important and believes that trust is being put in them to perform a job well.

☑ Delegation helps to train workers and they can then make progress in the organisation. It gives them career opportunities.

Despite the advantages of delegation, there are some managers who are reluctant to delegate. Bill Murray is not one of them. But he recalls that, when he worked for a large department store, his manager was reluctant to delegate tasks. Bill believes this was because he was afraid that the subordinates might fail and the manager wanted to control everything by himself. Also, there was a risk that the subordinates might do a better job than the manager! This could have made the manager feel very insecure.

There needs to be an increase in trust in order to reduce control over workers

a reduction in direct control by supervisors and managers once tasks are done by workers

Delegation must mean:

increasing trust of workers by supervisors and managers

Revision summary: delegation

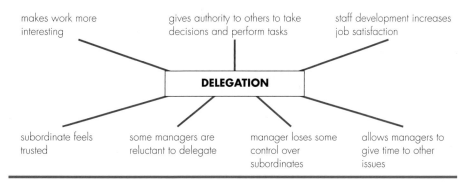

makes work more interesting

gives authority to others to take decisions and perform tasks

staff development increases job satisfaction

DELEGATION

subordinate feels trusted

some managers are reluctant to delegate

manager loses some control over subordinates

allows managers to give time to other issues

■ *Case study example*

Bill Murray's business had expanded rapidly. More employees had been appointed. Some of them managed the shop because Bill spent more time on office work. Shop opening hours were lengthened. Eventually, he decided to open four further stores in other towns. It became clear to Bill that his business needed the advantages of limited company status (see Unit 3). A business friend agreed to buy shares and become one of the directors of the company. As the organisation was growing, Bill decided it needed a clear structure. After discussions with his directors and senior managers he drew out the chart below.

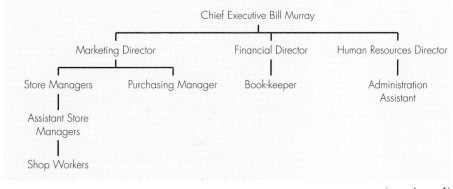

Chief Executive Bill Murray

Marketing Director   Financial Director   Human Resources Director

Store Managers   Purchasing Manager   Book-keeper   Administration Assistant

Assistant Store Managers

Shop Workers

(continued)

In fact, this is a typical organisation chart for many businesses. The most important features are as follows.

- It is a *hierarchy*. This means that there are different levels in the organisation. Each level has a different degree of authority. People on the same level of hierarchy have the same degree of authority. There are five levels of hierarchy from Chief Executive down to Shop Worker.
- It is organised into *departments*. Each of these departments has a particular job or *function*.
- As there are different levels of management there is a CHAIN OF COMMAND. This is how power and authority are passed down from the top to the lower levels in the organisation. Because Cosy Corner Ltd is still quite a small business, the chain of command is quite short as there are not many levels of management. Bigger businesses are likely to have many more levels of hierarchy and therefore a longer chain of command.

Bill decided to give a copy of this chart to all members of staff. He considered that there were several advantages in both constructing the organisation chart as a hierarchy and informing everybody of it.

■ **Definitions to learn:**
CHAIN OF COMMAND is the structure in an organisation which allows instructions to be passed down from senior management to lower levels of management.

The SPAN OF CONTROL is the number of subordinates working directly under a manager.

Advantages of an organisation chart

- ☑ The chart shows how everybody is linked together in the organisation. All employees are aware of which communication channel is used to reach them with messages and instructions.
- ☑ Every individual can see their own position in the organisation. They can identify who they are accountable to and who they have authority over. Employees can see who they should take orders from.
- ☑ It shows the links and relationship between different departments within the organisation.
- ☑ Everyone is in a department and this gives them a sense of belonging.

Chain of command and span of control

Look at the two organisational charts on page 147. There are two essential differences between them.

- Business A has a tall structure and a long chain of command.
- Business B has a wide structure and a short chain of command.

As a result of these two different structures, the SPAN OF CONTROL (the number of subordinates working directly under a manager) is wider in Business B than in Business A – in Business A this number is two and in Business B it is five.

There is therefore an important link between the span of control and the chain of command. The longer the chain of command, the 'taller' will be the organisational structure and the 'narrower' the span of control.

Business A –
organisational chart

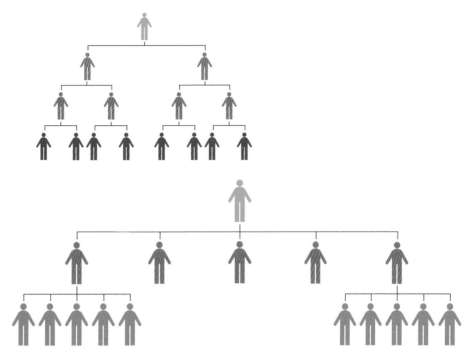

Business B –
organisational chart

When the chain of command is short, the organisation will have 'wider' spans of control.

There is no perfect organisational structure. In recent years many organisations have made their structure 'wider' and with a shorter chain of command. In some cases, this has been done by removing a whole level of management – called *de-layering*. These are the claimed advantages of short chains of command.

Advantages of short chains of command

☑ *Communication* is quicker and more accurate. Each message has fewer levels to pass through before reaching the intended person.

☑ Top managers are *less remote* from the lower level of the hierarchy. These top managers should be more in touch with people below them as there are fewer management levels to get to know.

☑ *Spans of control* will be wider. This means that each manager is responsible for more subordinates. Why is this an advantage?
  – If superiors have more people to manage, it will encourage managers to delegate more. This is because, as their department is larger, they cannot possibly do all the important work by themselves.
  – There will be less direct control of each worker and they will feel more trusted. They will be able to take more decisions by themselves. They may obtain more job satisfaction.

However, wider spans of control, with more people to be directly responsible for, could mean that the managers lose control of what their subordinates are doing. If they are poorly trained, the subordinates could make many mistakes.

■ *Activity 10.3: case study task*

Mustafa was bored with his work. He was a telephone operator in a large telephone banking firm. The business received calls from customers who wanted to use banking services but did not have time to go to a bank branch.

Mustafa worked in a team, called Team A, with other colleagues, Hammed and Asif. They were supervised by Aziz who was under the authority of Mohammed. There were two other groups of telephone operators, Team B and Team C. These two teams were the same size as Team A. They also had their own supervisors who reported to Mohammed.

All calls were recorded and supervisors could listen in to make sure that all workers were polite and helpful to customers. Telephone operators were only allowed to do certain tasks for customers. Other jobs, such as transfers of large sums of money, had to be referred to a supervisor or manager. Telephone operators had to aim to answer 20 calls each hour. No wonder Mustafa was bored with his work!

a) Draw the organisation chart for this telephone business.
b) What is the span of control of the supervisors?
c) What would be the advantages and disadvantages of removing the supervisors altogether? Your answer should include references to:

- chain of command
- delegation
- span of control.

Functional departments

■ *Case study example*

The newly opened branches of Cosy Corner plc proved to be just as popular as the first one. Profits increased and the business expanded in other ways. Bill and his fellow directors decided to open the first store in a foreign country, France. They had plans to open several more. The directors had also taken the step of opening a food processing factory to provide some of the goods sold by the Cosy Corner stores. It was found to be cheaper to produce these goods than to buy them from outside suppliers.

These expansion projects had required a great deal of capital. The business had 'gone public' several months ago. The sales of shares to the public raised the necessary finance. Bill was Chairman of the company as well as Chief Executive. He and his Board of Directors were accountable to the shareholders. The management structure below him was now more complicated than when the business was smaller. The current organisational chart is shown opposite.

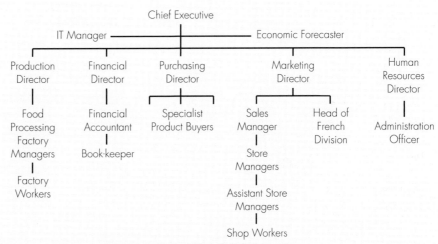

The key features of the current organisation chart, which is typical of many larger businesses, are as follows.

- It is still largely arranged into *functional departments*, such as Finance and Marketing. These departments are responsible for one important part of the work of the organisation. They use specialist skills in their work and are often efficient as a result. However, businesses organised in this way may find that workers feel more loyalty to their department than to the organisation as a whole. There could be conflict between departments. For example, Production may wish to purchase new machinery, but Finance do not make the necessary money available. Managers working in these departments are called LINE MANAGERS. They have the authority to give orders and to have their decisions put into effect in their department. They directly supervise subordinates in a clear line of authority.

- In addition to the functional departments, there is also a *regional division* responsible for the Cosy Corner stores in other countries. This department has the advantage of being able to use specialist knowledge to help them run the stores abroad. For instance, this department will be aware of which goods are likely to be most popular in each country or which goods may be illegal in some.

- There are other departments which do not have a typical function and which employ specialists in particular areas. Examples from Cosy Corner plc are the Economic Forecasting department and the Information Technology department. Some people include the Human Resources department in this group too. These departments report directly to the Board of Directors. The people in these departments are called STAFF MANAGERS because they provide specialist advice and support to the Board of Directors and to line managers of the functional departments. Staff managers tend to be very well qualified experts. They often know more about their particular specialist subject than they do about running the business.

■ **Definitions to learn:**

LINE MANAGERS have direct authority over subordinates in their department. They are able to take decisions in their departmental area.

STAFF MANAGERS are specialist advisers who provide support to line managers and to the Board of Directors.

The advantages and disadvantages of employing staff managers as well as line managers

☑ Staff managers can provide advice to line managers on particular issues, such as new computer systems or how economic changes may affect the Marketing department.

☑ This will help give line managers more time to concentrate on their main tasks – organising their department and taking decisions.

☒ However, there may be conflict and frustration between the two groups because they may have different points of view on important matters.

☒ Line employees may be confused about who to take orders or instructions from – the line or the staff manager.

Decentralisation

■ *Case study example*

Bill Murray was amazed by the success of the business he had started many years ago. The organisation he created was now one of the largest food processors and retailers in the country. When he was asked for the secrets of his success he replied:

'I have always believed in a DECENTRALISED decision-making structure. This has encouraged all of my managers to take important decisions and to use their own knowledge and skills to the full. For example, I allow my managers to take the following decisions:

■ new product ranges
■ new locations for stores
■ major marketing promotions.

The Board of Directors, including myself, are then free to concentrate on important policy matters such as business take-overs and new business opportunities.'

Definitions to learn:

A DECENTRALISED management structure means that many decisions are not taken at the centre of the business at all but are delegated to a lower level of management.

A CENTRALISED management structure means that most decisions are taken at the centre, or higher levels of management.

What did Bill mean by 'decentralised' and how is this different from a CENTRALISED system? A decentralised management structure means that many decisions are not taken at the centre of the business but are delegated to lower levels of management. A centralised management structure, on the other hand, means that most decisions are taken at the centre, or higher levels of management. There is, therefore, little effective delegation.

Advantages of a decentralised management structure

☑ Decisions are taken by managers who are 'closer to the action'. For example, managers who have closer contact with customers than the Board of Directors are more likely to know which products are going to be successful. Also, the decision on a new advertising campaign is perhaps best left to the experts in the Marketing department who have studied the most effective methods of promotion.

☑ As decentralisation is a form of delegation, the managers who are now able to take the decisions will feel more trusted and will have more satisfaction from their work.

☑ Decisions can be made much more quickly than if the Board of Directors or senior managers have to be given all the information before making a decision. When the environment in which a business operates is changing very quickly, for example, because of new competitors, then it is very important to be able to take speedy decisions.

■ *Case study example*

One of Bill's fellow directors is rather concerned about the policy of decentralisation. She wrote the following memo to Bill.

```
Memorandum
To: Bill Murray, Chief Executive
From: Sue Mason
Date: 8/8/03
Subject: Policy of decentralisation

Bill - can we discuss the current policy of
decentralisation at the next board meeting? I am
concerned in particular that:

• the Board of Directors is losing control of
  important decisions
• there is no common policy or consistency between
  departments or divisions of the business. All
  managers are taking their own decisions without
  enough central guidance
• as directors, we just do not know what is going
  on in some departments.

Could you let me know if you are happy for these
issues to be discussed at our next meeting?
```

■ *Activity 10.4: case study task*

Assume you are the Head of Operations for Cosy Corner plc in France. You are delighted at the independence you have been given by the policy of decentralisation. You have the authority to control location, human resources and marketing decisions in France. Write a memorandum to Bill explaining three major, successful decisions that you have taken. If these had been left to the Board of Directors, you consider that mistakes could have been made.

Taking decisions away from the centre of an organisation

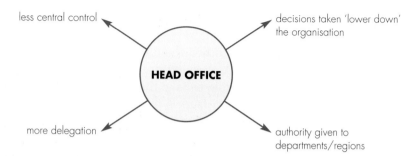

less central control

decisions taken 'lower down' the organisation

HEAD OFFICE

more delegation

authority given to departments/regions

Different forms of decentralisation

There are four different types of decentralisation.

Functional decentralisation

This is when specialist departments are delegated decision-making authority. These are the most common functional departments.

- Marketing – authority over market research, new product plans, packaging, promotion and distribution.
- Production – authority over production resources such as factories, machines and stocks.
- Finance – authority over raising finance, making payments such as wages and keeping accounting records.
- Human Resources – authority over recruitment, pay levels and training of staff.

Federal decentralisation

This is when authority is divided between different product lines of the business. For example, a vehicle manufacturer could have separate truck, car and bus divisions.

Regional decentralisation

This is when a business, such as a multinational, has bases in many different regions or countries. Each one has authority over its own operations.

Decentralisation by project teams

This is when a particular project, for example, the design of a new aircraft, is given to a team involving people from all functional areas.

Is complete decentralisation a good idea?

Should all decisions be taken by lower level management? This would be unwise for most businesses. In nearly all cases, some really important issues would need to be considered centrally. These could include major investment projects costing millions of pounds or decisions to take over other businesses. The overall aims of the business and long-term policy decisions would nearly always remain centralised. These could include the firm's growth strategy and the environmental objectives of the business. If such issues were *not* centralised then there could be a lack of common purpose and direction for the business.

■ *Revision questions*

1 What is meant by *organisational structure?* [2]

2 How, as a business expands and employs more people, will the organisational chart be likely to change? [3]

3 Explain how an organisational chart for a business could be useful when informing new employees about the business. [3]

4 What do you understand by the term *delegation?* [2]

5 Why might it be important for a busy manager to delegate to other members of staff? [3]

6 Examine *two* possible benefits to be gained from delegation, for the subordinate. [4]

7 Examine *two* possible benefits and *one* drawback that could result from delegation for the manager. [5]

8 Study the organisational chart for a company, shown below.

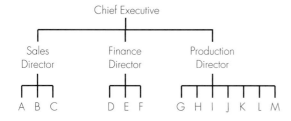

   a) Explain what is meant by the term *span of control.* [2]
   b) What is the span of control of the Production Director? [1]
   c) What could be the advantages to the business of this director having an even wider span of control? [3]
   d) What could be the disadvantages to the business of this? [3]

9 **a)** Explain the difference between line and staff managers? [3]
   b) Explain one benefit to a firm of all existing staff knowing the organisational structure of the business. [4]

10 **a)** Explain what is meant by the term *functional department.* [2]
   b) Give *two* examples of decisions that you think would be made by the Board of Directors and not decentralised to lower level managers. Explain your choice. [4]

11 Draw an organisational chart of your own school or college. Explain what your diagram shows about the chain of command there. [4]

12 What is meant by *decentralisation?* [3]

13 Explain *two* advantages to a business of adopting a decentralised structure. [4]

The CD-ROM (see details on page x) provides further tests, activities and Case study work on the topics covered in this unit.

11 Managing a business

This unit will explain:

- [?] what managers do and show why management is necessary in any business
- [?] the meaning of risk-taking and the role of entrepreneurs
- [?] how managers approach decision-making
- [?] the main functional areas for which managers are responsible.

By the end of this unit you should be able to:

- [✓] understand the main tasks of managers
- [✓] understand that decision-making involves taking risks
- [✓] show how a process of decision-making can help to reduce risks
- [✓] identify and explain the main functional responsibilities of managers.

What do managers do?

All organisations, including businesses, have managers. They may not be called managers because different titles can be used – leader, director, headteacher, and so on. Whatever their title, the tasks of all managers are very similar, no matter what the organisation. If you are a student in a school or college or if you are in full employment, the managers of your organisation will, at some time, have to fulfil the following tasks.

Planning

Planning for the future of the organisation involves setting aims or targets, for example, 'the school will aim to increase its sixth form to over 200 students in two years' time' or 'we should plan to increase sales of our new fruit juice range by 50 per cent in three years'.

These aims or targets will give the organisation a sense of *direction* or *purpose*. There will be a common feeling in the organisation of having something to work towards. It is a poor manager who does not plan for the future at all.

In addition to these aims, a manager must also plan for the resources which will be needed. For example, 'to achieve our aim of increasing student numbers in the sixth form, we will need to build a new sixth form centre' or 'increased advertising expenditure will be needed to increase sales of our fruit juices'. These are two examples of *strategies* which are designed to help the organisation achieve the aims set for it.

Organising

A manager cannot do everything. Tasks must be delegated to others in the organisation. These people must have the resources to be able to do these tasks successfully. It is therefore the manager's responsibility to organise people and resources effectively. An organisational chart can help here – as we saw in Unit 10.

An organisational chart can help to show who has the authority to do different jobs. It also helps to make sure that specialisation occurs and two people do not end up doing the same task. An effective manager will organise people and resources very carefully indeed.

Co-ordinating

Co-ordinating means 'working together'. A manager may be very good at planning and organising but may have failed to 'bring people in the organisation together'. This is a real danger with the functional form of organisation. Different departments can be working away in their own specialist area without making contact with people from other departments. For example, there is no point in the Marketing department planning the launch of a new product unless they have worked with (co-ordinated with) the Production department. It is the Production department that will have to produce the product at the right time in the right quantities.

A good manager will therefore make sure that all departments in the organisation work together to achieve the plans originally set by the manager. In the example above, this could be done by regular meetings between people in the different departments. Alternatively, a *project team* could have been set up to develop and launch the new product. The team would be made up of people from different departments.

Commanding

Many people think that this is all managers do! But, the task of management is more concerned with guiding, leading and supervising people than just telling them what to do – although this may be important too. Managers have to make sure that all supervisors and workers are keeping to targets and deadlines. Instructions and guidance must be provided by managers and it is also their responsibility to make sure that the tasks are carried out by people below them in the organisation.

Controlling

This is a never-ending task of management. Managers must try to measure and evaluate the work of all individuals and groups to make sure that they are on target. There is little point in planning and organising if managers then fail to check that the original aims are being met. If it seems that certain groups are failing to do what is expected of them, then managers may have to take some corrective action. This is *not* necessarily disciplining staff – although that might be important. There might be other reasons for poor performance other than inefficient workers – it is the manager's job to find out why targets are not being met and then correct the problem.

Do you now have a clearer idea of what managers *do?* Management is not easy to define, but the list of tasks above helps to demonstrate the varied and important work that good managers should be doing.

From studying the list of points on pages 154–55, it should also become clear why management is necessary to any organisation. Without clear and effective management, a business is going to lack:

- a sense of control and direction
- co-ordination between departments, leading to wastage of effort
- control of employees
- organisation of resources, leading to low output and sales.

In short, without management to take the business forward, the firm will drift and eventually fail.

■ Activity 11.1: case study task

Naomi is a student at a Sixth Form College. She recently took part in a work shadowing exercise to find out what it is like to be a manager. Work shadowing means that a student follows a manager for a day or more to experience the work that they do.

Naomi 'shadowed' Sabrina Choolun who is the manager of the sportswear section in Suresave plc, a large department store. Naomi kept the following diary for one day.

8.30 a.m.	Attended meeting with other departmental heads and Chief Executive to agree targets for the next two years. Departmental heads told to plan their own strategy to meet these goals.
9.15 a.m.	Two staff members failed to turn up for work. Sabrina asked other staff to cover these absences by working longer shifts today.
10.00 a.m.	Meeting with Sales Manager from big sports manufacturer. Sabrina discussed the range of goods she may purchase next year to meet the store's targets.
11.00 a.m.	New member of staff did not cope well with awkward customer. When customer had gone, Sabrina reminded the shop assistant of the correct procedure that should be followed. Asked worker always to follow company policy in these matters.
2.30 p.m.	Computer printouts of individual staff sales figures were studied. One worker in particular has failed to meet sales targets and it was agreed with him that further product training was necessary.
4.00 p.m.	Memo received from Sabrina's line manager. There was a problem with another department selling clothing including sports clothes. It was now possible for customers to find the same goods in the store in two departments at different prices! Sabrina needed to meet the other departmental manager to agree on a common policy.

For each of the tasks that Sabrina carried out, identify whether it was concerned with: planning, organising, co-ordinating, commanding or controlling.

What makes a good manager?

Can anyone become a good manager? Are the qualities of leadership – because that is what managers do – limited to just a few people? Why are some managers so much more successful than others? There are no easy answers to these questions. There is no general agreement on whether 'good managers are born' or 'good managers are made by training'.

There is some general understanding that good managers are likely to have some, or all, of the following qualities:

- *intelligence* to be able to understand difficult ideas and deal with different issues
- *initiative* to be able to suggest solutions to problems and take control of situations
- *self-confidence* to be willing and able to lead others and to set an example
- *assertiveness and determination* to be able to take command of others and to push through ideas and policies to their conclusion
- *communication skills* to be able to put ideas and messages across to subordinates in a clear way which will encourage them to respond positively
- *energy and enthusiasm* to set high standards of effort and involvement so that others are encouraged to act in similar ways.

It is possible to add to this list. Already you are probably thinking that not everyone will have the qualities and skills needed to become a successful manager. Training and human resources development programmes can help to give employees the skills needed to manage but, without the personal desire to lead and control, some employees are likely to remain in subordinate positions.

Styles of leadership

Different styles of leadership often call for different management styles. As the way in which a manager deals with a situation can have such an important impact on people and how they react to the manager, these different leadership styles are studied in Unit 13, *Motivation at work*. It is important to remember here that a good manager will adopt the style of leadership that best suits each situation.

Revision summary: effective managers

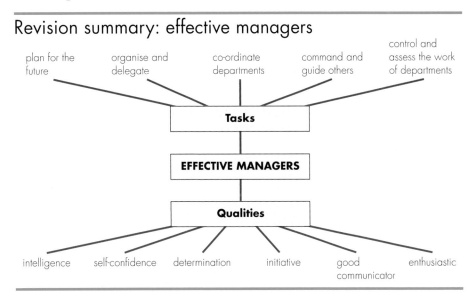

Management involves taking risks

All of the management tasks studied so far have involved *decision-making*. Planning, organising, controlling, commanding and co-ordinating will all require decisions to be made. Here are some examples of common business decisions.

■ Should we open a new factory in the south or the north of the country?
■ What price should we charge for the new product range?
■ Do we buy the new machine even though this will involve job losses for some of our workers?
■ Is expansion in another country going to be profitable?
■ Do we promote an internal applicant to the job or should we recruit from outside the business?
■ How much should we spend on developing new products?
■ How do we finance the take-over of this business?
■ How shall we measure the performance of the sales division?

■ *Activity 11.2*

a) Suggest six further decisions that might have to be made by the manager of a hotel business.
b) Indicate which of the management functions is being performed in each of the decisions you choose. For example, how should staffing levels of the hotel restaurant be changed for the holiday weekend? This will involve *organising* resources.

Are all decisions as important as each other?

This cannot be the case. Deciding to close a factory, involving hundreds of job losses, must be more important than deciding to close a shop for a staff lunch break. It is common to divide decisions into three types.

■ **Definitions to learn:**

STRATEGIC DECISIONS are very important decisions which can affect the overall success of the business.
TACTICAL DECISIONS are those which are taken more frequently and which are less important.
OPERATIONAL DECISIONS are day-to-day decisions which will be taken by lower level managers.

■ STRATEGIC DECISIONS are very important decisions which can affect the overall success of the business. They do not usually need to be taken very often. They could include: future plans for the business, long-term investments such as take-overs and expansion in other countries, changing the status of the business, for example, 'going public'. These decisions will be taken by senior managers and directors.
■ TACTICAL DECISIONS are those which are taken more frequently and which are less important. They will not determine the future plans of the business. They could include: ways of training new staff, methods of advertising to be used, which types of machines to purchase. These decisions are likely to be taken by 'middle management'.
■ OPERATIONAL DECISIONS are day-to-day decisions which will be taken by lower level managers. They tend to be repetitive decisions and previous experience can be used to guide the decision-maker. They could include: staffing levels, stock levels, methods of delivery of goods.

Taking decisions always involves *risk*. Time, money and other resources will be used as a result of a decision – unless the decision is to do nothing! The decision to do something always involves rejecting other options – and they *could* have been very successful. This can be explained by means of two examples, one decision taken by an individual and one decision taken by a manager.

■ *Case study examples*

■ Jonas is 18 years old and has passed his final school examinations. He now has a decision to make. He could either go straight to university or accept an offer of a job in a local bank. Going to university would cost him and his parents a lot of money because he could only take up a part-time job. However, if he gained a degree after three years, he could apply for a job in a City bank which pays a higher salary. If he takes up the local bank job now, he would be earning immediately. He would, though, be giving up the chance to work in the City.

Jonas must decide soon. Whatever he decides will involve a risk. The option he does not take could turn out to be even more worthwhile than the one he does decide on.

There are risks for Jonas with either option

■ Paul is a general manager of a construction firm. The business owns some land. Paul must decide what to use this land for. He has considered all of the options and has reduced these to two. He could either sell the land now for £2 million, or build houses on the land and sell these for £4 million. The houses will cost about £1.5 million to build. His problem is that he is not certain he can sell the houses. He is quite sure that he could sell the land now. Does he sell the land for a definite sum of money or does he try to make more profit by building and, hopefully, selling the houses?

He has to make a decision and accept the risks attached to it.

Should Paul take risks by building the houses?

It is not easy taking decisions, is it? Whether they concern personal or business matters, decisions have to be taken and the risks accepted. In a small business, such as a sole trader, the owner is the manager. This person will be taking risks with their own capital or savings. These people are referred to as true *entrepreneurs* or *risk-takers*. If the decision goes wrong, they could end up losing their own house and other assets. In a larger business, such as a public limited company, the manager taking the decision is not risking his or her own capital – but that of the shareholders. Although the manager is still taking risks, the cost of poor decisions will be felt differently. The manager may lose his or her job – but it is the shareholders' capital which is put at stake. Managers in these cases are not real entrepreneurs as the sole traders are.

How can managers reduce risks when taking decisions?

There will always be some risk – some *cost of failure* – when taking decisions. These risks can be reduced, but not eliminated, by following these steps when taking decisions. These steps are sometimes called the *decision-making process*.

1 *Establish the objectives of the organisation* It is not possible to take good decisions unless it is clear what the aims of the firm are.
2 *Identify and analyse the problem to be solved* All decisions are taken to solve a problem. In our examples above, Jonas had the problem of how to spend the next few years of his life. Paul had the problem of how most profitably to use a plot of land. Managers need to know what they are trying to solve before deciding on a 'solution'. For example, a Sales manager is worried about falling sales. The decision is taken to lower prices. This has no effect on demand but lowers the firm's profit margin. Only later does the manager discover that sales fell due to advertisements not appearing in papers when they were planned to. The wrong decision had been taken. The problem had not been correctly analysed.
3 *Collect data on all the possible alternative solutions* It is too easy to jump at the first solution thought of. Managers must collect data about all possible options before making a final choice. This data must include the limits (or constraints) on what is possible. There is no point in suggesting that the firm's stores should open all day on Sunday, to boost sales, if this is actually against the law.
4 Make the final decision and put it in to effect. This is called *implementing the decision*. The manager's job is not finished even when this has been done – it is important to check to see that the decision has been put in to effect and that it is working to plan.
5 Look back to see whether the right decision was made. This is called *review and evaluation of the decision*. This is sometimes very hard to do – especially if the wrong decision was made! But by looking back and evaluating what happened, lessons for the future can be learned.

A decision-making flow chart – there are many factors to consider when making decisions!

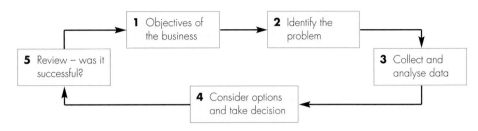

Revision summary: management decision-making

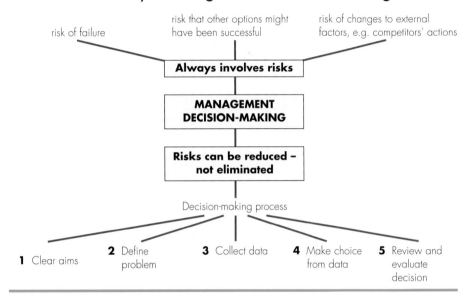

Management responsibilities in departments

Most businesses have departments organised on 'functional' lines. We studied the reasons for this in Unit 10. In addition, the work of each department was briefly referred to. It is useful to look in more detail at these separate responsibilities.

Human Resources department

Managers in this department will be responsible for:

- forecasting staffing needs for the business
- recruiting staff
- preparing job descriptions and job specifications
- planning and implementing staff training programmes
- interviewing and selecting staff
- negotiating with workers' representatives, such as union leaders, on pay and working conditions
- keeping staff records
- disciplining and warning staff if necessary.

The role of this department is very important in most businesses. With the increasing cost of recruiting staff, it is important for the Human Resources department to manage people firmly and fairly. A common sign of an ineffective Human Resources manager is when staff leave the firm after only a short period of employment. If the 'staff turnover' is high, it is often a sign that the wrong staff were appointed in the first place and efforts have not been made to keep workers in the business.

Marketing department

The managers in this department will be responsible for:

- market research into existing or new markets in order to identify new market opportunities
- planning new products, working closely with the Research and Development and Production departments
- deciding upon the best 'marketing mix' (see Units 19–22) for each product and making sure that this is put into effect
- keeping records of the sales of each product/service so that decisions can be made about 'extension' strategies or taking products off the market.

Without effective marketing, no business will survive. The Marketing managers have a key role in keeping in contact with customers so that products will meet their needs.

Accounting and Finance department

The main responsibilities include:

- recording all financial transactions with other firms and individuals
- collecting all of this data together and presenting it in the form of regular accounts
- preparing budgets for the whole of the business
- analysing the profitability of new investment projects
- deciding on the most appropriate methods of finance
- keeping control of the cash flow of the business.

Production department or Operations management

The managers in this department will have the following responsibilities:

- ordering stock of material and other resources to allow production to take place
- developing and designing new products to allow production to take place
- locating buildings in the most cost effective area
- deciding on production methods and machinery – the purchase of new machinery will involve the Finance department too
- controlling production to ensure high levels of efficiency
- maintaining the efficiency of all machinery
- making sure the quality of the product reaches the standard expected by the consumer.

Administration department

The work of the Administration department varies greatly from one business to another. In small businesses that might not have the resources for separate Finance or Human Resources departments it is common to find the Administration department handling these tasks. Larger businesses are likely to have a specialist Administration department. A typical Administration department will undertake the following functions:

- *Clerical and office support services.* The daily mail delivery will be distributed to different departments and offices. Outgoing mail will be sorted and franked (a process that puts the correct postal rate and date on each letter and parcel) and prepared for collection. Reception tasks will be to greet visitors, accept incoming telephone calls, respond to enquiries and schedule rooms for meetings. Office tasks will involve careful filing of all documents and keeping records, e.g. of visitors and telephone calls. Further duties are likely to include information and data processing. These functions are essential for the smooth and efficient operation of all the other departments in the business.
- *Responsibility for the Information Technology system.* It is common for a firm's Information Technology department to be a part of the Administration department. The efficient operation and maintenance of this system will not only allow information to flow accurately between departments but also provide managers with essential data to help their decision-making function.
- *Cleaning, maintenance and security.* These are all vital to safe, healthy working conditions within the business. Failure to maintain equipment or the building itself (e.g. air conditioning) can greatly reduce the efficiency of the other departments (see also information on Health and Safety, pages 66–67).

The widespread use of computers by workers in some businesses means that some of the above tasks can now be done by members of staff for themselves. This means that a separate Administration department – especially in the area of clerical and support services – is becoming less common in businesses.

■ *Activity 11.3: case study task*

As Managing Director of a business producing electrical kitchen goods, you are concerned that your departmental managers do not work together closely enough. You are concerned about three recent decisions in particular.

a) The Production department decided to make a new kettle without talking to the Marketing department at all.

b) The Marketing department decided to spend £1 million on a new advertising campaign for the kitchen mixer range – but had not told any of the other departments first.

c) The Human Resources department agreed a new pay rise for all workers without either gaining the approval of the Finance department or letting the Production and Marketing departments know.

Write a letter, to be sent to *all* departmental managers, explaining how the three decisions above had caused real problems for the business. Explain in the letter why it is important for the work of all departments to be co-ordinated.

Revision summary: the responsibilities of functions managers

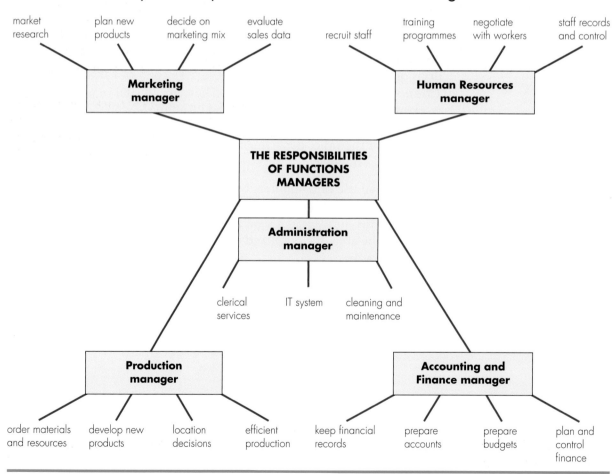

■ *Revision questions*

1 List *three* examples of management tasks. [3]

2 Refer to Activity 11.1 on page 156. Sabrina Choolun has recently resigned. The Chief Executive plans to replace her with another manager. What qualities should the Chief Executive look for in a new manager? Explain why each of the qualities that you choose is important. [8]

3 Give an example of *three* decisions that senior managers in a clothes retailing business might have to make. [3]

4 Explain the difference between strategic and tactical decisions, using your own examples. [5]

5 List *four* main functional departments usually found in a business. [4]

6 State *two* tasks carried out by the managers in each of the departments that you identified in Question 5. [8]

7 The directors of a shoe-making business are aiming to increase profits. They plan to make three important decisions which should increase profits. These are to:

- introduce a new range of shoes
- lower prices for existing shoes
- replace some factory workers with an automated machine.

a) For each of these decisions, list *four* items of information the managers will need before making a final decision in each case. [6]

b) Briefly explain, in each case, why the information you have listed is important. [12]

8 A manager has to decide whether to produce Product A or Product B. Finance has to be borrowed to pay for the new machines needed. The business cannot afford to produce both. Explain to the manager:

a) Why this decision will involve some risks for the business. [5]

b) How to reduce these risks by following a clear decision-making process. [6]

The CD-ROM (see details on page x) provides further tests, activities and Case study work on the topics covered in this unit.

12 Communication in business

What is effective communication and why is it necessary?

■ **Definitions to learn:**

COMMUNICATION is the transferring of a MESSAGE from the sender to the receiver, who understands the message.

The MESSAGE is the information or instructions being passed by the sender to the receiver.

COMMUNICATION occurs when a MESSAGE is transferred from one person to another, who understands the content of the message.

We all communicate with other people every day of our lives. We communicate with our families, at school or college, when we go shopping, or when chatting with friends. Communication with others is a natural part of life. Why do we need to study something which comes naturally to us? There is one important reason for this and that is: communication must be *effective*. This means that the information or message being sent is received, understood and acted upon in the way intended. This can be annoying for us when we communicate with our friends. For businesses, ineffective communication, or communication failure, between people in the firm can have serious consequences.

Why do people within a business need to communicate with each other?

In all organisations, it is necessary for people to communicate with each other in various ways. Without communication, we would all be working as individuals with no links with anybody else in the business we worked in. The tasks of management in guiding, instructing, warning and encouraging workers would become impossible.

Here are some examples of common messages communicated within businesses. The way in which each message is given is also shown:

■ 'Please do not smoke in this area.' (notice on a table)
■ 'How many hours did you work last week?' (manager asks a worker)

- 'There will be a Fire Drill at 11.00 a.m. today.' (notice on a board)
- 'The cutting machine has broken down. Can you send the engineer as soon as possible?' (telephone call)
- 'Sales last week reached a record level. You will need to increase output so that we do not run out of stocks.' (written memorandum to Production manager)
- 'Keep this door locked at all times.' (sign on a door)
- 'You have been sacked because of frequent absences from work. Please acknowledge receipt of this letter.' (letter written to an employee)
- 'Shoplifting is on the increase in our store – this meeting gives all employees a chance to give their ideas on how the problem can be reduced.' (meeting with all shop workers in a store)

The list could have been very long indeed, but these examples show the wide range of topics which need to be communicated in business. Can you imagine the serious problems that could occur if these messages were not communicated effectively to the people who need the information they contain?

The process of effective communication

Effective communication involves the following four features:

- a TRANSMITTER or SENDER of the message. This is the person who wishes to pass on the information to others. This person has to choose the next two features carefully in order to make sure that communication occurs effectively
- a MEDIUM OF COMMUNICATION or a method for sending the message, for example, a letter or noticeboard
- a RECEIVER of the information – the person to whom the message should be sent
- FEEDBACK, where the receiver confirms that the message has been received and responds to it. This ensures that the information has been correctly received by the right person and, if necessary, acted upon.

■ Definitions to learn:

The TRANSMITTER or SENDER of the message is the person starting off the process by sending the message.

MEDIUM OF COMMUNICATION is the method used to send a message, for example, a letter is a method of written communication and a meeting is a method of verbal communication.

The RECEIVER is the person who receives the message.

FEEDBACK is the reply from the receiver which shows whether the message has arrived, been understood and, if necessary, acted upon.

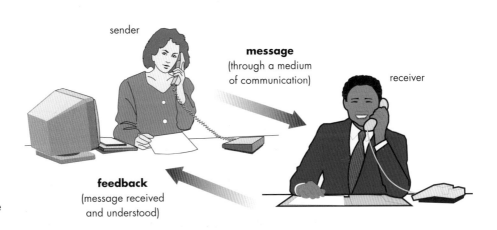

sender

message
(through a medium of communication)

receiver

feedback
(message received and understood)

The features of effective communication

■ Activity 12.1: case study task

Sales were below target at the Co-operative Retail Store. The manager was very concerned about this. She decided to write to every member of staff, about 30 in all, to warn them of the problem of falling sales and how jobs were now at risk. In the letter she asked for ideas on how to increase sales. Staff were asked to confirm that they had received the letter and tell her if they had any good ideas.

a) In this case study, identify:
   i) the transmitter of the message
   ii) the medium being used
   iii) the receiver of the message.
b) Did the communication involve feedback?
c) Do you think that the method used by the manager to communicate to the staff was the best one to use? If not, which method would have been more effective? Explain your answer.

■ **Definitions to learn:**

ONE-WAY COMMUNICATION involves a message which does not call for or require a response.

TWO-WAY COMMUNICATION is when the receiver gives a response to the message and there is a discussion about it.

One-way and two-way communication

ONE-WAY COMMUNICATION occurs when the receiver of a message has no chance to reply or respond to the message. An example would be an instruction to 'take these goods to the customer'. One-way communication does not allow the receiver to contribute to communication or to provide any feedback.

TWO-WAY COMMUNICATION is when there is a reply or a response from the receiver. This could be just simple confirmation of receipt of the message or it could be a discussion about the message. Both people are therefore involved in the communication process. This could lead to better and clearer information.

■ Activity 12.2

Refer to the list of messages on pages 166–67. The method used to send or transmit each message is also given. Which messages are most likely to lead to:

a) two-way communication?
b) one-way communication?

Give reasons for your answer in each case.

The advantages of two-way communication

When the receiver has to, or decides to, give feedback to the sender of the message there are two main benefits from this.

☑ It should become absolutely clear to the sender whether or not the person receiving the message has understood it and acted upon it. If they have not, then perhaps the message needs to be sent again or made clearer. Effective communication has not taken place until the message is understood by the receiver.

☑ Both people are now involved in the communication process. The receiver feels more a part of this process. He or she can make a real contribution to the topic being discussed or communicated. This may help to motivate the receiver.

The difference between one-way and two-way communication

one-way   two-way

Internal and external communication

INTERNAL COMMUNICATION is when messages are sent between people working in the same organisation. Examples include:

■ a manager talking to workers
■ a report sent from one director to another.

EXTERNAL COMMUNICATION is when messages are sent between one organisation and another or between the organisation and individuals other than employees, for example, customers. Some of the main examples of external communication are:

■ orders for goods from suppliers
■ sending information to customers about prices and delivery times
■ advertising goods or services – this is covered in detail in Unit 21
■ asking customers to pay bills on time.

Why external communication has to work well

External communication is very important to the *image* and *efficiency* of a business. If a firm communicates ineffectively with suppliers, it may be sent the wrong materials. If it sends inaccurate information to a customer, he/she may buy a product from another firm.

One type of communication is not more important than another. It is just as important for a business to have good external communication as good internal communication. The key features of both types are the same. The methods of communication which can be used are also the same. The main difference is *who* is being communicated with.

On page 170 there are some more examples of external communication. You can imagine how serious it would be if communication were not effective in all of these cases.

- A Finance Manager writes a letter to the tax office asking how much tax must be paid this year.
- A Sales Manager takes a telephone order from a customer for 330 items to be delivered by next Wednesday.
- A business must contact thousands of customers who have bought a product which turns out to be dangerous. An advertisement is put in all of the local papers asking customers to return the goods for a refund.

Revision summary: effective communication

sender or transmitter of the message   clear message   appropriate medium or method   receiver must be the right person

EFFECTIVE COMMUNICATION

Internal	**External**

to people in the same organisation   to people in other organisations or to consumers

Different ways of communicating: the communication media

Information can be sent or transmitted in a number of different ways.

- *Verbal* forms of communication involve the sender of the message speaking to the receiver.

- *Written* forms of communication include letters but may increasingly involve the use of information technology.

■ *Visual* forms of communication include methods such as diagrams, charts and videos.

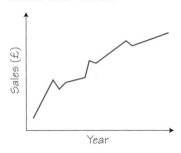 

Which is the best method of communication?

There is no simple answer to this question. Sometimes it is better to use verbal communication and on other occasions it is essential to use written communication. Different messages require different methods of communication, so there is no *best* method in all cases.

How is the appropriate method of communication selected? The sender of the message will need to consider the advantages and disadvantages of each method before deciding which one to use.

Verbal communication

Verbal, or oral, communication includes the following methods:

■ *one-to-one* talks between the sender and the receiver
■ *telephone* conversations
■ *video conferencing* where groups of people in different locations are able to see and hear each other through a video link
■ *meetings* which could involve a few people or hundreds.

Advantages of verbal communication

☑ Information can be given out quickly. When this happens at big meetings, it is an efficient way of communicating with a large number of people.
☑ There is opportunity for immediate feedback and two-way communication.
☑ The message is often reinforced by seeing the speaker. The *body language* of the speaker, how they stand and their facial expressions, can help to put the message across effectively. This, of course, does not apply to telephone conversations.

Disadvantages of verbal communication

✖ In a big meeting, there is no way of telling whether everybody is listening or has understood the message.
✖ It can take longer to use verbal methods when feedback occurs than to use a written form of communication.
✖ When an accurate and permanent record of the message is needed, such as a warning to a worker, a verbal method is inappropriate.

Written communication

Written forms of communication include:

■ *letters* used for either internal or external communication. They should follow a set structure – see *Introduction and guidance for students* on page viii

■ *memos* (an abbreviation of *memorandum*) written messages used only internally. Many businesses use computers to send these through the internal electronic mail system. An example is shown below.

```
MEMORANDUM
To: Sales Manager
From: Distribution Manager
Date: 3/8/2004
Subject: Delivery of damaged goods
The problem of damaged goods reaching our Newtown
branch has been solved. It was discovered that the
boxes were being loaded on to the truck without
any rope attaching them.
I have met with the loading supervisor to tell him
that this must not happen again.
```

■ *reports* detailed documents about a particular issue or problem. These are often produced by experts working in the business. They can be sent to managers to read before a meeting to discuss the issue. Very often these reports are so detailed that they could not be understood by all employees

■ *notices* pinned on boards. These are used to display information which is open to everyone. However, there is no certainty that they are read

■ *faxes* (facsimile messages) written messages sent to other offices by electronic means via telephone lines

■ *e-mail* and other forms of electronic communication using information technology. These have revolutionised communications in recent years. Written messages can be sent between two or more people with computing facilities. Printouts of messages can be obtained if a 'hard copy' is required.

Two examples of how information technology is transforming communication, both internal and external

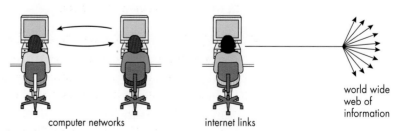

computer networks   internet links   world wide web of information

Advantages of written communication

☑ There is 'hard' evidence of the message which can be referred to in the future. This should help to reduce disagreements between the sender and the receiver about the contents of the message.

☑ It is essential for certain messages involving complicated details which might be misunderstood if, for example, a telephone message were given. Also, the law in many countries requires certain safety messages to be written and displayed in offices and factories. It is not sufficient to tell people about safety measures – they could be forgotten.

☑ A written message can be copied and sent to many people. This could be more efficient than telephoning all of those people to give them the same message verbally.

Disadvantages of written communication

☒ There is no opportunity for direct feedback. Two-way communication is either discouraged or takes a great deal longer than with verbal communication. It is often more difficult to check that the message has been received and acted upon than with verbal messages.

☒ The language used can be difficult for some receivers to understand. If the written message is too long it may be confusing and lose the interest of the reader. There is no opportunity for body language to be used to reinforce the message.

Visual communication

Visual forms of communication include the following.

■ *Films and videos* Often used by businesses to help train new staff or to inform sales people about new products.

■ *Posters* Can be used to explain a simple but important message by means of a picture or cartoon. For example, the dangers of operating an unguarded machine or the waste of leaving lights switched on.

■ *Charts and diagrams* Can be used in reports or letters to show numerical data or to simplify complicated ideas such as how the business is organised. Examples of these appear in other units of this book. Computers and relevant software packages can be used to present data in a wide variety of different tables, charts, graphs and diagrams. Printouts of these can then be obtained as a hard copy to add to reports and other documents.

Advantages of visual communication

☑ These methods can present information in an appealing and attractive way. People are often more prepared to look at films or posters than to read letters or notices because of the interesting way they communicate messages.

☑ They can be used to make a written message clearer by adding a chart or diagram to illustrate the point being made.

Disadvantages of visual communication

✖ There is no feedback and the sender of the message may need to use other forms of communication to check that the message is understood. For example, training videos are often followed by a written test for the new staff to check their understanding.

✖ Charts and graphs are difficult for some people to interpret. The overall message might be misunderstood if the receiver is unsure of how to read values from a graph or how to interpret a technical diagram.

■ Activity 12.3

Copy out this table and place a tick in the box which you think best describes each of the communication methods or media.

Communication methods or media

	Verbal	Written	Visual
Letter			
Video conference			
Meeting			
Facsimile			
Staff paper or newsletter			
Television			
Memorandum			
Notice			
Face-to-face			
Poster			
Telephone			

Revision summary: communication methods or media

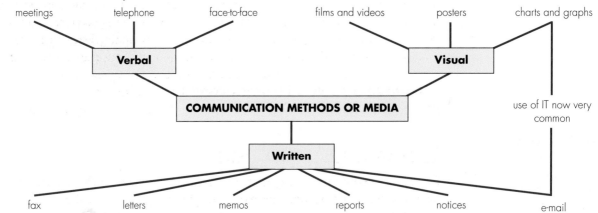

■ *Activity 12.4*

Which communication method might be most appropriate for the following messages? Give reasons for your answer in each case.

a) There should be no smoking in the staff canteen.
b) The management want to instruct all employees on how the new computer system works.
c) Details of the firm's sales figures for the last four years are being sent to shareholders.
d) The Finance Manager wants to remind the Production Manager that they have arranged a meeting for next week.
e) The Product Development Manager wants to inform directors of the market research into three new product ideas. He hopes that they will agree to launch one of these products.
f) The Office Manager wants to obtain views from all office workers on how paper waste could be reduced.
g) A supervisor plans to warn (for the last time) a worker who is always late for work.
h) Next year's holiday dates need to be made available to all workers.
i) The Human Resources Manager wants to invite an applicant for a job to an interview.
j) The Production Manager wants to send the plans for a new factory to the Managing Director who is on a foreign business trip.

Formal and informal communication

If you are a school student or in employment, how do you receive messages which are important to you? You may read notices on the noticeboard, receive reports or memos or attend official meetings. These are all examples of *formal communication*, which are channels of communication set up and recognised by an organisation such as a business or a school. As we have seen, these formal means of communication are very important. But are they the only way you learn of what is going on in your organisation? Almost certainly not.

You are also likely to receive messages through *informal* channels, such as meetings with friends or contact with others in the canteen or at break times. These informal, or unrecognised, meetings are sometimes referred to as the 'grapevine'. Sometimes these informal channels can be used by managers to 'try out' the reaction to new ideas, such as a new shift system in the factory, before communicating details of the new system formally. If the reaction to management from the grapevine is negative, they may not introduce the new idea at all. At other times, the informal channels can spread gossip and rumour which is unhelpful to managers. Managers, however, cannot prevent the informal links existing between people in the organisation.

Definition to learn:

COMMUNICATION NETS are the ways in which members of a group communicate with each other.

Communication nets

Groups of people in an organisation can communicate with each other in different ways. These links between people in a group are called COMMUNICATION NETS. Three examples are given on page 176.

Chain network

- ☑ It can be used to transmit important messages from the top of an organisation to the lower levels.
- ☒ This often leads to one-way communication and the message can become confused as it passes through several different levels. The more times a message is passed on the less accurate the message is likely to be.

Wheel network

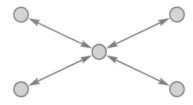

- ☑ It can be used to communicate with different departments or regions of a business. A solution to a problem discovered in one region can then be communicated to the other regions.
- ☒ The departments have no opportunity to communicate directly between themselves.

Connected network

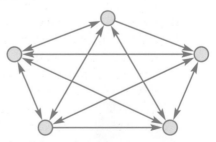

- ☑ Used to create and discuss new ideas as two-way communication is the key feature.
- ☒ Can be time-consuming and there is no clear leader or sender of messages.

Which network is best?

There is no one answer to this question. Different networks have different advantages. It is likely that organisations will use all forms of networks at different times or for different groups.

■ The chain network could be used to communicate important company policy.
■ The wheel network could be used to send different messages to different regional offices of the business.
■ The connected network might be of most use when the business is looking for new business ideas or solutions to problems where group discussion could be most effective.

The direction of communications

A typical organisational chart for a business is shown below.

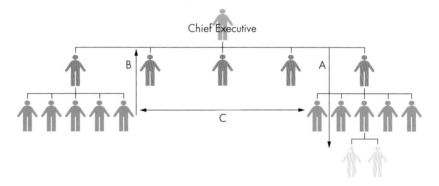

Look at the arrows. They indicate the *direction of communication*.

■ Arrow A shows *downward communication*. This is when messages are sent from managers to subordinates. It can be used for instructions or statements on important business decisions. It does not allow for feedback. As we saw in the section on communication nets, if these messages have to pass through many levels of hierarchy then the original meaning of the message could become distorted.
■ Arrow B shows *upward communication*. This is when a message or feedback is passed from subordinates to managers. As we have seen, such feedback can be an essential part of effective communication. Workers in an organisation have much to offer by being involved in the communication process. They should not be afraid of contributing to discussions or meetings. The organisation has much to gain when the managers are prepared to listen to and to act upon messages received from those lower down the organisation.
■ Arrow C shows *horizontal communication* (sometimes referred to as *lateral communication*). This occurs when people at the same level of an organisation communicate with each other. Information and ideas can be exchanged at both formal and informal meetings. This can be a

cause of conflict between departments; for example, if one department, Marketing, informs another one, Production, that the quality of their work is so poor that the consumers are returning goods as faulty!

Barriers to effective communication

As we saw on page 167, there are four parts to any successful communication – sender, receiver, medium used and feedback. Communication can fail if any one of these four parts does not operate as it should. If one part fails, it would be called a *barrier to effective communication*. This would cause a *breakdown in communications* which could lead to serious problems for the organisation.

The most common barriers to effective communication are listed in the table below. The most effective way of overcoming these barriers is also described.

Barriers to effective communication and how they can be overcome

Barrier	Description	How the barrier can be overcome
Problems with the sender	Language which is too difficult is used. 'Jargon' or technical terms may not be understood by the receiver	The sender should ensure that the message uses language which is understandable. Use of jargon or terms which are too technical should be avoided
	The sender uses verbal means of communication but speaks too quickly or not clearly enough	The sender should make the message as clear as possible. Feedback should be asked for to ensure the message is being understood
	The sender communicates the wrong message or passes it to the wrong receiver	The sender must make sure that the right person is receiving the right message
	The message is too long and too much detail prevents the main points being understood. This is again the fault of the sender	The message should be as brief as possible to allow the main points to be understood
Problems with the medium	The message may be lost	It is important to insist on feedback. If no feedback is received then the sender assumes the message was lost
	The wrong channel has been used, e.g. an important message was put on the noticeboard which most people did not read	The sender must select the appropriate channel for each message sent
	If the message is sent down a long chain of command, the original meaning of the message may be lost. It could become distorted	The shortest possible channel should be used to avoid this problem
	No feedback is received	This could be because, e.g., a letter was sent to workers asking for their opinions. A meeting would have been more useful
	Breakdown of the medium, e.g. computer failure or postal strike	Other forms of communication should, where possible, be made available

Barrier	Description	How the barrier can be overcome
Problems with the receiver	They might not be listening or paying attention	The importance of the message should be emphasised. The receivers should be asked for feedback to ensure understanding
	The receiver may not like or trust the sender. They may be unwilling to act upon his or her message	There should be trust between both the sender and receiver or effective communication is unlikely. Perhaps another sender should be used who is respected by the receiver
Problems with feedback	There is no feedback	Perhaps no feedback was asked for. Perhaps the method of communication used did not allow for feedback
	It is received too slowly or is distorted. As with the original message, perhaps the feedback is passing through too many people before being received by the original sender of the message	Direct lines of communication between subordinates and managers must be available. Direct communication is always more effective

Revision summary: barriers to effective communication

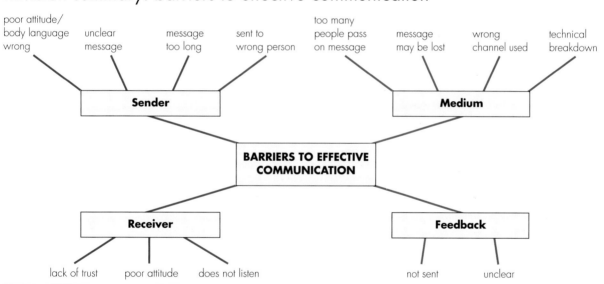

■ *Revision questions*

1 What is meant by communication? [3]

2 Outline the *four* features necessary for communication to be 'effective'. [4]

3 Explain the difference between one-way and two-way communication. [3]

4 Explain *one* situation in which two-way communication would be particularly useful. [4]

5 Explain the difference between internal and external communication. [3]

6 List *three* media that can be used for written communication. [3]

7 Imagine you are the Human Resources Director of a large department store. State *three* business situations where good internal communications would be important to you. [3]

8 Which method of communication would you use if you wanted to:
   a) Give an instruction to a large number of people.
   b) Explain a detailed plan to a few other people.
   c) Obtain a very quick reply to your message to another member of staff.
   d) Inform all staff about health and safety regulations.
   e) Tell an applicant for a job what the conditions of employment are. [5]

9 In each of the cases in Question 8, briefly explain the reasons for your choice. [5]

10 Draw *two* examples of communication nets – and state one advantage of each. [4]

11 Suggest advantages and disadvantages of each of the following methods of communication:
   a) letters
   b) memorandum
   c) meeting
   d) one-to-one conversation
   e) e-mail
   f) telephone [12]

12 Internal communications in your organisation are very poor. Messages are either not being received or not being acted upon. As Manager of Communications you have been asked to write a report to the Chief Executive. He wants your report to:
   a) Define *barriers to communication*. [2]
   b) Outline the *five* most likely barriers to effective communication in your organisation. [5]
   c) Give details of the steps you intend to take to remove these barriers. [4]

The CD-ROM (see details on page x) provides further tests, activities and Case study work on the topics covered in this unit.

Motivation at work

People work for a variety of reasons. The main reason why most people work is because they need to earn money to buy food and the basic necessities for life. But some work is voluntary and does not yield any money. This unit considers a wide range of MOTIVATIONS for work and how firms can make use of this motivation to encourage their workers to work more effectively. High productivity in a business usually comes from a workforce that is motivated to work effectively and from this comes increased profits.

Definition to learn:

MOTIVATION is the reason why employees want to work hard and work effectively for the business.

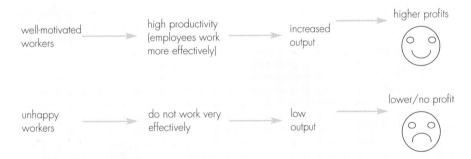

Of course improved organisation in a business and/or the increasing use of new technology, especially when it replaces workers, result in productivity gains. However, businesses also need to recognise that the value of their employees' output, in terms of how much they produce and the quality of it, comes from how well-motivated they are to work effectively. Employees are a firm's greatest asset!

Motivation theories

When people work for themselves they tend to work hard and effectively as they see the direct benefits of their labours. However, once people work for someone else then they may not work as effectively. One of the tasks of management is to get their workforce to contribute fully to the success of the business. To this end, many studies have been carried out to discover what makes employees work effectively. Three main theories are outlined below.

F.W. Taylor

Frederick Taylor started his working life as a labourer in a factory in America in the 1880s. He rose to become chief engineer. During this time he conducted experiments, at the steel company where he worked, into how labour productivity (see Unit 23) could be increased. His ideas and findings were published in 1911.

Taylor based his ideas on the assumption that all individuals are motivated by personal gain and therefore, if they are paid more, they will work more effectively. He was looking at workers who worked in factories. He broke down their jobs into simple processes and then calculated how much output they should be able to do in a day. If they produced this target output, they would be paid more money. Taylor saw employees rather like machines – when they were working hard, their productivity would be high and therefore their labour costs would be low. (This extra output would be worth more than the extra pay the workers received.)

Taylor's ideas resulted in big productivity gains at the company where he worked and many other businesses adopted his ideas. But there are several criticisms of Taylor's ideas, the main one being that his ideas were too simplistic – employees are motivated by many things and not just money. The other main weakness is that you can pay an employee more money, but if they are unfulfilled by their work in some way, there will be no increase in their effectiveness at work and there will be no productivity gains. Another practical problem is what happens if you cannot easily measure an employee's output?

Activity 13.1

a) From the following list of jobs, say which you could measure to find out how effectively the employees are working, i.e. how much output they are producing.
  i) Car production worker   ii) Shop assistant   iii) Waiter   iv) Tailor
  v) Teacher   vi) Police officer   vii) Soldier

b) Are there any jobs from the list for which output is difficult to measure? If so, explain why it is difficult to measure their output in each case.

c) If you cannot measure workers' output, how can you pay them more money if they work harder or more effectively?

d) Does this present problems for modern economies today where the majority of the workforce work in service sector jobs?

Maslow

Abraham Maslow studied employee motivation. His ideas were published in 1954 where he proposed a *hierarchy of needs*, shown in this diagram.

Maslow's Hierarchy of Needs

succeeding to your full potential	**self-actualisation**	being promoted and given more responsibility
having status and recognition, achievement, independence	**esteem needs**	being given recognition for a job well done
friendship, a sense of belonging to a team	**social needs**	work colleagues that support you at work
protection against danger, protection against poverty, fair treatment	**safety/security needs**	job security
food, rest, recreation, shelter	**physiological needs**	wages high enough to meet weekly bills

In Maslow's hierarchy:

- physiological needs are the basic requirements of food, shelter, warmth and sleep
- security needs are the needs to know that you are physically safe
- social needs are the needs to have rewarding relationships with other employees at work
- esteem needs are the needs for self-respect and to be respected and valued by other people
- self-fulfilment/self-actualisation needs are being able to be creative and feeling that you have done a good job. Maslow argued that everyone is capable of self-actualisation, but that in practice very few reach this level.

Businesses have begun to recognise that if employees are going to be motivated to work effectively then the higher levels in the hierarchy must be available to them, i.e. money alone will not be the single route to increased productivity as was thought by Taylor. Evidence for the hierarchy can be seen in people who are unemployed. They very often lose their self-respect and self-esteem and have the feeling of belonging to society, which often comes from working.

Maslow also suggested that each level in the hierarchy must be achieved before an employee can be motivated by the next level. For example, once social needs are met, this will no longer motivate the employee, but the opportunity to gain the respect of fellow workers and to gain esteem could motivate someone to work effectively. If this is true then there are important messages for management in the way employees are managed.

There are problems in that some levels do not appear to exist for certain individuals, while some rewards appear to fit into more than one level. For example, money allows basic needs to be purchased, but high pay can also be a status symbol or indicator of personal worth.

Managers must identify the level of the hierarchy that a particular job provides and then look for ways of allowing the employees to benefit from the next level up the hierarchy. For example, workers in agriculture who work on a temporary basis, when required, will probably have physiological needs fulfilled, but security needs may be lacking. If they were offered full-time jobs, they might feel more committed to the business and work more effectively for it.

Activity 13.2: case study task

- Miguel works as a farm labourer for a rich landlord. He has a small house on the estate and is allowed to grow his own food on a piece of land next to his house. He grows enough food to feed himself and his family and is paid a small wage, which pays for the other needs of the family such as clothes, shoes and medicines.
- Pierre works in a car factory on the assembly line. He works in a team of other workers welding the car body together. He is also a member of the company football team. He is well paid and his family can afford quite a few luxuries.
- Anya has a degree in Business Management and professional qualifications in human resources management. She is the Human Resources Manager of a large company. She has her own office with her name on the door and is in charge of the rest of the human resources staff. She works long hours but feels it is worth it if the right employees are recruited to the company.

Identify which of Maslow's needs are being satisfied for each of these employees. Explain the reasons for your choices.

McGregor

Theory X and Theory Y summarised

Douglas McGregor published his research findings in 1960. He identified two types of managers – those who believe in Theory X and those who believe in Theory Y.

Theory X	Theory Y
The average Theory X person dislikes work and will try to avoid it	The average Theory Y person thinks work is natural and does not dislike it in principle
People must be pressurised to work and threatened with punishment if they do not work	People will not need to be supervised and will use their own initiative; they are committed to hard work
These people will not want responsibility	They will accept responsibility and will then seek responsibility
These people are not ambitious and see security as their main need	Their greatest need is self-actualisation and these people have great creative potential which is mostly under-utilised at present

- Managers who believe in Theory X think that the willingness to work is mainly influenced by *external factors*, such as pay schemes which pay more if more output is produced. These managers think that people are naturally lazy and have to be motivated, pushed and urged to work.

- Managers who believe in Theory Y think that motivation is basically an *internal factor*. Most people want to do a good day's work but need a favourable environment in which to do it.
- Managers who believe in Theory X will look to introduce incentives and to have supervision to encourage employees to work hard.
- Managers who believe in Theory Y will try to provide a satisfactory environment in which people can work where they are not frustrated and can take an interest in their work.

▨ *Activity 13.3: case study task*

Two companies, Company A and Company B, are managed in very different ways.

- *Company A* Each office has at least one supervisor to check the work of the staff. The employees are set a target of work to complete each day and a log is kept of what is completed each day.
  Each process is broken down into its different tasks and these are assigned to individual employees to complete (this is a type of specialisation which was discussed in Unit 1).
- *Company B* There are a few group supervisors whose job it is to help the other staff if work builds up. The employees are encouraged to complete what they can. If a task needs more time than anticipated, the employee is encouraged to take the time required to do a good job.
  Employees are given a whole task to complete and they can choose how it is completed.

a) Which company employs managers who believe in Theory X and which has Theory Y managers? Explain your choice.
b) Which company would you rather work for and why?

Theories like Taylor's view employees as disliking work and conclude that they should be paid high wages and be closely supervised if they are to be made to work hard for the business. These are Theory X people. McGregor's own ideas are based on Theory Y – these employees, given the right conditions, will enjoy work, be creative and productive and will work effectively for the business. They will be committed, have self-control and will want to be part of the decision-making process.

The implications for management of McGregor's thinking is that they should create Theory Y working conditions so that the workers will be self-motivated and effective in their work. The role of management will be to help and support the employees rather than to be supervisory and to impose discipline.

Revision summary: motivation theories

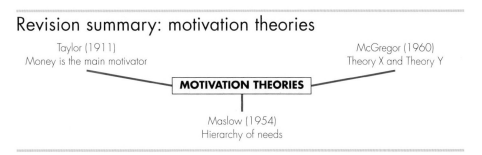

Taylor (1911)
Money is the main motivator

McGregor (1960)
Theory X and Theory Y

MOTIVATION THEORIES

Maslow (1954)
Hierarchy of needs

Why do people work?

The reasons why people work are summarised in the diagram below.

Money
to pay for necessities and some luxuries

Security
a sense of security, i.e. knowing that your job and pay are safe – you are not likely to lose your job

WHY WORK?

Social needs (affiliation)
feeling part of a group or organisation, meeting people, making friends at work

Esteem needs (self-importance)
feeling important, feeling that the job you do is important

Job satisfaction
enjoyment is derived from feeling that you have done a good job

Motivating factors

It is the responsibility of management, and often the Human Resources department, to motivate the workforce. A well-motivated workforce helps to raise productivity. Employees who are well-motivated tend to have fewer days off work and are less likely to have grievances which result in strike action.

So how can managers motivate their employees – whether it be in the office or on the factory floor? There are three factors which can motivate employees:

■ monetary rewards
■ non-monetary rewards
■ introducing ways to give job satisfaction.

Monetary rewards

Pay is seen as a main reason for working, but there are other reasons, as has been discussed in *Motivation theories* on pages 182–85. However, pay may be used to give incentives to employees to encourage them to work harder or more effectively. Payment can take various forms, the most common forms of which are outlined below.

Wages

> ▦ **Definition to learn:**
> A WAGE is payment for work, usually paid weekly.

WAGES are often paid every week, sometimes in cash and sometimes into a bank account. The worker gets paid on a regular basis and does not have to wait long for some money. Wages tend to be paid to manual workers, such as those who work in a warehouse. As the wages are paid weekly, they have to be calculated every week which takes time and money. Wages clerks are often employed to perform this task.

If the employee works longer than their normal hours, they will usually be paid *overtime*. This is their regular amount per hour plus an extra amount.

A typical wage slip for an employee in the UK

```
Name:...........................................    Employee no:.........................................

Employer:.......................................    Payment date:.......................................

Payments              Deductions                       To date

Basic wage  400.00    Income tax         100.00    Tax code  419L
Overtime     30.00    National Insurance  40.00    Tax week  3
                      Pension             40.00    Tax         289.54
                      Trade Union fees     5.00

Total       430.00    Total              185.00    Net pay £245.00
```

When calculating the wages to be paid, they can be worked out in a number of different ways.

■ *Time rate* Payment by the hour (payment for a period of time). For example, if an employee is paid £10 per hour and they work for 40 hours, then they will be paid £400.

  ☑ This makes it easy to calculate the worker's wages and the worker knows exactly what they will be paid for working a certain period of time. The hours worked are often recorded on a *time-sheet* which must be filled in and used to calculate the wages by the Accounts department.

  ☒ This system takes time. Good and bad workers get paid the same amount of money and often supervisors are needed to make sure the workers keep working and producing a good quality product. This is expensive because more supervisors are needed by the business. Also, a *clocking-in system* is needed to determine the number of hours worked by the employees.

  Time rate is often used where it is difficult to measure the output of the worker, for example, a bus driver or hotel receptionist.

A time-sheet for an employee who is paid by time rate

```
Name:...........................................    Employee no:.........................................

Department:.....................................    Standard rate of pay: £10 per hour
                                                    Overtime rate of pay: £15 per hour
                                                    Basic number of hours per week: 40

                Start time     Finish time        Total hours
Monday          16.00          24.00              8
Tuesday         16.00          24.00              8
Wednesday       16.00          24.00              8
Thursday        16.00          24.00              8
Friday          16.00          24.00              8
Saturday        16.00          18.00              2
Sunday          —

Total hours for week = 42    40 hours at £10 = £400
                             2 hours at £15  =  £30
                             Gross pay       = £430
```

In the example on page 187, the employee has worked two hours of overtime. This is paid at the overtime rate of £15 per hour and is added to the *basic pay* of £400, to give *gross pay* of £430.

However, the employee will not keep all of the £430. *Deductions* will be made. Some money will be paid:
– to the government in taxation
– into a pension scheme
– as a trade union subscription.

In the UK, National Insurance is also deducted from employees' wages (unless they are low paid) – this is like an insurance scheme which entitles the employee to unemployment benefit for a short time if they lose their job, or to sickness benefit if they are ill and cannot work, and it will entitle them to a state pension upon retirement.

■ *Piece rate* Where the workers are paid depending on the quantity of products made, i.e. the more they make, the more they get paid. A basic rate is usually paid with additional money paid according to how many products have been produced. Piece rate can be applied to bonus systems where employees who produce more than a set target of output can be rewarded. Piece rates can only be used where it is possible to measure the performance produced by an individual or a team.

☑ The advantage with this system is that it encourages workers to work faster and produce more goods.

☒ However, they may concentrate on making a large number of products and ignore quality, producing goods that may not sell very well because they are of a poor quality. This usually requires a quality control system and this is expensive. If poor quality goods are produced this could damage the reputation of the business.

Workers who are careful in their work will not earn as much as those who rush, which may not be seen as fair. Friction between employees may be caused as some will earn more than others. If the machinery breaks down, the employees will earn less money. Because of this, workers are often paid a guaranteed minimum amount of money.

Salaries

SALARIES are paid monthly, normally paid straight into a bank account. They are not paid in cash. It is usual for office staff or management (white-collar workers) to be paid salaries. It is calculated as an amount of money per year which is divided into 12 monthly amounts. It is paid for the job and extra work is not usually paid for – it is counted as part of the salary. The employer has the money in their bank account for longer than if they were paying their workers wages, as salaries are paid only once a month. Also, the payment has to be calculated only once a month instead of at least four times a month – as with wages.

Salaries are usually a standard rate, i.e. a set amount of money, but workers may get more money if the following rewards are added to the basic salary: COMMISSION; PROFIT-SHARING; BONUS; PERFORMANCE-RELATED PAY.

Commission

Commission is often paid to sales staff. They may be paid a small basic pay and then will be paid more money depending on how many goods they sell. It is similar to piece rate. The more sales they make, the more money they will make. This obviously encourages sales staff to sell as many products as possible which should be good for the business. Extra money is paid out to sales staff only if sales have increased, which is better for the business. However, if the sales staff are very persuasive and persuade people to buy goods they do not really want, the business may get a bad reputation – while in the short term they will have increased sales, in the long term they will see sales fall as their poor reputation spreads. It can also be very stressful for the sales staff because if they have a poor month, they will receive less pay.

Profit-sharing

In addition to a basic salary, the employee will receive a share of the profits – profit-sharing. If the business is successful, all the employees may receive a bonus. This will motivate the worker because if the business does well then they will all share in its success. The business will share only a portion of its profits and this is carried out either quarterly, half-yearly or yearly. (Some profits will need to be paid out as dividends and some may be required for reinvestment.) The benefit to the employees is that they feel a greater sense of being part of the business and that their efforts are being rewarded. Employees will hopefully work more effectively which is good for the business. This is often used in the service sector where it may be difficult to identify an individual employee's contribution to the increased profits, but they will all then benefit from more effective work.

Bonus

A bonus is usually a lump sum which is paid to workers when they have worked well. It can be paid at the end of the year if the company has had a successful year or it can be paid at intervals during the year.

Performance-related pay

In order to link the pay awarded to employees with their level of effectiveness in the organisation, performance-related pay is increasingly being used. The type of work where this is used is where output cannot readily be measured, for example police personnel, teachers, managers, or health workers. To assess their performance, businesses or managers often use a system of APPRAISAL. Appraisal is where an employee's immediate superior observes their work, talks to their colleagues and then carries out an interview with the employee to discuss their progress and their effectiveness. (Training needs may be identified at appraisal interviews and this helps to increase the employee's effectiveness in the future.)

▦ **Definition to learn:**
An APPRAISAL is a method of assessing the effectiveness of an employee.

Revision summary: methods of payment

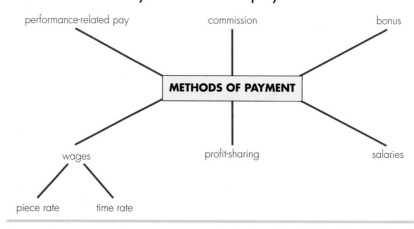

Non-monetary rewards

In addition to monetary rewards, firms may give non-monetary rewards, such as use of company cars, houses, expense accounts, or discounts on the firm's products. Non-monetary rewards vary according to the seniority of the job. Factory workers may get discounts on the firm's products, but they would not all have a company car, whereas a senior manager may have several non-monetary rewards, such as a house, a car and an expense account. These are sometimes called *perks* or FRINGE BENEFITS of a job.

Non-monetary rewards may include:

- children's education fees paid
- discounts on the firm's products
- health care paid for
- company vehicle (car)
- free accommodation
- share options (where company shares are given to employees)
- generous expense accounts (for food and clothing)
- pension paid for by the business
- free trips abroad/holidays.

▨ **Definition to learn:**
FRINGE BENEFITS are non-monetary rewards given to employees.

▨ *Activity 13.4*

For the following jobs, say which methods of reward (monetary and non-monetary) would be suitable and why. (Remember to consider whether it is easy to measure their output – this may affect how you decide to reward their efforts.)

a) Car production worker
b) Hotel receptionist
c) Teacher
d) Shop assistant
e) Managing Director
f) Taxi driver

Job satisfaction

There are other ways that people can be motivated to be more committed to their job and work more effectively – they need to get enjoyment from doing their job. However, there are some factors that will make employees unhappy and these must be satisfied before the employees can be motivated in a positive way. For example, if the management of the business is poor and the employees are treated badly, giving them fringe benefits will probably not motivate them. If their rates of pay are perceived by the employees as very poor relative to other similar workers, this will be a source of dissatisfaction to the employees. If these sources of dissatisfaction have been avoided, for example, reasonable wage rates are paid and employees are treated fairly at work, then these other sources of JOB SATISFACTION can motivate employees.

Employees have different ideas about what makes their jobs satisfying. They include:

- pay – the amount of money paid to an employee (already discussed earlier in the unit)
- opportunities for promotion
- working conditions
- fringe benefits (already discussed earlier in the unit)
- the way that the employee is managed (treated)
- working hours
- colleagues
- the nature of the work itself
- level of responsibility
- the sense of achievement derived from the job
- recognition for good work
- chance for training
- status of the job.

Individual employees will have different ideas about which of these is the most important.

Some of the motivation theories (particularly Maslow and McGregor) emphasise that the important aspects of jobs are that they should give recognition, responsibility and satisfaction to the people doing them and allow the employee to gain a sense of achievement from the work itself. Some jobs may seem dull and boring, but with a little thought and creativity they can be made more interesting and consequently increase motivation.

There are several ways in which a business can increase the job satisfaction of its employees.

- JOB ROTATION Workers on a production line may carry out simple but different tasks. Job rotation involves the workers swapping round and doing each specific task for only a limited time (for example, for one hour) and then changing round again. This increases the variety in the work itself and also makes it easier for the managers to move workers

Definition to learn:

JOB SATISFACTION is the enjoyment derived from feeling that you have done a good job.

Definition to learn:

JOB ROTATION involves workers swapping round and doing each specific task for only a limited time and then changing round again.

around the factory if people are ill and their jobs need covering. However, it does not make the tasks themselves more interesting.

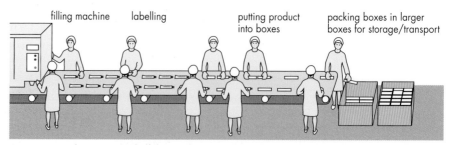

filling machine   labelling   putting product into boxes   packing boxes in larger boxes for storage/transport

every hour, or every half day, each person moves along and changes jobs

■ JOB ENLARGEMENT This is where extra tasks of a similar level of work are added to a worker's job description. The extra tasks should not add extra work or increased responsibility to the employee, but they should give greater variety to the work and therefore increase job satisfaction.

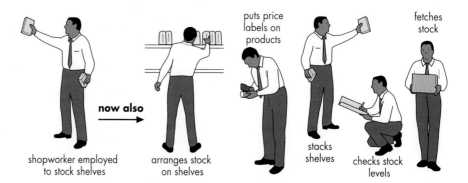

puts price labels on products   fetches stock

now also

shopworker employed to stock shelves   arranges stock on shelves   stacks shelves   checks stock levels

■ JOB ENRICHMENT This involves looking at jobs and adding tasks that require more skill and/or responsibility. Additional training may be necessary to enable the employee to take on extra tasks. For example, employees may be given responsibility for a whole area of the work. If managers can design jobs so that they provide scope for fulfilling higher human needs, workers will often become more committed because they get more satisfaction from their jobs, again raising productivity.

reception   now also   word-processes letters   takes orders   deals with telephone enquiries

receptionist employed to greet customers   training will be needed – receptionist will need to know about products sold in order to deal with enquiries

■ *Autonomous work groups or teamworking* This is where a group of workers is given responsibility for a particular process, product or development. They can decide as a group how to complete the tasks or organise the jobs. The workers can become more involved in the decision-making and take responsibility for this process. This gives a feeling of control over the jobs/tasks and the employees feel more committed, therefore increasing job satisfaction. An example of this way of organising employees is on a car production line where particular parts of the assembly line are given over to teams of workers and they decide how to organise themselves. Often this leads to job rotation and job enrichment. Working as a group helps improve morale as well as giving a greater sense of belonging to the company.

A team of workers is responsible for a particular part of the assembly
The team decides how the processes will be completed
The tasks are allocated by the team themselves – they make the decisions

Revision summary: motivating factors at all levels

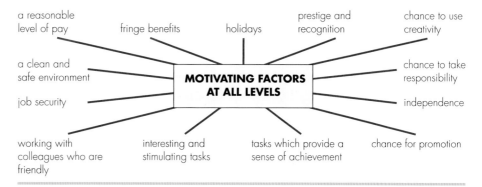

a reasonable level of pay

fringe benefits

holidays

prestige and recognition

chance to use creativity

a clean and safe environment

MOTIVATING FACTORS AT ALL LEVELS

chance to take responsibility

job security

independence

working with colleagues who are friendly

interesting and stimulating tasks

tasks which provide a sense of achievement

chance for promotion

Leadership

Studies on motivation have emphasised the importance of good management in business and the need for leadership. There are many leaders in society – from politicians, religious leaders, captain of the sports team, to leaders of large businesses. Many people take on the role of being a leader and some are more effective than others. A good leader in a large business is someone who can inspire and get the best out of the workforce, getting them to work towards a common goal.

Activity 13.5: case study task

■ Duncan is a computer programmer. He has a degree in Computer Studies and enjoyed writing programs as part of his degree course. He thought computer programming would be his ideal job. However, all he does is write simple programs for firms' Accounts departments which allow the processing of their paperwork.

   He is told what to do by his manager and is given little opportunity to visit the client to discuss their requirements and does not go to install the software at the business when it is finished. He is so fed up he is looking for another job.

■ Sita works in a clothes shop. She spends her time looking after the changing room where she checks customers into the changing rooms and takes the garments which are not going to be purchased from them when the customers have tried them on. There are several other employees in the shop, one takes the money from customers at the cash till, one puts out the clothes on the rails and does the shop displays, one person works in the stock room and there is a manager who does all the ordering and administration for the shop. The shop can be very quiet on some days and very busy on others. Sita is not happy. She does not care if customers find the right clothes for them or not – she gets paid whether they buy the clothes or not.

■ Tim works in a clothing factory. He cuts out the collars for shirts. The rest of the processes for making shirts are carried out by other employees. He has done this job for two years now and gets very fed up with what he is doing. He does not worry too much if the collars are slightly uneven as he thinks customers will not notice. The other employees who work with him in the shirt department feel the same as he does.

These three employees are not happy in their work. Describe how you would try to improve their job satisfaction. Explain the reasons for your suggestions. (You may suggest more than one way for each of the employees.)

Definition to learn:

LEADERSHIP STYLES are the different approaches to dealing with people when in a position of authority – autocratic, *laissez-faire* or democratic.

There are different approaches to leadership that are adopted and these can be summarised into three main LEADERSHIP STYLES:

■ autocratic leadership
■ *laissez-faire* leadership
■ democratic leadership.

Autocratic leadership

Autocratic leadership is where the manager expects to be in charge of the business and to have their orders followed. They keep themselves separate from the rest of the employees. They make virtually all the decisions and keep information to themselves. They tell employees only what they need to know. Communication in the business is mainly one way, that is, *top down* (see Unit 12, page 177), and the workers have little or no opportunity to comment on anything.

Laissez-faire leadership

Laissez-faire is French for 'leave to do'. This type of leadership tends to make the broad objectives for the business known to employees, but then they are left to make their own decisions and organise their own work. Communication can be difficult in this type of organisation as clear direction will not be given. The leader has only a very limited role to play.

Democratic leadership

This type of leadership will get other employees involved in the decision-making process. Information about future plans will be openly discussed before the final decision will be made, often by the leader. Communication will be both *top down* and *bottom up*.

The style of leadership used by a manager can vary depending on the employees being dealt with and the problem to be solved. Managers may not be autocratic leaders all of the time – it may be appropriate for them to be democratic over some issues, whereas other issues will need a decision imposing on the workforce.

Leadership styles

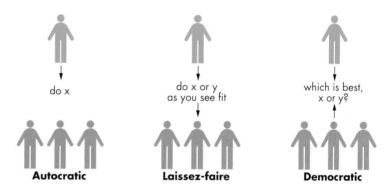

Activity 13.6: case study task

Sanjay is a hotel manager. He needs to introduce new shift patterns for the hotel's employees because the airline which uses his hotel has changed a number of its flight times and needs to be able to book in several of their staff in the middle of the night. This will particularly affect the kitchen staff because the airline employees will require food. He has decided just to tell them about the changes and if they do not like it they can get another job elsewhere and he will recruit and train some new staff.

a) What style of leadership is Sanjay using?
b) Do you think he was right to use this style of leadership?
c) What other leadership style could he have used to manage these changes?

Formal and informal groups

Students joining a school or college will join a particular tutor group. This is a FORMAL GROUP put together by the school or college. However, within this tutor group there will be sub-groups of students who get together because they have similar interests. These are INFORMAL GROUPS and they usually join together by choice. Several of these informal groups might play

▥ **Definitions to learn:**
A FORMAL GROUP is a group designated to carry out specific tasks within a business.
An INFORMAL GROUP is a group of people who form independently of any official groups set up within the business and who have similar interests or something else in common.

football at break times. If the school is trying to put together a team to represent the school, i.e. a formal group, then they may be more effective if informal groups are incorporated into the selected players. It will be the job of the football team manager to get these players to work well together.

Formal groups in business

A business divides itself up into different groups to carry out specific tasks and/or into different departments to deal with human resources or marketing or accounts. There may be other groups set up from time to time to deal with particular problems, for example, a group of people representing different departments might form a group to discuss how the introduction of new technology might be handled. They will come together to work on that particular project.

Informal groups in business

In business there are also informal groups who form by themselves. These will be groups of people with similar interests or they may have something else in common. If a group of doctors and nurses in a hospital wanted to help the poor in a local area where there is little or no medical provision, they might volunteer to go out and help the sick poor people. These volunteers will probably work better with each other when they are back in their formal group, i.e. their normal work in the hospital, as they will have worked with people from other departments and will co-operate and be more helpful.

If two departments are put together, employees from each of the original departments might not be willing to mix with employees from the other department. This official formal group of a single department may not be very effective if each former department still sees itself as two separate informal groups. For a business to work effectively, these informal groups need to be handled carefully.

Regular meetings between managers and employees, joint consultation on issues, organised social events for employees, joint fund-raising efforts, activity weekends for staff, and improved communication are all ways of using informal groups in a positive way rather than letting them become negative. Motivation can be improved if a positive solution can be found.

Formal and informal groups in business

Formal

Marketing department

Informal

some of the department also meet after work to play basketball

■ *Revision questions*

1 Why are well motivated employees good for a business? [2]

2 Match the statement to the person (A – Taylor, B – Maslow, C – McGregor) whose theory it best describes:
i) 'People have different needs, from the basic requirements of food and shelter to finding a self-fulfilment that comes from doing a good job.'
ii) 'Money is the main motivator; pay someone more money and they will work harder.'
iii) 'Some managers think that workers are lazy and need to be pushed to work – these are Theory X managers; other managers think employees just need a reasonable environment and want to do a good job – these are Theory Y managers.' [3]

3 State *five* reasons why people work. [5]

4 What *three* factors can be used by managers to motivate their employees? [3]

5 Joe is paid €3,000 per month whilst Kiran is paid €5.00 per hour and last week earned €20 extra as he worked overtime. Who is paid a wage and who is paid a salary? [2]

6 Name *two* deductions that may be made from an employee's total pay. [2]

7 After deductions of €50 Kiran's take-home pay for the week is €200. How much is his gross pay? [2]

8 Sarah is paid €5.00 per hour and works 40 hours a week, whilst Selina is paid €5.00 for every component she produces. Who is paid by piece rate and who is paid by time rate? [2]

9 Give *one* advantage and *one* disadvantage of using time rate. [4]

10 Give *one* example when time rate may be used by a business. [1]

11 Give *one* advantage and *one* disadvantage of using piece rate. [4]

12 Give *one* example when piece rate may be used by a business. [1]

13 Other than wages and salaries, describe *four* other methods of paying employees. [4]

14 What is meant by *appraisal*? [2]

15 What is meant by *non-monetary rewards*? [2]

16 Give *five* examples of non-monetary rewards. [5]

17 Give *three* ways in which a job might be satisfying for an employee. [3]

18 For each of the following three jobs state whether job rotation, job enlargement or job enrichment would be the most suitable way to increase job satisfaction:
a) shop worker
b) chef
c) production line worker in a car assembly plant? [6]

19 What are the *three* basic types of leadership? [3]

20 Which types of groups, formal or informal, are the following:
a) meeting between Human Resources and Production departments to plan a job advertisement for assembly workers
b) company football team practice at lunch time
c) staff organised fund-raising event for a local charity
d) Finance department monthly meeting? [4]

The CD-ROM (see details on page x) provides further tests, activities and Case study work on the topics covered in this unit.

14 Recruitment, training and human resources

This unit will explain:

- ? the role of the Human Resources department
- ? each stage of the recruitment and selection process
- ? different types of training
- ? dismissal and redundancy.

By the end of the unit you should be able to:

- ☑ understand the different functions of the Human Resources department
- ☑ draw up a job description
- ☑ draw up a job specification
- ☑ choose suitable ways of advertising a vacancy
- ☑ draw up a CV or resumé and an application form
- ☑ draw up questions for interviews
- ☑ design an induction programme
- ☑ explain the difference between on-the-job training and off-the-job training.

The work of the Human Resources department

Recruitment and selection are the most familiar roles of the Human Resources department, and this unit will look at these roles in detail, and at another important area of human resources work – the training of employees. Redundancy and dismissal are also the responsibility of the Human Resources department and these are discussed.

The responsibilities of the Human Resources department

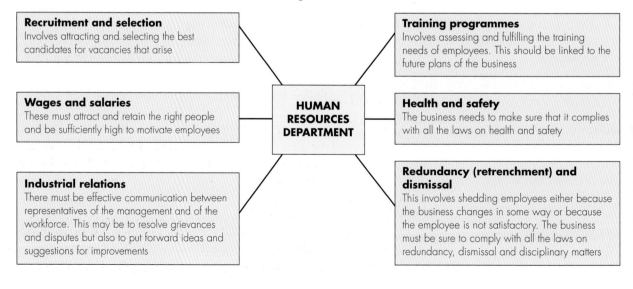

Recruitment and selection
Involves attracting and selecting the best candidates for vacancies that arise

Wages and salaries
These must attract and retain the right people and be sufficiently high to motivate employees

Industrial relations
There must be effective communication between representatives of the management and of the workforce. This may be to resolve grievances and disputes but also to put forward ideas and suggestions for improvements

HUMAN RESOURCES DEPARTMENT

Training programmes
Involves assessing and fulfilling the training needs of employees. This should be linked to the future plans of the business

Health and safety
The business needs to make sure that it complies with all the laws on health and safety

Redundancy (retrenchment) and dismissal
This involves shedding employees either because the business changes in some way or because the employee is not satisfactory. The business must be sure to comply with all the laws on redundancy, dismissal and disciplinary matters

Recruitment and selection

When an employee leaves a job, when a new business is starting up or when a business is successful and wants to expand, the process of recruitment and selection starts. The business will first of all have to decide if the employee leaving a job needs to be replaced. Sometimes the tasks that people do can be changed around and a different type of job can be created. For example, when an Administration Assistant leaves an office, the job may be changed to include more duties involving the computers in the office. Therefore the type of person that needs to be recruited will have had different training and skills to the one who is leaving. The start of the recruitment process gives the business time to reassess the nature of people's jobs and consider future requirements.

After all the duties of the job have been decided, the skills required for the job are assessed. Then an advertisement can be designed and placed in a suitable location. People will apply for the job, interviews will be held and finally a suitable person will be offered the job and appointed.

In a large business this process of recruiting and selecting staff is usually undertaken by the Human Resources department. Small businesses do not recruit enough people to make it worthwhile having a separate Human Resources department – often the managers who will be supervising the employee will deal with recruitment for their department. For example, in a hotel a restaurant manager might recruit the waiters and waitresses.

The more important the job is to the business, i.e. the more technical and senior the position, the more careful and time-consuming the recruitment and selection process will be.

The recruitment process is summarised in the diagram below.

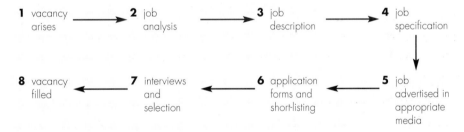

The recruitment process
Job analysis and description

■ **Definition to learn:**
A JOB ANALYSIS identifies and records the responsibilities and tasks relating to a job.

The first stage of the recruitment process is to carry out a JOB ANALYSIS to study the tasks and activities to be carried out by the new employee. If the business is recruiting an employee to fill an existing post, for example, if someone has left or been dismissed, an outline of the duties for the new employee will be relatively easy to draw up, and may even already exist. If the new employee is needed due to the business expanding or because the business has identified skills that it needs but no one in the business has these skills, more thought will have to go into the analysis of the job.

■ **Definitions to learn:**

A JOB DESCRIPTION outlines the responsibilities and duties to be carried out by someone employed to do a specific job.

A JOB SPECIFICATION is a document which outlines the requirements, qualifications, expertise, physical characteristics, etc. for a specified job.

Once all of these details about the job have been gathered, a JOB DESCRIPTION will be produced. A job description has several functions.

- It is given to the candidates for the job so they know exactly what the job entails.
- It will allow a JOB SPECIFICATION to be drawn up, to see if the candidates 'match up to the job', so that people with the right skills will be employed.
- Once someone has been employed, it will show whether they are carrying out the job effectively. If any disputes occur about what the employee is asked to do, it is something both the employee and the employer can refer to in order to settle any questions.

■ *Case study example*

Here is a job description for a housekeeper in a hotel.

Job title: Housekeeper
Department: Housekeeping
Responsible to: Hotel Manager
Responsible for: Cleaners, room attendants

Main purpose of the job:

Responsible for domestic services in the hotel, with an aim to keeping accommodation clean and maintained for the hotel guests. Responsible for the cleaners and room attendants. To take a supervisory role.

Main duties:

- allocation of duties, such as cleaning
- advising staff when queries arise
- sending soiled linen to the laundry
- organising repairs and replacement of worn items from rooms
- checking that belongings have not been left in rooms
- checking that the rooms are ready to receive guests
- informing reception when rooms are ready for occupancy.

Occasional duties:

- appointment of new staff
- training new staff in their duties
- training new staff to use the equipment
- disciplining staff as and when required
- dismissing staff if necessary.

The exact content of a job description varies from business to business, but generally it will contain:

- the title of the job, for example, secretary or waiter
- the department of the business in which the person will work, for example, Marketing department or restaurant
- who the job-holder is responsible to (the person who will be in charge of the employee)

- who the job-holder is responsible for (anyone the employee will be in charge of)
- the purpose of the job (a summary of the job itself)
- the main duties of the job (a list of the duties that the employee will be expected to carry out).

Job descriptions sometimes also contain information about:

- the conditions of employment – salary, hours of work, pension scheme and staff welfare
- training that will be offered
- opportunities for promotion.

Job specification

Once a job description has been drawn up, the qualifications and qualities necessary to undertake the job can be specified. This list of desirable and essential requirements for the job is called a job, or person, specification. The listed requirements will usually include:

- the level of educational qualifications
- the amount of experience and type of experience
- special skills, knowledge or particular aptitude
- personal characteristics, such as type of personality.

■ *Case study example*

Here is a job specification for the post of housekeeper in a hotel.

Job title: Housekeeper
Department: Housekeeping

Details of job:

Responsible for domestic services in the hotel, with an aim to keeping accommodation clean and maintained for the hotel guests. Responsible for cleaners and room attendants. To take a supervisory role.

Qualifications:

Essential: 4 GCSEs (A–C) including Maths and English
Desirable: Minimum 1 year's experience of working in hotels

Skills:

- Communicates effectively with people
- Ability to manage people

Physical fitness:

Fit, needs to be on feet all day

Personal characteristics:

- Honest and responsible
- Friendly, helpful, organised

■ *Activity 14.1: case study task*

a) Draw up a job description for *one* of the following:

- Accountant
- Hotel Manager
- Shop Assistant
- Teacher

Research information to help you by asking someone who does the job or from careers information.

b) Now draw up a job specification for the job you chose for a). The same research should help you to complete this task. Show which are essential and which are desirable requirements for the job.

Advertising the vacancy

The next stage is to decide how the post will be filled.

Internal recruitment

The post could be filled from inside the organisation – INTERNAL RECRUITMENT. The vacancy may be advertised on a company noticeboard or, if the business is large, in a company newspaper. This would be suitable for an employee who seeks promotion within the business.

Advantages of internal recruitment

- ☑ It saves time and money, rather than recruiting someone from outside the business (advertising, interviewing, etc.).
- ☑ The person is already known to the business and their reliability, ability and potential are known.
- ☑ The person also knows the organisation's way of working and what is expected from employees.
- ☑ It can be very motivating for other employees to see their fellow workers being promoted – it makes them work harder.

Disadvantages of internal recruitment

- ☒ No new ideas or experience come into the business. Other companies may have different ways of working and these ways may be better in some respects. This allows these working practices to be spread to other businesses and makes them more efficient.
- ☒ There may be jealousy and rivalry amongst existing employees.

External recruitment

Most vacancies are filled by EXTERNAL RECRUITMENT. This involves advertising the vacancy. There are several places the advertisement can be placed.

- *Local newspapers* These will usually be for clerical (office) or manual (factory) positions. These types of jobs do not require a high level of skill and therefore it is likely that many people locally could fill these vacancies.

- *National newspapers* These will usually be used for more senior positions where there may be few, if any, local people who have the right experience, skills and qualifications to do the job. The national newspapers will be read by many people who live in different parts of the country or sometimes by people who live in different countries. As the positions are senior, they will be highly paid and these people will be willing to move to another part of the country. Job vacancies in other countries are also sometimes advertised in national newspapers.
- *Specialist magazines and journals* These will usually be used for particular technical people such as scientists. These people will read the specialist magazines and see the advertisements. Again these can be for jobs in their home country or abroad.
- *Recruitment agencies* These are specialists in recruiting employees. They will advertise and interview people for particular types of jobs. They keep details of qualified people on their 'books'. When a suitable vacancy arises, they will put forward candidates to be interviewed for the job.

  Agencies are also approached by companies who need to employ a particular type of skilled worker. The agency will send along those people they think will be suitable. This method is often used when temporary contracts need filling and where the vacancy is in another country.

  The use of recruitment agencies has increased in recent years. Some businesses are happy to leave the recruitment process to someone else because they have a wide range of candidates on their register. However, the services of an agency are expensive – they charge a fee for recommending the applicant which is based on a percentage of the person's salary, if the person is successfully appointed to the job.
- *Centres run by the government (Job Centres)* These are places where job vacancies can be advertised. Details of vacancies are given to interested people. The vacancies are usually for unskilled and semi-skilled jobs.

Job advertisement

After the business has decided to advertise externally, the next step is to draw up the advertisement. When drawing up a job advertisement, the business will need to decide:

- what should be included in the advert
- where the advertisement should be placed
- how much the advertising will cost and is it too expensive? (Can they afford it?)

Answering the first question is straightforward – information about the job has to be included. This will usually be the duties involved, qualifications required, salary, conditions of employment, and information about the method of application (whether it is by letter of application and CV or should they request and fill in an application form from the business).

Answers to the other two questions will depend on the vacancy being filled and whether it is a senior position or one which does not require any qualifications.

■ *Activity 14.2: case study task*

Night Cashier for busy petrol station, 38 hours per week, Wed to Sat, 10.00 p.m.–7.30 a.m., £7.50 per hour. Start immediately. Tel.1122 44551

Industrial Engineering Professional

Multi-site role throughout the country: based in New City. Competitive rate of pay with fringe benefits. Qualityfoam Ltd is a leading manufacturer of polyurethane foam operating in 16 countries and a major supplier to the home country's furniture industry.

Appealing to results-orientated professional, responsibilities will include performance improvement, business analysis, project management and capital expenditure appraisal.

You will be a graduate of calibre, numerate and PC literate, with at least three years' experience in manufacturing.

Please write with full CV to: Mr M. Ahmed, MD, Qualityfoam Ltd, New Road, New City, 3412 8769.

Secretary required £10.00 per hour

Good all-round secretarial skills needed to undertake a variety of duties within the organisation. Knowledge of WORD or similar package essential. Immediate start.

Please write or telephone for an application form from:

Mr S. Singh, ZYT Ltd, 2341 Old Road, New City, 456723. Tel. 0892 557739

a) Which advert would have appeared in a national newspaper and which would have been in the local newspaper? Explain your choice.

b) Design your own advertisement for the job for which you drew up a job description and job specification (page 202). Where would you place this advertisement, and why?

c) Compare your advert with that of the other students in your group. Which would be most likely to attract the best people to apply for the job and why?

■ *Activity 14.3*

On a large sheet of paper, copy out the table below and then fill in the gaps.

Advantages and disadvantages of the different methods of recruitment

Methods of recruitment	Advantages	Disadvantages	Examples of suitable jobs for use with this method
Internal Noticeboard at the company (or company newspaper)			
External Local newspapers			
National newspapers			
Specialist magazines			
Recruitment agencies			
Government-run Job Centres			

Application forms and CVs/resumés

A job advertisement will require the applicant to apply in writing. This can either be by requesting, and then filling in, an *application form*, or by writing a *letter of application* and enclosing a *curriculum vitae (CV)* or *resumé*. A CV or resumé is a summary of a person's qualifications, experience and qualities, and is written in a standard format.

A business will use the application forms, or letters and CVs, to see which of the applicants match the job specification. The applicants who are the closest match are the ones who will be invited for an interview – the *selection stage*. A short-list will be drawn up.

A curriculum vitae (CV) or resumé must be well laid out and clear. It should usually contain the following details:

- name
- address
- telephone number
- date of birth
- nationality
- marital status
- education and qualifications
- work experience
- positions of responsibility
- interests
- names and addresses of referees (for references).

The letter of application should outline briefly:

- why the applicant wants the job
- why the applicant feels he/she would be suitable.

Application forms are sometimes completed in place of the CV and usually ask for the same information. They sometimes also ask if the person has dependants, for details of their medical history and whether they have a criminal record.

■ *Activity 14.4: case study task*

a) Study this job advertisement and the three application forms below. Which of the three people would be most suitable for the job? Give reasons for your choice of the successful applicant and why you rejected the other two applicants.

> **Senior Secretary**
> Salary in excess of £20,000 per year
> The General Manager at our New City office requires an experienced and highly skilled Secretary to provide a complete support service. In a typically busy day you will manage the General Manager's office, type a variety of documents, maintain an accurate diary and liaise with customers, clients and corporate contracts.
> You will need to be able to demonstrate excellent keyboard skills, knowledge of Microsoft Office and associated programs, a good standard of numeracy and literacy and have previous experience in a similar role.
>
> *If you enjoy working with a friendly team, please send your CV to Corinne Ogunbanjo, Human Resources, NYDB plc, 3286 New Street, New City, 467813.*

	Applicant 1	**Applicant 2**	**Applicant 3**
Name	Caroline Sharma	Pablo Gitano	Sara Gherman
Address	2144 Main Road, New City	4245 Long Row, New City	9876 New Road, New City
Age	19	29	38
Marital status	Single	Married	Single
Educational qualifications	5 GCSEs, including English, Maths and Computer Studies. Secretarial qualifications – Level 1	6 IGCSEs, including English, Maths and Computer Studies. Secretarial qualifications – Levels 1 & 2	5 O-levels, including English and Maths. Secretarial qualifications – Levels 1, 2 and 3
Previous employment	6 months as a secretary	1 year as office junior, 3 years on reception, 6 years as personal assistant	Switchboard duties – 2 years, Reception – 3 years, General office duties – 6 years, Head of secretarial section – 6 years, Personal Assistant – 2 years
Interests/ hobbies	Playing sports – member of several local teams, going to see friends, voluntary helper with a youth group	Reading, member of local football team, playing piano, rock climbing	Reading, going to the cinema, watching television

b) What additional questions do you think should have been on the application form? Why should they have been asked?

c) Design your own application form for the job for which you produced an advertisement on page 204.

Interviews

The applicants who are short-listed and invited for interview will have provided the names and addresses of referees. These are people who will be asked to provide a reference, i.e. give their opinion on the applicant's character, honesty, reliability and their suitability for the job. References are usually confidential, which means the applicant does not see what has been written about them. This should allow the person giving the reference to be honest in their opinions. References may be applied for before an interview, to help with the selection, or after, when an applicant may be offered the job subject to favourable references. Sometimes an 'open' reference or testimonial will be given. These are not confidential, indeed the applicant may bring these along themselves. They include the same sort of comments that a closed reference would contain but would not usually include critical comments about the person.

If the applicant is a school leaver, it is normal to give their school as a reference. If the applicant is older, usually a former employer will be used.

Interviews are still the most widely used form of selection. However, interviews are not always the most reliable way of choosing the best person for the job. The main purposes of an interview are to assess, in the shortest possible time:

- the applicant's ability to do the job
- any personal qualities that are an advantage or disadvantage
- the general character and personality of the applicant – will they fit in?

The types of question asked at an interview are likely to include:

- why have you applied for the job?
- what do you know about this company?
- what qualities do you have to offer the company? (Why should we offer you the job?)
- what ambitions do you have?
- tell me about your hobbies and interests. (What do you do in your leisure time?)
- do you have any questions to ask us?

Interviews can be one-to-one, two-to-one or a panel of people to interview the applicant. Panel interviews are usually used for more senior positions. Some businesses include tests in their selection process, for example:

- *skills tests* aim to show the ability of the candidate to carry out certain tasks
- *aptitude tests* aim to show the candidate's potential to gain additional skills. Either general intelligence tests or more specific tests are used to assess the candidate's ability to train for a particular job
- *personality tests* are used if a particular type of person is required for the job, if the job requires the ability to work under stress or if the person will need to fit in as part of a team of people

■ *group situation tests* give tasks to applicants to complete in group situations and the group is observed. Each applicant will be assessed on the way they work as a member of the team and the way they tackle the tasks themselves. Again, a job that requires the applicant to work as part of a team, for example on projects, will often use this type of selection procedure during the selection process.

■ Activity 14.5: case study task

Imagine that you are now going to interview candidates for the vacancy that you advertised in Activity 14.2.

You have drawn up the following six questions to ask the interviewees.

1 What is it about the job that attracted you to apply for it?
2 What do you know about the company?
3 Tell me more about your hobbies and interests.
4 Why do you feel you are particularly suitable for the job?
5 Where do you see yourself in five years' time?
6 Do you have any questions?

a) What is the purpose of each of these questions? What are you hoping to find out?
b) What other questions ought to be asked?
c) Get other students in your class to apply for the job you have advertised and then carry out a mock interview. Would you offer them the job?

Rejecting unsuccessful applicants

When the suitable applicant has been offered the job, the unsuccessful applicants should be informed that they have not got the job and thanked for applying.

■ Activity 14.6: case study tasks

a) An international construction company has just won a contract to build a dam in an African country. How might the Human Resources department recruit the following workers for the contract:
i) experienced engineers
ii) labourers?
b) An international airline is expanding its operations in Latin America. It needs to recruit staff to be based in just this continent, as the flights will not go all around the world. What recruitment and selection methods would it use to appoint:
i) airline pilots
ii) cabin crew (air stewardesses and stewards)?

Revision summary: the recruitment and selection process

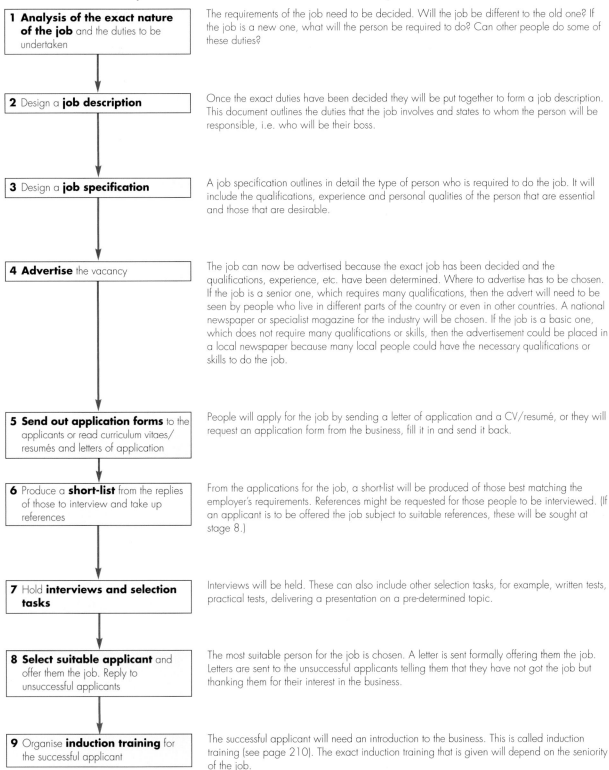

1 Analysis of the exact nature of the job and the duties to be undertaken

The requirements of the job need to be decided. Will the job be different to the old one? If the job is a new one, what will the person be required to do? Can other people do some of these duties?

2 Design a **job description**

Once the exact duties have been decided they will be put together to form a job description. This document outlines the duties that the job involves and states to whom the person will be responsible, i.e. who will be their boss.

3 Design a **job specification**

A job specification outlines in detail the type of person who is required to do the job. It will include the qualifications, experience and personal qualities of the person that are essential and those that are desirable.

4 Advertise the vacancy

The job can now be advertised because the exact job has been decided and the qualifications, experience, etc. have been determined. Where to advertise has to be chosen. If the job is a senior one, which requires many qualifications, then the advert will need to be seen by people who live in different parts of the country or even in other countries. A national newspaper or specialist magazine for the industry will be chosen. If the job is a basic one, which does not require many qualifications or skills, then the advertisement could be placed in a local newspaper because many local people could have the necessary qualifications or skills to do the job.

5 Send out application forms to the applicants or read curriculum vitaes/ resumés and letters of application

People will apply for the job by sending a letter of application and a CV/resumé, or they will request an application form from the business, fill it in and send it back.

6 Produce a **short-list** from the replies of those to interview and take up references

From the applications for the job, a short-list will be produced of those best matching the employer's requirements. References might be requested for those people to be interviewed. (If an applicant is to be offered the job subject to suitable references, these will be sought at stage 8.)

7 Hold **interviews and selection tasks**

Interviews will be held. These can also include other selection tasks, for example, written tests, practical tests, delivering a presentation on a pre-determined topic.

8 Select suitable applicant and offer them the job. Reply to unsuccessful applicants

The most suitable person for the job is chosen. A letter is sent formally offering them the job. Letters are sent to the unsuccessful applicants telling them that they have not got the job but thanking them for their interest in the business.

9 Organise **induction training** for the successful applicant

The successful applicant will need an introduction to the business. This is called induction training (see page 210). The exact induction training that is given will depend on the seniority of the job.

Training

There should be clear objectives for training employees. Training is often needed to:

- introduce a new process or new equipment
- improve the efficiency of the workforce
- provide training for the unskilled workers to make them more valuable to the company
- decrease the supervision needed
- improve the opportunity for internal promotion
- decrease the chances of accidents.

Employees should be clear about the benefits of the training or they will not work hard and take the training seriously.

Training covers many different needs. Some may be short-term, such as one-day courses on how to operate a new machine safely. Others may last a few days and some may be long-term where a programme of management training is involved.

Training is usually trying to either:

- increase skills
- increase knowledge
- change people's attitudes/raise awareness, for example, customer service.

There are three main types of training:

- INDUCTION TRAINING
- ON-THE-JOB TRAINING
- OFF-THE-JOB TRAINING.

Induction training

This is carried out when an employee is new to the post. When a new employee starts at a company, they will not know where anything is or who people are and what is expected of them. The induction programme will last sometimes for a day, sometimes for several days – it depends on the company and the particular job. When a person starts a new school, they are shown round, introduced to teachers and told about their lessons – this is the same type of information you would need to know if you had just joined a new company.

■ **Definitions to learn:**

INDUCTION TRAINING is an introduction given to a new employee, explaining the firm's activities, customs and procedures and introducing them to their fellow workers.

ON-THE-JOB TRAINING occurs by watching a more experienced worker doing the job.

OFF-THE-JOB TRAINING involves being trained away from the workplace, usually by specialist trainers.

■ *Case study example*

The following is an induction programme for a shop assistant.

8.30 a.m.	Introduction
8.45 a.m.	Company history
9.00 a.m.	Company structure
9.30 a.m.	Administration details:
	Company regulations
	Health and safety in the workplace
	Uniform
10.30 a.m.	Break
10.45 a.m.	Workplace:
	Map of the premises showing places of work
	Staffroom
	Staff canteen
	First aid point
	Fire exits
	Human Resources Manager's office
11.45 a.m.	Conditions of employment:
	Rate of pay
	Hours worked
	Sickness and holiday pay
	Pensions
	Trade Unions
	Disciplinary procedures
	Breaks
	Staff purchase/discounts
12.45 p.m.	Training:
	Opportunities
1.00 p.m.	Lunch
1.30 p.m.	Job training:
	Customer service
	Stacking shelves/presentation of shelves
	Pricing goods
	Using bar code reader
	Using tills
	How to deal with difficult customers
	Security
5.00 p.m.	Close

On-the-job training

This is where a person is trained by watching a more experienced worker doing the job. They are shown what to do. This method of training is only suitable for unskilled and semi-skilled jobs. It has the advantage that individual tuition is given and it is in the workplace so the employee does not need to be sent away (travel costs are expensive). The trainee will do some work whilst they are learning what to do, but the trainer will not be as productive as usual because they are showing the trainee what to do instead of getting on with their job. The trainer may have bad habits and they may pass these on to the trainee.

Off-the-job training

This is where the worker goes away from the place where they work. This may be in a different part of the building or it may be at a different place altogether, such as a college or specialist training centre. The techniques used to train workers are more varied and can involve more complex tasks. Off-the-job training often involves classroom learning using lecture, role play, case studies or computer simulations. This may be similar to how you are taught. A broad range of skills can be taught using these techniques. If these courses are taught in the evening after work, they are cheaper for the business because the employee will still carry out their normal duties during the day. The business will only need to pay for the course and it will not also lose the output of the employee.

Employees may be taught a variety of skills, they become multi-skilled and this makes them more versatile. They can be moved around the company when the need arises.

Training is necessary for the success of most businesses. It is a form of investment, but in human capital not physical capital. Investment usually leads to greater output in the future and this is true of employees as well as machinery.

■ *Activity 14.7*

Copy out the table below and fill in the gaps.

Advantages and disadvantages of methods of training

Method of training	Description	Advantages	Disadvantages
Induction training			
On-the-job training			
Off-the-job training			

Revision summary: training

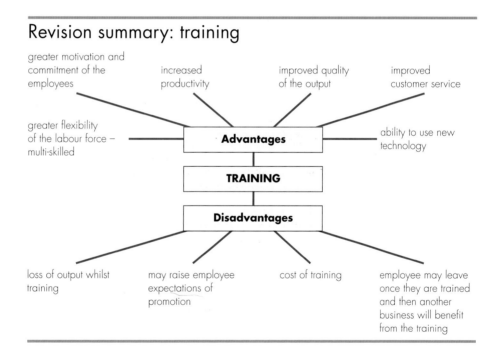

greater motivation and commitment of the employees

increased productivity

improved quality of the output

improved customer service

greater flexibility of the labour force – multi-skilled

Advantages

ability to use new technology

TRAINING

Disadvantages

loss of output whilst training

may raise employee expectations of promotion

cost of training

employee may leave once they are trained and then another business will benefit from the training

■ *Activity 14.8: case study task*

For each of the examples below, decide what type of training would be most appropriate and why.

a) S&S plc have just introduced a new computer program into the accounts offices. All the accounts employees will need to know how to use the new software.

b) Sandeep has been given a job as a trainee manager with a large retail company. The training will last for about two years.

c) James has just got a job as a hotel porter. He has never done this type of job before. He is starting work next week.

Manpower planning

The business will need to decide on the type and number of employees needed in the future. The number required will depend upon the firm's sales forecasts, its future plans such as expansion or automation, and its objectives, for example, introducing new types of products.

When it has been decided how many employees will be required and what their skills need to be, the Human Resources department can plan how this will be achieved by:

- finding out the skills of all the present employees
- counting out anyone who will be leaving soon, for example, due to retirement
- consulting with existing staff as to who could and would want to retrain to fill the new jobs
- preparing a recruitment plan to show how many new staff will be needed and how they should be recruited (internally or externally).

Dismissal and redundancy (retrenchment)

There may be occasions when a business needs to reduce the number of employees. This can be done in one of two ways:

- dismissal
- REDUNDANCY.

■ **Definition to learn:**
REDUNDANCY is when an employee is no longer needed and so loses their job. It is not due to any aspect of their work being unsatisfactory.

Dismissal

This is where a worker is told to leave their job because their work or behaviour is unsatisfactory. For example, an employee who was constantly late for work and who, despite being given warnings, continued to be late, would probably be dismissed. An employee who was caught stealing or who was unable to do the job to a satisfactory standard would be dismissed.

Redundancy

There may be occasions when a business needs to reduce the number of employees, either because it is closing down a branch/factory or because it is experiencing falling sales and profits and so needs to save money by getting rid of some employees. Another possible reason may be that a business has merged or been taken over and some jobs have become surplus to requirements in the newly combined business. Also, if a company has introduced new machinery that does the job of several workers, those workers may no longer be needed. A number of employees will therefore no longer be needed, through no fault of their own.

When an employee is made redundant, they are usually given some money to compensate them for losing their job. In some countries this is laid down in law, for example, one week's wages for every year that the employee has worked for the business. However, there is nothing to stop a business from paying more than the legal minimum and redundancy pay is often agreed with the trade union(s) involved.

If only some of the employees are to be made redundant, the trade unions will normally agree the fairest way to decide who goes. Sometimes this will be by *voluntary redundancy* where some employees will be willing to be made redundant. They are sometimes older workers or those who have other ideas for employment. The terms of the redundancy are usually agreed between the Human Resources department and the trade unions who represent the employees.

■ *Revision questions*

1 State *six* responsibilities of the Human Resources department. [6]

2 Give *three* reasons why a business recruits new employees. [3]

3 Why does a business carry out a job analysis before drawing up a job description? [2]

4 What is the purpose of a job specification? [2]

5 a) What is meant by the phrase 'recruit internally'? (2)
  b) State *one* other method of recruitment. [1]
  c) Explain *one* advantage and *one* disadvantage of internal recruitment. [4]

6 Identify *three* different places a business could advertise if it was recruiting externally. [3]

7 State *four* items that should go on a CV/resumé and explain why the information is needed by the business. [12]

8 State *four* items that should be in an advertisement for a job. [4]

9 A manager is needed for a new shop that is being opened in the city centre. What factors should be considered when selecting a manager for a new shop? [6]

10 Why does a business carry out interviews as part of the process of selecting staff? [2]

11 Name *two* tests that are sometimes also used in the selection process and explain how they help to decide who to recruit. [4]

12 Name *three* types of training that a business may use. [3]

13 What is meant by *induction training* and why is it used? [2]

14 A business is thinking of changing from on-the-job training to off-the-job training. Explain *two* advantages of this change. [2]

15 What is the difference between dismissal and redundancy? [2]

The CD-ROM (see details on page x) provides further tests, activities and Case study work on the topics covered in this unit.

15 Employee and employer associations

■ Definition to learn:

A TRADE UNION is a group of workers who have joined together to ensure their interests are protected.

Some businesses are very small and have very few employees working for them. An example might be a sole trader who owns and runs a small shop. If an employee has a problem, they would probably talk to the owner of the business directly. However, many people are employed by large businesses and it can become more and more difficult to discuss problems with the managers or owners of the business.

Imagine you were the Human Resources Manager for a large chemical company employing 500 people. If these employees had different skills and did different jobs, from a scientist to someone who kept the building clean, how would you agree everyone's wage rate? If a pay rise was going to be given, who would receive the most? Would everyone receive the same pay rise? It is much easier for managers if workers get together and are represented by an employee association, usually called a TRADE UNION. This saves the Human Resources Manager a lot of time by not having to see workers individually to agree their pay.

Employees might not be treated fairly at work. They may be given low wages, forced to work long hours or work in poor conditions. There are often laws passed by governments to protect employees but these vary from country to country. (Laws to protect employees were discussed in Unit 4.) Trade unions also exist to improve the pay, conditions of employment and the working conditions of their members.

Trade unions

Employees generally share many of the same interests, such as improving their pay, having a pleasant environment in which to work, being treated fairly by their employer, being given proper training, working in a safe environment. Forming a trade union is a way of helping employees to achieve improvements in these different aspects of their employment – a trade union is a type of *pressure group*.

Trade unions can be traced back to the Middle Ages, but it was in the nineteenth century in Britain, around the time of the Industrial Revolution, that trade unions as we know them today were developed. Conditions for workers were very harsh in Britain at this time and so workers got together in groups and tried to negotiate with their employers to improve the pay and working conditions of the workers. Any worker who complained risked being dismissed but there was strength in numbers. If all the workers got together and complained, it was much less likely that they would all be sacked.

The first trade unions were for skilled craftsmen. Today CRAFT UNIONS still exist for workers who have undergone lengthy training and are skilled workers, such as electricians and plumbers. Sometime there have been disputes between different craft unions in a workplace as each tried to protect their skilled jobs from being carried out by other workers.

Workers who were unskilled or semi-skilled also wanted to be represented by a union and so these workers formed GENERAL UNIONS. These unions represent many different types of workers who work in many different industries regardless of skill, type or place of work. They tend to have been formed by different unions merging together and they are usually large unions. Because they are so large their leaders can feel out of touch with their members' views. This is especially true because their members tend to be spread over a large number of industries and are located in different parts of the country.

In addition, there are also INDUSTRIAL UNIONS who represent all the workers (skilled, semi-skilled and unskilled) who work in a particular industry. For example, if all the workers who worked for the railways were represented by one trade union, this would be an industrial union. Management like this type of union because they have to deal with only one trade union instead of several. From the workers' point of view, the union tends to be large and therefore has more power to improve conditions of employment.

However, many employees are non-manual workers. These include office workers and those in management and professional occupations. Their unions are called WHITE-COLLAR UNIONS. An example would be a union for civil servants who work for the government.

Today, trade unions are found in many different countries around the world from the USA to Papua New Guinea.

■ **Definitions to learn:**

A CRAFT UNION is a trade union which represents a particular type of skilled worker.

A GENERAL UNION is a trade union which represents workers from a variety of trades and industry. They are often unskilled but also include semi-skilled workers.

An INDUSTRIAL UNION is a trade union which represents all types of workers in a particular industry.

A WHITE-COLLAR UNION is a trade union which represents non-manual workers, for example, office workers, management and professional people.

Revision summary: types of trade union

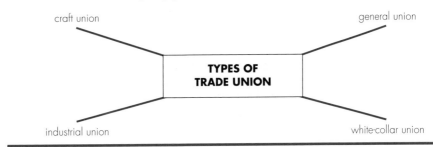

craft union

general union

TYPES OF TRADE UNION

industrial union

white-collar union

■ *Activity 15.1: case study task*

a) Each of the following workers needs to be advised on which type of trade union to join. Decide which trade union would be the best type of union for them to join and explain your choice.

- ■ John is a skilled electrician and works for a large public limited company. He could join a craft union for electricians or a general union. There is no industry union to join.
- ■ Jai works in a small shop and has not had any training.
- ■ Misha works for the government in their taxation office. She has many qualifications and has several people working for her in the department.

b) Carry out some research in the area where you live. Do workers who work in local businesses belong to trade unions? If they do, find out which type of union they are and what benefits they give to their members.

Why do workers join a trade union?

When a person starts work they may be asked by someone who represents a trade union if they want to join. In a factory this will usually be a SHOP STEWARD. If the worker decides to join the trade union, they will pay an annual subscription (a yearly fee). This money can be paid in one lump sum at the beginning of the year or can be taken out of the employee's pay every week or month. Part of this subscription will go towards employing union officials. These officials will represent the views of the union to the employers in a bid to achieve their aims.

So what benefits does the employee receive in exchange for paying their subscription? It varies from union to union, but generally includes many of the following benefits.

■ **Definition to learn:**

A SHOP STEWARD is an unpaid representative of a trade union at factory/office level.

Advantages to an employee of trade union membership

☑ Strength in numbers.
☑ Improved conditions of employment, for example, rates of pay, holidays and hours of work.
☑ Improved environment where people work, for example, health and safety, noise, heating.

☑ Improved benefits for members who are not working because they are sick, retired or have been made redundant (retrenchment).

☑ Improved job satisfaction by encouraging training.

☑ Advice and/or financial support if a member thinks that they have been unfairly dismissed or made redundant (retrenchment), have received unfair treatment, or have been asked to do something that is not part of their job.

☑ Benefits that have been negotiated or provided for union members such as discounts in certain shops, provision of sporting facilities or clubs.

☑ Employment where there is a CLOSED SHOP.

Trade unions also seek to:

■ put forward their views to the media and influence government decisions, for example, minimum wage legislation, employment laws

■ improve communications between workers and management.

Closed shop

In some countries a closed shop may be in operation in certain businesses. A closed shop is where all the employees have to be a member of a particular trade union. To gain employment in these businesses you would have to agree to become a union member. These agreements are made because some employees feel that it is unfair if non-union members gain increases in pay or improved working conditions that the union has achieved for its members. Union members pay their annual subscription and yet non-union members will get the same improvements if they work for the company and pay nothing. Trade unions also have greater strength when negotiating to improve pay or conditions if all the firm's employees are members of the union. However, many people consider that it is unfair that they are forced to join a particular trade union – they feel they should be allowed to make their own choices.

Single-union agreements

Some firms now have a SINGLE-UNION AGREEMENT where the firm deals with only one particular union. Employees who want to join a trade union would join this union. These are becoming increasingly popular today as employees are trained to do several jobs, i.e. are becoming multi-skilled. This makes the employees more flexible and the business can use them in different areas of production as and where needed. It becomes more difficult to know which trade union to join, so a single-union agreement is often more suitable. There are advantages to the employees and the employers in this arrangement.

Advantages to employees of a single-union agreement

☑ There is only one union to negotiate with management – discussions are clearer.

☑ Most employees are in one union and not spread across several unions and therefore have greater power.

■ **Definition to learn:**
A CLOSED SHOP is where all employees must be a member of the same trade union.

■ **Definition to learn:**
A SINGLE-UNION AGREEMENT is when a firm will deal with only one particular trade union and no others.

☑ There are no disagreements between different unions.
☑ A better working relationship should develop between the management and the union.
☑ Disputes are probably solved more quickly as only one union is involved in negotiation.

Advantages to employers of a single-union agreement

☑ There is only one union to negotiate with management – discussions are clearer.
☑ A better working relationship should develop between the management and the union.
☑ Disputes are probably solved more quickly as only one union is involved in negotiation.
☑ It is easier to agree changes to the working conditions and less time is wasted in arguments.
☑ A better relationship between management and employees mean fewer industrial disputes which is better for both employees and employers.

Far Eastern companies, for example Japanese companies, often have single-union agreements with their employees.

■ *Activity 15.2: case study task*

You work in the Human Resources department of a large company. The company wants to introduce a single-union agreement. You have been asked by your Managing Director to write an article for the company magazine explaining what is meant by a single-union agreement and why it will be a good move for the employees as well as the company.

(You could include your own examples of companies that have adopted single-union agreements if you know of any.)

Revision summary: benefits of joining a trade union

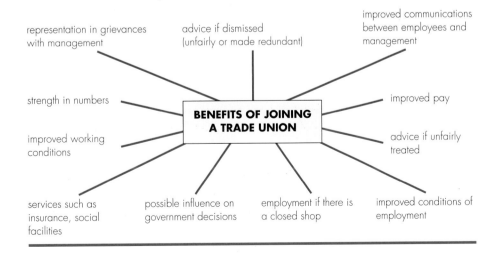

representation in grievances with management

advice if dismissed (unfairly or made redundant)

improved communications between employees and management

strength in numbers

BENEFITS OF JOINING A TRADE UNION

improved pay

improved working conditions

advice if unfairly treated

services such as insurance, social facilities

possible influence on government decisions

employment if there is a closed shop

improved conditions of employment

■ *Activity 15.3: case study task*

Shona has just started work as an Administrative Assistant in a government department and has been asked if she wants to join the trade union that represents the workers in that business. She does not know what to do as she knows nothing about trade unions. Write her a letter outlining the advantages and disadvantages of joining a trade union. Include a recommendation to Shona as to whether to join the trade union or not.

The structure of a trade union

This varies widely but generally a President or General Secretary will be elected and they will work full-time for, and be paid by, the trade union. They will work at the headquarters of the union.

If the union is large, it may have full-time officials working in each district or region. These people will support and help members in the branches.

The branches of a union are often at each work site, i.e. factory or offices, or based in the local region if the members do not all work for the same employer. The branches will have a shop steward or a union representative, as they are sometimes called. Unions are usually democratic and all the officials (people working for the union) will have been elected to their position by the union members. Shop stewards are often given paid time off work to carry out their union duties. Managers can find it helpful to have shop stewards because they have someone through whom to work when dealing with the employees. In large factories, the shop stewards may elect someone to represent them – this person is called a *convenor*.

Revision summary: the structure of a trade union

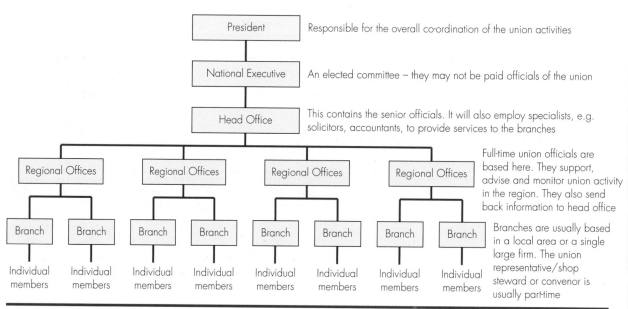

Employer associations

Many industries in different countries have EMPLOYER ASSOCIATIONS, EMPLOYER FEDERATIONS or TRADE ASSOCIATIONS. Businesses join together to form their own association or federation. Their members pay an annual subscription and in return they will receive benefits.

Advantages of joining an employer association

- ☑ They represent employers and negotiate with the trade unions on behalf of their members.
- ☑ They give advice to members on issues such as employment law, the effects of trade agreements, health and safety regulations, and taxation laws.
- ☑ They act as a pressure group and have greater strength, because they are a large group, to put arguments to government when changes are requested (one small business alone would be ignored by government).
- ☑ Sometimes these organisations share ideas and they will help each other, usually when they are not in direct competition or in different sectors of the market. They may share research facilities when one small firm alone could not afford to do this research.
- ☑ They sometimes organise bulk buying for their members and can therefore obtain a discount on the goods purchased.

Employer associations act as pressure groups on the government to try to influence their policies. They represent business interests and therefore want the government to create an economic environment which will allow their businesses to prosper.

- ■ They will want the government to keep control of the economy in such matters as inflation, to provide services such as law and order, health and education for the workforce.
- ■ Taxation should not be too much of a burden on business.
- ■ Rules and regulations on business should not be too great.
- ■ Economic policies should ensure fair competition between firms.
- ■ There should be a good transport infrastructure (roads, ports, rail, bridges), access to overseas markets and reliable sources of power.

■ *Activity 15.4: case study task*

Paul owns a small factory which produces wooden furniture. He finds it very difficult to buy his raw materials at low prices. He also has problems selling the furniture. Most of his output is sold to a large company that exports the furniture overseas. In the area where he lives, there are many furniture producers and they are in a similar position to himself. He thinks it would be a good idea if all the small furniture producers in the local area got together to form a trade association.

Prepare a letter for Paul to send out to all these other small businesses in the area outlining the advantages and disadvantages of them joining together and asking them to attend a meeting to discuss the matter further.

Collective bargaining

As mentioned earlier, it is not feasible or economic to NEGOTIATE with each worker separately, when discussing issues such as improvements in pay and conditions. Therefore agreements are made between representatives of the different interested groups and a 'collective' agreement is made. This is called COLLECTIVE BARGAINING.

The bargaining can take place on a local or national level. The relevant parties get together, usually the trade union(s) and employers or employers' associations, and discuss the particular issue. They discuss the problem and negotiate an agreement, for example, about a pay increase or to improve particular working conditions.

Trade unions usually argue for a wage increase for one of the following reasons.

- Prices have been rising (inflation) and their members need more money to keep their present standard of living.
- It is difficult to recruit qualified workers and a pay rise is necessary to attract the right sort of people.
- Pay differentials need to be maintained. There will be distinct differences between the wage rates of different skilled, unskilled and semi-skilled workers, and also between public and private sector employees.
- If there have been changes in the workplace, such as the introduction of new machinery, the unions may argue that the workers need to be compensated for the changes.
- If there have been increases in workers' productivity, the unions will argue that the workers should get their fair share of the increase. Increased productivity means that the employees will be producing a larger output in the same time as before (see page 326). Sometimes the management will link increases in pay to increases in productivity as a way of motivating the workers to work harder. These are called PRODUCTIVITY AGREEMENTS.

If the discussions are about a pay increase then both sides often start off at a position higher (trade union) or lower (employer) than they are willing to settle at. This is like bartering in the street over the price of a product for sale. The person interested in buying offers a low price for the item and the seller asks a high price. Discussion and negotiation takes place and a price somewhere in the middle may be agreed and the item purchased. In the case of pay, the employees will start at a high rate and are usually willing to come down a little, whereas the employers will start off at a low pay increase, but if necessary will be willing to increase their offer a little. If the two sides are not too far apart in the beginning, they will meet in the middle and there will be a negotiated settlement or agreement. Both sides are happy and they both feel they have gained something.

However, this does not always happen. If the two sides are far apart over an issue then negotiations may break down. The workers may take INDUSTRIAL ACTION to try to force the employers to agree to their demands.

Definitions to learn:

NEGOTIATION is another name for collective bargaining. It is when there is joint decision-making involving bargaining between representatives of the management and of the workforce within a firm. The aim is to arrive at a mutually acceptable agreement.

COLLECTIVE BARGAINING is negotiations between one or more trade unions and one or more employers (or employers' associations) on pay and conditions of employment.

Definitions to learn:

A PRODUCTIVITY AGREEMENT is where workers and management agree an increase in benefits, in return for an increase in productivity.

INDUSTRIAL ACTION is action taken by the trade unions to decrease or halt production.

Industrial action

Industrial action can take various forms and differs from industry to industry, firm to firm and country to country. It may take at least one of the following forms.

Strike action

STRIKE action may take the form of:

- *a token strike* – a short stoppage of half a day, one day or even an hour to indicate the strength of feeling about the claim
- *a selective strike* – only a few selected workers walk out; these will be chosen by the trade union in order to cause a lot of disruption to the workplace
- *an all out strike* – all members of the union stop working and leave the workplace until the dispute or claim is settled.

Workers may be paid out of the trade union's strike fund if the strike is official, i.e. it has the backing and agreement of the trade union. If it is an unofficial strike, sometimes called a 'wild-cat strike', strike pay will not be paid. If strike action is called by the trade union, then the members are sometimes sent a ballot paper on which they can vote whether they want to strike. Alternatively, a meeting may be called where members vote on whether they want to strike or not. If the majority of workers are in favour of the strike, all the trade union members should go out on strike. However, some may carry on working because they disagree with the strike or they may not be able to afford to go without wages.

Picketing

PICKETING is carried out to support strike action. Workers, who are on strike, stand outside the factory gates and try to persuade the other workers not to go in to work. If they are successful then production at the factory may be halted altogether. The strikers gain publicity for their grievances and can give the firm a bad image. This puts pressure on the firm to settle the dispute.

■ **Definition to learn:**
A STRIKE is when employees refuse to work.

■ **Definition to learn:**
PICKETING is when employees who are taking industrial action stand outside their place of work to prevent or protest at the delivery of goods, arrival and departure of other employees, etc.

■ **Definition to learn:**

A WORK TO RULE is when rules are strictly obeyed so that work is slowed down.

Work to rule

In a WORK TO RULE, workers stick rigidly to the rules and regulations laid down by the company. For example, there may be several checks that should be made to a delivery lorry before it goes out on delivery. All these checks may take a very long time and therefore some checks will normally not be carried out every time the lorry goes out. If the employees want to slow down the amount of work done, they could stick rigidly to the rule book and carry out all the checks necessary every time the lorry goes out. Workers still get paid their normal wages or salaries as they are doing nothing wrong while working to rule, but it causes a lot of disruption to the business.

■ **Definitions to learn:**

A GO SLOW is when employees do their normal tasks but more slowly than usual.

NON-COOPERATION is when employees refuse to comply with new working practices.

An OVERTIME BAN is when employees refuse to work longer than their normal working hours.

Go slow

A GO SLOW is similar to a work to rule. This is where employees do their job more slowly. They deliberately take longer to complete their normal tasks.

Non-cooperation

NON-COOPERATION is when workers refuse to have anything to do with new working practices which they do not approve of. For example, a new administration procedure may involve the workers filling in more paperwork. They would refuse to fill in the new forms.

Overtime ban

An OVERTIME BAN is when trade union members only carry out their normal duties in the normal hours of work. They will not carry out additional work after hours. It can be very damaging for a company if it needs to complete an order quickly, if workers are not willing to remain behind after normal hours and work until the order is finished. Workers still receive their normal pay but not any overtime earnings.

Possible harmful consequences of industrial action

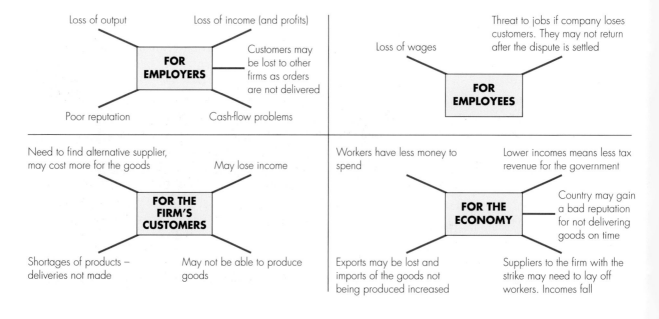

Definitions to learn:

A NO-STRIKE AGREEMENT is reached when trade unions and management agree to have pay disputes settled by an independent ARBITRATOR instead of taking strike action.

An ARBITRATOR listens to both sides in the industrial dispute (trade union and management) and then gives a ruling on what they think is fair to both sides.

In a LOCK-OUT employees are locked out of their workplace by the employers.

Because strikes are so damaging to both employers and employees there are now more and more examples of trade unions and management signing NO-STRIKE AGREEMENTS. These agreements usually involve pay rises being determined by an independent ARBITRATOR. The independent arbitrator is rather like a judge, who hears both sides of the argument (for what the pay rise should be). For example, the trade union may say it wants an increase of €2.00 per hour, whilst the management offers an increase of €1.00 per hour. The arbitrator may decide that €1.50 is fair. Both sides have agreed to accept the decision of the arbitrator. Some trade unions see this as the way forward in the future as managers and trade unions work more closely together. However, others disagree.

The main weapons an employer has are:

■ to dismiss the workers – this is drastic action and would leave the business in rather a mess; it would probably be unable to produce anything and it would not be able to satisfy any orders for goods
■ to lock the workers out of the workplace (a LOCK-OUT) or to prevent any who want to come back to work (and be paid) from doing so. This may be useful if the workers are working to rule or are going slow – the employer will save on wages by not paying them
■ to institute a pay freeze – used if there are disagreements over work practices, for example, when new machinery is introduced.

■ *Activity 15.5: case study task*

a) In each of the situations below, collective bargaining is being carried out but negotiations have broken down. For each situation, advise the trade union on the form of industrial action it should take and give reasons why you think it will be the most effective action to take. Also consider what the employer might do.

■ C&C plc has offered its workers a 2 per cent wage increase. The trade union has asked for 20 per cent. They have asked for a large pay rise because over the last year inflation has been at 12 per cent. Workers are finding that they cannot afford to buy as many goods now, as everything is more expensive. There have been negotiations for several weeks and the employers have not been willing to offer more than the original 2 per cent.
■ The employees at Spartacus Sports plc have been working more efficiently due to new working practices and output has recently increased. The employees want to be rewarded for their extra efficiency with a wage rise but the manager has refused to grant them one.
■ TTS Bank employs several office workers at their head office. When the office is very busy, the secretaries take home unfinished work and complete it in the evening, or some stay late in the office to finish off. They are paid a salary and do not receive any overtime pay. The union which represents these secretarial staff has asked the managers at the bank to reward the extra work undertaken. The management are not prepared to do this. They say that the secretaries should be able to complete the work in their normal hours. The secretaries are very unhappy about these comments.

b) Look in newspapers for reports of industrial disputes. Find out what the disputes are about and whether they have been settled yet. What forms of industrial action were taken?

All forms of industrial action are designed to put pressure on one party in the negotiation to give in to the demands of the other party. In the end, some middle way may be found, or else one party may have to compromise because the other party is in a stronger position and refuses to give in. Successful negotiations usually involve a compromise on both sides – the compromise being satisfactory to both sides but not necessarily what either of them wanted.

Conflict in business organisations

Conflict in an organisation will certainly make it less efficient and may even result in a complete halt in production. Strike action is an extreme example of conflict but there are other indicators of conflict existing in an organisation. Factors like the levels of absenteeism amongst employees, labour turnover (the percentage of the employees leaving each year), the number of rejects produced, even customer complaints are indicators of possible conflict. It is one of the functions of management to find ways of avoiding these conflicts.

To help to avoid conflict building up and causing problems for the business, formal grievance and dispute procedures should be adopted. However, although these procedures help to avoid conflict, the real sources of conflict might still exist.

Examples of the sources of conflict include:

■ poor wage rates, poor conditions of employment and poor working conditions
■ rigid and authoritarian management where orders are issued and those at the bottom of the chain of command tend not to know what is happening. This can cause problems to build up as people become frustrated (authoritarian leadership as discussed in Unit 13, *Motivation at work*)
■ rapid change or poorly planned change in the business, where employees find themselves downgraded or moved from one position to another without consultation
■ lack of involvement in the decision-making process. If employees do not feel their contribution to the business is important, they can get bored and feel alienated. They will not care about the business as it doesn't care about them
■ decline in the business' market share. This may cause employees to worry about losing their jobs.

Until workers get fair rates of pay, conflicts will continue to exist. However, it must be recognised that what counts as a fair wage will vary from country to country. The average wage rates in developed countries are very different to those in developing countries. Union membership is growing quite fast worldwide (although it is falling in some countries) and this is vital if there are to be changes in the balance between rich and poor in some countries in the world, to produce more equal societies.

■ *Activity 15.6: case study task*

T & G plc is an insurance company. It has seen its profits fall slightly each year over the last three years. The management have decided to reorganise the departments and downgrade some of the jobs (i.e. put them on to lower pay scales) to save money on wages. These changes have just been announced to the employees and they have had no chance to discuss them. Some of the employees will have their salaries reduced and their job descriptions changed. The employees are not happy!

a) Why has conflict arisen in this situation?
b) What could the workers and the employer do to resolve the conflict?

Consultation

This is where employees' views are asked for when a decision that will affect them is going to be made. The people responsible for taking the decision will listen to the employees' views, but they do not have to do what the employees want and it is not essential that the employees agree with the final decision as to what course of action will be taken.

Consultation is different from collective bargaining or negotiation in that managers do not usually seek the formal agreement of employees; they simply ask for their views and may or may not take these into account in making the decision.

Worker participation

The management need to get everyone feeling a part of the business and a way of doing this is by WORKER PARTICIPATION – the involvement of employees in the decision-making process. This can take various forms, both formal and informal.

- *Worker directors* can be appointed, but they are not usually allowed to attend all board meetings.
- WORKS COUNCILS are where representatives of the workforce get together and discuss proposals by the managers and then put forward their ideas and comments. Issues such as health and safety and the introduction of new machinery are typical items for discussion. Works councils, or European committees, will be used increasingly in European Union countries in the future – multinational firms employing at least 1,000 employees or at least 100 workers at branches in two or more European countries have to set up a works council, or European committee. They are to be informed or consulted on any matters that affect the interests of the employees.
- *Quality circles* are used by many companies, especially Japanese companies, to encourage continuous improvement in the product. This involves the employees working in teams and meeting regularly to discuss improvements that could be made in the ways jobs are carried

■ **Definitions to learn:**

WORKER PARTICIPATION occurs when employees contribute to decision-making in the business.

WORKS COUNCILS are committees of workers who are consulted or informed on matters that affect employees.

out or the product is assembled. This will also improve the employees' feeling of being part of the company and being able to voice their opinions.

■ More *democratic styles of leadership* (this was discussed in Unit 13). In offices more decisions could be delegated to individual departments. They could be responsible for running their own areas of work as teams and discuss what needs to be done. Everyone will feel that they can contribute to the success of the business.

Advantages of worker participation

✓ It increases the flow of information and therefore improves relations between employer and employees.

✓ It increases motivation as workers feel more involved and committed to the company.

✓ There is increased satisfaction for the workers and for the company as it makes use of the knowledge and experience of the employees.

Disadvantages of worker participation

✗ It is very time-consuming.

✗ The workers may lack the necessary technical knowledge.

✗ If the representation is via the trade unions, non-union members will lose out.

✗ There could possibly be a conflict of interest on some occasions when decisions that may be good for the company, such as increased mechanisation or changes to work practices, may be bad for the employees.

■ *Activity 15.7: case study task*

K & H plc is a large private company that produces computer components. The computer components industry is very competitive. The company quite often changes its products and this involves the workers having to undertake different jobs and sometimes also change their working hours to fit in with new production procedures. The employees do not like the frequent changes and complain that they just get changed around without being told in advance. Staff turnover is high – people frequently leave because they feel unhappy and do not feel a valued part of the company. There are also frequent disputes between the employees and the management and industrial action is quite often used.

It has been suggested that one way of improving this situation would be to introduce worker participation. You have been asked to prepare a report for the Board of Directors of K & H plc advising them of the advantages and disadvantages of worker participation. Also include a consideration of how it might be introduced and make a recommendation to the Board as to whether they should go ahead with the introduction of worker participation or not.

(You may want to carry out additional research to find examples of ways employees are involved in, or consulted about, the decisions made by the business. *Include these examples in your report.*)

Major UK organisations involved in industrial relations

Trades Union Congress (TUC)

In some countries trade unions got together and formed a single group to represent trade union aims in general. In the UK it is called the Trades Union Congress (TUC). It has full-time employees, administrators, economists and solicitors. It is made up of representatives from all the trade unions who are its members and it meets at regular intervals during the year. It is more powerful than just a single union on its own.
Its aims are to:

■ act as a pressure group
■ represent trade union views in general
■ influence employers' associations
■ influence government policy, e.g. over the level of a minimum wage.

Confederation of British Industry (CBI)

In the UK there is an organisation called the Confederation of British Industry (CBI) that represents many UK industries. It represents industry in rather the same way as the TUC represents trade unions. Their aims are similar to those of the TUC in that they:

■ act as a pressure group
■ represent employers
■ try to influence government decisions.

Advisory, Conciliation and Arbitration Service (ACAS)

In some countries there are special organisations whose job it is to help an agreement to be reached when negotiations in industrial disputes break down. In the UK this organisation is called the Advisory, Conciliation and Arbitration Service (ACAS). This is an independent body which is financed by the government and has the role of trying to improve industrial relations. It provides its services free and it is impartial. If a dispute goes 'to arbitration' then both sides must agree to abide by the rulings of ACAS. The service provides:

■ *advice and information* on all areas of employment to both employees and employers
■ *conciliation* – ACAS talks to both sides in a dispute to try to find areas on which both sides can agree. This will allow both sides in a dispute to start negotiating again if discussions have broken down
■ *arbitration* – if a dispute has reached a position where there is deadlock and neither side will agree on a settlement, they may go to arbitration. ACAS arranges for an independent group to listen to both sides in the dispute and to propose what they think is a fair settlement. Both sides must agree in advance to accept the arbitrator's findings.

■ *Revision questions*

1 What is meant by a trade union? [2]

2 Name *four* different types of trade union. [4]

3 Why do employees join a trade union? [4]

4 What is meant by a single union agreement? [2]

5 What are the benefits of a single union agreement to:
a) employees?
b) employers? [8]

6 Why do businesses join employer associations? [4]

7 Why do businesses negotiate with their employees over pay and conditions? [4]

8 What is a productivity agreement? [3]

9 Name and describe *four* types of industrial action and say why they might be effective. [12]

10 Give *two* examples of why conflicts might arise in a business. [2]

11 How may conflicts within a business be avoided? [3]

12 L & B plc want to invest in new technology which will reduce the number of employees.
a) What problems might the company have with their employees if they go ahead with their plans? [6]
b) How could they deal with these problems? [6]

The CD-ROM (see details on page x) provides further tests, activities and Case study work on the topics covered in this unit.

16 The market and marketing

What is a market?

■ **Definition to learn:**

A MARKET is where buyers and sellers come together to exchange products for money; this will not usually be a single location.

You may think of a MARKET as a place outside in the open air, where you can go and buy things from stall holders. This is the oldest form of a market but only one type of market.

The term 'market' is used to describe all the people to whom products are sold and this may not involve face-to-face selling. It may include, for example, buying products over the telephone, purchasing products in shops, ordering on the internet, or ordering by post. To have a market for a product, buyers and sellers simply have to be brought together in some way to exchange products for money. For example, the market for computers will cover many different customers, both domestic consumers and business users. Computers will be sold in many different countries and through many different shops or ordered by post or telephone in response to adverts in magazines or newspapers.

In Units 16–22, products will be discussed. The term 'product' includes providing a service for the customers. Services need to be marketed but sometimes in a different way to physical goods. However, the principles are the same. To simplify the discussion in these marketing chapters, 'product' will be used to mean both goods and services.

■ Activity 16.1

a) *Coca-Cola* has a very large market. List all the different types of shop and any other places you can think of where it is sold. Try to include examples from other countries as well as your own country. What type of people drink *Coca-Cola*?

b) Suggest a local product that does not have a large market. Why do you think it is not sold to many people?

Product-orientated and market-orientated businesses

Some businesses produce the product first and then try to find a market for it. This is known as being PRODUCT-ORIENTATED. This is not common today. Product-orientated businesses often produce basic necessities required for living, such as agricultural tools or fresh foods. These products may not have their own name or brand (brand names will be discussed later in this unit) and are general products that consumers need to buy. The manufacturer and retailer are mainly concerned with price and quality of the product. Sometimes when new technologies are being developed, this is done without first investigating possible markets. People may not want this product until it has been developed and advertising has persuaded them to buy it.

Businesses whose markets are national or international cannot afford to produce products and hope that they will sell, without first carrying out MARKET RESEARCH (see Unit 17) to find out if the consumers will want the product. This is called being MARKET-ORIENTATED and it means that the business must have a MARKETING BUDGET. The businesses have to identify the wants and desires of customers, both now and in the future, in order to produce the right goods which will sell well and make a good profit for the business.

Market-orientated businesses are better able to survive and be successful because they are usually more prepared for changes in customer tastes. They are able to take advantage of new market opportunities which may arise. New products are launched with more confidence when customer needs have already been identified, *before* the product is introduced on to the market.

What is marketing?

MARKETING is not just advertising, promotion and selling. Marketing actually covers many more activities that are carried out by businesses. It includes the development of a product, finding out what sort of customers might buy the product, what packaging should be used, what price should be charged, where it should be sold, as well as the advertising and promotion that should be used. All of these marketing activities will be discussed in this and the following units.

■ *Activity 16.2: case study task*

Joshua invents a new tool for planting seeds. It is much easier to use than existing tools. However, it has high manufacturing costs, twice as much as existing tools.

a) Is Joshua's business product-orientated or market-orientated? Give reasons for your answer.
b) What would you advise Joshua to do before he starts to manufacture the new tool? Explain your answer.

Businesses can make products and hope that they will sell but this is very risky. Marketing usually means going out and *finding out what consumer requirements are*, because if they do not satisfy customers' needs, they will be unlikely to sell many of their products. To do this, the Marketing department will carry out market research (see Unit 17).

To be successful, the Marketing department also has to *predict future consumer requirements*. Again, this is identified by market research. The Marketing department will have to look at the market research information and try to predict what consumers might want to buy. This is often based on past trends. An example of this is the toy market – manufacturers must try to predict which toys they think children will want. There have been many trends in children's toys, often based on successful television programmes or books. The Marketing department have to anticipate which programmes will be popular and which will not be popular and therefore which toys will sell well.

Once the consumer requirements have been identified, these customer needs must be met by new products being developed or changes to existing products. If this is not carried out successfully, the business will not sell many products.

Revision summary: the function of marketing

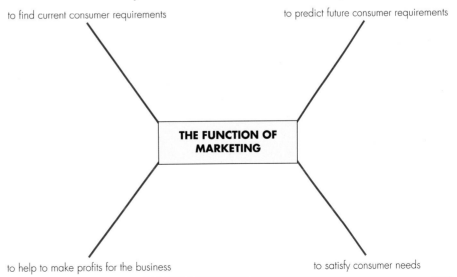

to find current consumer requirements

to predict future consumer requirements

THE FUNCTION OF MARKETING

to help to make profits for the business

to satisfy consumer needs

The Marketing department

Most businesses, unless they are very small, will have a Marketing department. In a large public limited company, the Marketing Director will have people responsible for research and development of new products, promotion (including promotions and advertising), distribution, pricing and sales. An example is shown below.

The structure of a typical Marketing department

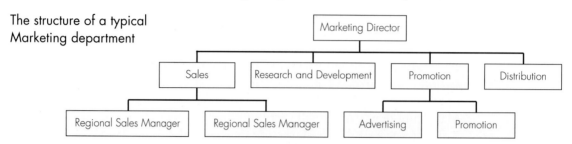

The bigger the company, the more people will be employed in the Marketing department and the more sections there are likely to be.

■ The *Sales department* is responsible for the sales of the product. It will usually have separate sections for each region to which the product is distributed. If the product is exported, there may also be an Export department.

■ The *Research and Development department* is usually responsible for market research and testing new products to see if they might be suitable to start selling to consumers. Existing products are also researched to see if they can be improved in order to remain popular.

■ The *Promotion department* deals with organising the advertising for products. It arranges for advertisements to be produced. For example, adverts are filmed if they are to be on television, or designed if they are to be in newspapers. The department also decides on the types of promotion that will be included in campaigns. It will have a marketing budget – a fixed amount of money to spend. It has to decide which types of advertising media will be the most effective to use because there will only be a certain amount to spend; the department cannot spend what it likes!

■ The *Distribution department* transports the products to the market.

■ Activity 16.3

In which department – Sales, Research and Development, Promotion or Distribution – do each of the following people work?

a) Anya spends most of her time in other countries showing the product to people who buy stock for large retail groups.

b) Mohamed spends his time arranging for adverts of the product to be placed in newspapers and magazines.

c) Paul spends his time producing new products.

d) Mary organises the airline flights for the products to be sent to their markets abroad.

The objectives of marketing

If the Marketing department is successful in identifying customer requirements and predicting future customer needs, it should enable the business to meet one of the following objectives, i.e. what the business is trying to achieve.

■ To increase sales revenue and profitability
■ To increase or maintain market share
■ To maintain or improve the image of products or a business
■ To target a new market or market segment
■ To develop new products or improve existing products.

Increasing sales revenue and therefore profits is the most obvious objective for a Marketing department. It will also want to maintain its current share of the market, especially if the market is very competitive, or may even be trying to increase its share.

■ *Case study example*

A fizzy drinks manufacturer has 60 per cent of the market and wants to expand its operation and increase its share of the market still further. The Marketing department will be vital in deciding how this can be achieved. Will it need to develop new varieties of fizzy drinks? Who will its new customers be? What advertising and promotions will be effective? These are the questions it will need to answer, if it is to be successful.

A business will have to take action to maintain its market share whenever there is growth amongst its competitors. This may also be necessary if the image of the business has been harmed by bad publicity in the newspapers or on television, for example, if a particular toy doll had harmed a child. Then the business will need to find ways to convince customers that the problem has been corrected. If it does not, then the sales revenue and profits would obviously go down. Improving or maintaining image is an important factor in improving or maintaining market share.

■ *Case study example*

Pepsi have been trying to increase their market share against *Coca-Cola*. To do this their advertising has focused on young people. They have created an image of people who are lively, energetic and adventurous being associated with drinking *Pepsi*.

A business might want to sell its products in new markets. These could be markets in other countries or they could be different markets in their own country.

■ Case study example

A chocolate bar manufacturer, well-known for its original advertisement with cartoon characters aimed at children, might want to try to sell chocolate bars aimed at adults. They try to sell to different parts of the market in order to increase total sales.

In order to remain successful, a business may need to keep improving its existing product. This is especially true if its competitors improve their products. Businesses also may need to bring out new products to keep the customers' interest in their company rather than their competitors. This will help them to keep, or even increase, their market share. An example of this would be Microsoft which keeps on improving and developing its operating systems.

■ Activity 16.4: case study task

S&S plc is a large company that sells computers in many different countries. They have been using an advert in one particular country that shows an old woman using their computer and looking very happy. (The people who buy the computers in this country are mainly businessmen.)
What do you think might be the marketing objective of this company? Explain your answer.

SWOT analysis

This is a technique used to help the Marketing department to assess a product. It is a way of assessing the strengths, weaknesses, opportunities and threats (SWOT) of the product. It can also be applied to the business as a whole.

To carry out a SWOT analysis, four boxes are drawn up. The top two boxes, strengths and weaknesses, relate to the actual position of the product and are internal factors, while the bottom two boxes, opportunities and threats, relate to the product's future potential and are external to the business.

For example – a SWOT analysis for a chocolate bar:

Strengths	Weaknesses
■ good brand image ■ sales in the home market are rising	■ necessary updates to production equipment would mean production costs will rise
Opportunities	**Threats**
■ could sell in new markets abroad ■ could merge with a competitor to increase market share	■ foreign chocolate producers are very competitive

■ *Activity 16.5*

Carry out a SWOT analysis on a product of your choice.

Market segments

MARKET SEGMENTATION is when a market is broken down into sub-groups which share similar characteristics. For example, chocolates are eaten by young children, teenagers and adults of both sexes. Different brands of chocolates will appeal to these different groups of people. The marketing people divide the whole market into different groups and categories, these are called *market segments.*

Each segment is investigated in great detail. When it comes to advertising, the marketing people know the best places to advertise and the most likely place the particular market segment will see the advertisement. They will also know how to design the advertisement to appeal to the particular market segment they are aiming at. An example might be teenagers buying pop music. They might be asked questions about which magazines they read, which television programmes they watch and general questions about what they like. This will enable the Marketing department to select the best times to advertise, if television advertisements are to be used, and the type of adverts that will appeal to teenagers. They can advertise in magazines that are usually read by teenagers.

Here are some of the most common ways a market can be segmented.

■ *By income group* Income groups can be defined by grouping people's jobs according to how much they are paid. For example, managers are usually paid more than office staff. Office staff are usually paid more than production workers. Unemployed people will obviously be the lowest income groups. This often means that products are priced differently to target certain income groups. If the product is aimed to appeal to people on a high income, the price might be set high to emphasise that this is a luxury product. If the product is aimed to appeal to people on very low incomes, its price has to be low or they will not be able to buy it.

- *By age* The products bought by people in different age groups will not be the same. Young people buy different products to adults. The products bought for babies will vary from those bought by old people. Age grouping is a very common way to segment a market.
- *By region* In different regions of a country people might buy different products. For example, if there are dry and wet parts of the country then waterproof clothing would be sold in the rainy part of the country but not in the dry part. If the product is exported then it may need to be changed slightly (for example, a different name or different packaging) in order to appeal to the tastes of people in other countries.
- *By gender* Some products are bought only by women or only by men. For example, a shaving razor would normally be bought by a man, whereas perfume would normally be bought by a woman. In some cases, products are bought by both sexes but the advertising is aimed at just males or females – car adverts are often used in this way.
- *By use of the product* For example, cars can be used by consumers for domestic use or for business use. The advertising media and promotions methods used will differ. Cars for business use may be advertised by sending brochures out to the businesses, whereas cars for domestic use may be advertised on television. These cars may be the same models, but they will be marketed in a different way.
- *By lifestyle* For example, a single person earning the same income as a married person with three children will spend that income differently, buying different products.

A marketing person would take all these factors into account when deciding which segments might buy new products or improved products. Therefore, once the segments have been identified, this will influence how they package and advertise the product. It will also affect the choice of shops they sell the products in, in order to get maximum sales and therefore make maximum profits.

The business can use market segmentation to sell more products. They do this by making different brands of a product and then aiming it at different market segments. As can be seen in the example of soap on page 241, a business could produce various brands of soap to satisfy most of the market segments. Customers will be happy with a brand that meets their needs and the business will have made more sales.

By finding out the different segments in a market, a business can sometimes identify a segment whose needs are not being met, i.e. there is a *gap in the market*. They can then produce a suitable product to meet these customer needs and again increase sales. They need to identify this gap before a competitor can find it.

■ *Case study example*

This is an example of how the market for soap may be segmented.

Type of soap	Characteristics of market segment
Beauty soap	People who buy beauty soap will be people who want to keep their skin soft and therefore buy soap which contains moisturisers. This will be bought mainly by women.
Baby soap	This is mild soap which will not harm a baby's skin. Bought mainly by mothers for their babies.
Medicated soap	Sometimes soap is sold to help fight acne. This tends to be bought mainly by teenagers, both male and female.
Non-branded soap	This is an economy product which is plain soap with no extra perfume added. This will probably be bought by people on low incomes.

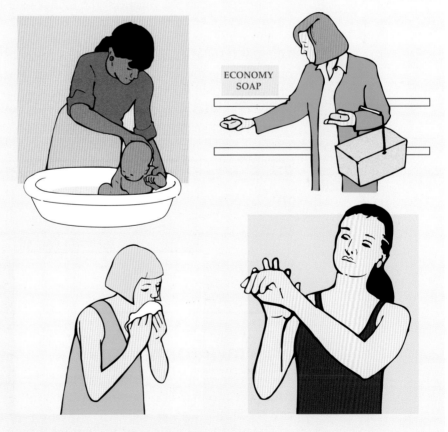

There may be other types of soap you can think of which are aimed at different groups. Sales of soap will be affected by income groups, gender and also age.

■ *Case study example*

A market could be segmented by social groups. Social groups are based on the job of the head of the household, and this gives an idea of how much income the household receives, as shown in the table below.

Social group	Job description
A	Higher managerial, administrative, professional
B	Intermediate managerial, administrative and professional
C1	Supervisory or clerical and junior managerial, administrative and professional
C2	Skilled manual
D	Semi-skilled and unskilled manual
E	Casual labourers, state pensioners and the unemployed

Social groups A, B and C1 are office-type jobs. Depending on how senior you are in the business, the higher your income and therefore the higher the social group. A manager of a small shop may be in group C1, whereas the senior manager of an airline would be in social group A. Groups C2 and D are jobs that are manual, i.e. physical labour. These people generally get paid less money than groups A and B, but may not always get paid less than C1, hence the C grade is split into office-type jobs and factory-type jobs even though the pay may be the same. Grade E is for people who are not working or low-paid temporary workers.

Revision summary: ways of segmenting markets

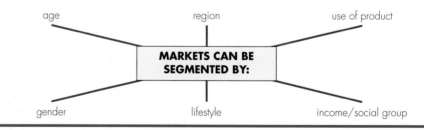

The marketing mix

The *marketing mix* is a term which is used to describe all the activities which go into marketing a product (remember that this includes goods and services).

The producer might need to find out through market research what customers want from the product, then they may change the product to produce what consumers want. Once this is achieved, the producer has to convince the consumers that their product is the one that they want and that it meets their needs better than any of their competitors' products. Producers do this by *branding* their product. This involves giving a product a unique name and packaging. It is then advertised to make consumers believe that it is different to any of the competitors' brands. The product also has to be sold in places that reinforce the *brand image* (see Unit 19).

All of these activities are part of the *marketing mix* for a product. They are often summarised as the four Ps.

- *Product* This applies to the product itself, i.e. its design and quality. How does the product compare with its competitors' products? What is the packaging like? (See Unit 19.)
- *Price* This is the price at which it is sold. A comparison must be made with the prices of competitors' products. Price should, in the long run, cover costs. (See Unit 20.)
- *Promotion* This is how the product is advertised and promoted. What types of advertising media will be used? It includes discounts that may be offered or any other types of sales promotion, such as money-off vouchers or free gifts. (See Unit 21.)
- *Place* This refers to the channels of distribution that are selected. That is, what method of getting the products to the market are to be used? Will the manufacturer sell their products to shops who sell to the public, or to wholesalers, or direct to the customers? (See Unit 22.)

Some people also talk about packaging as being a fifth P, but it can be included as part of both product and promotion.

Each part of the marketing mix has to be considered carefully to make sure that it all fits together and one part does not counteract the other. For example, a high-priced perfume should be wrapped in expensive-looking packaging, and advertised by glamorous women, but then it should not be sold in small food stores. The 'Place' would not fit in with the other parts of the marketing mix.

Revision summary: the marketing mix

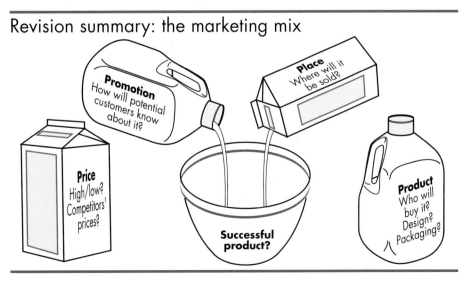

■ *Revision questions*

1 Does a market have to be in one place? Explain your answer. [3]

2 Give an example of a market. [1]

3 What is the difference between a product-orientated and a market-orientated business? [4]

4 Why might a business that is entirely product-orientated find it difficult to survive? [4]

5 State *three* advantages to a business of being market-orientated. [4]

6 Why is it necessary for a business to set a marketing budget? [3]

7 State *five* objectives of marketing. [5]

8 Why does a business carry out a SWOT analysis? [8]

9 ■ Just Juicy is a new fruit drink that is to be launched on to the market.
  ■ The product requires new production techniques.
  ■ There are many competitors, but this new drink has added vitamins and flavourings that make it taste really good.
  ■ There is growing trend for people to drink healthy drinks.
  ■ The economy is booming and unemployment is falling.

   Carry out a SWOT analysis for the possible launching of Just Juicy. [8]

10 Describe, using your own examples, what is meant by *market segments* and explain their importance to the process of marketing. [8]

11 How could a market for
   a) furniture   b) breakfast cereal
   be segmented? [10]

12 Explain the term *market gap*. [2]

The CD-ROM (see details on page x) provides further tests, activities and Case study work on the topics covered in this unit.

This unit will explain:

- ? **why market research is needed**
- ? **what is meant by primary research**
- ? **what is meant by secondary research**
- ? **who carries out this research**
- ? **why the information collected may not be accurate.**

By the end of the unit you should be able to:

- ☑ **identify whether primary or secondary research would be suitable to gather data for a particular purpose**
- ☑ **conduct your own market research – primary and secondary**
- ☑ **evaluate the accuracy of the data gathered.**

Why is market research needed?

A business needs to find out how many people would want to buy the product it is offering for sale. If there is not a very big market for the product, a great deal of money could be wasted producing goods that not many people will buy. It could even cause the business to go bankrupt. Therefore, it is very important that market research is carried out accurately.

Market research is used to try to find out the answers to these questions.

- What feature of my product do people like or dislike?
- Would they be willing to buy my product?
- What price would they be prepared to pay?
- Where would they be most likely to buy my product?
- What type of customer would buy my product?
- What type of promotion would be effective with these types of customers?
- What is the competition like?

If you are going to undertake coursework then you will also need to carry out your own research using some of the methods outlined in this unit.

Types of information

Market research can find out:

- *quantitative information*, which answers questions about the *quantity* of something, for example, 'How many sports shoes were sold in the month of December?' or 'What percentage of children drink a certain sort of cola?'
- *qualitative information*, which answers questions where an *opinion* or *judgement* is necessary, for example, 'What do customers like about a particular product?' or 'Why do more women than men buy the company's products?'

■ **Definitions to learn:**

PRIMARY RESEARCH is the collection and collation of original data via direct contact with potential or existing customers. Also called field research.

SECONDARY RESEARCH is the use of information that has already been collected and is available for use by others. Also called desk research.

A QUESTIONNAIRE is a set of questions to be answered as a means of collecting data for market research.

CONSUMER PANELS are groups of people who agree to provide information about a specific product or general spending patterns over a period of time.

Both types of information can be gathered as a result of:

■ PRIMARY RESEARCH, or field research
■ SECONDARY RESEARCH, or desk research.

Primary research

Primary research, or field research, is the collection and collation of *original data*. It involves *direct contact* with potential or existing customers.

This research will usually have been planned and carried out by the people who want to use the data; it is first-hand. It can be an expensive way to gather information and will usually be for a specific purpose, for example, to test the market to see if a new product would be likely to succeed.

There are various types of primary research method:

■ QUESTIONNAIRES – postal, face-to-face or by telephone
■ interviews – individual face-to-face or by telephone, group interviews
■ CONSUMER PANELS
■ observation – recording, watching or audits
■ experiments.

Note: Questionnaires, interviews and consumer panels are all different types of *survey*.

The process of primary research

To undertake primary research, a business will normally go through a number of stages, as summarised in the diagram below.

The stages of primary research

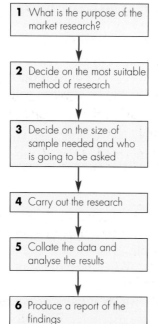

1 What is the purpose of the market research?	What do they want to find out? What information will be needed? What action will be taken as a result of the research? This will affect the type of market research undertaken.
2 Decide on the most suitable method of research	Will more than one method be necessary? Will just secondary research be sufficient or will primary research be needed as well? The cost of the research and the time required will need to be taken into account.
3 Decide on the size of sample needed and who is going to be asked	How big will the sample size need to be to keep costs down but get a sufficiently accurate result? Which different groups of people will need to be included in the survey? Different age groups? Different income groups?
4 Carry out the research	
5 Collate the data and analyse the results	The information will need to be put together and the data analysed. What does it seem to show?
6 Produce a report of the findings	A report will need to be produced showing the findings. Included in the report will be a summary of the research findings and conclusions drawn based on these results. Recommendations should be made as to what actions are necessary as a result of the research; these should be based on the conclusions.

Methods of primary research

Questionnaires

Questionnaires form the basis of most primary research. Questionnaires may be conducted face-to-face, for example, in the street, by telephone or by post.

Deciding *what questions to ask* is difficult if you are to be sure of getting accurate results. Some questions may not be very clear, some questions may lead the respondents to answer in a certain way which may not be what they really think. The researcher also needs to decide who to ask.

Advantages of questionnaires

☑ Detailed qualitative information can be gathered about the product or service.

☑ Customers' opinions about the product or service can be obtained.

Disadvantages of questionnaires

☒ If questions are not well thought out, the answers to them will not be very accurate. It may be very misleading for the business if it is thought that a product is liked by consumers, when in fact the respondents were only saying they thought the product was quite attractive but they would not actually buy it.

☒ Carrying out questionnaires can take a lot of time and money. Collating and analysing the results is also time-consuming.

Interviews

When interviews are used, the interviewer (the person asking the questions) will have ready-prepared questions for the interviewee (the person answering the questions).

Advantages of interviews

☑ The interviewer is able to explain any questions that the interviewee does not understand.

☑ Detailed information about what the interviewees like and dislike about the product can be gathered.

Disadvantage of interviews

- ☒ The interviewer could lead the interviewee into answering in a certain way, this could be done consciously or unconsciously, resulting in inaccurate results due to *interviewer bias*.
- ☒ Interviews are very time-consuming to carry out and, therefore, they are often an expensive way of gathering information.

Interviews can be carried out with one person or they can be done in groups, where there is a single interviewer putting the questions to a group of people. This is less expensive than asking people individually, but it does run the risk of the answers from people not being what they really think but being influenced by what the others in the group say.

When deciding who to ask to fill in the questionnaire or who to interview, a *sample* would have to be selected as it would be too expensive and impractical to try to include all the relevant population. This could be:

- ■ a RANDOM SAMPLE. This means that every member of the population has an even chance of being selected. People are selected at random (often by computer), for example, every 100th name in a telephone directory. The advantage is that everyone has an even chance of being picked, but not everyone in the population may be a consumer of the particular product being investigated.
- ■ a QUOTA SAMPLE. This is when people are selected on the basis of certain characteristics, for example, age, gender or income. Researchers are given a quota. If they were carrying out street interviews, the researchers can choose who to interview, providing they ask a certain number of people with certain characteristics. For example, they may be required to interview 20 people from the age group 10–25, 30 people from the age group 26–45, 20 people from age group 46–60. The researchers can then find out the views of these specific groups.

Consumer panels

This is where groups of people agree to provide information about a specific product or general spending patterns over a period of time. Panels may also test new products and then discuss what they think of the product, explaining what they like and dislike about it.

Advantage of consumer panels

- ☑ They can provide detailed information about consumers' opinions.

Disadvantage of consumer panels

- ☒ They can be time-consuming, expensive and biased if some people in the panel are influenced by the opinions of others.

Observation

This can take the form of:

- ■ *recording* For example, meters can be fitted to monitor which television channels are being watched

- *watching* Which includes such activities as counting how many different types of vehicles pass particular billboards or posters, counting how many different types of people go into a particular shop and also come out having bought something
- *audits* For example, the counting of stock in the shops to see which have sold well.

Advantage of observation

☑ It is quite an inexpensive way of gathering data.

Disadvantage of observation

☒ The information only gives basic figures. It does not provide the business with *reasons* for consumer decisions.

Experiments

An example of this type of research is where samples of new products are given out to consumers in supermarkets to taste, and then they are asked to say what they think.

Advantages of experiments

☑ They are relatively easy to set up, carry out and gather consumers' first reactions to the products.

Disadvantages of experiments

☒ People might not give their real feelings so as not to cause offence.
☒ A representative sample of consumers may not be asked, as only the people who shop in those particular supermarkets are asked.
☒ Many other potential customers may shop elsewhere and they will not be asked.

Whether questionnaires, interviews, consumer panels, observation or experiments are used to find out about a product or service depends very much on the type of product or service. Experiments are much easier to carry out with food products than with a service, while questionnaires can be used for most products and services.

■ *Activity 17.1*

The following products require some primary research. Decide which type of research would be the most appropriate to use and why.

a) The possible success of a new chocolate bar.
b) Whether to introduce a new style of watch which uses fashionable bright colours.
c) Whether to extend an existing taxi service to cover a new town.
d) The feasibility of opening a new restaurant.
e) Why the sales of a sports shoe are falling.

Secondary research

Secondary research, or desk research, is the use of information that has already been collected and is available for use by others. This is either from internal sources or external sources.

Internal sources of information

A lot of information may be readily and cheaply available from the firm's own records. The type of qualitative information available will be from the Sales department, which will hold detailed data on which brands of products have been selling well and in which area. The Finance department could give detailed information on the costs of manufacturing products or providing services.

Examples of internal sources of information include:

- Sales department sales records, pricing data, customer records, sales reports
- opinions of distribution and public relations personnel
- Finance department
- Customer Service department.

External sources of information

These are sources of information which are obtained from outside the company. These sources are many and varied and tend to depend on the type of product that is being researched. This type of data is inevitably of a general nature as it has been gathered for some purpose other than the research that is being undertaken. It can still be useful, as long as the limitations are taken into account when using the information.

Examples of external sources of information include:

■ trade and employers' associations
■ specialist journals
■ research reports
■ newspapers
■ government reports and statistics
■ media reports
■ market research agencies' reports.

Government statistics are a detailed source of general information about such things as the population and its age structure. This is available in most countries.

Newspapers may have useful articles, for example, about the general state of the economy and whether customers are expected to increase or decrease their spending in the near future.

If there is a trade association for the industry, it often provides information for the businesses in that industry. For example, there might be an agricultural association which helps farmers who grow particular crops.

Market research agencies are specialist agencies who carry out research on behalf of companies or anyone who commissions them. They sometimes publish reports of their research into particular markets. However, whilst being very detailed information about the market, it is expensive to buy.

Secondary research is often a much cheaper way of gathering information as the research has already been done by others and you are also just making use of it. It may be needed to help assess the total size of a market by finding out the size of the population and its age structure. Newspapers may carry vital economic forecasts if you are trying to assess when a recession might end and your sales increase again. This type of information could not be obtained by primary research.

■ *Activity 17.2: case study task*

L&I plc manufacture fizzy drinks. They want to start selling in your country. To help them assess the size of the market, you have been asked to find out the following information:

■ size of total population
■ how many people there are in the age groups 1–10, 11–20, and 21–30 in your country
■ how many different fizzy drinks are sold in your country (how many competitors there are)
■ where these competitors come from – are they local companies or are the drinks imported?

What other research would you advise the company to undertake before starting to sell in your country? Explain your answer.

■ *Activity 17.3*

Which of the following sources of information gathered by a business are primary data and which are secondary?

Data	Primary or secondary?
The *Daily News* article on a competitor's new product	
Sales department's monthly sales figures	
A shop's daily stocktake figures showing on which days sales are at their highest	
A traffic count to see how many vehicles pass your billboard advertisement in a week	
Postal questionnaire results researching into your new product	
A market research agency's report on what customers like and dislike about your product	
Annual government population statistics	
Data on customer complaints	

Who carries out market research?

Businesses can carry out their own research into different aspects of the market for their existing product or the possible market for a new product. Secondary research is often easier and cheaper for the business to carry out itself, as primary research may be too expensive to undertake on its own.

The business may decide that it can afford to pay a *specialist market research agency* who will carry out whatever research it is asked to do. (These agencies also carry out opinion polls to see who they predict will win political elections.) They will find out consumers' spending habits as well as what they think about an individual business' products and their competitors' products.

Accuracy of market research information

The reliability or accuracy of the information that has been collected depends largely on how carefully the sample is drawn up and the way in which the questions in the questionnaire are phrased to ensure honest responses.

The sample selected is unlikely to be truly representative of the total population, but it needs to be as near as is possible. If a quota sample is used, rather than a random sample, it is easier to get more accurate replies.

The size of the sample is also important. It is not possible to ask everyone in a population and therefore only a sample has to be asked. The larger the sample, the more accurate the results are likely to be, but the more expensive will be the research. If only a small sample is asked, the results are unlikely to be as accurate. Therefore, the researchers need to decide how many people will give them the accuracy they want and can afford!

Trying out questionnaires on a small group of people before they are carried out on a large sample can help to see if any of the questions could be misinterpreted. The questions can then be rephrased and used with the main sample.

Secondary research may not be as accurate as first thought because it was initially carried out for some other purpose and you would not know how the information was actually gathered. Articles in newspapers sometimes have a bias and important information is left out deliberately. Statistics can quickly become out of date and not relate to current trends in consumers' buying habits, but reflect what they used to be spending their money on.

These are just some of the reasons why information collected from all sources, both primary and secondary, should be used with care and it should not be assumed straightaway that it is correct.

Revision summary: methods of market research

postal   telephone   face-to-face   audits   watching   recording

Questionnaires   **Experiment**   **Observation**

PRIMARY RESEARCH (FIELD RESEARCH)

Interviews   **Consumer panels**

individual   group

pricing data   Finance department   customer records   sales records   public relations personnel

Internal sources

SECONDARY RESEARCH (DESK RESEARCH)

trade and employers' associations   **External sources**   government reports and statistics

research reports   newspapers   specialist trade journals   media reports   market research agencies' reports

■ Activity 17.4

Copy out the table below and fill in the boxes.

Advantages and disadvantages of different types of market research

Method	Examples	Advantages	Disadvantages	Examples of appropriate use	Why the information may not be accurate
Primary research	Questionnaires				
	Interviews				
	Observation				
	Consumer panels				
	Experiments				
Secondary research	Internal souces				
	External sources				

How to design a questionnaire

Ask yourself the following questions.

- What do I want to find out?
- Who do I need to ask? (Age group, male/female, particular income or occupations)
- Where will I carry out my questionnaire?

Writing the questions

- When deciding what questions to ask, it is advisable to ask *no more than 12 questions*, as the interviewee can get impatient if asked a lot of questions and answer them quickly without thinking about their replies.
- *Keep the questions short and clear*. It is a good idea to *keep the answers simple* too, for example, ask for yes/no answers or provide a choice from which the respondents have to choose. This also makes it is easier to collate the results.
- If you want to know the age of the interviewee, give a *choice of age groups*, for example 21–40, as people do not always like to tell you how old they are.
- *Avoid open-ended questions* unless people's opinions are sought. It can be very difficult to collate a wide variety of responses. For example, 'What would make you buy this product?' might be better worded as 'What do you like about this product?' with a choice of answers, including 'other' to allow for people who want to give a choice that you have not offered.

- *Be careful not to lead the interviewee* into an answer that may not be true by asking too direct a question. For example, 'Would you buy this product?' often leads the interviewee to answer 'yes', even when they would not actually buy it, because they may not want to offend you.
- Think about the order in which you ask the questions. Be logical!

Examples of questions:

Have you seen the television advert for product X?

Yes ☐

No ☐

Don't know ☐

What do you think of the taste of product X?

Excellent ☐   Poor ☐

Good ☐   Bad ☐

Quite good ☐

How often do you buy Product X?

Every day ☐   Every two weeks ☐

Several days a week ☐   Once a month ☐

Once a week ☐   Less than once a month ☐

Carrying out the questionnaire

Before going out and asking the questions, think about how you will ask the questions and how you are going to record the results. You may need to create a grid to put the respondents' replies on. It is a good idea to practise what you are going to say before you go out. Think carefully about who you can ask – will it be safe for you in that particular area? Do you need permission to ask people questions? Can someone go with you? You should not go alone. Do not be upset if people are too busy to answer the questions and just walk by.

Questionnaires do not usually ask for the person's name to be put on it and so they will be more willing to give honest answers to the questions. You should reassure the respondents that you are not going to give their answers to anyone else, it is just for your use.

Finally, consider:

- how many people you are going to ask
- at what time of the day you are going to carry out the questionnaire. Will this affect who will answer the questions?
- where you are going to carry out the questionnaire. Will this have an influence on who you ask?

■ *Activity 17.5: case study task*

Below are some of the results of a questionnaire that was carried out to look into the feasibility of opening a fast food restaurant in a city centre. One hundred people were asked at random to answer the questionnaire. The aim of the questionnaire was to identify the particular market segment to be targeted in any promotional campaign.

Analyse the results and answer the questions that follow.

(i) Responses to question 1:
Age structure of persons in the sample

Age group (years):	No. of persons:
0–9	5
10–19	40
20–29	20
30–39	20
40–49	10
50+	5

(ii) Responses to question 2:
'How often do you eat out?'

Response:	No. of persons:
Never	5
Occasionally	20
Once per month	30
Once per week	20
More than once per week	25

(iii) Responses to question 3:
'Where do you purchase meals most often?'

Response:	No. of persons:
Hotel	20
Cafe	15
Fast food restaurant	35
Food stalls (in street)	25

(iv) Responses to question 4:
'How far do you usually travel when eating out?'

Response:	No. of persons:
1 km	30
2 km	40
5 km	12
5–10 km	8
over 10 km	5

Looking at the results above:

a) Which age group would be most likely to eat in fast food restaurants?
b) How will this information affect where the business will advertise their restaurant?
c) Why did the questionnaire contain the question 'How often do you eat out?'?
d) How will the responses to questions 2 and 3 be useful to the fast food restaurant?
e) Suggest two additional questions that could have been included in the questionnaire. Explain why the information they provide would be useful to the business.
f) Explain why the questionnaire results might not be very accurate.

■ *Activity 17.6*

You have been asked to carry out some research into the feasibility of opening a new restaurant in your local area. Design your own questionnaire to carry out on friends and/or family.

Complete the following steps.

a) Design the questionnaire.
b) Decide who you are going to ask.
c) Decide how many people you are going to ask (it is a good idea to carry out the questionnaire with friends and then put the results together so that you have a greater number of replies).
d) Produce a summary sheet on which to collate the results.
e) Collate the results.
f) Present the results you have found. You may need to read Unit 18 on presenting data before you do this.
g) Evaluate your findings. What does the data tell you? Should a new restaurant be opened? If so, what type of restaurant would be successful?
h) Evaluate your questionnaire. How accurate were your results? Would you redesign the questionnaire if you were carrying out the questionnaire again?

■ *Revision questions*

1 What do you understand by the term *market research*? [6]

2 Explain why a business might carry out market research. [4]

3 What is the difference between qualitative and quantitative information? [4]

4 What is the difference between primary research and secondary research sources of market research data? [4]

5 Give *four* examples of primary research. [4]

6 Describe how a business could carry out primary market research to find out if there is a market for a new toy. [10]

7 Give *two* advantages of using primary source data to a company producing a new chocolate bar. [4]

8 List *four* sources of secondary data that could be used by a business planning to open a new sports centre. [4]

9 Give *one* example to show how a company can benefit from using secondary source data. [4]

10 Why might the information collected from market research be inaccurate? [4]

11 Why is it important for a business to conduct market research before locating a new branch in an overseas country? [6]

12 What has to be taken into account when drawing up a questionnaire? [6]

The CD-ROM (see details on page x) provides further tests, activities and Case study work on the topics covered in this unit.

This unit will explain:

? **different ways of presenting data gathered from market research**
? **alternative ways of presenting information for use in coursework.**

By the end of the unit you should be able to:

☑ **select the most suitable way of presenting information**
☑ **draw charts and plot graphs.**

During any business studies course it is likely that you will be required to present data, either that you have collected or have been given. You will often be required to interpret data that has been presented to you in an examination. You may even be required to present data yourself from information that has been provided as part of an examination. If you undertake coursework, you will certainly have to present the information that you have collected. This unit aims to help you to choose appropriate ways to present the data that you have collected or have been given.

Presentation of data from market research

When information has been gathered as part of market research, it may be difficult to make sense of what it means. The raw data will need to be converted into a form which is easy to understand. The significant points need to be made clear. For example, after conducting a questionnaire, it may not be clear which answer has the greatest number of 'yes' responses.

The type of data that has been collected and what it is to be used for will affect the form of presentation which will be used. Information can be displayed in the form of:

- a *table* Usually used to record the data in its original form, i.e. the raw data that has been collected. Sometimes, if the data is brief and does not contain a lot of different information, a table may be a sufficient form of presentation. However, it is often better to convert the data into a chart or graph
- a *chart* Shows the total figures for each piece of data or the proportion of each piece of data in terms of the total number. For example, if a company sells its product in several countries, a chart can show at a glance which countries have the biggest percentage of sales and which have the lowest
- a *graph* Used to show the relationship between two sets of data. For example, how total cost changed over the last five years. The two variables are 'total cost' and 'time'.

A selection of the most often used forms of presenting data are explained below.

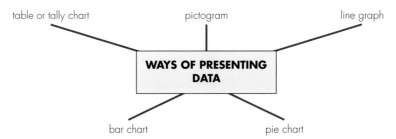

Table or tally chart

When data is collected, a table or tally chart is used to record the information. This makes it clear what data has been gathered. It allows the information to be put into an order so that sense can be made of the data. An example is shown below.

■ *Case study example*

A survey was carried out of the type and number of vehicles and people passing a particular shop. The researcher wanted to investigate possible customers that could be attracted to the shop, that is, possible passing trade. The results were recorded by putting a mark on the table for each vehicle that passed by in each of the time periods. The tally chart is shown below.

Time	Car	Lorry	Van	Bicycle	Person walking by
1.00–1.59 p.m.	卌 卌	卌 卌 卌	III	卌 III	卌 卌 卌 卌
2.00–2.59 p.m.	卌 卌 卌	卌 卌 卌 卌	卌 卌	卌	卌 卌 卌
3.00–3.59 p.m.	卌 卌 卌 卌	卌 卌 卌	卌 卌 卌	卌	卌 卌 卌
4.00–4.59 p.m.	卌 卌 卌 卌 卌 卌	卌 卌 卌	卌 卌 III	卌 卌 卌	卌 卌 III
5.00–5.59 p.m.	卌 卌 卌 卌 卌 卌 卌 III	卌 卌	卌 III	卌 卌 卌 卌 卌	卌 卌 卌 卌 卌 卌 III

Are the results of the traffic count clear? When are the most lorries and vans passing the shop?

The answers to questions which might be asked are not clear from the table and the information would be better displayed in the form of a chart. You need to show the total number of each type of passer-by for each hour in the afternoon.

Bar chart

Charts are eye-catching and enable information to be presented in a form which can be easily understood. They allow information to be seen in a more meaningful way. The data from the tally chart is displayed on the bar chart below. It can be clearly seen at what time of the day the different vehicles and people are passing the shop.

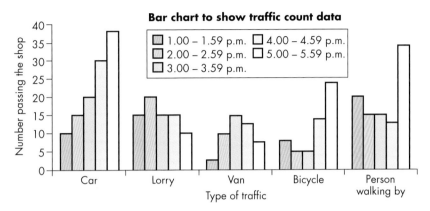

To draw a bar chart, follow the steps below:

1 Add up the tally marks for each section of the table.
2 The highest number will allow you to decide the scale for the vertical (y) axis. In this case, 38 cars passed the shop between 5.00 and 5.59 p.m. So a scale up to 40 was constructed and equal spaces of 5 were marked on the axis, which allows all the other totals to be drawn.
3 The horizontal (x) axis needs to be divided by how many different totals are to be shown. In this case five types of passer-by are to be shown, each with five different time periods.
4 After the axes have been drawn, the information from the table can be drawn on the chart.
5 The axes need to be labelled and a title should be added so that anyone looking at the chart will know what it shows.
6 If necessary, add a key to show what each bar represents.

Pictogram

A pictogram shows the data in a similar way but, instead of using columns, a symbol for the item (or number of items) is used. A key must be included to explain what the symbol is showing. A selection of the above data has been used to draw the pictogram below.

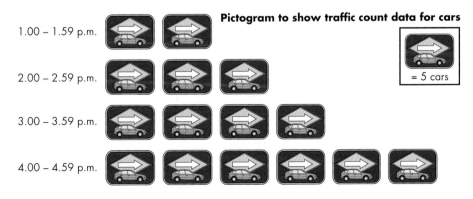

A pictogram is not usually used if a lot of data has to be presented or if the data involves odd numbers, such as 5679 or 4523.

However, a pictogram is a very effective form of presentation if the data is simple and in numbers that can be easily represented by a scale.

Pie chart

A pie chart can be used to show what proportion of the total figure is made up by each component. Each slice of the pie chart represents a particular component's contribution to the total amount. For example, a pie chart could represent the total costs of running a factory for a year, and each slice of the pie chart could represent the cost of each of the elements. The bigger the slice, the bigger the proportion of the total cost.

To draw a pie chart, follow the steps below:

1 Add up all the numbers in the data to find the total figure.
2 Take each figure separately and divide it by the total figure.
3 Multiply your answer by 360. The number you get represents the number of degrees of the circle that the item will take up. This calculation should be done for each piece of data.
4 Draw a circle.
5 Using a protractor, draw the proportion of the circle each piece of data will take up.
6 Label each segment of the circle.
7 Add a title to the pie chart clearly stating what it shows. Include a key if necessary.

An example of a pie chart is shown opposite, based on the information in the following case study example.

■ *Case study example*

Company A sells its products to a number of different countries. The table shows the data collected by the Sales department regarding the value of sales to each country.

Company A: value of sales

Country	Sales figures (£000)
UK	2
Belgium	3
USA	5
Tanzania	3
Egypt	2
Saudi Arabia	4
Argentina	1

From the table, the Sales department carried out the following calculations in order to draw a pie chart:

1 Total sales = 20
2 For the first country in the table:

$$UK = \frac{2}{20} = 0.1$$

(The answer to this calculation also provides the percentage of total sales if multiplied by 100; so the UK percentage = 10%)

3 UK = 0.1 × 360 = 36 degrees
   The same calculation was then done for the other countries:

$$Belgium = \frac{3}{20} = 0.15 \rightarrow 0.15 \times 360 = 54 \text{ degrees}$$

$$USA = \frac{5}{20} = 0.25 \rightarrow 0.25 \times 360 = 90 \text{ degrees}$$

$$Tanzania = \frac{3}{20} = 0.15 \rightarrow 0.15 \times 360 = 54 \text{ degrees}$$

$$Egypt = \frac{2}{20} = 0.1 \rightarrow 0.1 \times 360 = 36 \text{ degrees}$$

$$Saudi\ Arabia = \frac{4}{20} = 0.2 \rightarrow 0.2 \times 360 = 72 \text{ degrees}$$

$$Argentina = \frac{1}{20} = 0.05 \rightarrow 0.05 \times 360 = 18 \text{ degrees}$$

4

5

6/7

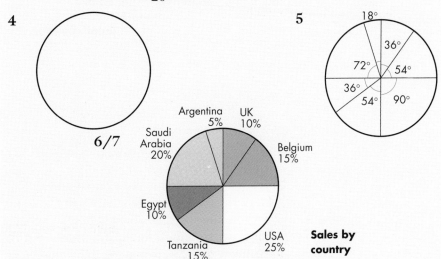

Sales by country

■ *Activity 18.1: case study task*

Using the tally chart on page 260, draw a pie chart to show the types of traffic that passed the shop between 1.00 and 1.59 p.m.

Line graph

Graphs show the relationship between two variables and can be drawn either as a straight line or as a curve.

To plot a line graph, follow the steps below.

1 Decide what scale to use on the vertical (y) axis.
2 Decide what scale to use on the horizontal (x) axis.
3 Label the axes.
4 Plot each point on the graph.
5 Join up the points.
6 Add a title, clearly stating what the graph shows.
7 If necessary, add a key to show what information each line represents.

It is easier to see the relationship between sales over time if the data is shown as a graph rather than just as figures. It is also easier to see trends in the data. That is, what the data has been doing over the last five years – has it been increasing steadily, increasing slowly, staying steady or decreasing?

The relationship between two sets of figures can be shown on a line graph. Look at the following case study and complete Activity 18.2 to see how effective a line graph can be.

■ *Case study example*

The company directors have asked the Sales department to show them how the sales last year compare with the previous four years. The Sales department first produced a table.

	Sales revenue (£)
Year 1	5,000
Year 2	6,000
Year 3	8,000
Year 4	11,000
Year 5	15,000

Note: Year 5 represents last year's figures.

Have the sales been rising faster in the last two years or has the growth in sales been at a steady pace? The answer to this question is much easier to find if the information is put onto a graph. The Sales department did this, following the steps below.

1 The sales figures go from 5,000 to 15,000 and so a scale up to 15,000 is needed on the vertical axis. The scale could go up in steps of 5,000 or perhaps 2,000.
2 Five points need to be marked, equally spaced, on the horizontal axis – one for each year.

3 The axes are labelled. Here are two alternative methods:

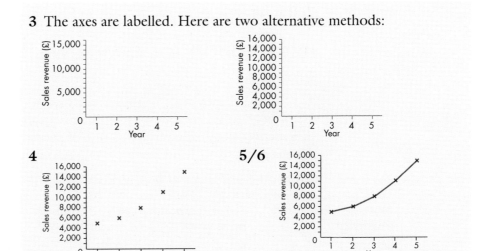

Sales revenue over the last five years

■ *Activity 18.2: case study task*

A company wants to see if paying the workers bonuses, when they achieve output targets, has increased profits for the company. Draw a line graph showing the following set of data. (The months should be along the horizontal axis and money (£) should go on the vertical axis.)

Months	Total wages (£000)	Profits (£000)
January	50	10
February	60	15
March	60	20
April	70	20
May	50	12
June	50	10
July	70	18

Revision summary: when to use different types of presentation

	Show a small number of simple figures	Show proportions	Show the changes over time (relationship over time – trends)	Show several total figures with large variations in the numbers	Compare the changes in different sets of data
Table	✔				
Pictogram	✔				
Bar chart	✔			✔	✔
Pie chart		✔			✔
Line graph			✔	✔	✔

Alternative ways of presenting information for coursework

Tables

As you have already seen, a table can be used to show how different items of information are related to each other. For example, a table could be very useful if you had interviewed several people about what motivated them at work. A table on this topic might look like the one below.

Four people were asked 'What would motivate you to work harder?'

	More money	Promotion	Praise/recognition of hard work	Threat of dismissal	Pleasant working conditions
Person 1	✔		✔		✔
Person 2	✔				✔
Person 3	✔	✔	✔		
Person 4	✔			✔	

This table would be much clearer to the person reading the coursework than just writing down everything that the person said in the interview.

Photographs

Photographs can be used to illustrate the points you are making in your coursework. They should be relevant to the work, i.e. they should support what you are saying and you should refer to them. They should not just be included to make the work look attractive.

Diagrams

Diagrams can be used to simplify information. For example, if a business had been asked what different types of finance it had used to pay for a new factory, the information could be displayed as in the diagram below.

Instead of writing out a list of the types of finance used by the company, a diagram could be used.

Maps

Maps are another way of presenting information in a different form to that in which it was gathered.

As part of an assignment, a map of an area where a business is located could be drawn. Instead of just including the map in its original form and then writing about the area around the business, it could be annotated. This involves adding notes onto the map itself. This can often make points about the area very clear to the person reading the assignment. An example might look like the one below.

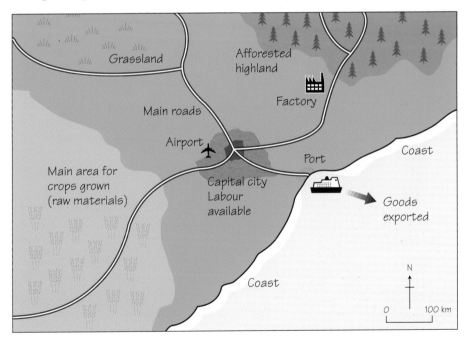

The aim of presenting data is to make information clear for the reader. Words and numbers alone are not always the best way of doing this.

■ *Activity 18.3: case study tasks*

For each of the following situations, choose the most appropriate method of presentation to use. Present the data using your chosen method. Say why you think it would be the most suitable method.

a) A questionnaire has been carried out and you have this information on the age groups of the respondents.

Age group	No. of persons
0–9	5
10–19	40
20–29	20
30–39	20
40–49	10
50+	5

b) A questionnaire has been carried out and you have many different answers to the question 'What did you like best about the product?'. The answers are 'tastes good', 'looks nice', 'nice packaging', 'value for money', 'free gifts', 'nicer flavour than others', 'like the colour', 'packet is colourful', 'money-off token', 'nice taste', 'cheap'.

c) The Sales department have given you this information on product sales over the past ten years.

Year	Sales revenue £(000)
1	10
2	15
3	18
4	21
5	25
6	30
7	32
8	31
9	30
10	29

d) You are concerned about wage rates rising and have obtained all the different costs of producing the product for the last two years. How important are wages in relation to the other costs? You want to see if wages have increased as a proportion of the total costs.

	Year 1	Year 2
Wages	20	30
Materials	40	44
Overheads	30	20
Advertising	10	16

NB All figures are in £000

19 The marketing mix: product and packaging

This unit will explain:

- the role of product in the marketing mix
- product development
- the importance of branding
- the importance of packaging in the marketing mix
- the product life cycle
- how the product life cycle can be extended.

By the end of the unit you should be able to:

- identify the different types of products which are sold
- understand what makes a product successful
- understand how a new product is developed
- understand what is meant by a brand name and why it is important
- identify the important characteristics of the packaging for a product
- draw a product life cycle
- identify the different stages of the product life cycle from information about sales, pricing, promotion and profitability
- suggest ways of extending the product life cycle.

The role of product in the marketing mix

The product itself is probably the most important element in the marketing mix – without the product, the rest of the marketing mix is pointless. As discussed in Unit 16, some businesses are product-orientated. They will develop a product and then try to decide who might buy it. Today most companies are market-orientated when developing new products. They spend a lot of money researching consumers' buying habits, their likes and dislikes, to see if they can design a product which people will want to buy. After deciding the market segment for the product, the other parts of the marketing mix – price, promotion and place – will be determined.

Large companies often have a department which spends all its time developing new products. It will also look at competitors' products to see what they are successfully selling.

The important thing about the product is that it must fulfil a want. Consumers buy products for the pleasure, satisfaction or benefits they provide. Therefore, a product must give satisfaction of some sort or it will not be purchased. The satisfaction given to consumers can vary. For example, some products are bought because they satisfy a basic need, like food which stops hunger. Other products, like a refrigerator, in addition to keeping food cool, would be expected to be reliable and last a long time. An expensive perfume would give a certain image to the consumer when they used it and it would be expected to be of high quality.

Types of product

There are several types of product. Some products are sold to consumers and some can be sold to other businesses, i.e. to other producers. In addition to goods, services are also sold to consumers and to other producers. Products are usually grouped into the following types.

■ *Consumer goods* These are goods which are consumed by people. They can be goods that do not last long, such as food and cleaning materials. Some goods last a long time and give enjoyment over a long time, such as furniture and computers.
■ *Consumer services* These are services that are produced for people. Examples include repairing cars, shoe-shining or education.
■ *Producer goods* These are goods that are produced for other businesses to use. They are bought to help with the production process. Examples include lorries, machinery or components.
■ *Producer services* These are services that are produced to help other businesses. Examples include accounting, insurance and advertising agencies.

Activity 19.1

Copy this table and tick the correct box for each product.

Product	Consumer good	Consumer service	Producer good	Producer service
Tube of toothpaste				
Bottle filling machine				
Bank accounts				
A pair of sports shoes				
A chocolate bar				
Doctor's treatment of a patient				
Office cleaning				
Factory building				
Purchase of a hospital bed				
Television programme				

Defining the type of product the business is producing is important when deciding how the product will be developed and marketed.

Promotion of a producer good will be quite different to promotion of a consumer good – this is discussed in Unit 21.

Producing the right product at the right price is an important part of the marketing mix.

■ The product needs to satisfy consumer wants and needs. If it does not then it will not sell.
■ The product also needs to be of the right quality so the price is what consumers are willing to pay.
■ The costs of production must enable a price to be set that will produce a reasonable profit.
■ Design of the product is obviously very important. Not only does the quality need to be appropriate for the brand image, i.e. high price = high quality, cheaper price = lower quality, but it also has to last a reasonable length of time. If the product is not reliable and breaks down, or breaks soon after it is purchased, then it will get a bad reputation and is unlikely to sell well. The product also needs to perform to a standard expected from it, i.e. soap powder for washing clothes should do so effectively!

What makes a product successful?

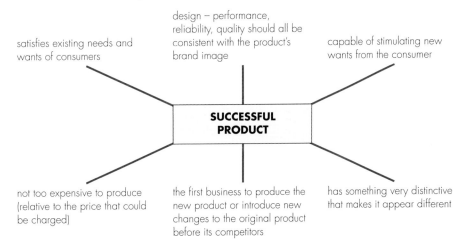

satisfies existing needs and wants of consumers

design – performance, reliability, quality should all be consistent with the product's brand image

capable of stimulating new wants from the consumer

SUCCESSFUL PRODUCT

not too expensive to produce (relative to the price that could be charged)

the first business to produce the new product or introduce new changes to the original product before its competitors

has something very distinctive that makes it appear different

Activity 19.2

Choose *three* products that you have bought.
Do you think they have been successful? Why?
Try to analyse their success using the above criteria. For example, does it have a good design? Is it reliable? Is it very distinctive from other brands?

Product development

Large businesses are looking for new products all the time. Smaller businesses are also trying to stay competitive and therefore need to keep up with other companies. When developing a new product most businesses go through the process outlined on page 272.

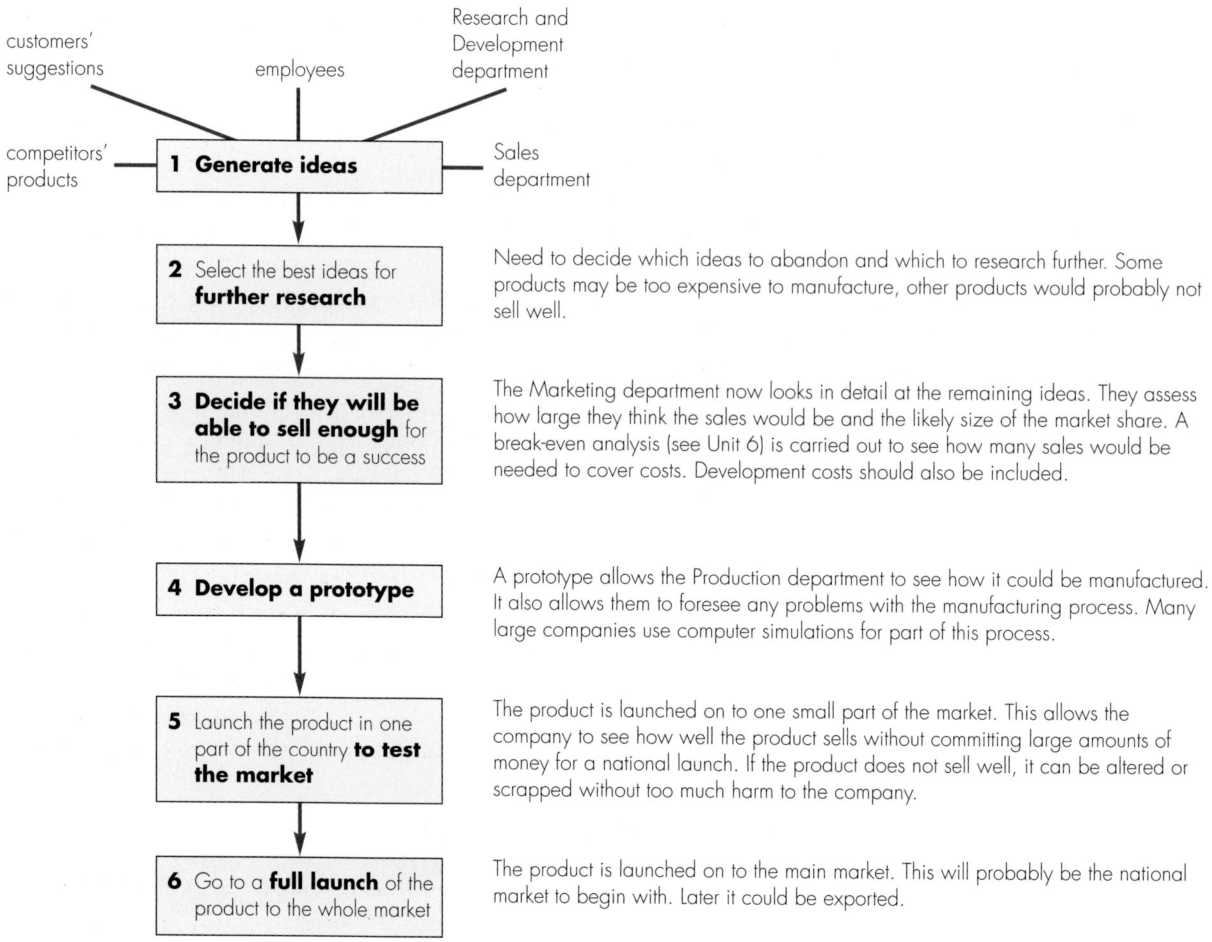
customers' suggestions
employees
Research and Development department
competitors' products
1 Generate ideas
Sales department
2 Select the best ideas for further research
Need to decide which ideas to abandon and which to research further. Some products may be too expensive to manufacture, other products would probably not sell well.
3 Decide if they will be able to sell enough for the product to be a success
The Marketing department now looks in detail at the remaining ideas. They assess how large they think the sales would be and the likely size of the market share. A break-even analysis (see Unit 6) is carried out to see how many sales would be needed to cover costs. Development costs should also be included.
4 Develop a prototype
A prototype allows the Production department to see how it could be manufactured. It also allows them to foresee any problems with the manufacturing process. Many large companies use computer simulations for part of this process.
5 Launch the product in one part of the country to test the market
The product is launched on to one small part of the market. This allows the company to see how well the product sells without committing large amounts of money for a national launch. If the product does not sell well, it can be altered or scrapped without too much harm to the company.
6 Go to a full launch of the product to the whole market
The product is launched on to the main market. This will probably be the national market to begin with. Later it could be exported.

Activity 19.3: case study task

You work for a company which manufactures ice cream. You have been given the task of designing a new ice cream on a stick (a lolly) suitable for small children.
Describe in detail how you would do this.

The importance of branding

Selling a product directly to the customer makes it easy to inform the customer of the product's qualities and good points. The salesperson can persuade the customer to buy the product. If a small business produced hand-made jewellery and sold it on a street stall, it could be explained to customers how the jewellery was made and why it was a good product to buy.

Today, the manufacturers of most products do not sell them directly to the customer – they are sold to other businesses or retailers, who sell them on to the customer. This means that the product's unique features and the

Definitions to learn:

The BRAND NAME is the unique name of a product that distinguishes it from other brands.

BRAND LOYALTY is when consumers keep buying the same brand again and again instead of choosing a competitor's brand.

BRAND IMAGE is an image or identity given to a product which gives it a personality of its own and distinguishes it from its competitors' brands.

reasons for buying it must be conveyed in a different way. This is done by creating a *brand* for the product. It will have a unique name, a BRAND NAME, and advertising will need to make consumers aware of the qualities of the product to try to persuade them to buy it. Branded products are normally sold as being of higher quality than unbranded products. It is the assurance of a standard quality that makes consumers confident in buying branded products. They may not be sure that an unbranded product will always be of the same quality. If you bought a hamburger from a street seller, it might not always be very nice. On the other hand, if you bought a McDonald's hamburger you would be confident that the quality would always be the same, no matter where in the world you bought one.

Businesses use brands for their products to encourage consumers to keep buying their products and not those of their competitors. Consumers may have BRAND LOYALTY, which means they will keep buying the same brand of a product instead of trying other similar products.

BRAND IMAGE is important. The brand is more than just an assurance of guaranteed quality, it will have a whole image which surrounds it and will be reinforced by advertising. *Coca-Cola*, for example, is sold throughout the world and has an image of being a superior quality cola drink which tastes better than its rivals' drinks. Advertising shows people having fun when they drink it and emphasises that it is a fashionable drink for young people.

▦ *Case study example*

Sweetie plc manufacture chocolate bars. They want to introduce a new chocolate bar which will appeal to young children. They have decided to call the bar 'CrocoChoc' and on the front of the packaging there will be a picture of a smiling chocolate covered crocodile. The advertising will be on television and the adverts will feature ChocoCroc – he will be a friendly, likeable character and the chocolate bars will be crocodile shaped. The image of the chocolate bar will be embodied in ChocoCroc as he has been created to appeal to young children.

Revision summary: branding

needs advertising to reinforce the brand's qualities

unique name (brand name)

higher price than unbranded products

higher quality than unbranded products

BRANDING

creates a brand image (an image associated with consuming the product)

always of the same standard (assured quality)

unique packaging

encourages customers to keep buying it (brand loyalty)

▨ *Activity 19.4*

Select *two* products that have brand names. For each of the products identify:

a) who the customers of the product are
b) what it is that attracts them to the product
c) what brand image the manufacturer is trying to create
d) how the name and the packaging of the product helps to reinforce the brand image
e) where it is sold.

▨ **Definition to learn:**

PACKAGING is the physical container or wrapping for a product. It is also used for promotion and selling appeal.

The role of packaging in the marketing mix

Getting the PACKAGING right is just as important as getting the other parts of the marketing mix right. The packaging has two functions to perform.

- It has to be suitable for the product to be put in. Packaging has to give protection to the product and not allow it to spoil. It also has to allow the product to be used easily. It is no good having hair shampoo in a tin which will not allow the liquid to pour out easily. It has to be suitable for transporting the product from the factory to the shops, so preferably the packaging should not be too delicate or the product could easily get damaged.

- Packaging is also used for promoting the product. It has to appeal to the consumer, therefore the colour and shape of the container is very important. It is the packaging that catches the customer's eye, not usually the product inside! The brand image will be reinforced by the packaging in which the product is sold. An expensive product will have a luxurious-looking container, often a gold colour. A low-cost product may have basic simple packaging with plain colours.

The labels on products sometimes have to carry vital information about the product, such as how to store or use it and what ingredients it contains.

▨ *Case study example*

C&D plc manufacture breakfast cereals. The packaging used is bright and colourful and has the brand name clearly printed on the front of the packet in large letters. The outer packet is made of cardboard to keep its shape, so it will stand up on the shelves in shops and prevent the contents from being crushed. The side of the packet contains information about the nutritional qualities of the product. There is also a special offer printed on the outside of the packet to encourage consumers to buy the cereal. There are tokens on the packet to be cut out, collected and then sent off to receive a free gift. The cardboard packet has inner packaging to keep the product sealed in and fresh until it is purchased and consumed by the customer.

Revision summary: packaging

PACKAGING

protects the product

easy to transport the product

easy to open the container and use the product

suitable for the product to fit in

eye-catching

carries information about the product

promotes the brand image

▨ *Activity 19.5: case study task*

S&B Food Products plc have decided to produce a new fruit-flavoured milk drink especially for young children. The market segment that it expects to buy the product is parents, for their children. It is a healthy drink which contains vitamins and minerals.

a) Which of the possible containers drawn above would you use for the new fruit-flavoured milk drink? Explain your choice.

b) Suggest another container that might be more suitable for the new milk drink.

c) What colour(s) should the container be? Explain your choice.

d) Choose a brand name for the new milk drink. What image does the name give to the product?

e) Design a label for the container. Why do you think the design of the label will help the product to sell?

f) What information will need to be put on the label?

The product life cycle

Products do not last forever. A typical cycle for a product is as follows:

1 First a product will be *developed*. The prototype will be tested and market research carried out before it is launched on to the market. There will be no sales at this time.

2 It is then *introduced* or launched on to the market. Sales will grow slowly at first because most consumers will not be aware of its existence. Informative advertising is used until the product becomes known. Price skimming (see Unit 20) may be used if the product is a new development and there are no competitors. No profits are made at this point as development costs have not yet been covered.

3 Sales start to *grow* rapidly. The advertising is changed to persuasive advertising to encourage brand loyalty. Prices are reduced a little as new competitors enter the market and try to take some of your customers. Profits start to be made as the development costs will have been covered.

4 Sales now increase only slowly. Competition becomes intense and pricing strategies are now competitive or promotional pricing (see Unit 20). A lot of advertising is used to maintain sales growth. Profits are at their highest.

5 Sales have reached *saturation* point and stabilise at their highest point. Competition is high but there are no new competitors. Competitive pricing is used. A high and stable level of advertising is used but profits start to fall as sales are static and prices have to be reduced to be competitive.

6 Sales of the product will *decline* as new products come along or because the product has lost its appeal. The product will usually be withdrawn from the market when sales become so low and prices have been reduced so far that it becomes unprofitable to produce the product. Advertising is reduced and then stopped.

This process of what happens to a product is called the PRODUCT LIFE CYCLE. It is usually drawn as a graph like the one below.

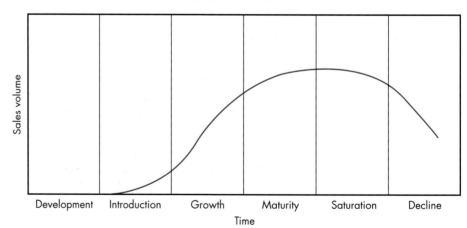

▥ **Definition to learn:**

The PRODUCT LIFE CYCLE describes the stages a product will pass through from its introduction, through its growth until it is mature and then finally its decline.

A typical product life cycle

The exact length of the life cycle, in terms of time, varies a great deal from product to product. It is affected by the type of product it is, for example, fashionable items will go out of fashion quickly whereas food products may last a very long time. The life cycle of some very popular brands, such as *Coca-Cola*, is many years, whereas the life cycle of fashionable clothes is often less than a year. New developments in technology will make original products obsolete and their life cycle will come to a quick end as new products are purchased in preference to old technology.

The exact stage that a product is at needs to be identified by the business so that it knows what it can do to prices or promotion. In the different stages, the business will need to react differently. For example, when the product is in decline it is no good putting up its price, or if the product is in the growth phase it would be foolish to cut the amount of advertising that is being undertaken.

▓ *Case study example*

Compute plc invented a new computer game. It had been developed over several months before it was finally launched on to the market. Initially it was expensive, being bought by only a few people who wanted to be the first to play the new game. It quickly became successful – a lot of advertising was used to promote the game and sales grew rapidly. Over the next few months, more and more shops ordered copies of the game and competition between the shops was fierce. The shops offered the game at cheaper and cheaper prices to attract customers and prices for the game started to fall. Sales grew steadily now, not at the fast rates of increase that were first seen. Once most computer users had purchased the game, the market was saturated and sales began to fall, even though prices by now were low. The game was making little or no profit for the company and so they decided to withdraw the game from sale and concentrate on their new games that had been introduced.

Extending the product life cycle

When the product reaches the mature or saturation stage of its product life cycle, businesses may stop sales starting to fall by adopting *extension strategies*. These are ways that sales may be given a boost. Some possible ways businesses might extend the life cycle of their products are shown in the diagram below.

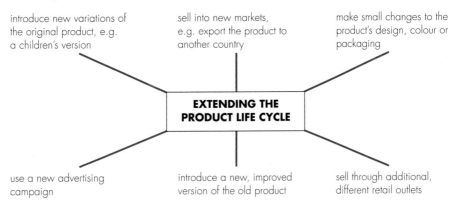

introduce new variations of the original product, e.g. a children's version

sell into new markets, e.g. export the product to another country

make small changes to the product's design, colour or packaging

EXTENDING THE PRODUCT LIFE CYCLE

use a new advertising campaign

introduce a new, improved version of the old product

sell through additional, different retail outlets

■ *Activity 19.6*

Copy out the table on a large sheet of paper. You should select the correct answer from the list below to fit each stage of the product life cycle.
The choices for **Sales** have already been filled in to get you started.

	Introduction	**Growth**	**Maturity**	**Saturation**	**Decline**
Sales	Low sales because the product is new	Sales rise rapidly	Sales increase more slowly	Sales level off as market saturation is reached	Sales fall as new products become available or the product goes out of fashion
Pricing policy/ competition					
Promotion/ advertising					
Profits					

Pricing policy/competition
■ Price skimming as few/no competitors
■ Penetration pricing by competitors as a few competing products are introduced, small reduction in your prices to compete with these products
■ Competitive pricing/promotional pricing as competition becomes intense
■ Price reductions to encourage sales as sales are falling. Some competitors stop making the product
■ Competitive pricing/prices are reduced to compete with existing competitors, no new competitors enter the market

Promotion/advertising
■ Advertising reduced or may stop altogether as sales fall
■ Informative advertising as the product is new, free samples may be given out to get customers to try it
■ A lot of advertising to encourage brand loyalty and to compete with other very competitive products
■ A high and stable level of advertising, may be promoting new improved versions of the original product
■ Informative advertising changed to persuasive advertising to encourage brand loyalty as sales start to rise rapidly

Profits
■ Loss made due to high development costs
■ Profits fall as sales fall
■ Profits fall as sales are static and prices have been reduced
■ Profits start to be made after development costs have been covered
■ Profits at their highest as sales growth is high

If the extension strategies are effective, the maturity phase of the product life cycle will be prolonged. An example of what might happen is shown in the diagram below.

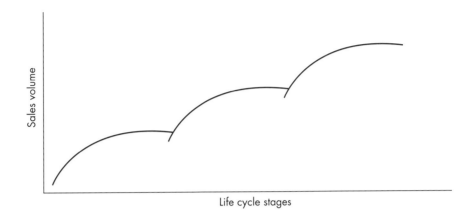

Businesses will not usually manufacture just one product. They will have a range of products at different stages of the product life cycle. For example, a business will need to have products coming up into the growth phase to counteract those that are in decline.

▨ Activity 19.7

Suggest possible ways to extend the product life cycles of each of the following products. State which extension strategy you would use for each product, and explain why you think it would be successful in boosting sales.

a) A chocolate bar which has been sold for many years in the same packaging and has the same brand image. There are several competitors' brands of chocolate bars also sold in the market and sales have stabilised.

b) A sports shoe that is worn when playing a particular sport. This sport is no longer very popular with young people.

c) The sales of a new model of a car have stagnated. It is only sold in the home country where it is manufactured.

d) A children's toy which is only sold in toy shops saw steady growth in its sales but now the sales are stable and not increasing any further.

■ Revision questions

1 Products can be grouped into four different types. Name the *four* types. [4]

2 What has to be taken into account to improve the chances of the successful development of a new product? [4]

3 Describe *six* steps to developing a new product. Start with 'Step 1 – generate ideas'. [5]

4 What do you understand by the term *brand*? [2]

5 a) Give *six* examples of famous brands that have been established for many years. [6]
  b) Why do you think each of these brands has lasted so long? [6]

6 What are the risks of launching a new brand? [2]

7 What has to be taken into account, and why, when deciding the packaging for:
  a) a new toy
  b) a new chocolate bar? [8]

8 Draw and label the stages of a typical product life cycle. [3]

9 Why do some products have much longer life cycles than others? Use examples to illustrate your answer. [6]

10 Explain the difference in the sales performance of products A and B below. [4]

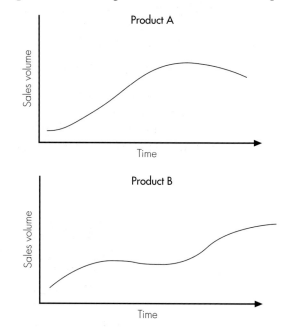

11 Explain what factors might influence the length or shape of the life cycle of a product. [5]

12 Pricing is a very important element of the marketing mix of a company. How and why might a company change its pricing during the stages of the product life cycle? [5]

The CD-ROM (see details on page x) provides further tests, activities and Case study work on the topics covered in this unit.

This unit will explain:

- ? the role of price in the marketing mix
- ? the determination of market prices (supply and demand analysis)
- ? pricing strategies that businesses can use.

By the end of the unit you should be able to:

- ☑ understand how prices are determined in the market and what influences demand for and supply of products
- ☑ understand the different pricing strategies a business can use
- ☑ select a suitable pricing strategy for a particular business situation/objective.

The role of price in the marketing mix

When deciding a price for an existing product or a new product, the business must be very careful to choose a price which will fit in with the rest of the marketing mix for the product. For example, if a new product is of high quality, is to be aimed at consumers who have a lot of money, is wrapped in luxurious packaging but has a low price, consumers will not think it is a good quality product and will not buy it. Some products are sold in very competitive markets and prices will have to be set near to their competitors' prices. Other products are the only ones available in their market and so consumers may be willing to pay a high price to have one of these products.

 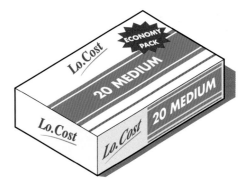

Price determination in a free market

How are prices determined in the free market? If one product is the same as other products, for example, rice, wheat, potatoes, cassava, then its price will probably be determined by the interaction of demand for and supply of the product. If there are many competitors in a market, then prices will also probably be determined by *demand and supply*. This will mean that businesses have to charge the *market price* for their products and not necessarily what they want to charge.

■ Case study example

If a farmer produced rice, he would take the rice to market and sell it for the price that rice was selling for in that market. The farmer could not charge a much higher price because no one would buy his rice – consumers would buy from other farmers who were charging the lower market price.

To understand how price is arrived at, demand and supply will be looked at separately.

Demand

What is meant by demand? Demand is not just what people want to buy, they must also have the money to be able to purchase the product. You might want to buy a yacht, but unless you have the money to buy one, you do not form part of the demand for yachts!

The demand for a product varies with how much is charged for the product. If the price increases, normally fewer will be bought and if the price goes down, more will be demanded.

This relationship is shown in the table below. When the price of a chocolate bar is only £1.00, 7,000,000 chocolate bars will be bought. But if the price of each chocolate bar was £2.00, only 3,000,000 would be demanded. The table shows what would be demanded if the price was at different levels, but the exact market price is not known yet because we do not know what the producers are willing to supply at different prices.

Price of chocolate bar (£)	Quantity demanded of chocolate bars per week (000s)
2.50	1,000
2.25	2,000
2.00	3,000
1.75	4,000
1.50	5,000
1.25	6,000
1.00	7,000

The table can be changed into a graph. Price will be put on the vertical axis and quantity demanded will be put on the horizontal axis. The graph will look like the one on page 283.

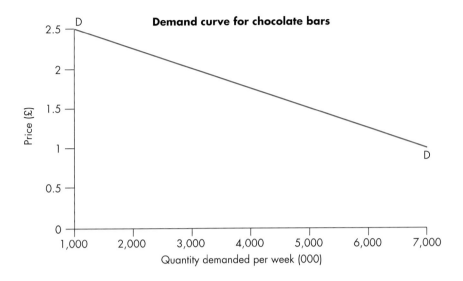

It can be seen from the graph that at high prices there will be less demand for chocolate bars than at low prices.

Supply

The supply curve shows a different relationship. As the price goes up, the producer will plan to supply more of the product to the market to take advantage of the higher price. A supply curve will therefore slope in the opposite direction to the demand curve.

This relationship is shown in the table below. When the price is only £1.00 then 1,000,000 chocolate bars will be supplied. If the price of each chocolate bar is £2.00, 5,000,000 would be supplied. The table shows what would be supplied if the price was at different levels, but the exact market price is not known because we have not yet added demand. Therefore, the actual quantity supplied is not known.

Price of chocolate bar (£)	Quantity supplied of chocolate bars per week (000s)
2.50	7,000
2.25	6,000
2.00	5,000
1.75	4,000
1.50	3,000
1.25	2,000
1.00	1,000

The table can also be changed into a graph. Again price will be put on the vertical axis and quantity supplied will be put on the horizontal axis. The graph will look like the one on page 284.

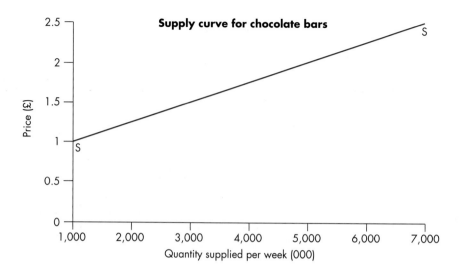

It can be seen from the graph that at high prices there will be more chocolate bars supplied to the market than if prices are low.

The market price

For the market price to be decided, the supply curve and the demand curve must be put together on the same graph. When the curves are plotted on the same graph, the two lines (supply and demand) will usually cross. Where they cross is where the demand for the product just equals the supply of the product to the market and this will give the market price. Look at the diagram below.

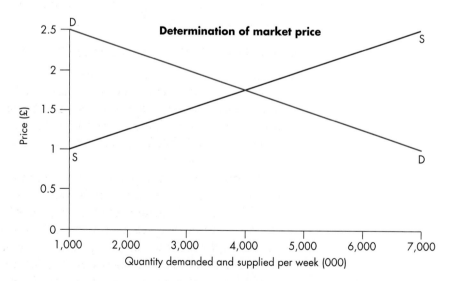

For this diagram, demand and supply are equal at £1.75. This means that 4,000,000 chocolate bars are supplied to the market at £1.75 and 4,000,000 chocolate bars are demanded. There are no chocolate bars left over and there is no demand that has not been satisfied at this price.

■ *Activity 20.1: case study task*

This table shows the demand for and supply of packets of cereals.

a) What will the market price be?
b) Plot the demand and supply on a diagram and show the position of the market price.

Price (€)	Demand (000s)	Supply (000s)
0.50	10,000	2,000
0.75	9,000	3,000
1.00	8,000	4,000
1.25	7,000	5,000
1.50	6,000	6,000
1.75	5,000	7,000
2.00	4,000	8,000
2.25	3,000	9,000

Factors that affect demand and supply

When these tables and graphs are drawn it is assumed that nothing else changes. But what would happen if consumers had increases in their income or the price of other products changed? The demand curve can move to a position to the right or left of the original curve. That is, the demand curve moves due to factors that affect demand other than price.

Changes in the price of products affect where you are on the demand curve (whether you move up or down the curve), but changes in other factors affect the position of the curve on the graph.

Factors that affect the position of the demand curve

■ *Changes in the prices of other products*
  – These can be *substitute* products. These are bought and used in place of another product. If the price of a substitute product decreases then more of the substitute product is bought and so demand for this product will fall. This means the demand curve will move to the left of the original curve.

  Assuming beans and peppers are substitute goods; if the price of beans falls then more beans will be bought and demand for peppers will fall, i.e. the demand curve for peppers will move to the left.
  – Products can be *complementary* goods. These are products that tend to be bought and consumed together. If the prices of complementary products increases then less of the complementary product is purchased and therefore less of your product will be purchased. The demand curve will move to the left.

  Assuming coffee and milk are complements; if the price of coffee rises, then less coffee will be bought and therefore there will be less demand for milk. The demand curve for milk will move to the left.

■ *Changes in income* If consumers' income falls (perhaps because there has been an increase in the tax on their income), there will be less demand for many products. When consumers have less money to spend, they will reduce their demand for products and this will mean demand curves will move to the left. Less income will usually mean there will be less demand for meals in restaurants as people economise. The demand curve for meals in restaurants will move to the left.

■ *Changes in taste and fashion* If a product becomes more popular, demand will increase and the curve will move to the right. A particular type of sports shoe might become more fashionable, its demand will increase and the curve will move to the right of the original one.

■ *A change in advertising* If there has been a successful advertising campaign, for example, for a particular brand of breakfast cereals, the demand curve will move to the right.

These are just a few of the influences on the demand curve – there are others.

If demand increases, due to one of the reasons outlined above, and the curve moves to the right, then the market price will usually increase and sales will increase. If demand falls and the curve moves to the left then the market price will usually fall and sales will fall. This is illustrated on the graphs below.

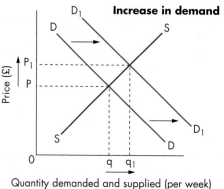
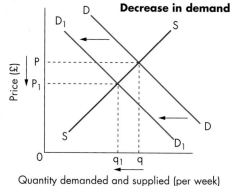

Revision summary: factors affecting demand

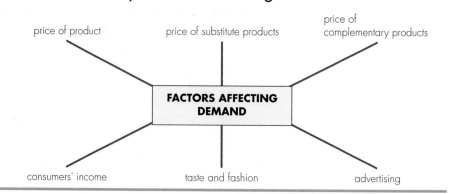

How responsive the quantity demanded is to changes in price is affected by how many close substitutes there are. If there are many close substitutes for the product then, if price rises a little, the consumers will respond by buying the substitute product and so quantity demanded will fall a lot. For example, if the price of a chocolate bar rose by 5 per cent, some customers would buy alternative chocolate bars and sales might fall by 15 per cent. This product would be said to have an *elastic demand curve* – the percentage change in quantity demanded is greater than the percentage change in price.

If, however, there are not really any substitutes, for example, petrol, then an increase in price of 15 per cent will not cause much of a fall in sales – perhaps 5 per cent, as most consumers will carry on buying the product at the higher price. This is said to be an *inelastic demand curve* – the percentage change in quantity demanded is less than the percentage change in price.

Factors that affect the position of the supply curve

Changes in the costs of supplying the product to the market will have the effect of moving the supply curve. An increase in the costs will make it more expensive to supply the goods to the market, and so supply will fall. This will move the curve to the left. A fall in the costs will make it cheaper to supply the goods to the market and supply will increase. This will move the curve to the right.

For example, if the cost of raw materials increased, the supply curve would move to the left – supply would decrease. If the wage costs fell, the supply curve would move to the right – supply would increase. Improvements in technology would make it cheaper to produce the product and supply would increase, moving the curve to the right. Taxes would result in it being more expensive to supply the product to the market and so supply would decrease.

If supply increases, and the curve moves to the right, the market price will usually decrease and sales will increase. If supply falls and the curve moves to the left, the market price will usually increase and sales will fall. When the product is scarce, the price will usually increase. When the product is in abundant supply, the price will usually fall.

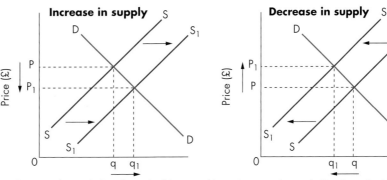

Quantity demanded and supplied (per week)   Quantity demanded and supplied (per week)

Revision summary: factors affecting supply

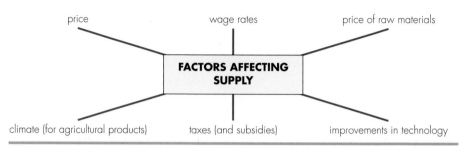

How responsive the quantity supplied is to changes in price is affected by how easily and quickly supply can be changed when price changes.

If it is difficult to change supply when price rises – for example, natural rubber prices rise by 20 per cent, but the quantity supplied only increases 5 per cent, it is very difficult to suddenly produce more natural rubber – the product would have an *inelastic supply curve* (the percentage change in quantity supplied is less than the percentage change in price). If, however, it is easy to increase supply when there is an increase in price then this is said to be an *elastic supply curve*. For example, the price of chocolate bars increases by 5 per cent and the quantity supplied increases by 15 per cent, it is relatively easy to increase the output of chocolate by adding extra production workers. The percentage change in quantity supplied is more than the percentage change in price.

■ *Activity 20.2*

Copy and complete the table. For each of the changes say whether:

a) it is demand or supply that is affected
b) prices increase or decrease
c) sales increase or decrease.

The first example has been done for you.

The change that has taken place	Demand or supply affected?	Will price increase or decrease?	Will sales increase or decrease?
There has been a bad harvest for coffee beans	Supply decreases	Price increases (in short supply)	Sales decrease (in short supply)
Jeans go out of fashion			
A government report is published which says eating rice is very good for your health			
New technology is introduced into the production of computers which increases efficiency			
The costs of components has increased			
A competitor's prices increase			

Pricing strategies

If the product that is manufactured can easily be distinguished from other products in the market then it is probably a branded product. If the product is branded, it will have a distinctive name and packaging, and be aimed at a particular part of the market. It will be important to select an appropriate price to complement the brand image; a value-for-money brand should have a low price. Today many products have a brand image. Price will not just be determined by demand and supply in the market. The producer will have a lot of influence over the price of the product.

If a product has a lot of competitors in its market, the price it charges will be very important. The business must constantly monitor what its competitors are charging for their products to make sure its prices remain competitive.

A business can adopt pricing strategies for several reasons:

■ to try to break into a new market
■ to try to increase its market share
■ to try to increase its profits
■ to make sure all its costs are covered and a particular profit is earned.

The business objective being sought will affect which of the pricing strategies it decides to use. The price the business chooses to charge may not be related to the cost of manufacturing the product. Sometimes they might charge what they think the consumer will pay and this may be well above what it has cost them to manufacture the product.

Here are some pricing strategies that a business could use for its products.

Cost-plus pricing

Definition to learn:
COST-PLUS PRICING is the cost of manufacturing the product plus a profit mark-up.

COST-PLUS PRICING involves estimating how many of the product will be produced, then calculating the total cost of producing this output and finally adding a percentage mark-up for profit.

☑ The method is easy to apply.
☒ You could lose sales if the selling price is a lot higher than your competitor's price.

For example, if the total cost of making 2,000 chocolate bars is £2,000 and you want to make a 50 per cent profit on each bar, you would need to use the following calculation:

$$\frac{£2,000}{2,000} + 50\% = £1.50 \text{ per bar is the selling price}$$

$$(1 + 0.50 = £1.50)$$

The calculation to find 50 per cent of £2,000/2000 is as follows:

$$\frac{£2,000}{2,000} \times \frac{50}{100} = 1 \times \frac{50}{100} = 0.50$$

$$\left(\frac{\text{Total cost}}{\text{Output}} \times \% \text{ Mark-up} = \text{Selling price}\right)$$

Penetration pricing

Definition to learn:
PENETRATION PRICING is when the price is set lower than the competitors' prices in order to be able to enter a new market.

PENETRATION PRICING would possibly be used when trying to enter a new market and the price would be set lower than the competitors' prices.

☑ It ensures that sales are made and the new product enters the market.
☒ The product is sold at a low price and therefore the sales revenue may be low.

For example, a company launches a new chocolate bar at a price several pence below the prices of similar chocolate bars that are already on the market. If this is successful, consumers will try the new bar and will become regular customers.

Price skimming

With PRICE SKIMMING, the product is usually a new invention, or a new development of an old product, and therefore it can be sold on the market at a high price and people will pay this high price because of the novelty factor. The product will often have cost a lot in research and development, and these costs need to be recouped. Sometimes the high price can be due to the high quality of the product.

☑ Skimming can help to establish the product as being of good quality.
☒ It may put off some potential customers because of the high price.

For example, a new computer games system is invented. It will be sold in the shops at a very high price, much higher than the existing computer games systems. Because it is new and with better graphics than the old systems, consumers will be willing to pay the high price. This way the business will earn high profits which will make the research and development costs worthwhile.

Competitive pricing

COMPETITIVE PRICING involves putting prices in line with your competitors' prices or just below their prices.

☑ Sales are likely to be high as your price is at a realistic level and the product is not under- or over-priced.
☒ In order to decide what this price should be, you would have to research what price your competitors are charging and this costs time and money.

For example, a company wants to sell a brand of soap powder. It needs to sell it at a similar price to all the other brands available or consumers will buy their competitors' brands.

Promotional pricing

PROMOTIONAL PRICING would be used when you want to price the product at a low price for a set amount of time.

☑ It is useful for getting rid of unwanted stock that will not sell.
☑ It can help to renew interest in a business if sales are falling.
☒ The sales revenue will be lower because the price of each item will be low.

For example, at the end of summer, a shop might have a lot of summer clothes left unsold. It might have a sale offering 'Buy one, get one free'. This will encourage customers to buy one item in order to get the second one free and it will clear the end-of-season stock. However, the shop will not make much, if any, profit on the clothes. But at least it will get some money for clothes that otherwise it might not have been able to sell at all.

Pyschological pricing

PSYCHOLOGICAL PRICING is an approach when particular attention is paid to the effect that the price of a product will have upon consumers' perceptions of the product.

This might involve charging a very high price for a high quality product so that high income customers wish to purchase it as a status symbol.

It could also involve charging a price for a product which is just below a whole number, for example, 99p is just below £1 and creates the impression of being much cheaper.

Supermarkets may charge low prices for products purchased on a regular basis and this will give customers the impression of being given good value for money.

■ *Case study example*

Wizzit plc is a large company that produces soft drinks. It has developed a new drink which contains an ingredient that gives people energy when they drink it. The company decided to target young people who like to go out dancing. They put the drink in a new shaped bottle which had bright colours on the outside so that it would be easily identified. The drink was advertised regularly on TV and was shown as a fashionable drink for young people. Teenagers were shown as happy, lively and enjoying life. The drink had a clearly identified brand name and was sold at a higher price than the other soft drinks that young people drink.

The company had developed a clear brand image for the product and spent a lot of money advertising the drink. As the product was new, fashionable and different, it could charge a high price for it – price skimming.

Wizzit also manufacture a traditional soft drink that is consumed mainly by children. Sales have been falling due to more varieties of soft drinks becoming available. The company decide to reduce the price for a few months to try to attract the lost customers back – promotional pricing.

The company uses prices to help it fulfil different aims at different times. The same product could have very low prices when entering a new market, until it is established, and then it might have competitive pricing for a while, and from time to time promotional pricing might be used if the company wants sales to be given a boost.

Revision summary: pricing strategies

■ *Activity 20.3*

What pricing strategy would most probably be used for the following products? Explain your choice in each case.

a) A watch that is very similar to other watches sold in the shops.
b) A new type of radio that has been developed and is a lot higher quality than existing radios.
c) A chocolate bar which has been on the market for several years and new brands are being brought out which are competing with it.
d) A shop, which sells food, wants to get its money back on buying the stock and make an extra 75 per cent as well.
e) A new brand of soap powder is launched (there are already many similar brands available).
f) A toy sold for £1.99.

■ *Activity 20.4*

Copy out the table and fill in the blank boxes.

Pricing strategy	Examples and when they might be used	Advantages	Disadvantages
Cost-plus pricing			
Penetration pricing			
Price skimming			
Competitive pricing			
Promotional pricing			
Psychological pricing			

■ *Revision questions*

1 What is meant by demand? [2]

2 Draw and label a diagram to show how market prices are determined. [5]

3 Give *three* reasons why the demand curve could rise (i.e. move to the right). [3]

4 What happens to market price when the demand curve decreases (moves to the left)? [2]

5 What is meant by *elastic demand* and *inelastic demand*? [6]

6 Explain *three* reasons why the supply curve could decrease (move to the left). [6]

7 What happens to the market price when the supply curve increases (moves to the right)? [2]

8 Why might a firm's supply curve be inelastic? [4]

9 Explain *two* pricing methods that a company could use. [6]

10 What factors should a company take into account when determining its selling price? [6]

11 The costs of production for a new toy is £10. The price of competitors' products are: Product A – £25, Product B – £20, Product C – £23, Product D – £22.

a) What price should the company sell the new toy at if it prices at cost plus profit at 100 per cent profit mark-up?
b) What price should the company sell the new toy at if it prices using competitive pricing?
c) What price should the company sell the new toy at if it prices using penetration pricing?
d) What price should the company sell the new toy at if it prices using price skimming? [4]

12 For each of the following, state the pricing strategy the business should use. Justify your answer.
a) XYZ plc are introducing a new brand of chocolate bar that has a luxurious taste. It contains ingredients that have not been used in chocolate bars before and gives this new product a special taste.
b) A wooden furniture manufacturer wants to achieve a £50 profit on each table produced.
c) T&Z plc have been established for many years selling a well known brand of washing powder. Its sales are starting to fall. It uses competitive pricing at the moment, but should it change? [9]

13 Often shops decrease their prices at certain times of the year. Why do they do this? [5]

The CD-ROM (see details on page x) provides further tests, activities and Case study work on the topics covered in this unit.

21 The marketing mix: promotion

The role of promotion in the marketing mix

Promotion gives the consumer information about the rest of the marketing mix – without it, consumers would not know about the product, the price it sells for or the place where the product is sold. It is often thought that promotion is just about advertising the product, but it includes several different types of promotion as well as advertising (see pages 297–306).

It is difficult to think of products that are not advertised and promoted. Most products are produced for the mass market and therefore need advertising and promoting. Producer goods are often sold directly by sales representatives visiting businesses but even these products are advertised in trade magazines, or leaflets are sent out to businesses informing them about the product.

Promotion is essential when a brand image is being created for a product. It must be remembered that advertising does not necessarily increase sales and profits. A lot of money can be spent on advertising and not be effective. Advertising may increase sales, but if prices have been reduced and advertising expenditure increased then profits may not increase.

Promotion as part of the marketing mix includes:

- *advertisements* These can take different forms, such as television adverts or magazine adverts. These are discussed later on pages 297–300
- *promotion* This includes examples such as giving money-off coupons. More examples are discussed on pages 303–306
- *personal selling* This usually involves sending out sales representatives to businesses to talk directly with the customer
- *public relations* This involves making the public aware of the product or company, for example, through sponsorships or publicity in the media.

The aims of promotion

As you can see, promotion includes many activities that are undertaken by businesses. They all have one thing in common – their *purpose*, which is to raise awareness of the firm's products and encourage consumers to make a purchase. The aims are summarised in the diagram below.

Advertising
The advertising process

When planning an advertising campaign the business will need to go through the steps shown in the diagram below.

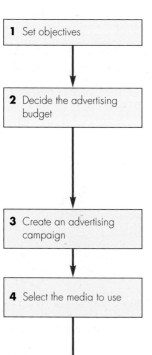

The business will have to decide the purpose of the advertising. Is it to capture a new market? Is it to increase market share? Is it to improve the image of the company? Is it to create or improve a brand image?

The business will need to decide how much to spend on advertising. This is a difficult task, too much and money is wasted, too little and the advertising will not be effective. One way, used most often, is to predict how much sales will be in the future and then spend a certain percentage of the predicted sales on advertising the product. This way the expense of advertising is related to the revenue brought in by sales of the product. The percentage used is usually between 2–10 per cent of sales revenue. Sometimes the budget will be set by how much competitors are spending on their advertising. Or sometimes it is simply what the business can afford to spend. This is particularly true of small businesses.

The business will need to decide what sort of advertising campaign to run. For example, will the adverts be to attract young people? The target audience (the people who the advertisers think might buy the product) and the purpose of the advertising must be kept in mind when creating the campaign.

The business will need to decide which is the best type of advertising media to use. The target audience will determine the most suitable forms of media to use to make sure that the adverts are seen by the people intended. The business will also need to decide how often the adverts will appear in order to make sure the target audience sees them and is encouraged to buy the product. The type of media selected has to be *cost effective*. It is pointless spending a lot of money on television advertising when the business is not trying to reach a mass audience, but only wants to target bicycle riders. It would be more cost effective to advertise in bicycle magazines which would be cheaper and seen by the people who are the potential customers and no one else.

The business needs to see if sales have increased as a result of the advertising campaign or see if the product's brand image has improved, i.e. has the advertising campaign met its objective?

■ *Activity 21.1*

a) Collect at least *ten* examples of either:

- magazine/newspaper advertisements, or
- examples of promotions, or
- details of television adverts.

b) Identify what appear to be the aims of the adverts. An advert may appear to cover more than one aim, for example, it might be creating a brand image of being expensive and also trying to increase sales.

Try to find examples for each of the different aims of promotion.

■ **Definitions to learn:**

INFORMATIVE ADVERTISING is where the emphasis of advertising or sales promotion is to give full information about the product.

PERSUASIVE ADVERTISING is advertising or promotion which is trying to persuade the consumer that they really need the product and should buy it.

Different types of advertising

Advertising can be either INFORMATIVE or PERSUASIVE or have elements of both. 'Celcius' is an expensive aftershave. It is not sold by telling people all about what it will do for the skin. It is meant to make consumers think that when wearing the aftershave they will smell nice to the opposite sex and make them more attractive. The adverts for the aftershave used in magazines show a picture of an attractive man which is meant to *persuade* the readers to buy the aftershave so that they will be attractive like the man in the advert.

Would consumers buy a computer that was shown in adverts as being used by an attractive person, but with no technical information provided? Probably not. When buying computers, consumers want to know what speed it will run at and what memory it has. They want *information* about the product and its price.

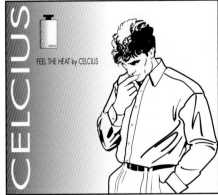

FEEL THE HEAT by CELCIUS

CELCIUS

Grrr.

RAW POWER ON YOUR DESKTOP.
450MHz • 4.5 GB HD
128MB RAM • 32x CD ROM
Tornado Rip™ Graphics Accelerator

Dual processor™
True cross-platform
inter-operability
Open upgrade path

AxisNT™ PPC
WORKSTATION SOLUTION

The types of advertising media that businesses can use are as follows.

Television

This is a very powerful medium to get across a message. The advert will often go out to millions of people and can show the product in a very favourable way, making it look very attractive. It is a very expensive form of advertising but reaches the biggest number of potential consumers – the TARGET AUDIENCE. The time of day the advert is broadcast affects who sees the advert. For example, if the advert is broadcast when children's programmes are being shown, it is likely only children and perhaps their parents may see the advert. If your product is chocolate bars, this might be suitable, but if your product is cars, the target audience will probably not see the advert and it will have been a waste of money. Therefore, it is very important that the time of day that the advert is broadcast is chosen carefully. It must also be considered that when most people watch television, at peak viewing times, adverts are most expensive. When the least number of people are viewing, they tend to cost the least amount of money.

To summarise, when preparing to place an advert on television the producer must consider:

- the advert itself – is it getting the right message across to the audience?
- the time the advert is broadcast – will the target audience be watching then?
- how many times the advert should be shown.
- how many adverts the budget will allow.

Radio

Radio has similar considerations to television: the time the advert goes out, the number of times the advert is played, how many adverts the budget will allow. Radio is cheaper than television, but cannot put across a visual message. A tune or song is often played with a radio advert to help to get the attention of the audience. The audience may not be as large as for television, but this may vary from country to country.

Newspapers and magazines

These are often produced every day and sold to different groups of people. Some newspapers are aimed at business people, whilst others may be aimed at the majority of people. Newspapers can be national or local. The national newspapers will be purchased and read by a lot more people than local ones and therefore they are a lot more expensive to advertise in than local newspapers. However, the cost of the advert per reader is often lower for national newspapers than for local newspapers. Also, particular national newspapers are usually read by certain social groups (see Unit 16) and if these people are the potential customers (target audience), this may be a very cost effective way to reach them. If the business is small and is selling only to the local population, an advert in the local newspaper will be cheaper and more cost effective than one in a national newspaper because it needs to be read only by local people.

■ **Definition to learn:**
The TARGET AUDIENCE is the people who are potential buyers of the product or service.

Magazines are often bought by specific groups of people, such as bicycle enthusiasts, and therefore adverts can be placed in magazines that are specifically aimed at these groups of people. This means that the adverts are seen by the target audience and the money spent on advertising is cost effective and is not wasted. Magazines are often colourful and can make adverts look more attractive than they do in newspapers. Magazines are usually only published once a week or once a month.

The adverts in newspapers and magazines are permanent and can be cut out and kept. Far more information can be put into a newspaper or magazine advert than on television or radio. However, it is less attention-grabbing than an advert on television and may not even be read.

If the product or service is sold to other businesses, trade magazines are a useful place to advertise. They will be cost effective in reaching their target audience.

Posters/billboards

These are large adverts on boards usually placed at the side of roads. They are permanent but can easily be missed as people go past them. The message of the advert has to be simple and visual or passers-by will not grasp what is being advertised. No detailed information can be included, only a persuasive type of picture or slogan.

Businesses pay to have their advert on the board for a certain length of time and then someone else might place an advert there. The board could be owned by the business itself and then they can decide when to change their own adverts.

This can be quite a cheap form of advertising, but it is seen by everyone, not just the target audience and is therefore more suitable for products that are bought by a wide range of people. Posters can also be used to advertise local events. The position of the poster can vary, for example, it could be by a main road/highway or it could be by a quieter road. There will be different amounts of people seeing the poster if it is in different places, and therefore the cost of placing the poster on the billboard will be higher if more people are going to see the advert.

Cinemas

This can be an effective form of advertisement but will only be seen by a limited number of people. The type of film being shown will obviously affect who is watching it and therefore who sees the advert. Because only a limited number of people see the advert, the cost is lower but it can be a very effective way of advertising if your target audience are likely to go and see the film being shown.

Leaflets/direct mail

These can be given out to anyone in the street and therefore many of the leaflets will not be read. They can also be delivered to people's homes (called direct mail if sent to people's homes) and can be targeted at particular neighbourhoods. For example, if the leaflets were advertising a local expensive restaurant, leaflets could be delivered or sent to an area where the houses are expensive to buy. It is likely that more wealthy people live in these areas.

Leaflets have the advantage of being permanent and can be kept for future reference; this is especially useful if a promotional offer is put on the bottom of the leaflet which offers money off the product or service.

Internet (E-commerce)

The internet is indispensable for many businesses as a medium for advertising. It has the advantage that a large amount of information can be placed on a web site and orders can be placed instantly. This route makes the advert theoretically accessible to vast numbers of people, although in some countries internet access is limited, and even where potential customers do have access, it cannot be guaranteed that they will find one particular site. Any company's site is inevitably one of a large number offering related products and services so the response rate may not be high. The use of key words in a web site means that potential buyers searching for a particular product or related topics may find the site. Once they do, there are still obstacles to overcome for those selling online; for example, possible security problems in purchasing with a credit card on the internet discourages some customers from buying online. (See also page 315.)

Other types of advertising

There are several other types of advertising that are carried out in different parts of the world. Examples include bright lit-up (neon) signs, sometimes flashing, which show the name of a product, for example, *Coca-Cola*. These can be found at city centre sites or outside the businesses themselves.

Bags which have the name of the shop on them are given out with purchases. This advertises the shop as customers walk down the street. Delivery vehicles can have the company name or product on their side.

■ Case study example

The T&G Partnership sell insurance to households and businesses. They use direct mail to businesses, sending out letters and brochures about the services they offer. In addition, they advertise on local radio and in local newspapers to attract both customers from the general public and business customers. As they are only a small business, they cannot afford to advertise on television or in the national newspapers. However, they are considering setting up a web site on the internet.

Revision summary: types of advertising media

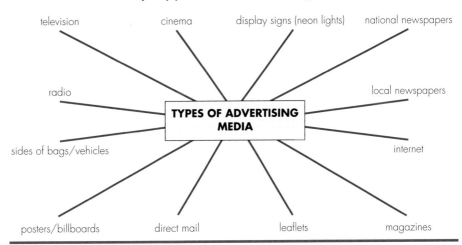

television cinema display signs (neon lights) national newspapers

radio

TYPES OF ADVERTISING MEDIA

local newspapers

sides of bags/vehicles

internet

posters/billboards direct mail leaflets magazines

■ **Definition to learn:**
The AIDA MODEL is a simple way of planning an advert's design. It stands for attention, interest, desire, action.

Design of adverts

When deciding on the exact design of an advert the designer will have to think very carefully about who they are trying to attract to the product. A simple way of planning an advert's design is to use the AIDA MODEL. This is short for:

A attention – consumers have to be made aware that the product exists
I interest – consumers need to be made interested in the product
D desire – consumers need to be made to want to buy the product
A action – consumers are prompted into action. They actually buy the product.

The AIDA model is usually used with more expensive products that are not purchased very often, such as televisions or CD players. Products that are bought frequently, such as bread, are bought out of habit and the AIDA model will be less successful in these cases.

■ *Activity 21.2*

Look at some adverts in newspapers and magazines and decide whether the AIDA model is present in them. Consider:

■ how the advert catches your attention
■ what is in the advert that made you look at it
■ what it is about the advert that made you interested in the product
■ what it is that makes you want to buy the product
■ whether the advert tells you where the product can be purchased.

■ Activity 21.3

a) Choose *ten* products which you and your friends buy regularly. Collect examples of the advertising and write down where the products are advertised. Copy out the table below and fill in the blanks when you have all your examples.

Product	TV	Radio	Newspapers	Magazines	Cinemas	Posters/ billboards	Leaflets	Internet	Other
1									
2									
3									
4									
5									
6									
7									
8									
9									
10									

b) What can you observe from the table?
c) Do the places where the adverts are found suggest a particular target audience for the products?
d) Is the target population a very large number of people or a relatively small number of people?
e) Do the places suggest the product is only sold locally or also nationally?
f) Are these findings what you expected? Explain your answer.

■ Activity 21.4

For each of the following products, decide on the best advertising media to use. Explain your choice in each case.

a) The owners of a company who produce an established brand of sports shoes, which is sold to teenagers as a leisure shoe, want to become more competitive with rival companies. This product is sold in many areas of the country.
b) A new bicycle has been produced which is suitable for using over rough ground and for cycling up mountains.
c) A new computer game has been developed.
d) A new restaurant in a small town has opened.
e) A famous brand of fizzy soft drink wants to expand its sales.
f) A local town is holding a festival.

■ *Activity 21.5*

Copy out the table and fill in the gaps.

Advantages and disadvantages of different types of advertising media

Advertising media	Advantages	Disadvantages	Examples of suitable products/ services to advertise using this method
Television			
Radio			
Newspapers			
Magazines			
Posters/billboards			
Cinemas			
Leaflets			
Internet			
Others			

Promotion

Different types of promotion

Promotion is used to support advertising and encourage new or existing consumers to buy the product. It is used in the short term to give a boost to sales, but it is not used over long periods of time. An example of this might be when a new chocolate bar has been introduced on to the market and is being advertised on television. In the shops where the chocolate bars are to be sold, free samples may be given out to encourage the customers to try the new chocolate bar and, if they like it, to become regular buyers.

There are several different types of promotion that can be used by businesses.

Price reductions

Examples include reduced prices in shops and money-off coupons to be used when a product is next purchased. Money-off coupons are sometimes found on the bottom of leaflets, in newspapers or on the packet of the product itself, for example, '€1.00 off your next packet'. This encourages the consumer to try the product and, with luck, to become a regular customer.

Gifts

Sometimes small gifts are placed in the packaging of a product to encourage the consumer to buy it. This is often used with products like breakfast cereals and the gifts are usually aimed at children. Sometimes coupons are put on the back of packets and have to be cut out and collected. When a specific number have been gathered they can be exchanged for a gift, such as a book. If the item on offer is more expensive, the coupons may be exchanged for the item but a small additional charge may also have to be paid. Collecting coupons requires several packets of the product to be purchased before the gift can be claimed and so several packets of the product will be sold. The aim is that the customer may continue buying the product even after the promotion has ended.

Competitions

The packaging of a product may include an entry form which allows the customer to enter a competition. The prize is often an expensive item, such as a car. This again obviously encourages the consumer to buy the product.

Point-of-sale display and demonstration

Point-of-sale is the place where the product is being sold – usually a shop. In the shop, there may be a special display of the product. With some products it can be an advantage to show how they should be used and therefore a demonstration in the shop can be a good way of encouraging customers to buy.

After-sales service

With expensive products, like cars or computers, providing an after-sales service can be a way of encouraging the customer to buy. They can be reassured that, if the product goes wrong in the first few weeks or months after they have bought it, they will be able to take it back and get it repaired with no additional charge to themselves. This may make the customer buy from a shop that offers an after-sales service rather than from somewhere that does not.

Free samples

This is most commonly used with products like food, shampoo and cleaning products. A free sample can be handed out in the shop to encourage the customer to try the product and hopefully buy it. Free samples can be delivered to people's houses – although this would not be to every person's house, just the neighbourhoods that they think will buy the product. Free samples can also be given away with other products. For example, new washing machines often contain a free sample of washing powder.

■ *Case study example*

Dolly Dee sell a range of dolls for young children. They are sold through toy shops where a special stand is provided for the shop to display the dolls, so that they are easily seen by customers. A new doll in the range has just been introduced that will eat special food provided with the doll. To show children what the doll will do, a representative of the company is visiting toy shops to demonstrate the doll. Also, with each purchase of the new doll there is a chance to enter a prize draw – the first prize is a trip to Disneyland.

Revision summary: types of promotion

The advantages of promotion

- ☑ It can promote sales at times in the year when sales are traditionally low (off-season purchases).
- ☑ It encourages new customers to try an existing product.
- ☑ It encourages consumers to try a new product.
- ☑ It encourages existing customers to buy a product more often or in greater quantities.
- ☑ It encourages customers to buy a product instead of a competing brand.

Which type of promotion should be used?

When deciding which type of promotion (advertising and promotional methods) will be most suitable to use for a particular product, the following points need to be considered:

■ *The stage of the product life cycle that has been reached* Read Unit 19, pages 275–79, to see which stages of the life cycle require different methods of promotion. If the product is new and has just been launched, the advertising may be more informative, but if the product is well-established and is at maturity then the advertising may be persuasive.

■ *The nature of the product itself* If the product is a producer good, the type of promotion that would be used when promoting the product to other producers will be quite different to the methods used with consumer goods. For example, money-off coupons would not be suitable, but discounts when goods are purchased in bulk would be appropriate. Businesses would not be influenced by collecting money-off coupons, but they will buy in large quantities and will be influenced by a discount. A product sold to other businesses, for example, a machine to wrap perfume, will not be advertised in the same way as the perfume itself, which will be bought by consumers. The advertising for the machine will be informative, while the advertising for the perfume will be persuasive.

■ *The advertising budget* If the business cannot afford a very high budget, this will limit the places where the business can advertise. If the budget is small, television advertising will not be possible. The number of times adverts appear in a magazine could be higher if the budget was larger. With only a small promotion budget, a business will need to plan very carefully where the money will be spent.

■ *The cultural issues involved in international marketing* If the product is to be sold abroad then different types of promotion may be appropriate. The advertising media used will be dependent on factors such as the number of televisions owned, literacy of the population, availability of radio and cinema. It is no use advertising in a national newspaper if most of the population do not read and cannot afford a newspaper. Free samples, competitions, special offers, etc. will also have to be suitable for the culture of the population. In some countries it might not be usual to enter competitions and therefore this promotional route would not act as an attraction to buy the product. The business might need to consider the types of promotion in terms of what is acceptable to people in the countries where the product is being sold. The use of women in adverts or the promotion of alcohol would not be allowed in some parts of the world.

■ *The nature of the target market* Whether it is local, national or international and its size – a local market will require different media to a national one or an international one. Is the product quite a specialist product such as water skis or sold to the majority of the population such as cola?

■ *Activity 21.6*

Choose *ten* products which you and your friends buy regularly. (Use the same ten as for Activity 21.3.) Collect examples of promotions that have been used for these products and explain why these methods of promotion were being used.

■ *Activity 21.7*

For each of the following five products decide the best method of promotion to use. Explain your choice in each case.

a) A new magazine aimed at teenage boys.
b) A new type of pen which is very comfortable to use and does not smudge.
c) A company making a famous brand of football boots wants to expand sales.
d) A new fast food takeaway opens in a small town.
e) A soft toy has been invented that changes colour when hugged and can be dressed in different clothes which also change colour when warmed.

Personal selling

This is used when the exact nature of the product can vary, for example, alterations to a house will be individual to that property and a standard version will not be available. Customers need to be able to discuss their specific requirements before they buy from the business. Also, the price can vary due to the differing requirements from customers. If the product sold does not vary from customer to customer, for example, packets of biscuits, personal selling will not usually be used.

When consumers buy services, such as insurance, they may also need advice on which is the most appropriate for them. Here, personal selling will usually be used.

If the product is expensive, personal selling is usually used. The customer will want to be reassured that they are making the right purchase if they are spending a lot of money. For example, when selling a car, a sales person will be used to advise the customer and make sure that they are happy.

Personal selling is used extensively when selling to other businesses. The items bought may need to be individually tailored to that customer's needs, for example, specialised machinery. If large orders are to be placed, discounts will be negotiated to ensure that the sale is made. For example, discounts are given when bulk-buying computers.

If the business has a stand at a trade fair (a place where many similar businesses come together and show off their products to other businesses, for example, a toy fair for trade customers of toys), personal selling will be used. The sales staff will offer advice on the products and will negotiate prices with the customers.

Public relations

This is concerned with promoting a good image for the company and/or its products. Public relations can take many forms, from sponsoring events such as football matches, to publicity stunts where employees, or owners of the company, take part in a sponsored activity for a good cause.

Another example is where companies donate some of their products to charity – for relief when there has been a natural disaster, or food for victims of a famine.

All these types of activity raise the public's awareness of the company and its products, and increases the likelihood of their choosing its products over its competitors.

Customer service

It is far more expensive to attract a new customer than to keep an existing customer. An important objective of the business is to retain its customer base. In today's business climate many products are similar, making it more difficult to show how one product is different from another. For a business to stand out from competitors it may consider using other promotional activities to add extra value to the product, which could involve providing a good customer service.

Good customer service means not only producing a good quality product that meets the needs of customers but also the following:

■ *Giving advice about the product,* along with care and attention towards the customer, allows the sales person as well as the business to fulfil the customer's requirements. For example, when buying a car it is important that the sales person listens to what the customer wants so that the right choice of vehicle is made to meet their needs. They will need information on the size, performance, price, etc. of the vehicle to decide which will be the best one for them. This care and attention may result in repeat business in the future and positive comments being passed on to the customer's friends.

■ *Delivering goods for customers* has become a common occurrence in the market place. This makes it more convenient for the customer and may encourage a form of impulse buying because the customer does not have to worry about getting the newly purchased product home.

■ *Providing credit facilities,* for example, 'buy now, don't pay anything for 6 months', 'buy this product and pay in instalments'. Credit is usually provided with more expensive goods such as electrical equipment. This makes the product more affordable and consequently widens the market segment as disposable income may become less of a factor in purchasing the product. The credit facilities may incur extra interest charges for the privilege or else interest-free credit may be part of the promotion of the product.

■ *Providing product information* is important whether the customer is purchasing a product for the first time or is an existing customer. Passing on relevant information as well as any helpline numbers will give the customer confidence in the staff and their ability to meet their needs. Helplines are particularly useful to customers purchasing computer equipment.

■ *After-sales service* shows the dedication to customer satisfaction which will ultimately lead to repeat business and potential new customer purchases through reputation and word of mouth. Examples include giving guarantees, giving advice, providing checks on the products to see if they are working correctly, giving a refund if the product proves faulty, exchanging goods if they are not what the customer wants (for example, because the colour of something purchased does not match the colour scheme of their house). Customer service is concerned with keeping the customer happy, by putting emphasis on making the customer feel important and creating a relationship between the business and customer based on trust, reliability and value.

Revision summary: customer service

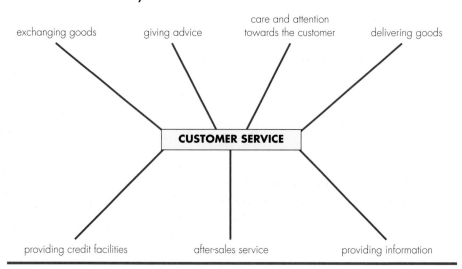

exchanging goods giving advice care and attention towards the customer delivering goods

CUSTOMER SERVICE

providing credit facilities after-sales service providing information

■ *Activity 21.8*

a) Draw up a list of what you would consider to be good customer service.

b) Choose an electrical product you may want to buy for yourself, for example, a CD player, mini-disc player, television. Then visit three places that sell your chosen item. Use your list to see how good their customer service is. Do any of the places have ticks against your whole list?

c) Write a summary of the three places you visited, saying how able they are at providing good customer service. Include any recommendations for improvement that you think they should consider.

■ *Revision questions*

1 Why is promotion an important part of the marketing mix? [3]

2 What *four* types of promotion form part of the marketing mix? [4]

3 State *three* aims of promotion. [3]

4 Describe the *five* steps involved in the advertising process for a new breakfast cereal. [5]

5 a) What is the difference between informative advertising and persuasive advertising? [4]

b) Which would be most suitable for a new computer, and why? [3]

6 What is a *target audience*? [2]

7 Name *eight* different types of advertising media. [4]

8 What *four* types of media might be used for the launch of a new fruit drink, and why? [4]

9 The following graph shows the sales of a company and the amount it spends on advertising.

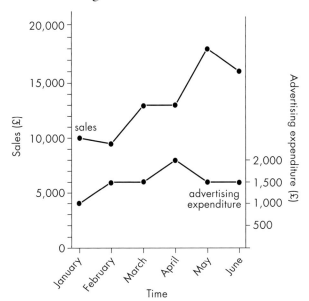

a) Describe the relationship that appears to exist between advertising expenditure and the level of sales. [4]

b) What conclusions can you draw from this information? [2]

10 Explain why advertising is likely to be very important in determining the success of a new product. [4]

11 The management of a company is planning to increase its marketing budget. It is unsure whether to spend more on advertising or to improve packaging. What factors should influence its decision? [5]

12 Why do businesses use different types of promotion? Use examples to help to explain your answer. [5]

13 When should a business use personal selling to promote its product? [2]

14 How does Public Relations (PR) help to promote a business? Include an example to explain your answer. [2]

15 A new restaurant has opened very near to your own restaurant business and has taken many of your customers. What can you do to attract more customers to your restaurant? [6]

The CD-ROM (see details on page x) provides further tests, activities and Case study work on the topics covered in this unit.

22 | The marketing mix: place

This unit will explain:

- ? the role of place in the marketing mix
- ? the channel of distribution
- ? the function of the wholesaler
- ? methods of transporting goods
- ? marketing plans.

By the end of this unit you should be able to:

- ☑ understand the different channels of distribution
- ☑ understand the role of wholesalers
- ☑ select the most suitable channel of distribution for a given product
- ☑ select the most suitable method of transporting goods for a given product
- ☑ draw up a marketing plan.

The role of place in the marketing mix

After deciding on the product and right price, the business has to get the product to the consumer. The product or service has to be available *where* and *when customers want to buy*. Where consumers can buy the product will affect how well it will sell. Think of your local shop where you buy food. Would expensive luxury chocolates sell well? If many of the customers who use the shop are on low incomes then not many chocolates will be sold. If the product is not available where customers want to buy it, and they have to go searching in different shops, then they may give up and buy a competitor's product. It is very easy for a business to get the place wrong and therefore lose sales, or even fail altogether.

How consumers get to know about the product through promotion is important, but they must also be able to buy the products easily.

Channels of distribution

■ **Definition to learn:**

A CHANNEL OF DISTRIBUTION is the means by which a product is passed from the place of production to the customer or retailer.

Businesses have to decide where to sell their products. They also have to decide how to get the product to the consumer, that is, what CHANNEL OF DISTRIBUTION to use. Large expensive products like a house or a yacht will usually be sold by the producer directly to the consumer. If the product is low cost and sold regularly, for example, clothes, it would be difficult for a manufacturer to sell to millions of individual customers, while also being inefficient and not cost effective. Therefore these types of products are often sold to wholesalers or very large retailers who have their own warehouses. The channel of distribution used must be cost effective and efficient.

The channel of distribution can vary – from being directly to the consumer or via intermediary channels. The diagram below summarises the main distribution channels that are used.

The main channels of distribution

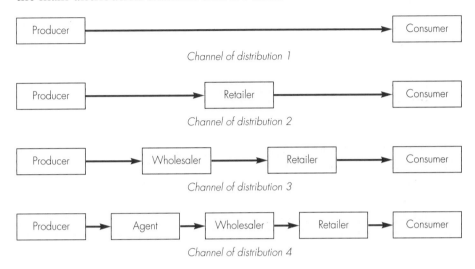

Producer ⟶ Consumer

Channel of distribution 1

Producer ⟶ Retailer ⟶ Consumer

Channel of distribution 2

Producer ⟶ Wholesaler ⟶ Retailer ⟶ Consumer

Channel of distribution 3

Producer ⟶ Agent ⟶ Wholesaler ⟶ Retailer ⟶ Consumer

Channel of distribution 4

Channel of distribution 1

This channel of distribution is very simple. It involves manufacturers selling their products directly to the consumer. This is usually impractical for most products because the consumers probably do not live near to the factory and could not go there to buy the products. It is also particularly true of products that are exported, where the consumers live in another country and cannot buy directly from the producer.

The types of product which may be sold in this way include certain types of agricultural products which are sometimes sold straight from the farm. Products can be sold by mail order catalogue (where the consumers are sent a copy of a catalogue, they order products by post and then products are sent from the factory to the consumer) or via the internet (where products are advertised, orders can be placed and then the goods will be sent by post to the customer). This method may not be suitable for products which cannot easily be sent by post. It may be very expensive to send the products by post and therefore it will not be cost effective.

This channel is also common when selling directly from one manufacturer to another manufacturer. For example, car components are sold directly to the car producer.

If the manufacturer wants to keep control over the way the product is presented to consumers, then they may use their own shops to sell their products. This tends to apply to expensive items such as designer clothes and would be an example of direct selling from the manufacturer to the consumer. It could also apply to perishable items like bread. The bakery makes bread and then sells it through its own shop(s) because the bread needs to be sold quickly before it goes stale.

Channel of distribution 2

The second channel of distribution is where the producer sells directly to the retail outlets and then they sell the product to the consumer. This is most common where the retailer is large, such as a large supermarket, or when the products are expensive, such as furniture or jewellery.

Channel of distribution 3

This channel of distribution involves using a wholesaler, who performs the function of *breaking bulk*.

Breaking bulk is where wholesalers buy products from manufacturers in large quantities and then divide up the stock into much smaller quantities for retailers to buy. Many smaller retailers, especially food retailers, do not want to buy large quantities of different products because they cannot sell them very quickly. Also, they do not have enough space to store large quantities of products. Some food products can only be purchased by retailers in small quantities because they have a relatively short 'shelf life' before they deteriorate.

Channel of distribution 4

When products are exported, the manufacturer sometimes uses an AGENT in the other country. The agent sells the products on behalf of the manufacturer. This can allow the manufacturer to have some control over the way the product is sold to consumers. The manufacturer may export to many countries and may not know the best way to sell the product in other markets. Agents will be aware of local conditions and will be in the best position to select the most effective places in which to sell.

■ **Definition to learn:**
An AGENT is an independent person or business that is appointed to deal with the sales and distribution of a product or range of products. The agent will either put an additional amount on the price to cover their expenses or will receive a commission on sales.

■ *Case study example*

Glaciers Ltd manufacture ice cream and they are located in a city famous for its quality ice cream. The company sells some ice cream directly to local shops because they sell a large amount of ice cream to tourists. Glaciers Ltd mainly sell their tubs of ice cream to wholesalers who sell to small shops in other towns and cities. Very large retailers, for example supermarkets, buy the ice cream in bulk and purchase it directly from Glaciers Ltd. A variety of channels of distribution are used by the company, depending on the customer and the quantity of ice cream purchased.

E-commerce

This is the use of the internet and electronic communications to carry out business transactions. Businesses also use e-mail to inform potential customers of new promotions or to answer queries about products. E-commerce can be used by manufacturers to sell straight to customers (channel of distribution 1) or can be used by large or small retailers to sell to customers (channel of distribution 2).

■ *Activity 22.1*

Choose *six* different products that you or your family buy and find out what channels of distribution are used to get the products from the manufacturer to you, the customer.
Are the channels of distribution used the ones you would expect? Explain your answer.

The role of wholesalers

The wholesaler is very helpful to small retailers and manufacturers in a number of ways.

■ By breaking bulk and buying in large quantities from the manufacturer, the wholesaler can sell small quantities of the product to the retailer. A small retailer would not have the storage space or money to buy in large quantities from the manufacturer. A small retailer is unlikely to sell several thousand tins of beans in a few weeks. Where would it all be stored?
■ The wholesaler buys in bulk from the manufacturer. It is cheaper and easier for the manufacturer to process a few large orders than many small ones. Far fewer transactions are needed.

The diagrams on page 316 show that there is a lot less paperwork for the manufacturer when a wholesaler is used and there are also fewer deliveries to make.

It might be thought that using a wholesaler would mean that products were more expensive for the retailer than buying directly from the manufacturer. The wholesaler has to add their profit on to prices. But, in fact, prices may not be higher because the manufacturer will make savings on administration and delivery costs. This will allow them to sell their products more cheaply to the wholesaler than if they were supplying many thousands of small retailers directly.

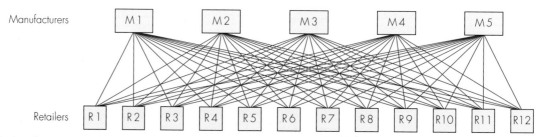

Without a wholesaler, a manufacturer has to process many orders from retailers

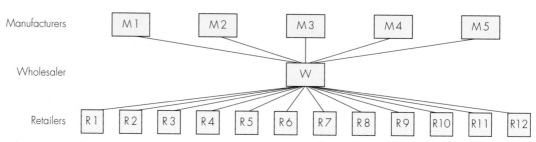

With a wholesaler, a manufacturer has less paperwork

- Storage is provided by the wholesaler instead of the manufacturer having to store the finished products. This also reduces costs for the manufacturer.
- Promotion may be carried out by the wholesaler instead of the manufacturer. This will save the manufacturer having to spend money on promoting the products.
- The wholesaler can give advice on how well the manufacturer's products are selling compared to competitors' products. The wholesaler will know which products are selling well and which ones are not popular. This will help the manufacturer to decide which products need to be changed or even ended altogether.

■ *Activity 22.2: case study task*

You have been asked by a manufacturer of children's toys whether they should use a wholesaler to sell their products. They originally manufactured just a few different types of toys and sold them to a small number of large retailers. They have expanded and are now selling many different types of toys to a large number of small retailers.

Write to the company advising them why you think it might be advantageous to use a wholesaler. They need persuading that a wholesaler will be beneficial, so give detailed explanation and examples to support your point of view.

Selecting the channel of distribution to use

When deciding which channel of distribution to use, manufacturers have to ask themselves a number of questions. This will help them to decide which channel will be the most successful for their products. These are the types of question that need to be answered.

- *What type of product is it?* Is it sold to other producers or to ordinary customers?
- *Is the product very technical?* If it is, it should be sold to the customer by someone with technical knowledge who can explain how it works and what it will do. Direct selling from the manufacturer will probably be selected in this case. An example might be an aeroplane engine; this will be sold to aircraft manufacturers by sales people employed by the manufacturer of the engines.
- *How often is the product purchased?* If it is bought every day, it will need to be sold in many retail outlets. This is so that it is convenient for customers and it will encourage them to buy the good. An example would be a product like newspapers which are purchased daily and are sold in many outlets. Customers do not want to have to travel far to buy a newspaper every day. If they were not readily available, customers might not bother to buy them at all.
- *How expensive is the product? Does it have an image of being expensive?* If the product is marketed as being expensive and of high quality, it will probably be sold through only a limited number of outlets. These shops will be in expensive shopping areas. For example, if the product is an expensive watch, it is no good selling it in discount jewellery shops – it would need to be supplied to superior jewellery shops.
- *How perishable is the product?* If the product goes rotten quickly, such as fruit or bread, then it will need to be widely available in many shops so that it can be sold quickly.
- *Where are the customers located?* If most of the customers are located in the cities, it is no good selling the product in only rural areas. If the customers are located in another country, then different retail routes might be appropriate. The internet might be used for 'on-line trading', for example.
- *Where do the competitors sell their products?* The retail outlets that competitors use will need to be considered. Each manufacturer will probably sell their products in the same outlets as their competitors so that they can compete directly for customers. An example is different brands of soap powder which will all be sold in shops selling household goods.

■ *Activity 22.3*

Choose a channel of distribution for each of the following products. Explain your choice in each case.

a) A farm tractor
b) Children's clothes for export
c) Tins of peas
d) Made-to-measure suit

Revision summary: factors affecting channels of distribution

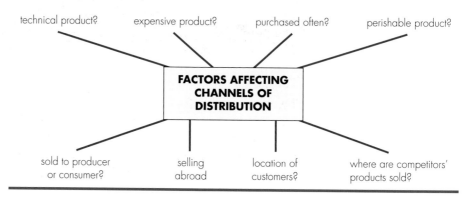

Methods of transporting goods

The method of transportation, that is, the type of transport that the manufacturer uses to deliver the products to the market, varies depending on the product being delivered and the value of the product. Distribution needs to be efficient to make sure that shops do not lose sales because the product is not available and the shelves are empty. Therefore, the method of transport used must be carefully selected to ensure the product arrives at the shop on time and in good condition.

There are several forms of transport which can be used to distribute products.

Road haulage

Lorries and vans are the most versatile type of transport as they can go from and to different places even when there are no rail links – road use is not affected by timetables. The products can be delivered at any time. It is relatively cheap and fast. Some businesses have their own lorries, whilst other businesses use specialist businesses who transport the products for them.

If a business uses its own lorry, it can put the company name on the side of the lorry, which is free advertising. To buy the lorries, a business can use its own profits, take out a loan, for example, from a bank, or it could lease the lorries (rather like renting). If the business owns its own lorries, it will have to pay all the costs of running the lorries such as wages, fuel, depreciation and repairs. When the lorries are not being used, the business still has most of these costs to pay. Therefore, if the lorries are not going to be used most of the time, it might be cheaper to hire a specialist transport business to transport the products.

Railways

These are suitable for long-distance transport and are often cheaper than road transport over long distances. It is faster than by road over a direct route. However, once the freight has reached its destination, it often still has to be transported by road to its final delivery point; the factory or shop may not be near to the railway station.

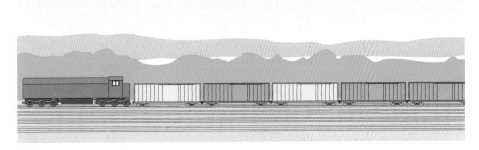

Canal and river

This is quite a slow way to transport products but it is cheap. It is particularly cheap for large, heavy products which would be expensive to transport by road or rail. A suitable river or canal has to be available and going where the business needs to deliver its products.

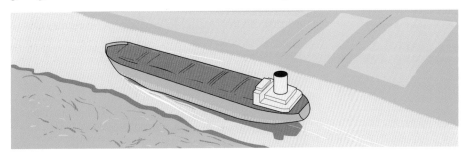

Sea freight

This is used mainly for international trade and carries a lot of different types of products around the world. Today many of these products are carried in containers. These are large metal boxes into which products are packed and then loaded on to ships (or trains and lorries) ready for transport. The containers make it very quick, and therefore cheap, to load and unload the ships. All the cranes need to do is pick up the container and load it on to a train or lorry, which is much quicker than loading and unloading individual crates.

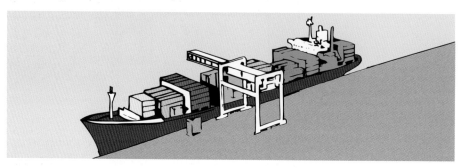

Air freight

This is used for small, expensive goods, or products that are perishable and/or will deteriorate quickly. This is a very expensive form of transport but is also a very quick way of transporting products.

Pipelines

These are used to transport liquids or gas over a long distance. For example, they are used for pumping oil over long distances from the oil fields to the oil refinery or docks. This is much cheaper than pumping crude oil into tankers and then transporting it by road to the coast. Roads are not always available and a pipeline can take the most direct route.

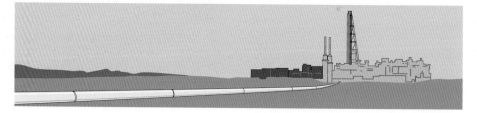

■ *Case study example*

Sengo plc manufacture televisions. Shops in the surrounding area receive their stock of televisions by lorry. Roads in the area are not good and so, if the shops purchasing the televisions are located a long distance away, rail is used for most of the journey. Some of the output is exported and then sea transport is used.

Revision summary: methods of transporting goods

■ *Activity 22.4*

For each of the following products, state the type of transport which would be most appropriate. Explain your choice in each case.

a) Tins of vegetables from the cannery to the wholesalers.
b) Cocoa beans from the plantation to the chocolate factory in another country.
c) Fresh cut flowers from the farm to the retailer in another country.
d) Crude oil from the oil field to the refinery.
e) Cars from the factory to the car showrooms.
f) Coal from the coal mine to the steel mill.
g) Logs from the forests to the saw mills.
h) Soft toys from the factory to the retailer in the same country.

Drawing up a marketing plan

You have now studied all four Ps of the marketing mix – product, price, promotion and place – and you know that getting the right marketing mix is very important. The way the Marketing department would bring everyone's ideas together would be to produce a *marketing plan*. They take a selected product and consider how each of the parts of the marketing mix will be adapted to suit the overall image and target market for this product. If this is successful, sales of the product will improve and so will profits.

■ *Case study example*

Here is an example of a brief marketing plan for a new tennis racquet. The proposed name for the tennis racquet is 'ProAm'. It is supposed to create an image of being suitable for the professional tennis player as well as the keen amateur.

Marketing plan for the 'ProAm' tennis racquet

Product

The product is a tennis racquet which is made of a new light, hard-wearing material.

The design is new and is claimed to allow the player to make the tennis ball go even faster than present tennis racquets. The performance of the player should be improved and this is the brand image that will need to be created through promotion. A logo or symbol which is associated with this brand of tennis racquet will need to be designed so that it will be easily recognisable on the racquet face.

It is likely to be purchased by people who are very skilled at tennis, the keen amateur, in addition to professional tennis players. (A labelled drawing of the product could be included in the marketing plan.)

Price

The tennis racquet is made of a new material and is, therefore, a new development which should mean that price skimming as a pricing strategy could be adopted. The new product offers the possibility of an improved performance and will mean that players will be willing to pay a higher price. Competitive pricing will not be necessary owing to the uniqueness of the new product. Therefore, a high price, well above that of the competing brands of tennis racquets, will be charged for the new product.

Promotion

The main form of advertising will need to include a famous tennis player, probably one of the top three tennis players in the world. The brand image has to be one of being a quality product and by using a top professional tennis player it will attach their success to the product.

The advertising media to use will not be television or newspapers as these are expensive and will be seen by many people who will not be potential customers, thus a waste of money. It will be advertised in specialist tennis magazines and at the point of sale, for example, sports shops and shops at tennis clubs. Promotion in the form of paying a top tennis player to use the tennis racquet will be the best form of advertising as this will be seen by tennis fans all over the world when the player is in tournaments.

Place

The tennis racquet will be sold only through specialist sports shops. This is to emphasise the high quality of the product. The channel of distribution used will be direct from the manufacturer to the retailer to the customer. It is an expensive product which will need to be sold by people who can provide technical information about the product and therefore specialist shops will be used. The manufacturer will want to have some control over the information that is given out about the product and therefore it will sell through shops where it has confidence in the ability of the sales staff to be able to give out accurate information about the new technical qualities of the racquet.

■ *Activity 22.5: case study task*

Choose *one* of the following products:

- a new breakfast cereal
- a new toy for a baby
- a new computer game
- a new chocolate bar
- a range of sports shoes.

Construct a marketing plan for your chosen product. Outline each part of the marketing mix and explain how they link together to create the desired brand image.
  Use the format below to help you to complete the activity.

Format for the marketing plan

1 Choose a name for the product. Decide on the brand image you wish to create.
2 *Product*
   - Describe the appearance and packaging of the product.
   - Who is your target customer? (Consider age, social group, lifestyle.)
   - What is the purpose and use for the product?
3 *Price*
   - What price will be charged for the product? (Give reasons, for example, undercutting competitors.)
4 *Promotion*
   - Where and how will the product be advertised? (Make reference to the different types of advertising media.)
   - Will you use different types of sales promotion? Money-off vouchers? Free gifts?
   - Will your packaging have promotions on it?
5 *Place*
   - Where will the product be sold? For example, a large department store in the city centre? (Give reasons.)
   - What channels of distribution will be used? For example, will you use a wholesaler or sell to retail outlets or sell directly to consumers? (Again, give reasons.)

■ *Revision questions*

1 Describe the channel of distribution you might use if your products are to be sold abroad. [2]

2 Describe the channel of distribution you might use if the product needs to be discussed in detail with the customer to determine exactly what it is that the customer requires. [2]

3 Why do some businesses choose to buy from a wholesaler? [6]

4 What are the advantages to a manufacturer of using a channel of distribution as shown below?
Manufacturer – wholesaler – retailer – customer. [8]

5 A food processing business is thinking of ending the sales of their meals to a retail chain and selling them directly to the consumer on a home delivery basis. What are the advantages and disadvantages of doing this? [8]

6 State and explain *five* factors which should be considered when selecting the channel of distribution to use. [10]

7 State *six* ways products can be delivered to customers or other businesses. [6]

8 What factors influence which method of transportation to use? Include an example to illustrate your answer. [6]

9 Instead of using its own lorries, a business could use a specialist transport company to deliver its products. Give *one* advantage and *one* disadvantage of doing this. [6]

10 Using an example, explain why a business might use more than one method of transportation to deliver its product to the customer. [6]

The CD-ROM (see details on page x) provides further tests, activities and Case study work on the topics covered in this unit.

This unit will explain:

- ? **what is meant by production and productivity**
- ? **methods of production**
- ? **lean production**
- ? **new technology**
- ? **quality control and quality assurance.**

By the end of the unit you should be able to:

- ☑ **understand the concept of value added**
- ☑ **identify factors that can increase productivity**
- ☑ **identify and explain the method of production used in a given situation**
- ☑ **identify and explain ways of implementing lean production**
- ☑ **understand the implications of new technology to business**
- ☑ **identify and explain different ways of ensuring the quality of the product.**

What is meant by production?

Production is the provision of a product or a service to satisfy consumer wants and needs. The process involves firms adding value to a product. ADDED VALUE is the difference between the cost of inputs (e.g. raw materials or components) and the final selling price of the product or service.

Definition to learn:

ADDED VALUE is the difference between the costs of inputs (e.g. raw materials or components) and the final selling price of the product or service.

For example, a firm that produces matches will buy tree trunks. These will be sawn up into smaller and smaller pieces of wood. Eventually match sticks will be produced and the phosphorus ends of the matches will be added. Finally the matches will be packed into boxes and packaged ready for shipment out to the shops. If the wood costs £1,000 for a batch and it produces matches that are sold for £4,000 then the added value is £3,000 (£4,000 selling price – £1,000 for the inputs = £3,000 added value).

■ *Case study example*

A factory manufacturing matches

Logs are bought by
the factory
£1,000

Logs are cut down
into match sticks

Phosphorus ends
are added

Matches are packed
into boxes

Matches are sold
to customers
£4,000
Value added = £3,000

The same process happens for services.

■ **Definition to learn:**

PRODUCTIVITY is the output measured against the inputs used to create it.

Productivity

The level of production is the output of the business. PRODUCTIVITY is the output measured against the inputs (usually labour) used to create it. This is measured by dividing the output over a given period of time by the number of employees:

$$\frac{\text{Output (over a given period of time)}}{\text{Number of employees}}$$

As employees become more efficient the amount of output produced per employee will rise and therefore costs of producing the product will fall.

Productivity is also measured against the capital employed. This is measured by working out the output per machine per period of time. Today this is very important as many firms are capital intensive, i.e. the production process consists mainly of machines and not people.

Businesses strive to increase productivity in order to become more competitive. Different levels of success at being *productively efficient* account for the differences between firms' ability to remain trading and being able to generate profits. For example, the UK had a motorbike industry in the 1960s but Japanese motorbike producers could manufacture their products much more cheaply than the UK firms. This led to the UK producers going out of business by the 1970s as their productivity was not as high as that of the Japanese firms.

Methods of production

■ *Case study example*

Tara wanted to start her own business. She knew that Thai food restaurants were very popular and she was an excellent cook of Thai food. She decided to start cooking dishes of Thai food and selling them to local people for dinner parties. She advertised in the local newspaper and used her own kitchen to prepare the food. Customers would ask her to cook particular dishes of their choice and she would cook it especially for them just how they wanted it. The food was extremely popular and soon she had many more orders for dinner parties than she could cope with and had to turn down customers.

So Tara decided to rent a small factory unit in which she could put large cookers. She expanded and took on several employees to help her. The number of orders received continued to grow as her reputation for producing excellent food spread. She also started to sell more and more to shops who would place orders for the food. The shops would order a large quantity of a particular dish and they would sell it to customers in smaller containers as a takeaway dinner which they could heat up at home. In the new premises she did things slightly differently. Now instead of making one pan of a particular dish, she would make a large quantity in one go and then divide it into large containers ready to be sent out for sale. She would then make a large quantity of another dish, and so on. Still the popularity of the food grew! After about two years of expanding at the small factory unit, Tara decided she could afford to buy much larger premises and invest in new automated machinery to cook the food. The demand was there, the food sold to airlines, hotels, supermarkets as well as the original shops. The new automated process would produce particular dishes in very large quantities, and would produce the same dish continually.

Tara used three main methods of production during the growth of her company:

- JOB PRODUCTION
- BATCH PRODUCTION
- FLOW PRODUCTION.

Job production

This is where products are made specifically to order, for example, a customer would order a particular dish and Tara would make it. Each order is different, and may or may not be repeated. Other examples include: specialist machinery manufacturers who will manufacture a machine for another business to meet a particular specification, bridges, ships, made-to-measure suits, cinema films, or individual computer programs that perform specialised tasks.

Advantages of job production
☑ The product meets the exact requirements of the customer.
☑ The workers often have more varied jobs (they don't carry out just one task).
☑ More varied work increases employee motivation – gives them greater job satisfaction.

Disadvantages of job production
☒ Skilled labour is often used.
☒ The costs are higher because it is often labour intensive.

Batch production

This is where similar products are made in blocks or batches. A certain number of one product is made, then a certain number of another product is made, and so on. Tara made a batch of one type of dish and then made a batch of another type of dish, etc. Other examples include a small bakery making batches of bread, several houses built together using the same design, furniture production – a certain number of tables are made, then a certain number of chairs, or clothing – a batch of a particular size of jeans are produced and then a batch of another size.

■ **Definitions to learn:**

JOB PRODUCTION is where a single product is made at a time.

BATCH PRODUCTION is where a quantity of a product is made at one time, then a quantity of another item will be produced, i.e. batches, usually as orders come in.

FLOW PRODUCTION is where large quantities of a product are produced in a continuous process. Sometimes referred to as mass production.

Advantages of batch production

☑ It is a flexible way of working and production can easily be changed from one product to another.

☑ It still gives some variety to workers' jobs.

☑ Production may not be affected to any great extent if machinery breaks down.

Disadvantages of batch production

✖ It can be expensive as semi-finished or finished products will need moving about.

✖ Warehouse space will be needed for stocks of raw materials and components. This is costly.

Flow production

This is when large quantities of a product are produced in a continuous process. It is sometimes referred to as mass production because of the large quantity of a standardised product that is produced.

It is called flow production because products look as if they are flowing down the production line, i.e. they move continuously along a production line. The basic ingredients are put together at one end of the production line and then the product moves down and more parts are added, and so on, until the product is finished and packaged ready for sale. Large numbers of identical products are made and the costs of production are low (the business will gain from *economies of scale* which were discussed in Unit 6). Examples of products produced in this way include cars, cameras, televisions, packaged foods and drinks; in fact any mass produced, standardised product which is sold to a mass market will be produced in this way.

Advantages of flow production

☑ Costs are kept low and therefore prices are also lower.

☑ It is easy for capital-intensive production methods to be used – reducing labour costs and increasing efficiency.

☑ Capital-intensive methods may only need relatively unskilled workers and therefore little training is needed.

☑ Low costs and therefore low prices usually mean high sales.

☑ Goods are produced quickly and cheaply.

☑ There is no need to move goods from one part of the factory to another as with batch production, so time is saved.

Disadvantages of flow production

✖ It is a very boring system for the workers, there is little job satisfaction.

✖ The capital costs of setting up the production line can be very high.

✖ If one machine breaks down the whole production line will have to be halted.

The most important factor which determines which method of production to use will be the *demand* for the product.

- If a fairly unique product or an individual service is required (in fact many services are individual to the customer and will be specifically tailored to their requirements), job production will be used.
- If demand is higher and more products can be sold but not in very large quantities, batch production will be used. The product will be produced in a certain quantity to meet the particular order.
- If, however, there is a large and fairly steady demand for the product, it becomes economic to set up a production line and continuously produce the product.

job production

batch production

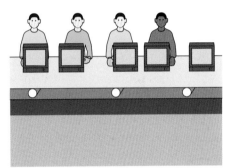

flow production

■ *Activity 23.1: case study tasks*

a) What method of production is used by each of the following businesses? Explain the reasons for your choice.

- ABC plc manufacture a well-known brand of chocolate bar. The chocolate bars are sold in many different shops and other outlets, and millions are sold a year.
- Alexander is a hairdresser. He styles men's hair and has a number of regular customers.

b) Hudson Limited have been in business for ten years manufacturing components for cars. They sell to several large car producers. Hudson Limited want to expand and manufacture components for aircraft engines. They have decided to build a new factory abroad, near to where aircraft engines are manufactured. Some of the new components they plan to produce will be designed for only one type of engine, whereas most of the other components will be standardised and used in several different models of engine.

Hudson Limited have chosen the new site for the factory but have not decided on the method of production to use. You have been asked to advise them on what to use. Explain your choice of the method(s) of production they should use.

Stock control

Have you ever gone into a shop and found they have run out of what you wanted? If so, then the shop might have had higher sales than usual or else their delivery of stock might have been late. To ensure that there is always enough stock to satisfy demand, stock levels must be carefully controlled. Similarly, in a manufacturing business, stocks of raw materials or components must be available with sufficient LEAD TIME to meet the needs of the Production department. This is particularly true of batch and flow production where there will be delays in production if there are not enough raw materials or components at hand.

Stock can take various forms, including raw materials, components, partly finished goods, or finished products ready for delivery. It can even include stocks of spare parts for machinery in case of breakdowns.

When stock levels get to a certain point (reorder point) they will be reordered to bring stocks back up to the maximum level again. The business must reorder before stocks get too low to allow time for the goods to be delivered. If stock levels get too low they might actually run out if there is an unexpectedly high demand for the goods. If too high a level of stocks are held then this costs a lot of money; the business has bought the goods but they are not being used and the money could be put to better use. The following graph demonstrates how stock levels can be managed:

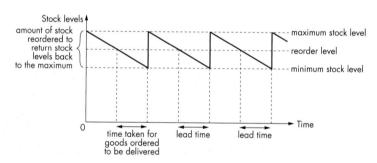

Effectively managing stock levels is very important to all types of businesses, especially manufacturing and retail businesses.

Lean production

Flow production or mass production concentrates on producing a large volume of a product using a production line. The workers and the machines are highly specialised and because of this the workers' jobs are boring. The Japanese way of manufacturing used a different approach to this called lean production.

LEAN PRODUCTION covers a variety of techniques used by business to cut down on any waste and therefore increase efficiency. It tries to reduce the time it takes for the product to be developed and become available in the shops for sale, so that it is as quick as possible.

■ **Definition to learn:**

LEAD TIME is the margin of time between the date when stock is obtained and the date when it is sold on.

■ **Definition to learn:**

LEAN PRODUCTION Techniques used by business to cut down on any waste and therefore increase efficiency, for example, by reducing the time it takes for the product to be developed and become available for sale.

Lean production might include using:

■ Kaizen
■ just-in-time production techniques
■ cell production
■ Kanban.

Kaizen

■ **Definition to learn:**

KAIZEN is a Japanese term meaning 'continuous improvement' through the elimination of waste.

KAIZEN means 'continuous improvement' in Japanese and its focus is on the elimination of waste. The improvement does not come from investing in new technology or equipment but through the ideas of the workers themselves. Small groups of workers meet regularly to discuss problems and possible solutions. This has proved effective because no one knows the problems that exist better than the workers who work with them all the time, so they are often the best ones to think of ways to overcome them.

Kaizen eliminates waste, for example, by getting rid of piles of stock or reducing the amount of time taken for workers to walk between jobs so that they eliminate unnecessary movements. When Kaizen is introduced, the factory floor is reorganised by repositioning machines tightly together in *cells* (see *Cell production* below), in order to improve the flow of production through the factory. The floor will be open and marked with colour-coded lines which map out the flow of materials through the production process.

The Kaizen effect: before

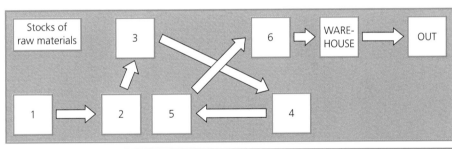

The Kaizen effect: after

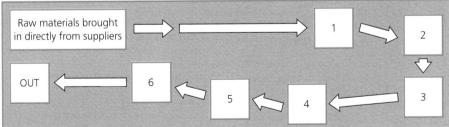

■ *Activity 23.2*

Identify the changes that have taken place in the reorganisation of the factory floor using Kaizen principles.

Advantages of Kaizen might be:

■ Increased productivity
■ Reduced amount of space needed for the production process
■ Work-in-progress is reduced
■ Improved layout of the factory floor may allow some jobs to be combined therefore freeing up employees to carry out some other job in the factory.

Just-in-time

JUST-IN-TIME or JIT is a production method whose focus is on reducing or virtually eliminating the need to hold stocks of raw materials or components and on reducing work-in-progress and stocks of the finished product. The raw materials or components are delivered just in time to be used in the production process, the making of any parts are just in time to be used in the next stage of production and the finished product is made just in time to be delivered to the customer. All this reduces the costs of holding stock, as no extra stock is ordered to keep in the warehouse just in case it is needed. Therefore warehouse space is not needed, again reducing costs. The finished product is sold quickly and so money will come back to the business more quickly, helping its cash flow.

To operate just-in-time, stocks of raw materials, work-in-progress and finished products are run down and no extra stock is kept. The business will therefore need very reliable suppliers and an efficient system of ordering raw materials or components. Just-in-time is usually implemented along with the introduction of cell production.

Cell production

Cell production is where the production line is divided into separate, self-contained units (cells) each making an identifiable part of the finished product instead of having a flow or mass production line. This method of production improves the morale of the employees and makes them work harder so they become more efficient. The employees feel more valued and are less likely to strike or cause disruption.

Kanban

Kanban is a system of ordering that is used alongside JIT production. It often operates by having two component bins, one on the production line and one being made ready. When the first is empty it is wheeled with its Kanban order card to the section of the factory that produces those components. This triggers the production of the components, which should then be ready before the second component bin is empty. This reduces the amount of part-finished stock and means that everyone has to work together and efficiently so that production is not held up.

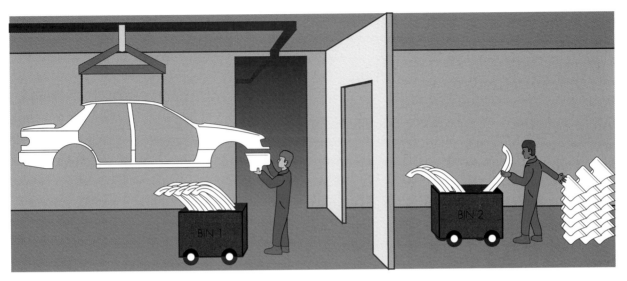

The Kanban method

Bin 1 is used on the production line until it is empty

Bin 2 is taken to the production line when Bin 1 is empty; Bin 1 is then filled and ready to go back

Improvements in technology

Technological advances have allowed the mechanisation and automatisation of production methods in many industries. For example, the car industry is almost entirely automated. The use of automation, robotics and CAD/CAM keeps businesses ahead of the competition, keeps costs falling, reduces prices and improves the products manufactured.

- *Automation* is where the equipment used in the factory is controlled by a computer to carry out mechanical processes such as paint spraying on a car assembly line. The production line will consist mainly of machines and only a few people will be needed to ensure that everything proceeds smoothly.
- *Mechanisation* is where the production is done by machines but operated by people, for example, a printing press. Robots are machines that are programmed to do tasks, particularly useful for unpleasant, dangerous and difficult jobs. They are quick, very accurate and work non-stop 24 hours a day.
- *CAD (computer aided design)* is computer software that draws items being designed more quickly and allows them to be rotated to see the item from all sides instead of having to draw it several times. It is used to design new products or to restyle existing products. It is particularly useful for detailed technical drawings.
- *CAM (computer aided manufacture)* is where computers monitor the production process and control machines or robots on the factory floor. For example, on the production line of a car plant computers will control the robots that spot-weld the car body together or the robots that spray paint the car.

The advantages of new technology

☑ Greater productivity as new production methods are used.

☑ Greater job satisfaction stimulates workers, as routine and boring jobs are now done by machines.

☑ The types of jobs have changed as more skilled workers are needed to use the new technology. Business must offer training to existing workers in the use of new technology. The workers are more motivated and therefore improve the quality of their work.

☑ Better quality products are produced owing to better production methods and better quality control.

☑ Better consumer service results from computers being used to monitor stock levels.

☑ Quicker communication and reduced paperwork, owing to computers, lead to increased profitability.

☑ The information that is available to managers is much greater and this results in better and quicker decision-making.

☑ New products are introduced as new methods of production are introduced. The market and tastes of the consumer have changed.

The disadvantages of new technology

☒ Increased unemployment as machines/computers replace people on the factory floor and in offices.

☒ Expensive to invest in which also increases the risks as large quantities of products need to be sold to cover the cost of purchasing the equipment.

☒ Employees are unhappy with the changes in their work practices when new technology is introduced.

☒ New technology is changing all the time and will often become outdated quite quickly and need to be replaced if the business is to remain competitive.

■ Activity 23.3

a) Choose a business that manufactures a product and find out what new technology/equipment has been installed in the Production department over the last five years.

b) What are the advantages and disadvantages of these changes?

c) How have these changes affected the business (e.g. employment, profits, sales, quality of the products)?

■ Activity 23.4

a) Choose a business that produces a service and find out what new technology/equipment has been installed in the business over the last five years. (This will probably be computers or specialised computer software.)

b) What are the advantages and disadvantages of these changes?

c) How have these changes affected the business (e.g. employment, profits, sales, quality of service)?

Quality control and quality assurance

Imagine you went to the shops and bought a music CD, took it home and found that it would not play any music – you would not be a very happy customer! The business would get a bad reputation if this happened very often and would lose sales. A business needs to try to ensure that all the products it sells are free of faults or defects. This will ensure that the business will maintain a good reputation and will help to increase sales. The business needs a product with a good design, then it needs to ensure that it is manufactured without any faults and finally the product needs to satisfy the wishes of the customer.

Quality is a very important part of any business in both the manufacturing and service sectors. There are several ways businesses can ensure that they produce a good quality product or provide a good service.

Quality control

A traditional way to make sure that products went out of factories with no defects was to have Quality Control departments whose job it was to take samples at regular intervals to check for errors. If errors were found then a whole batch of production might have to be scrapped or reworked. This was expensive for the business. The Quality Control department would check that quality was being maintained during the production of goods, try to eliminate errors before they occurred, and find any defective products before they went out of the factory to customers.

Quality assurance

This takes a slightly different approach to quality. The business will make sure quality standards are set and then it will apply these quality standards throughout the business. The purpose of quality assurance is to make sure that the customer is satisfied, with the aim of achieving greater sales, increased added value and increased profits. To implement a quality assurance system several aspects of production must be included. Attention must be paid to the design of the product, the components and materials used, delivery schedules, after-sales service and quality control procedures. The workforce must support the use of this system or it will not be effective. TQM is one approach to implementing a quality assurance system.

TQM

■ Definition to learn:

TOTAL QUALITY MANAGEMENT (TQM) is the continuous improvement of products and processes by focusing on quality at each stage of production.

Again it is the influence of the Japanese that has changed the way quality is ensured in many businesses today. It is the idea of TQM (TOTAL QUALITY MANAGEMENT) that is at the heart of many practices. TQM is the continuous improvement of products and processes by focusing on quality at each stage of production. It tries to get it right first time and not have any defects. There is an emphasis on ensuring that the customer is always satisfied, and the customer can be other people/departments in the same business that you are completing tasks for, not just the final customer.

This should mean that quality is maintained throughout the business and no faults should occur, as all employees are concerned with ensuring that a quality good or service is delivered. TQM should mean that costs will fall. It is closely linked with Kaizen and the use of quality circles. Quality circles are where groups of workers meet regularly and discuss problems and possible solutions.

| TOTAL QUALITY MANAGEMENT | Encourages everyone to think about quality
Quality is the aim for all staff
Customers' needs are paramount |

| QUALITY ASSURANCE | Inspection during and after production
Aim is to stop faults from happening
Aim is to ensure products attain a pre-set standard
Team working and responsibility |

| QUALITY CONTROL | Inspectors checking finished goods
Detection of components or products that are faulty
Involves considerable waste |

■ Activity 23.5

Look at products or services that are supplied locally. Do any of them have any marks on them to show that they are a quality product? How do you as a customer know that something has been well made?

Revision summary: ways to increase productivity

improved quality control/assurance reduces waste

improve employee motivation

introduce more modern equipment

WAYS TO INCREASE PRODUCTIVITY

use machines instead of people to do jobs (labour-saving machinery)

train staff to be more efficient

improve stock control

■ *Revision questions*

1 What is meant by *added value*? [2]

2 A new machine has been introduced into a factory and 100 workers can now produce 1,500 units per day. Using the old machine 100 workers could only produce 1,000 units per day. How much has output per head increased? [2]

3 How might a business benefit from increasing value added? [2]

4 What is meant by *job production*? [2]

5 Output expands and a business changes from job to batch production. What are the advantages of doing this? [4]

6 What problems would a cake manufacturer have if it changed to flow production? [4]

7 What factors influence the type of production a business should use? [6]

8 What are the advantages and disadvantages of holding high levels of stock of finished products? [8]

9 What are the advantages and disadvantages of holding low levels of components and raw material stocks? [8]

10 How should a business decide when to re-order stock? [2]

11 What is meant by *lean production*? [2]

12 What is meant by 'an increase in productivity'? Give an example. [4]

13 Who benefits from a business increasing its efficiency? [6]

14 The technology used in production machinery has improved over recent years. Discuss how this might affect the Production and Human Resources departments. [4]

15 Why should a business use quality control systems in their production process? [4]

The CD-ROM (see details on page x) provides further tests, activities and Case study work on the topics covered in this unit.

24 Factors affecting location

This unit will explain:

- ❓ **what factors affect the location of manufacturing business**
- ❓ **what factors affect the location of retailing business**
- ❓ **what factors may cause a business to relocate (home or abroad)**
- ❓ **what factors affect the location of a service sector business.**

By the end of the unit you should be able to:

- ☑ **identify the relevant factors that affect the location of a manufacturing business**
- ☑ **identify the relevant factors that affect the location of a retailing business**
- ☑ **identify the relevant factors that cause a business to relocate at an alternative site in the home country or abroad**
- ☑ **identify the relevant factors that affect the location of a service sector business.**

Location of industry

The location of a business is usually considered either when the business is first setting up or when its present location proves unsatisfactory for some reason. The business may decide to look for an alternative site or may decide to set up additional factories/shops either in the home country or abroad.

Many businesses operate on a large scale and look at location on a world level not just a national or continental level. This is often termed *globalisation* because firms plan many aspects of their business, such as location decisions, marketing and sales, on a global scale. (See Unit 25 for further discussion of these issues.)

In these circumstances, a variety of factors will influence the location decisions of the business. The various factors will not have an equal influence, some will be of critical importance whilst others will only be preferences. These differences will depend on the type of business making the decision. For example, if the business is expanding and changing from batch production to flow production to manufacture its products it may need to move to larger premises in order to make space for an automated production line. Skilled labour may no longer be important to the business as machinery is used instead of people.

Factors affecting where a manufacturing business chooses to locate will usually be different from those factors affecting where a retailing business will set up, and so these are discussed separately even though some factors will be common to both.

Factors affecting the location of manufacturing business

Production methods and location decisions

The type of production methods used in a manufacturing business is going to have a significant influence on the location of that business.

- If job production is used, the business is likely to be on a small scale and so the influence of the nearness of components, for example, will be of less importance to the business than if flow production is used.
- If production will be on a large scale, the location of component suppliers might be of greater importance because a large number of components will need to be transported and the cost will be high.

Market

Locating a factory near to the market for its products used to be thought important when the product gained weight, i.e. when it became heavier and, therefore, more expensive to transport than the raw materials/components. An example might be a drinks manufacturer, where the bottles and ingredients are lighter than the filled bottles and so the factory may have to be located near to the main markets for the product.

Today, because transport is much improved, being near to markets is of less importance, even for weight-gaining or bulk-increasing products. If the product perishes quickly and needs to be fresh when delivered to the market, such as milk, bread or cakes, the factory might be located close to its retail outlets. However, ways of preserving food for longer have reduced the importance of this factor.

Raw materials/components

Similar to the weight-gaining or bulk-increasing products discussed above, the raw materials may be considerably heavier or more expensive to transport than the finished product. Where a mineral is processed from the ore, there will usually be considerable waste produced in this process. It is often cheaper to process the ore near to the mining site than to transport it elsewhere.

If a particular process uses many different components, a business might look very carefully at its location. If many of these component suppliers are located near to one another, it might be preferable to locate near to these suppliers. This was often a factor in car manufacturing, where many different components are used to assemble a car, but again improved transport has lessened this influence.

If the raw material needs to be processed quickly whilst still fresh, locating near to the raw material source is still important. An example is frozen vegetables or tinned fruits, which need to be processed quickly. There will also be a lot of waste generated which does not go into the packaging.

External economies of scale

In addition to component suppliers, firms who can support the business in other ways might need to be located nearby. Support businesses which install and maintain equipment may be better if nearby so that they can respond quickly to breakdowns. The local education establishments, such as universities, might have research departments who work with the business on developing new products – being in close contact may help the business to be more effective.

Availability of labour

To be able to manufacture products at least some labour will be necessary, even if it is not a great number. If particular skilled labour is needed, it may be easier and cheaper to recruit these employees if the business sets up in an area where people with the relevant skills live. If the manufacturing process requires a large number of unskilled workers, an area where there is high unemployment may be more suitable. Also, the wage rates paid to employees might vary and an area where wages are lower might be preferable.

Government influence

When a government wants to encourage businesses to locate in a particular area it will offer state-funded grants to encourage firms to move there. This can be a favourable influence. If an area has high unemployment, the government might give money to businesses who locate in that area. However, the government influence might be negative in that there might be regulations or restrictions on what businesses can do. In fact, a government can refuse to allow a business to set up altogether. An example might be where the business produces a harmful waste product during the manufacturing process and the government will not want the waste product to poison the surrounding area, for example, nuclear waste. (Government influence on location is discussed in Unit 4.)

Transport and communications

Businesses usually need to be near to a transport system, be it road, rail, inland waterway, port or airport. Where the product is for export then the ability to easily get to a port will be important, indeed some businesses establish themselves in the surrounding buildings of the port for ease of access to the ships. A nearby motorway can reduce costs by speeding up the time spent delivering the products to market even when the market is quite a distance away.

Power

Today electricity is available in most places and therefore the availability of power is not so important. But to some industries having a *reliable* source of power, i.e. no regular power cuts, may be essential.

Water supply

The same could be said of water as for power, a reliable supply will be needed. If large supplies of water are needed as part of the manufacturing process, for example, for cooling purposes with a power station, then being near to a water supply, such as the sea or a river, will be important. Also, the cost of the water supply might be important in some areas where it is expensive.

Personal preferences of the owners

Since it will be the owners of the business who usually decide where to locate the business, their personal preferences will often influence their decision. They may originate from a particular area and wish to stay in the area due to family links or they may want to live in an area that is particularly pleasant for some reason, for example, good climate or a lot of nearby entertainments.

Climate

This will not influence most manufacturing businesses but occasionally climate might be important. Silicon Valley in the USA has a very dry climate which aids the production of silicon chips. Also warmer climates reduce the heating costs that would be incurred in colder climates – for some businesses this will be an important consideration when deciding where to locate within the country.

Revision summary: factors affecting the location of manufacturing businesses

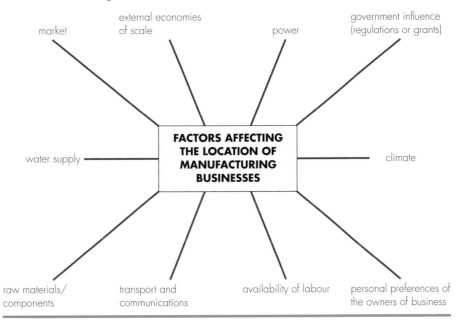

■ *Activity 24.1: case study task*

B&B plc manufactures food products. It wants to set up a factory to make a new ice cream. The new ice cream uses fresh ingredients – mainly freshly picked fruit – to maintain the fruits' flavour. The fruit used comes from one particular region of the country. This region is quite a long way away from the main cities where most of the country's population lives.

The production process is mainly automated and requires only a few skilled workers to supervise the equipment. It uses a lot of water in the mixture and also a lot of water to wash out the machinery every day to keep it clean.

The new ice cream is sold to domestic customers through supermarkets and other food stores. It is not sold abroad.

a) Which factors affecting the location of manufacturing plants will be most important to this business when deciding where to locate? Explain why you think they will be important.
b) Which do you think will be the most important factor and why?

Factors affecting the location of a retailing business

Shoppers

Whether an area is visited regularly by many shoppers or whether it is only visited occasionally is going to make a big difference to whether a retailer decides to locate in a particular area. Most retailers will want an area which is popular, such as a shopping mall/centre. The type of shopper an area attracts will also influence the attractiveness of the area to particular types of retailers. If the retailer sells expensive goods, it needs to be in an area where people on high incomes might visit, or if the goods are small gift-type products, the retailer might want to be in an area visited by tourists.

Nearby shops

Being able to locate near to shops/businesses which are visited regularly, such as a post office or popular fast food outlet, will mean that a lot of people pass your shop on the way to other shops and businesses. They may look in your window as they pass and may go in and make a purchase. There may be many competitors nearby. You may think that this is bad for business, but it can also be a positive situation. If the business sells clothes, then being located near to many other clothes shops encourages people to visit the area as there is a lot of choice, therefore increasing business. If the clothes shop is in a position where there are no other similar shops nearby, it may not attract people to visit the shop as there will be limited choice.

Customer parking available/nearby

Where many of the customers use their cars, the ability to park their vehicle will be very important as to whether they visit particular shops.

Where parking is convenient and near to the shops, this will encourage shoppers to that area and therefore possibly increase your sales. Lack of parking may put people off visiting the area and sales will be lower.

Availability of suitable vacant premises

If a suitable vacant shop or premises are not available for purchase or rent, the business may not be able to locate in the area it wishes. Prime sites in the centre of shopping areas will be in short supply.

Rent/taxes

The more central the site of the premises, the higher the rent and taxes will usually be. If a retail area is popular, there will be a high demand for sites in this area and therefore the cost of renting these sites will be higher. If the area is less popular, i.e. on the edge of town, the demand and therefore the rents will be lower. If the government also imposes taxes on the premises, the more popular sites will attract higher taxes.

Access for delivery vehicles

Access for delivery vehicles might be a consideration if it is very difficult for them to gain access to the premises.

Security

The rate of crime in an area might be of importance to a business. High rates of crimes such as theft and vandalism may deter a business from locating in a particular area. Insurance companies may not want to insure the business if it is in an area of high crime. A shopping area which is patrolled by guards, even though it will be more expensive to rent the premises, might prove preferable.

Revision summary: factors affecting the location of retailing businesses

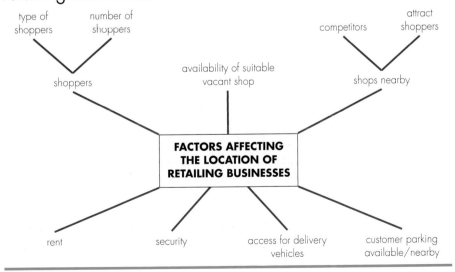

■ *Activity 24.2: case study task*

B&C Limited are going to open a new shop selling fashion shoes. The shoes are good quality and are aimed at younger women. B&C Limited have narrowed down the choice of where to locate the new shop to two nearby towns.

a) Read the information on the two towns and then select which one will be the best location for the new shop. Explain your choice.

	Town Y	**Town Z**
Population	30,000	10,000
% in age group 0–9 10–25 26–40 41–65 66+	15 30 30 20 5	20 35 30 10 5
Unemployment	low	high
Crime rate	low	low
Shopping centre	large – about 100 shops	small – about 40 shops
Parking facilities	large car parks but queues build up at busy times	plenty of parking available – no problems at busy times
Types of shops in the shopping centre	clothes shops, shoe shops, banks, household goods, food shops	food shops, household goods, clothes shops, post office, banks

b) What other information is needed to help make the final decision? Explain why the information is needed.

Factors that influence a business to relocate either at home or abroad

The present site is not large enough for planned expansion

When a business sees a steady increase in its sales, it may invest in its present site and produce more products, but there will be a limit to how much it can expand within its present location. There will come a point when, if it cannot buy or rent adjacent premises, it will probably move to a bigger site. *Note:* It may choose to set up an extra factory elsewhere and then the original factors that affect location of a business will be important.

Raw material source runs out

If the raw material source runs out, a business must either bring in alternative supplies from elsewhere or move to a new site where it can more easily obtain these supplies. This is particularly true of mineral sources such as oil wells.

Difficulties with the labour force

If the business is located in a country where wages keep on rising, there might come a point when the business decides to relocate overseas to take advantage of lower wage costs. This has been true of many Western businesses moving their manufacturing plants to poorer countries where the wages paid are much lower. If particular types of skilled labour are needed by the business, it might need to relocate to a different area where it can recruit the right type of labour to enable the business to expand.

Rents/taxes rising

If other costs such as rents or taxes keep rising, this might also cause the business to consider relocating to keep its costs down.

New markets open up overseas

If new markets open up in different countries, it may be more cost effective to locate a manufacturing plant there than to transport the goods overseas.

Government grants

Governments may want to encourage foreign businesses to locate in their country to bring in investment and jobs to the country. They may be willing to give money to businesses to induce them to come to their country rather than go elsewhere.

Tariff barriers

If there are tariff barriers, such as quotas (where a limit is placed on the quantity of imports of a particular good), then by locating in that country there will be no restrictions. An example of this is the investment by Japanese car companies in Europe in order to get around the European Union's strict quotas for the import of cars.

Revision summary: factors that influence a decision to relocate

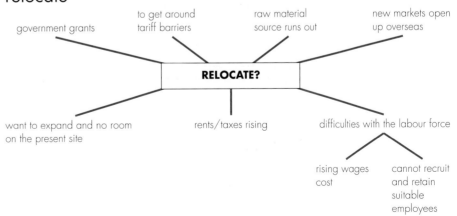

■ *Activity 24.3: case study task*

MT Furniture Limited wants to expand. Presently it is located in a small factory in the old part of the city. New markets are opening up abroad and it has experienced a steady increase in its sales for the last five years. There is no room to build onto the existing factory and none of the adjacent factories are for sale. The business has been forced to look for another site if it wants to grow.

Because more and more of its sales are exported, it is considering whether to build a factory abroad or whether to build one in its home country. The following information has been gathered about two sites, one near its existing factory and one abroad in the country where most of its products are exported.

Your task is to study the information provided and then write a report to the Board of Directors of MT Furniture Limited advising them of the advantages and disadvantages of each of the sites. Include a recommendation of which you think is the best site to choose. Remember to give reasons for your choice.

	Site A – on the outskirts of the city near to the original factory	Site B – in main export market
Market	Large local market	Large export market and growing
Communications	Good communications – main roads connect to all parts of the country and main port, which is several miles away	Good communications – main roads connect to all parts of the country and ports are very close to the site
Raw materials/ Components	Raw materials and components are close to the site – easily available	Raw materials and components are not close to the site – not easily available – some will need to be imported
Wage rates	High	Low – labour is very cheap
Skilled labour	Skilled workers employed at the present site – not too far from this site. Also additional skilled workers are available in the area.	Very few skilled workers are available.
Unemployment	Low	High
Rents/land taxes	High	Low
Government grants	No grants available	Grants paid towards capital investment when a new company is setting up in their country

Factors affecting the location of a service sector business

Customers

Locating a service sector business near its customers will be very important for certain types of services. These are usually services where direct contact between the business and the customer is required. If a quick response time is needed to serve the customers then the business needs to be located nearby. This would be true for plumbers and electricians who serve the local area in which they live. Other examples of personal services that need to be convenient for customers to use are hairdressers, beauticians, caterers, restaurants, cafés, gardeners, builders, post offices.

Some services do not need to be near to customers. Direct personal contact is not necessary as these services can be contacted by telephone, post or the internet. These businesses can therefore be located in different parts of the country or in different countries to where their customers live.

Personal preference of the owners

The owners can influence where particular services choose to locate. They often locate the business near to where they live.

Technology

Technology has allowed some services to locate away from their customers. Some services are now conducted by telephone or via the internet and therefore the business itself does not need to be near to customers. These service businesses can locate anywhere and can therefore choose to locate on the outskirts of cities or even in remote areas (dependent on how many employees are required), so that they can take advantage of cheaper rent.

Availability of labour

If the service business requires a large number of employees then it cannot locate in remote areas. It will need to locate near to a large town or city. If a particular type of skilled labour is required then it may also have to locate near to where this labour is found. However, it is more likely that the particular skilled labour will move near to the business for work rather than the other way round.

Climate

Climate will affect some businesses particularly if they are linked to tourism in some way. Hotels often need to locate themselves where the climate is good in order to serve the needs of their customers.

Near to other businesses

Some services serve the needs of large businesses, such as firms that service equipment found in big companies. They will need to be nearby to respond quickly to a call to repair equipment. Services such as banks and post offices need to be near busy areas for the convenience of customers and this often means being near to retail shops that people visit regularly.

Rent/taxes

If the service does not need to be on the main streets in a town or city centre then they will locate on the outskirts of town to benefit from lower rents and taxes, e.g. doctors, dentists, lawyers.

Revision summary: factors affecting the location of a service sector business

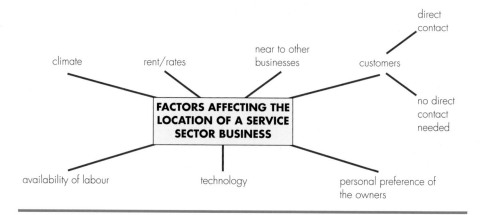

■ *Activity 24.4*

For each of the services listed below:
a) Choose four factors that you think are likely to affect its location.
b) Explain how you think each factor will influence the location decision.

■ Electrician (sole trader) serving domestic customers
■ Computer software firm which writes computer games that are sold all over the world
■ Small firm that trains people to scuba-dive and hires out scuba-diving equipment.

■ *Revision questions*

1   The directors of a company are planning to
expand production. A decision must be
made between building a new factory in
their own country or building one overseas
in Country B. Country B is seen as a
potential new market for the company's
products.
   a)   What would be the advantages to the
   company of exporting its products to
   Country B rather than producing them
   there?   [6]
   b)   'Our products have always sold well in
   our country so I think they will sell well
   in Country B,' says the Marketing
   Director. Explain why this may not be
   true.   [4]

2   Governments often intervene in companies'
location decisions. Why do you think this
happens?   [8]

3   Choose *two* factors affecting a business
location decision and explain why each of
them is important.   [6]

4   Why does the type of product influence
where it is produced?   [6]

5   Explain *six* factors that would affect the
location decision of a manufacturing
business.   [12]

6   A new shop selling computers is going to be
opened in the local town. What factors will
influence whether it decides to locate on the
outskirts of the town or in the centre?   [6]

7   What factors affect where a business
providing computer training for other
businesses will locate?   [6]

8   Why do the factors affecting the location of
a service sector business differ from those
affecting a primary sector business?   [6]

*The CD-ROM (see details on page x) provides further tests, activities and Case study work on the
topics covered in this unit.*

Business in the international community

The international dimension

There is an old expression which says 'no one is an island'. This means that none of us can live our lives without being affected by – or affecting – other people. So it is with businesses – no manager can operate a business

Case study example

Consider this simple business example to see how business activities so often involve an international dimension. All of the references to international issues are in **bold**:

Asif managed a manufacturing business. He bought many of his supplies **from abroad – as imports**. Over one half of the output of the business was **sold abroad – as exports**. Some of his products had been changed to meet **different safety laws which operated in other countries**. Some of the exports had to pay a **tariff** as they entered certain countries. Interest rates had been increased recently to stop the **value of the currency** falling, compared to foreign currencies. Asif's business faced increased competition from **other countries' producers** which had lower labour costs. He had heard that his country's government was planning to join an **economic union with other countries**. This might increase competition even further.

by completely ignoring the rest of the community. It was seen in Unit 4 how government and legal controls had a very important part to play in influencing what businesses were able to do. This unit considers the international community and how this can both control and help managers in running their businesses.

In the case study on page 350 there are several examples of how the international community has an impact on the success of one business. It is true to say that 'no business is an island'.

Exchange rates

Definition to learn:

The EXCHANGE RATE is the price of one currency in terms of another, for example £1:$1.5.

If you have ever travelled abroad then you will know that it is usually necessary to change your money into *foreign currency*. Every country has its own currency and to be able to buy things in other countries you have to use the local currency. How much of another currency do you get in exchange for your own country's money? This will depend on the EXCHANGE RATE between your currency and the foreign currency you wish to buy.

Assume that the exchange rate between the £ sterling and the US $ is £1:$1.5. This means that for each £1 being changed into dollars, $1.5 would be received in exchange. In effect, this exchange rate is the *price* of one currency in terms of another.

How are exchange rates determined?

Most currencies are allowed to vary or *float* on the foreign exchange market according to the *demand* and *supply* of each currency. Just as the prices of goods can vary according to supply and demand in a free market – as was seen in Unit 20 – so exchange rates will vary between currencies on a day-by-day basis depending on supply and demand for currencies.

For example, if the demand for £s was greater than the demand for $s, then the price of the £ would rise. Compared to the exchange rate in the first example, the new rate might now be £1:$1.75. Each £ now buys more $s than before.

How are businesses affected by changing exchange rates?

Changes in the exchange rate affect businesses in several different ways. For one, consider the impact on an *exporting business* – one which sells goods and services abroad.

▨ *Case study example*

Lion Trading Co. produces washing machines. The retail price of these machines is £300. They export many machines to France and the price there has to be in euro. The current exchange rate is £1:€1.6. The firm will therefore set a price of €480 for its machines in France (ignoring additional distribution and marketing costs).

Assume that the exchange rate for £s now rises compared to the euro and £1 is now worth €2.

The Marketing manager for Lion Trading now has two main options:

- to keep the price in France at €480 – this will mean that each machine is only earning the business £240, not £300 as previously
- to raise the price in France to €600 and continue to earn £300 from each machine. This higher price in France could now lead to fewer sales and exports to France are likely to fall.

▨ **Definitions to learn:**

CURRENCY APPRECIATION occurs when the value of a currency rises – it buys more of another currency than before.

CURRENCY DEPRECIATION occurs when the value of a currency falls – it buys less of another currency than before.

The change in the exchange rate described above is called a *£ appreciation* because the value of the £ has increased. Exporters have a serious problem when the currency of their country APPRECIATES.

▨ *Activity 25.1: case study task*

A business currently sells men's coats for £100. It also exports them to Japan. It sells them there for 8,000 yen as the exchange rate is currently £1:80¥.

a) The exchange rate for the £ now appreciates to £1:100¥. Calculate the new ¥ selling price for the coats, assuming that the Marketing manager wishes to earn the same amount of £ from each coat.

b) What might be the effect if the exchange rate for £ fell? This is called a DEPRECIATION. Calculate the new ¥ price if £1 falls to 60¥, assuming that the same amount of £ is earned from each coat.

How do changes in exchange rates affect an importer?

▨ *Case study example*

Nadir Imports Co. is based in the UK and buys fruit from other countries to sell to supermarkets. One tonne of bananas from abroad costs $250 and at the current exchange rate of £1:$2.5 this costs Nadir Imports £100.

If the value of the £ were now to *depreciate* what would happen to Nadir Imports' costs? Assume that the value of the £ now falls to £1:$2, how much will a tonne of bananas now cost? The answer is £125, which is a substantial increase in costs for the importing firm.

▩ *Activity 25.2*

a) Calculate the cost to a business in the UK of importing goods costing $500 if the exchange rate is £1:$2.

b) What will the cost of these imports be if the value of the £ were to appreciate to £1:$2.5?

We have shown that an importing firm will have *higher* costs if the exchange rate of its currency *depreciates*, but will have *lower* costs if the exchange rate *appreciates*.

You can now see how seriously businesses can be affected by *exchange rate movements*. This helps to explain why some international organisations such as the European Union (EU) are trying to reduce exchange rate movements. In the case of the EU, it has introduced a *common currency* which removes the need for separate currencies and exchange rates amongst its members.

Revision summary: exchange rates

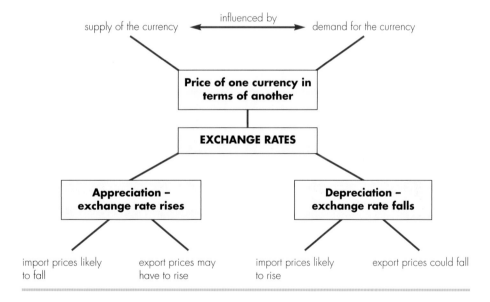

International economic organisations

These are some of the international organisations which countries have joined in recent years. It is important to study the impact of these on business:

- economic and political unions, such as the European Union (EU)
- free trade areas, such as the North American Free Trade Association (NAFTA)
- organisations working for free trade between countries, such as the World Trade Organisation (WTO).

The European Union

The EU is an organisation of 15 European countries. Several others have applied to join. There is a European Parliament and Commission to take decisions and to make laws which affect all member states. Listed below are some of the decisions that have been taken.

- *A single market within Europe* This means that selling products anywhere in the member states should be as easy as selling goods to the domestic market. There are no tariffs or controls over trade between the 15 members. The impact of this on European businesses has been to:
  - create a huge market for goods and services. This should make it possible to gain from economies of scale (see Unit 6)
  - increase competition amongst all European industries. This should give consumers more choice and help to keep prices low. Businesses have to develop new and better products to keep consumers buying their goods.
- COMMON CURRENCY – *the euro* From January 2002 most of the members of the EU replaced their own currencies – such as francs, lira and pesetas – with the euro. All transactions within or between these countries are now in euros. There is one European Central Bank in control of the issue of euros. It also fixes interest rates for all countries using the euro. They no longer have different interest rates. Eventually, this common currency could lead to the same tax rates in all EU countries.

  The UK has not yet joined. The UK government wants to see if the euro will be a success before asking the British people to vote on whether the UK should join the common currency. If the UK joined, there would be advantages and disadvantages.

Advantages for UK firms of the UK joining the euro

- ☑ Lower costs as one price list throughout Europe can be used.
- ☑ Lower costs as the charges for converting one European currency into another will disappear.
- ☑ Easier to trade with other European countries.
- ☑ Easier to compare costs of supplies from different EU countries.
- ☑ No risks of losing out from exchange rate changes between European currencies.

Disadvantages for UK firms of the UK joining the euro

- ▢ More competition from European firms in the UK. It will be easier for them to sell goods in the UK.
- ▢ Consumers in Europe will be able to compare prices easily between all countries – they will tend to buy at the lowest prices. This will again increase competition for UK firms.
- ▢ Interest rates might be at a level that does not suit UK firms – the Bank of England will no longer be able to set interest rates to suit UK economic interests.

- *The Social Charter* The EU does not just aim to make life easier for businesses. It also has the aim of improving working conditions for European workers and for making these equal throughout Europe. The Social Charter does this. The main conditions include:
  - workers can look for work anywhere within the EU
  - workers must be consulted on important issues
  - equal treatment for full- and part-time workers
  - limits on the maximum working week
  - improved health and safety rules at work.

  It is easy to see how these rules might affect businesses in Europe. The aim is not only to improve workers' living standards but also to make sure that all European businesses 'play by the rules'. The Social Charter forces all employers to keep to the same regulations.

Case study example

Mercury Electronics makes computer monitors. The business is located in a European country which is not a member of the EU. All raw materials are imported and many of the completed monitors are exported to EU countries. The Chief Executive, Benazir, works very hard and she expects all of her workers to put in long hours to help make the business a success. Some weeks, workers are expected to work for 60 hours. When the business is very busy, part-time workers are employed. They have no job security and receive no holiday pay. Currently, demand for the monitors is at a very high level and Benazir cannot find enough skilled staff to fill all of the vacancies. Her other major worry is the high exchange rate of the country's currency. This high value against some other currencies is making her exports seem very expensive.

How would Benazir's business be affected if her country joined the EU and also agreed to accept the euro? The most likely effects are as follows.

Advantages of joining the EU

- Free trade to the markets of all EU countries means the exports of the business could increase.
- The business is able to recruit labour easily from other EU member countries.
- There are no exchange rate problems as there would be just one currency in the EU.

Disadvantages of joining the EU

- Benazir would have to give part-time workers the same benefits and job security as full-time workers – this could raise business costs.
- The maximum hours worked would have to be reduced to 48 unless the workers agreed to overtime.
- Monitors from other EU countries could now be sold in Benazir's country with no import controls.

Revision summary: impact on business when a country is in the EU

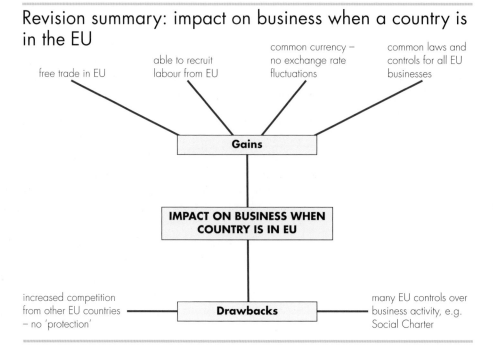

Free trade associations

These organisations have the aim of reducing all barriers and limits on international trade. This is called *free trade*. Countries which sign these agreements have to reduce all tariffs, quotas (limits on the *quantities* of imports) and other import restrictions. The agreements can be between a few countries – such as NAFTA – or between many countries. There are over 100 members of WTO, for example.

Why is free trade between countries considered so important? Because it allows every country to specialise in those goods and services in which it is most efficient. The prices of all imports and exports will be at their competitive level – not changed by controls or import taxes. Free trade is very helpful to developing nations which are attempting to build up their industries. They will now be able to sell their goods to consumers in richer countries and earn revenue which will help them expand.

Businesses are affected in the following ways by these agreements:

- more competition from foreign firms – consumers have more choices and prices must be kept low to attract them
- no 'protection' by governments. Firms cannot ask their own government for subsidies or special treatment because this would be against the rules of the organisation
- more opportunities exist for exporting which will help to increase sales. Efficient firms are likely to be very successful.

The long-term effect of these organisations is to encourage trade between all countries. This trade, by encouraging competition, makes all consumers better off than before and living standards are likely to rise as a result.

Globalisation

In many ways the world is becoming one large market rather than a series of separate national markets. The same goods and services can be found in many countries throughout the world. There are several reasons for this increasing global competition (GLOBALISATION).

- Free trade agreements and economic unions have reduced protection for industries. Consumers can now purchase goods and services from other countries with no import controls.
- Improved travel links and communications between all parts of the world have made it easier to compare prices and qualities of goods from many countries. This will further develop as the internet becomes more widely available worldwide.
- Many countries which used to have very undeveloped manufacturing industries have been building up these businesses very rapidly. Countries in SE Asia and China itself used to import many of the goods they needed. Now that their own manufacturing industries are so strong they can export in large quantities. This creates much more world competition.

▨ *Activity 25.3: case study task*

Jacques was pleased to find out last year that his employer had accepted a new EU Social Charter rule. This had the effect of reducing the number of hours he worked each week. He and his fellow workers already enjoyed excellent working conditions and high pay rates. Jacques worked in a clothing factory. The manager was always complaining about cheap imports taking away customers. The lowest priced imports were from countries outside of the EU which had no laws like the Social Charter. Workers had to work very long hours in these countries, with low wages and few, if any, benefits. As there were free trade agreements between the EU and most other countries, Jacques' employer could not ask for protection from imports from the government. The manager was overheard to say 'cheap imports and globalisation of the clothing industry will put European jobs at risk'.

a) In this case study, who is benefiting from free trade agreements?
b) What did the manager mean by the term 'globalisation of the clothing industry'?
c) Is Jacques likely to be in favour of the EU Social Charter? Give reasons for your answer.

Globalisation has led to more choice and lower prices for consumers. It has forced firms to look for ways of increasing efficiency. Inefficient producers have gone out of business. Many firms have merged with foreign businesses to make it easier to sell in foreign markets. This is one of the reasons behind the growth of multinational organisations.

This process of more and more free trade does lead to some problems. Many workers, often in the poorest countries, have lost their jobs owing to globalisation. Big foreign corporations can often produce goods more cheaply and efficiently, so other countries' workers lose out. As governments can no longer 'protect' their own industries against foreign competition this process can lead to serious social problems.

Multinational businesses

Definition to learn:

MULTINATIONAL BUSINESSES are those with factories, production or service operations in more than one country. These are sometimes known as TRANSNATIONAL businesses.

It is important to remember that a MULTINATIONAL (TRANSNATIONAL) BUSINESS is *not* one which just *sells* goods in more than one country. To be called a multinational, a business must produce goods or services in more than one country.

Multinational businesses are some of the largest organisations in the world. They include:

■ oil companies: Shell, BP, Exxon
■ tobacco companies: British American Tobacco, Philip Morris
■ car manufacturers: Nissan, General Motors.

Activity 25.4

Make a list of at least four businesses operating in your country which are multinational. You can check this list with your teacher or by contacting some businesses themselves. Ask which other countries they operate in.

Why do firms become multinational?

These are some of the reasons why firms become multinational organisations:

■ to produce goods in countries with low costs, such as low wages. For example, most sports clothing is produced in SE Asia because wages are lower than in Europe
■ to extract raw materials which the firm may need for production or refining. For example, crude oil from Saudi Arabia is needed to supply oil refineries in the USA
■ to produce goods nearer the market to reduce transport costs. For example, tiles and bricks are expensive to transport so the producer sets up a factory near the market in another country
■ to avoid barriers to trade put up by countries to reduce the imports of goods. For example, sales of cars made in Japan are restricted in Europe. Japanese manufacturers now make cars in Europe too
■ to expand into different market areas to spread risks. For example, if sales are falling in one country the business may move to another country where sales are rising.

So, there is no doubt that the *businesses gain* from becoming multinational. But what is the impact on the *countries* they operate in? There are both advantages and disadvantages to the countries as a result of multinationals operating there.

Advantages of multinationals operating in a country

- ☑ Jobs will be created which will reduce the level of unemployment.
- ☑ New investment in buildings and machinery will increase output of goods and services in the country.
- ☑ Some of the extra output may be sold abroad which will increase the exports of the country. Also, imports could be reduced as more goods are now made in the country.
- ☑ Taxes will be paid by the multinational which will increase the funds to the government.

Disadvantages of multinationals operating in a country

- ☒ The jobs created are often unskilled assembly line tasks. Skilled jobs, such as those in research and design, are not usually created in the 'host' countries receiving the multinationals.
- ☒ They may force local firms out of business. Multinationals are often more efficient and have lower costs than local businesses.
- ☒ Profits are often sent back to the multinational's 'home' country and not kept in the country where they are earned.
- ☒ They often use up scarce and non-renewable primary resources in the host country.
- ☒ As the businesses are very large they could have a lot of influence on both the government and the economy of the country. They might ask the government for large grants to keep them operating in the country.

▤ *Activity 25.5: case study task*

Should we allow the XYZ Corporation to set up a factory in our country?

- *About the business* The XYZ Corporation is applying for planning permission to build a factory in your country. The factory is expected to be very profitable. One thousand new jobs should be created for assembly-line work. Many of the goods made could be sold abroad. Some of the supplies for the factory will come from your country.
- *About your country* In your country unemployment is high, especially amongst skilled workers. The government cannot afford any new building projects. There are several local competitors producing goods similar to the XYZ Corporation. Import levels are very high. Land for new building is very limited. New developments would have to be built in beautiful countryside.

a) List *three* groups in your country who may benefit from allowing the XYZ Corporation to build the factory.
b) List *three* groups in your country who may lose from the building of the factory.
c) Would you advise your government to allow the new factory to be built? Explain your answer by judging between, or evaluating, all of the evidence.

Revision summary: advantages and disadvantages of multinational businesses

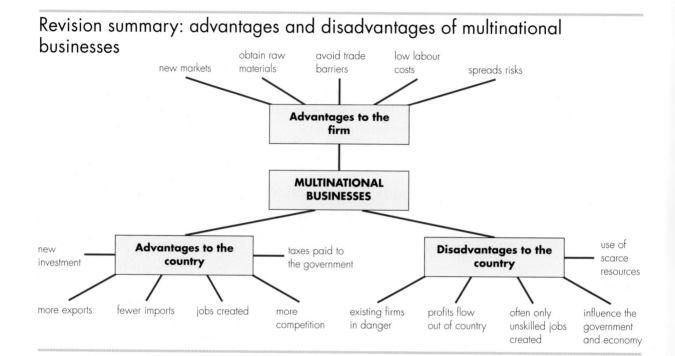

▦ *Revision questions*

1 What is meant by the term *exchange rate*? [2]

2 Explain the difference between a currency appreciation and a currency depreciation. Use numerical examples to support your answer. [5]

3 How will a currency appreciation affect an exporting firm? [3]

4 How will a currency depreciation affect an importing firm? [3]

5 Explain what is meant by the EU single market. [3]

6 State and explain *two* possible advantages to a UK firm of being part of the EU single market. [6]

7 What is meant by a common currency between countries? [2]

8 Imagine that you own a manufacturing business in the UK. Make a case for the UK joining the euro. [6]

9 Why might some businesses be opposed to the UK joining the euro? [6]

10 What is the EU Social Charter? [3]

11 Do you think globalisation is a good idea? Explain your answer. [6]

12 Using *one* example of a multinational with a base in your country, briefly explain why you think it is operating in more than one country. [4]

13 Give *three* possible effects on local businesses of a multinational fast food company setting up operations in your country. [3]

14 a) Explain the difference between an import quota and an import tariff. [2]
   b) 'Controlling imports will make prices higher. Governments should never do this.' Do you agree or disagree with this statement? Give reasons for your answer. [6]

The CD-ROM (see details on page x) provides further tests, activities and Case study work on the topics covered in this unit.

Answers to activities

Unit 1

Activity 1.1
Student's own answer

Activity 1.2
a) Student's own illustrations. For example, division of labour in clay pot making could include: one person preparing clay; one person spinning or making pots; one person firing pots; one person decorating pots; one person packing pots for sale to customer.

b) Advantages: specialised labour able to concentrate on one task; output is likely to rise as specialisation leads to faster output; workers' skills at one particular job are improved.
Disadvantages: tedious and repetitive work may lead to demotivated workers; it often results in the production of many items of the same style but the market may demand very different styles and designs; workers can become inflexible – that is, unable to perform other tasks which could cause problems during periods of staff absence.

Activity 1.3
a) Student's answers may vary but typical answers could include:
i) Survival: as the firm is about to experience an increase in the number of competitors
ii) Growth: there appear to be opportunities for expansion for a firm run by ambitious people
iii) Profits: by keeping out competitors, there should be the opportunity to maintain high profits
iv) Public service: to provide a postal service in all areas of the country even in unprofitable ones.

b) Student's answers will vary but suggested answers include:
i) Keep prices competitive, increase advertising, offer additional services to attract new customers
ii) Develop new and original products, emphasise quality and service to potential customers
iii) Attempt to keep competitors out of the market, possibly by using low prices which they cannot match. The firm may have to be careful of government action, however. Some policies to maintain monopoly power will be against the law.
iv) Keep prices as low as possible, offer the same services to all customers in all areas of the country.

Unit 2

Activity 2.1
Primary: forestry, coal mining
Secondary: computer assembly, brewery
Tertiary: insurance, travel agent, car showroom.

Activity 2.2
a) Health: provide health services to everyone, consistent standards in all areas, improve health of the population.
b) Education: to raise educational standards, provide educational services to everyone, consistent standards in all areas.
c) Defence: prevent private armies, to control defence forces in times of danger, maintain high standards of equipment to meet threats from other countries.
d) Public transport: to offer a public service in all areas, to increase mobility of the population, to reduce private car use by keeping fares as low as possible.
e) Water supply: to ensure that the whole country has access to clean water, to keep high standards for water, to prevent monopolies making high profits from the supply of an essential commodity.
f) Electricity supply: to keep control of an essential service, to ensure continuous supplies, to prevent monopolies making high profits from the supply of an essential good.

Activity 2.3
Student's own answer

Activity 2.4
Correct letter presentation essential.
Student's own answer based on the advantages and disadvantages of privatisation. The final recommendation must be justified.

Activity 2.5
Correct report format essential.
Findings should include: Company A employs more workers than any of the other businesses. It has the lowest value of capital invested in the business. It is the third most profitable business. It has the lowest sales figures.

There can be no overall conclusion regarding the size of Company A compared to the other companies but it does appear to be 'labour intensive' compared to the other businesses – as it employs more workers but less capital than the others.

Each of the methods of comparing the size of businesses should be assessed for advantages and disadvantages.

The figures seem to show that Company A is less efficient than the other companies. Despite employing most workers, its sales level is lowest. Each worker produces less output than workers in the other businesses. Perhaps this is because there is little capital equipment for each worker to use in Company A.

Activity 2.6

a) Horizontal
b) Horizontal – assuming that it is another bicycle shop!
c) Backward vertical integration
d) Forward vertical integration for the manufacturer
e) Backward vertical integration
f) Conglomerate merger resulting in diversification

Unit 3

Activity 3.1

a) Advantages: independence – able to take decisions and to control his own working life; chance of making profits; able to show enterprise; motivating to work for oneself.

Disadvantages: risk of own business failing and losing savings; no regular salary or work benefits from a large employer.
b) Student's own answer
c) Advantages: more capital; experience and advice from his uncle; he may be able to provide specialist support to Amin's business.

Disadvantages: uncle may try to dominate and take important decisions himself; profits must be shared; all partners are responsible for the decisions of any one partner.

Activity 3.2

a) Protects shareholder's possessions should the business go bankrupt.

b) Easier because shareholders are offered the opportunity to share the profits of the business. If losses are made the shareholders may lose their original investment in shares but cannot lose their other assets.
c) The owner may wish to keep complete control. The owner may not wish to share profits with partners.
d) To avoid losing control of the business to other shareholders. To avoid the separation of control and ownership. To keep more of the activities and accounts of the business secret.

Unit 4

Activity 4.1

a) £750
b) i) £22,000
ii) His real income fell because the rise in his income (10%) was less than the rate of inflation (15%). Prices rose by more than his income.
c) i) Imports
ii) Exports
iii) Exports
iv) Exports – the hotel services are being 'exported' to foreign tourists

Activity 4.2

TVs; foreign holidays; jewellery; home computers. These products are often bought by consumers 'on credit' with borrowed money. Higher interest rates will discourage some consumers from buying these goods.

Activity 4.3

a) Will reduce consumer demand for products.
b) Will leave more profits to be invested back into the business or to pay to shareholders.
c) Will make imports more expensive and will increase the cost of making computers.
d) Will reduce consumer demand. May cause the exchange rate to appreciate – could lead to higher export prices.
e) Will lower prices of computers and consumers may be encouraged to buy at lower prices.
f) Easier to employ well qualified workers – more able to expand production.
g) Will lead to more competition.

Activity 4.4

Student explains why protection is or is not needed in each case.
a) Trade Descriptions Act 1968
b) Weights and Measures Act 1951
c) Sale of Goods Act 1979
d) Consumer Protection Act 1987
e) Consumer Credit Act 1974

Activity 4.5

a) Student's own answer
b) Student's own answer
c) Points made could include: loyal staff, few staff leaving (low staff turnover), few disputes with staff, high output and productivity, few staff absences.

Activity 4.6

a) Local community and residents; suppliers; customers; government; workers.
b) Local residents – likely to oppose danger from new plant and extra traffic it may cause.
Suppliers – will support it as it could lead to additional orders from DEF.
Workers – likely to support it as there should be additional chances of employment.
Customers – likely to support it as it might lead to lower prices if the plant is efficient.
Government – will need to consider all of the wider employment and environmental issues before deciding.
c) Three reasons: may wish to encourage creation of new jobs; may want to see additional exports from the country; may wish to control the exact location and method of manufacture to protect the environment.

Unit 5

Activity 5.1

a) IT equipment in the office, e.g. computers, internet, e-mail, computer operated machines, automated equipment.
b) Fear of change; fear of need to retrain and learn new skills; danger of losing jobs and having to give up using existing skills.
c) Secrecy is probably unwise. This is because the workers may become suspicious and, when they do find out, they will feel that Ranjit did not trust them. If they had been involved then they might have been able to make some useful suggestions.

d) Obtain all of the necessary information, e.g. costs, how many staff are needed to operate machines; consider the impact on the market of moving away from traditional methods of manufacture; consult the staff to obtain their ideas and, possibly, their support.

Activity 5.2

a) Student's own, justified, answer but reference could be made to:
Yes – if the government wanted to encourage more business and jobs to the country.
No – if the government wanted to protect the environment and control polluting business activity.
b) It might have considered it too expensive to change policy. Extra costs could have reduced profits. This might be bad for shareholders. The management might decide not to expand the business if profits fall too low.
c) Pressure groups are groups formed by people who share a common interest and who will take action to achieve the changes they are seeking.
d) Yes – the good publicity will be 'free' advertising for the company and consumers may be more likely to buy its products. The extra revenue could help to pay for the additional costs resulting from the change of policy. Workers may prefer to work for an environmentally friendly business.
No – the extra costs could reduce profits and reduce the chances of the business expanding.

Activity 5.3

a) From tax revenue. In some countries there may be tolls on motorways to pay for improvements in the road system.
b) Social costs could include: noise and pollution during construction for local residents; noise and air pollution from cars for local residents; loss of countryside to road building; further loss of countryside if new factories are built once the road is completed.
   Social benefits could include: shorter journey times; less congestion, noise and pollution in city centres; faster and cheaper delivery of goods; employment for road builders and, later, factory workers, if the factories are built.
c) Depends on student's choices for **b)**.

Unit 6

Activity 6.1

Student's own answer but could include: workers' wages; distribution/transport of goods; taxes; advertising; market research; electricity and other utilities; machinery.

Activity 6.2

Student's own answer

Activity 6.3

a) x 30,000; y 30,000; z 0; a 50,000; b 80,000
b) Break-even chart

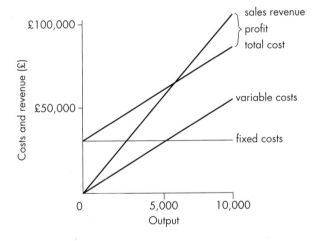

c) i) 6,000 units
ii) £20,000

Activity 6.4

a) 900
b) £2,400
c) 1,200

Activity 6.5

a) Y = £36,000,000; Z = £20,000,000
b) Y = £3,000; Z = £4,000
c) £2,800
d) £2,800

Activity 6.6

a) x = (£1,000); y = (£4,600)
b) No. Costs are above budget as shown by the negative cost variances. Greater cost control is needed. It could be that the original budget was unrealistic and this may need to be revised.

c) Those with the greatest negative variances: staffing, equipment, electricity and telephone.

Unit 7

Activity 7.1

a) £1,500
b) £9,000
c) £60,000
d) £75,000

Activity 7.2

b) £11,000
c) £1,000
d) £60,000

Activity 7.3

£70,000 = retained profits

Activity 7.4

a) In the trading account
b) In the appropriation account
c) In the balance sheet
d) In the profit and loss account
e) In the profit and loss account
f) In the balance sheet

Activity 7.5

Company vehicles – fixed assets
Cash in the till – current asset
Ten-year bank loan – long-term liability
Ordinary share capital – share capital
Money owed by customers – current asset
Unsold goods – current asset
Factory – fixed asset
Retained profit – reserves
Amounts owed to suppliers – current liability
Tax owed to government – current liability

Activity 7.6

a) i) 21.1%
ii) 28%
iii) 15.6%
b) The company performed less well in 2005 as all of the performance ratios are lower than in the previous year. Costs may have risen faster than prices and this has led to lower profit margins. Lower profit margins will lead to a lower return on net assets if sales do not increase at a fast rate.

Activity 7.7

a) i) 1.08
ii) 0.46
iii) 11.25
b) The liquidity of the company has fallen since 2004. The company has a liquidity problem as the acid test ratio shows that it could not afford to pay off all of its short-term debts from its liquid assets. The company has been less efficient in the management of stock and has been turning stock into sales less quickly.

Unit 8

Activity 8.1

Inflows are: sale of goods for cash; debtors paying bills; additional shares. The remainder are outflows.

Activity 8.2

a) £33,000
b) £10,500
c) Only half of sales were for cash.

Activity 8.3

a) $x = £2,000$; $y = £4,000$; $z = £22,000$
b) Rent might be paid every 3 months – this could cause a larger cash outflow in March, June, September and December. There could also be an additional cash expense forecast for March, such as an advertising campaign.

Activity 8.4

a) Helps in planning financial requirements. Action could be taken to prevent serious negative cash flows or financing could be arranged.
b) Student's own answer (forecast)
c) A negative closing bank balance is expected. The manager could attempt to reduce cash outflows or increase cash inflows. If these changes were not possible then the bank manager must be informed of the situation before April.

Activity 8.5

a) To assist in financial planning of the business
b) Bank manager. Reasons: to see if the bank balance is likely to become negative so that financing can be arranged. If Manuel is planning to take on partners into his business then they would also be

interested in looking at the cash flow forecast to see if the business is likely to be successful.
c) i) Wages as the same number of employees are employed every month.
ii) Seeds and composts as these will vary with the seasons of the year.
d) Cash outflows will increase and the bank balances will be lower each month.
e) Student's own answer which could include: changing to cheaper suppliers; raising prices; using seasonal labour; diversifying into other services in winter months.

Unit 9

Activity 9.1

Water rates, staff wages, maintenance of equipment are all revenue expenditures. The remainder are capital expenditures.

Activity 9.2

Student's own answer

Activity 9.3

a) New businesses have no retained profits.
b) As a sole trader he cannot sell shares and he may find it difficult to obtain bank loans for all of his firm's financial requirements.
c) Taxi firms provide a service and do not hold stock.

Activity 9.4

a) No interest and no loan to repay
b) When the profits likely to be made are greater than the cost of the loan. When retained profits are not high enough for the investment required.

Activity 9.5

Short term: overdraft, trade credit
Medium term: three-year bank loan, hire purchase
Long term: debentures, shares issue.

Activity 9.6

Student's own answer

Activity 9.7

a) Correct layout necessary. The letter should explain how each of these pieces of information will enable the manager to decide whether to offer the loan.

b) i) Cash flow forecast – to show the expected financing requirements of the business and the likely changes in the bank balance.
ii) Profit and loss account to see if the business is expected to make a profit and survive.
iii) Balance sheet to see how much capital the owners are investing in the business and to check the liquidity of the business.

Activity 9.8
Student's own answer which should refer to all of the relevant data. Correct report format should be used.

Activity 9.9
a) Student's own answer which should refer to all of the data provided.
b) Information about other companies share prices and dividend payments. Economic information which could affect the value of share prices.

Unit 10
Activity 10.1
Student's own answer

Activity 10.2
Student's own answer

Activity 10.3
a)

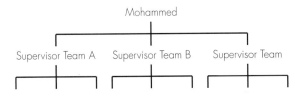

b) 3
c) Shortens chain of command – advantages are quicker and more accurate communication; increases the degree of delegation and hence the feeling of responsibility felt by the workers; widens the span of control – less direct control but more trust is being shown.

Activity 10.4
Student's own answer; correct memo format essential.

Unit 11
Activity 11.1
Student's own answer, but should include planning, organising, co-ordinating, commanding and controlling.

Activity 11.2
Student's own answers

Activity 11.3
Correct letter format required.

a) No market research had been undertaken. There might not be a market for the product. No advertising or promotional material had been prepared.
b) The finance may not be available. The Production department might not be able to produce the additional output.
c) The finance may not be available. The budgets of these two departments will now need to be adjusted. The costs of each product will need to be recalculated and prices may have to rise.

Unit 12
Activity 12.1
a) i) Manager
ii) Letter
iii) All staff
b) Feedback was asked for, but it was not clear how the staff were meant to 'feedback' their answers.
c) Student's own answer

Activity 12.2
a) Student's own answers and reasons
b) Student's own answers and reasons

Activity 12.3
Verbal: video conferencing; meeting; face-to-face; telephone
Written: letter; fax; staff newspaper; memo; notice
Visual: poster; television.

Activity 12.4
Student's own answers and reasons

Unit 13

Activity 13.1

a) A car production worker, a tailor and possibly a waiter could have their output measured.

b) A shop assistant would give difficulties as some consumers may not buy any goods.

For a teacher, police officer and soldier it is very difficult to measure what they produce. The difficulties arise when they provide a service and not a measurable output.

c) Alternative ways of rewarding efficient employees will have to be found, for example, sharing bonuses, or sharing profits.

d) It does present problems for modern economies because, as economies develop, more and more employees work in the service sector.

Activity 13.2

Miguel: physical needs and security needs
Pierre: physical needs, security needs and social needs
Anya: physical needs, security needs, social needs, esteem needs and self-actualisation

Activity 13.3

a) Company A – Theory X manager; Company B – Theory Y manager

b) Student's own answer

Activity 13.4

a) Car production worker: probably piece rate because where the output is measurable it is easier to implement pay related to the output produced; non-monetary reward would be discounts on new cars purchased.

b) Hotel receptionist would probably be paid a salary, it would be difficult to pay by the number of bookings taken. They could be given a share of the profits or some scheme in the hotel for sharing out money when they have had a successful year. Free accommodation at other hotels if they are in a chain, discounts on meals are the possible non-monetary benefits.

c) Teacher: paid a salary as output is not really measurable. Non-monetary rewards depend on the country the school is in, they may include free accommodation, free education at the school for their own children, pension, health care paid for,

limited free trips home if working at a foreign school.

d) Shop assistant: would probably be paid a salary, but pay could be related to the number of sales made. Non-monetary rewards would most likely be staff discounts on purchases.

e) Managing Director: paid a salary, profit-related pay, bonus if a good year. Non-monetary rewards include share options, free health care, company vehicle, generous expense account.

f) The taxi driver would just get paid by the number of journeys made, also possibly use of the taxi for their own use if the car belongs to a taxi firm.

There needs to be explanation of the above – discussion of whether output can be measured, seniority of the job, whether non-monetary rewards are expected in certain jobs.

Activity 13.5

Suggestions could include: job enlargement for Duncan; job rotation and/or job enrichment for Sita; job rotation for Tim. Students should explain the reason for each of their choices.

Activity 13.6

a) Autocratic leadership

b) Student's own answer

c) Student's own answer, but probably democratic leadership is the best option.

Unit 14

Activity 14.1

Student's own answers

Activity 14.2

a) The night cashier and the secretary are both jobs that would be advertised locally. There will probably be a large number of people locally who have the qualifications and skills required to carry out the job. The industrial engineering professional is more highly qualified and this job will be more difficult to fill. The advert will be in national newspapers to reach a wider number of people.

b) Student's own answer

c) Student's own answer

Activity 14.3

Methods of recruitment	Advantages	Disadvantages	Examples of suitable jobs for use with this method
Internal Noticeboard at the company (or company newspaper)	Do not have to pay to advertise. Fewer applications therefore less time spent looking through application forms/CVs. The person is already known to the company – they know if they are punctual, reliable, etc. The person already knows the organisation's way of working and what is expected from employees. It can be very motivating for other employees to see their fellow workers given a chance.	No new ideas are brought into the business. No new business practices will be brought from elsewhere. There could be jealousy and rivalry between existing employees.	This would be suitable for most levels of employees within a large business. However, the more senior the position the more likely it is that someone from outside the organisation will be appointed.
External Local newspapers	Cheap to advertise in. Seen by many local people who are likely to be able to apply for the job.	Only seen by people in the local area and only those who buy the newspaper.	Jobs that do not require a high level of skill. Clerical and manual positions, e.g. secretary, van driver, production worker.
National newspapers	The national newspapers will be read by many people who live in different parts of the country or even abroad.	Expensive to advertise in national newspapers.	Usually more senior positions where a high degree of skill and/or qualifications are required, e.g. senior manager, accountant.
Specialist magazines	Seen by people who have the right skills for the job.	Quite expensive to advertise in. Could be missed by people who do not read the specialist magazine.	The same types of job as for newspapers, except these will usually be for well qualified people, e.g. a research scientist, engineer.
Recruitment agencies	They advertise and interview people for you. They use their expertise to select suitable people. It saves the business time in not having to interview people.	Expensive because often a proportion of the person's salary in the first year will have to be paid to the agency.	This varies but usually the same types of jobs as for national newspapers and specialist magazines.
Govt-run Job Centres	Cheap to advertise in – usually does not cost anything.	Many people may not visit the centre and therefore may not know about the job.	Unskilled or semi-skilled jobs, e.g. production worker, warehouse worker, cleaner.

Activity 14.4

a) Student's own answers: there are advantages and disadvantages to each applicant and these should be discussed.

b) References so as to confirm the person's reliability;

health record or criminal record to assess their suitability; nationality in case there are restrictions on employing them.

c) Student's own design of advertisement.

Activity 14.5

a) Question 1 was asked to find out what the applicant thinks about the job.

Question 2 was asked to find out how keen the applicant is. Were they bothered enough about the job to do some research into the company's background, to know if it is a good company to work for?

Question 3 was asked to find out what sort of person they are. Are they sociable? Will they fit in with the other employees?

Question 4 was asked to find out what qualities the applicant thinks they possess that will make them suitable for the job. What can they offer the company?

Question 5 was asked to find out if the applicant is very ambitious.

Question 6 was asked to see how keen the applicant is. They should be keen to know about the job and ask their own questions.

b) and **c)** Student's own answer

Activity 14.6

a) Discussion about recruiting the experienced engineers from foreign countries if they are not available locally. The labourers would be recruited locally as there should be plenty of workers able to do the jobs required.

b) If possible the airline pilots will be recruited from a Latin American country so that they can return home easily. The airline may need to advertise in several countries to attract sufficient applicants of the right qualifications. The cabin crew will also be recruited from Latin America but these should be easier to recruit and they may come from just one country where the airline's operations are based. Discussion of the appropriate methods to use to recruit these employees should also be included.

Activity 14.8

a) S&S plc might send all their employees on an off-the-job training course. They will all need to go so it may be cheaper to get someone to come into their workplace and train them there, i.e. on-the-job training.

Activity 14.7

Method of training	Description	Advantages	Disadvantages
Induction training	Training carried out when the employee is new to the post.	Introduces the employee into the company. They will quickly settle into their work.	A lot of information is given out in one go and it may be too much for the new employee to remember.
On-the-job training	The person is trained by watching a more experienced worker doing the job. They are shown what to do.	Individual tuition is given. Trained in the workplace which may be cheaper. Some work will be carried out whilst the trainee is learning what to do.	Only really suitable for unskilled or semi-skilled jobs. The trainer will not be as productive as they would be whilst showing the trainee what to do and not working as fast as normal. The trainer may have bad habits that they may pass onto the trainee.
Off-the-job training	The employee goes away from the place of work. Varied techniques are used to train the workers, e.g. lecture, simulation, role play, case study, often in a classroom.	A broad range of skills can be taught. Evening courses are cheaper as the employee can still complete their normal work in the day – only the course fees will need to be paid, there will not be lost output.	Evening classes are tiring for employees and they may be less effective at work the next day. May be less control over what is being taught.

b) Sandeep will also have a combination of on-the-job and off-the-job training. He will probably go to college to learn some of the theories behind retail management. He will also learn from other managers in the workplace.

c) James will probably need induction training to be shown around and introduced to other staff, and on-the-job training to be shown what to do. It is not a very skilled job and it will not take him very long to learn the requirements of the job.

Unit 15

Activity 15.1

a) John: consideration of the advantages and disadvantages of joining a trade union which only represents skilled workers, and the advantages and disadvantages of joining a general union which is large and represents many different types of employees. Which one is preferable is left up to the student.

Jai: probably the only option is to join a general union because he is not skilled and there is unlikely to be an industry union which represents just shop workers.

Misha would probably join a white-collar union because she is an office worker.

b) Student's own answer

Activity 15.2

Student's own answer

Activity 15.3

Student's own answer

Activity 15.4

Student's own answer

Activity 15.5

a) C&C plc: the trade union could try using an overtime ban or work to rule (if appropriate) to increase the pressure on the company to settle the dispute. If this doesn't work then a strike may be necessary to put further pressure on the company. Success often depends on how committed the employees feel about their demands. Picketing would be used alongside a strike to increase its effectiveness. The company may look at its operations to see if it can switch production to another factory. It may also consider, if it is forced to raise the wage increase, what level of increase it could afford to pay and whether it could raise its prices in compensation.

Spartacus Sports plc: the trade union will probably try a go slow, working to rule or some form of non-cooperation. Strike action is less likely initially but may be a last resort especially if the employees felt strongly about the issue. The company could look into the feasibility of making a productivity deal with the trade unions. Increased productivity would probably increase profits which would pay for a wage increase.

TTS Bank: an overtime ban would seem to be the most effective as this would soon mean that tasks were not all completed. Discussions need to take place between the trade unions and the management to see if there is some way to change work practices so that work can be completed in the time allotted. If this is not possible then some agreement over rewarding additional work needs to be agreed.

b) Student's own answer

Activity 15.6

a) Conflict has arisen because the employees feel that they are not being treated fairly. The employer is worried about profit levels and seems to be less concerned about how it treats its employees.

b) The employees and employer need to negotiate a settlement, possibly they can find ways to improve productivity and then profits may be increased. Well motivated employees may be worth more to the business (even though they cost more to employ) than ones that are unhappy and will not work effectively (even though these cost less to employ).

Activity 15.7

Student's own answer

Unit 16

Activity 16.1

Student's own answer

Activity 16.2

a) Product-orientated because the product was invented. No market research was undertaken to see if there is a market for this product. It is not known if customers want the product or what price they are prepared to pay.

b) Before Joshua starts to manufacture the product he needs to carry out market research to establish whether there is a need for the tool and also what price customers are prepared to pay. He will have to compare the price customers might be willing to pay with his production costs to see if it will be profitable to produce the tool.

Activity 16.3

a) Anya: Sales department
b) Mohamed: Promotion department
c) Paul: Research and Development department
d) Mary: Distribution department

Activity 16.4

The marketing objective of S&S plc is likely to be to target a new market segment. The existing market segment is mainly businesses and the computers are mainly used by men. By changing the advert to an old woman they are trying to target customers for home use of the computers. The old woman is used to show that older people can use a computer.

Activity 16.5

Student's own answer

Unit 17

Activity 17.1

a) New chocolate bar: consumer panels to test product and ask about taste. The business would be interested to know if customers like the taste and this will get qualitative information about what consumers think.

b) New style of watch: questionnaires to see what people think about the colour of the watches and what colours people see as fashionable. A quota sample could be used to ask mainly younger people, if they are seen as the target population.

c) Extended taxi service: possibly questionnaires to find out who might use the extended service. However, the taxi firm could use experiments and run the new service on a trial basis. Customers might not have thought of using the service until it is offered and therefore experiments might be the better choice.

d) New restaurant: questionnaires could cover a wide selection of the local population. Questionnaires would also find out consumer preferences about the type of food they like and the prices they are willing to pay for restaurant meals.

e) Sports shoe: interviews would gain more in-depth opinions of consumers. They would be able to obtain qualitative information about what it is about the shoe which makes them unpopular and/or what makes their competitors' shoes popular.

Activity 17.2

Possible other information you should gather would be: actual sales figures for the different drinks to see the total size of the market; where the drinks are sold, the type of outlets that customers use could determine the distribution channels that could be used; prices charged for the drinks to work out how profitable the market might be.

Activity 17.3

Data	Primary or secondary?
The *Daily News* article on a competitor's new product	Secondary
Sales department's monthly sales figures	Secondary
A shop's daily stocktake figures showing on which days sales are at their highest	Secondary
A traffic count to see how many vehicles pass your billboard advertisement in a week	Primary
Postal questionnaire results researching into your new product	Primary
A market research agency's report on what customers like and dislike about your product	Primary (if carried out on your behalf)
Annual government population statistics	Secondary
Data on customer complaints	Secondary

Activity 17.4

Method	Examples	Advantages	Disadvantages	Examples of appropriate use	Why the information may not be accurate
Primary research	Questionnaires	Detailed qualitative information can be gathered, customer opinions can be obtained.	If questions are not good then the answers will not be very accurate, can be time consuming and expensive to carry out.	To find out if consumers like a new product, or what they dislike about an existing one; are competitors' products better?	Some questions may not be clear, some may be misleading; may not ask a representative sample.
	Interviews	Detailed qualitative information can be gathered, customer opinions can be obtained and it is usually more detailed than questionnaires. If questions are not understood they can be explained. Group interviews are cheaper.	Time consuming and expensive to carry out.	To find out if consumers like a new product, or what they dislike about an existing one; are competitor's products better? Especially useful where detailed information on people's opinions is required.	There may be interviewer bias. If carried out in groups the respondents may influence each other's answers.
	Observation	Quite cheap to carry out. Useful data about the total number of people doing certain things, e.g. passing a particular billboard.	Only total numbers are gathered, no information on customer's opinions is gathered.	Used when raw data is required, such as number of vehicles that pass a particular billboard.	The raw data does not tell you anything about how the data is broken down, for example, the type of people passing the billboard.
	Consumer panels	Can provide detailed information about customers' opinions.	Can be time consuming, expensive and may be biased if consumers in the panel are influenced by the other panel members.	To find out if consumers like a new product, or what they dislike about an existing one; are competitor's products better? Especially useful where detailed information on people's opinions is required.	If carried out in groups, the respondents may influence each other's answers.
	Experiments	Relatively easy to set up, gather consumers' first reactions to products.	A representative sample may not be asked to test the product.	Used when first impressions of new products are needed. Often used with new food products.	Customers may not give their true feelings for fear of upsetting the person carrying out the testing. A representative sample may not be asked. Many other potential customers may shop elsewhere and will not be asked to test the new product.

Activity 17.4 continues on page 374

Method	Examples	Advantages	Disadvantages	Examples of appropriate use	Why the information may not be accurate
Secondary research	Internal sources	Information is readily available, cheap to collect. Relates to the business's own products.	Most probably out of date. It is often information from the past. Doesn't tell you anything about the rest of the market/ its competitors.	Used when detailed information on sales is required or information on costs when considering pricing.	Out of date.
	External sources	Often cheap to gather. Useful information if limitations taken into account. Already exists so may be quicker to obtain. Information is obtained that would not be available from primary research.	Information gathered is of a general nature and not specifically about their product. It has been gathered for some other purpose, therefore its usefulness may be limited. Specialist reports from market research agencies are expensive to buy.	Used when general information about the population is required (size and age structure) – census statistics are used.	May be out of date. Gathered for some other purpose and so may have inaccuracies in it. It will not be clear exactly who was questioned if questionnaire information is used. Company reports may be misleading, the accounts show total figures, not data that has been broken down.

Activity 17.5

a) You cannot obtain this information in its present form. If you broke down the answers into the answers from each age group questioned, then you would have a better chance of answering this question.

b) You will advertise your restaurant where the age group who are likely to use the restaurant will see the advert.

c) To find out how often people are likely to use the restaurant. Customers might use a restaurant but only once a year, in this case you would not have a very high demand!

d) To estimate the number of potential customers. Whether they use restaurants and how often.

e) Examples might include – 'What price would you usually pay for a meal?' to get an idea of possible prices to charge. 'What time of the day do you eat out?' to find out if customers would eat in the evening or in the daytime, i.e. when would the restaurant be busy? 'What type of food do you like to eat?' to find out if the restaurant should serve different types of food.

f) The results might not be accurate due to the small sample size. Asking only 100 people would not be enough to get accurate information about the population as a whole. Also, the questions do not obtain very detailed information about the

consumers' current habits with respect to eating out, options such as 'occasionally' are too vague to be sure what the respondents meant.

Activity 17.6
Student's own answers

Unit 18
Activity 18.1

Pie chart to show traffic count data

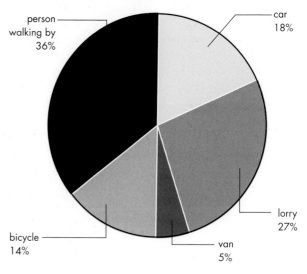

person walking by 36%

car 18%

lorry 27%

van 5%

bicycle 14%

Activity 18.2

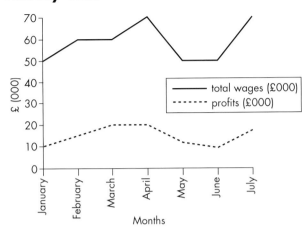

c) The information is showing a trend in the sales revenue figures and so a line graph shows this most clearly.

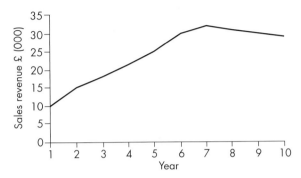

Activity 18.3

a) A bar chart shows clearly the number of people in the different age groups. The different proportions are not needed just the total figures.

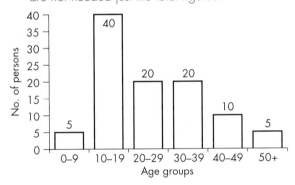

b) A table where the answers have been grouped together would be the clearest way to display this information. A graph would not be suitable as each category has only one answer. It would have been better if the questionnaire answers had option boxes to tick and then the answers could have been collated much more easily. The information could have then been graphed and the opinions of the respondents would have been clearer too.

d) Pie charts are used so that the proportions can clearly be seen. Two pie charts are used so that the differences can be observed. A bar chart could have been used instead but this would show the differences in the totals rather than the differences in the proportions.

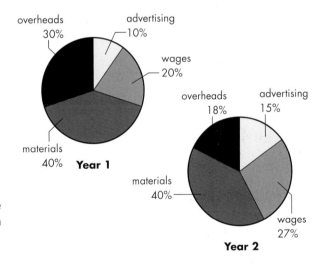

Different types of answers	Actual responses given	Number of answers
Appearance	Looks nice, like the colour, nice packaging, packet is colourful	4
Taste	Tastes good, nicer flavour than others, nice taste	3
Price	Value for money, cheap	2
Promotions	Free gifts, money-off token	2

Unit 19
Activity 19.1

Product	Consumer good	Consumer service	Producer good	Producer service
Tube of toothpaste	✓			
Bottle filling machine			✓	
Bank accounts		✓		✓
A pair of sports shoes	✓			
A chocolate bar	✓			
Doctor's treatment of a patient		✓		
Office cleaning				✓
Factory building			✓	
Purchase of a hospital bed			✓	
Television programme		✓		

Activity 19.2
Student's own answers

Activity 19.3
Student's own answers

Activity 19.4
Student's own answers

Activity 19.5
Student's own answers

Activity 19.6

	Introduction	Growth	Maturity	Saturation	Decline
Sales	Low sales because the product is new	Sales rise rapidly	Sales increase more slowly	Sales level off as market saturation is reached	Sales fall as new products become available or the product goes out of fashion
Pricing policy/ competition	Price skimming as few/no competitors	Penetration pricing by competitors as a few competing products are introduced, small reduction in your prices to compete with these products	Competitive pricing/ promotional pricing as competition becomes intense	Competitive pricing/ prices are reduced to compete with existing competitors, no new competitors enter the market	Price reductions to encourage sales as sales are falling. Some competitors stop making the product
Promotion/ advertising	Informative advertising as the product is new, free samples may be given out to get customers to try it	Informative advertising changed to persuasive advertising to encourage brand loyalty as sales start to rise rapidly	A lot of advertising to encourage brand loyalty and to compete with other very competitive products	A high and stable level of advertising, may be promoting new improved versions of the original product	Advertising reduced or may stop altogether as sales fall
Profits	Loss made due to high development costs	Profits start to be made after development costs have been covered	Profits at their highest as sales growth is high	Profits fall as sales are static and prices have been reduced	Profits fall as sales fall

Activity 19.7

a) Chocolate bar:

- selling into new markets to increase sales of the well-known brand
- introduce new improved version of the old brand to increase interest again
- introduce variations of the chocolate bars to increase interest from other market segments.

Students should include their own examples.

b) Sports shoe:

- introduce variations of the sports shoe which is used with other more popular sports or as a shoe bought by other market segments (leisure shoes). This should encourage people, who were not previously customers, to buy the shoe thus increasing sales.

c) New model of car:

- selling into new markets overseas may increase sales
- use a new advertising campaign to renew interest and possibly increase sales.

d) Children's toy

- sell through additional, different retail outlets. Different people may use these outlets and may buy the toy when previously they were not customers, therefore increasing sales

- use a new advertising campaign to encourage sales by people who were not previously customers
- increase the range of the toy by adding extras that could be purchased. Existing customers may be encouraged to make further purchases.

Unit 20

Activity 20.1

a) The market price is €1.50.

b)

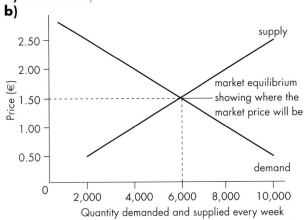

Activity 20.2

The change that has taken place	Demand or supply affected?	Will price increase or decrease?	Will sales increase or decrease?
There has been a bad harvest for coffee beans	Supply decreases	Price rises (in short supply)	Sales decrease (in short supply)
Jeans go out of fashion	Demand decreases	Price falls	Sales decrease
A government report is published which says eating rice is very good for your health	Demand increases	Price rises	Sales increase
New technology is introduced into the production of computers which increases efficiency	Supply increases	Price falls	Sales increase
The cost of components has increased	Supply decreases	Price rises	Sales decrease
A competitor's prices increase	Demand increases	Price rises	Sales increase

Activity 20.3

a) Watch: probably competitive pricing as the watch is very similar to its competitors.

b) New type of radio: probably price skimming to earn high profits to recoup some of the research and development costs.

c) Chocolate bar: probably promotional pricing to increase interest in the chocolate bar. Possibly competitive pricing to maintain sales.

d) Shop: will probably use cost-plus pricing to ensure that it covers its costs and makes the target profit of 75% mark-up on the cost of stock.

e) New brand of soap powder: probably penetration pricing as there are already similar brands available and they will need to get the new brand established in the market.

f) Toy: probably psychological pricing as although £1.99 is just below £2.00, it appears to be much cheaper.

Unit 21

Activity 21.1, 21.2 and 21.3

Student's own answers

Activity 21.4

a) Leisure shoe: the shoe is sold to teenagers and must therefore be advertised in places where it will be seen by teenagers, places such as the cinema, radio, magazines for teenagers, possibly television if it is not too expensive and can be shown at times when teenagers will be watching. These methods of advertising cover the whole country and will probably be seen by most teenagers.

Activity 20.4

Pricing strategy	Examples and when they might be used	Advantages	Disadvantages
Cost-plus pricing	A shop may add a certain percentage on to the cost of buying in the stock, e.g. food retailing, clothes retailing. This may be used when there is not a lot of competition between shops.	Easy to apply.	Could lose sales if the selling price is a lot higher than the competitors' prices.
Penetration pricing	A new product is launched on to the market where there are already several competing products. For example, a new chocolate bar.	Should ensure that sales are made and brand loyalty may be established.	Because prices are low the sales revenue may also be low.
Price skimming	Used when there is not a lot of competition for the new product, e.g. computer systems and computer games when they are first introduced on to the market.	Helps establish the product as a high quality product. High profits may be made.	The high price may reduce the number of customers.
Competitive pricing	An established product that is sold in a market where there are already several competing products. For example, a brand of soap powder.	Sales are likely to be high as your price is similar to your competitors and your product is not over or under priced.	Need to research the prices of your competitors and this will cost time and money.
Promotional pricing	Sales at the end of a season, such as end of winter sales to clear winter clothes. Old stock which has not sold very well might be sold in a clearance sale.	Gets rid of unwanted products or slow selling stock. Renews interest when sales are falling.	Sales revenue will be lower because prices are lower.
Psychological pricing	A high price is charged for a high quality product, for example, a luxurious face cream.	The price establishes the product as exclusive and reinforces the brand image.	The high price may reduce the number of customers.

b) A new bicycle: this will probably be purchased mainly by enthusiasts and therefore specialist bicycle magazines would be the best place to advertise as it will be seen just by the target audience. Other places to advertise will be seen by many people who would not consider buying the bicycle and therefore the advert could be a waste of money. Posters and leaflets to be placed in shops which sell the bicycle would also be helpful as it will draw the attention of the potential purchaser to their particular bicycle when at the point of sale, i.e. the bicycle shop.

c) A new computer game: this will probably be purchased mainly by younger people and therefore similar places to the sports shoe could be used. However, adults and possibly younger children might also be part of the target audience and therefore television may be used, particularly if it is an expensive computer game suitable for use on PCs rather than a specific system. A PC game would have a wider target audience and therefore the places to advertise would be more varied.

d) A new local restaurant: this will probably be used by adults and only local people, therefore only local sources of advertising need to be used. Any form of national advertising would be a waste of money. Advertising on local radio, local newspapers and possibly local billboards and leaflets handed out around the town should reach the target audience.

e) Fizzy soft drink: this is aimed at a wide section of people from younger children to older adults. It may be targeted particularly at younger people but television advertising would probably be used so that a wide selection of people would see the advert. Billboards, cinema and radio may also be used to target, more specifically, the younger population.

f) Local town festival: this is similar to the local restaurant, only local sources will be used, local radio, local newspapers, billboards and possibly leaflets.

Activity 21.5

Advertising media	Advantages	Disadvantages	Examples of suitable products/services to advertise using this method
Television	The advert will go out to millions of people. The product can be shown in a very favourable way, making it look attractive. It reaches the biggest number of customers and can target a specific audience by advertising at times when the programmes they are likely to be watching are being shown.	Very expensive form of advertising.	Food products and drinks that are bought by most people, cars that are bought by a large number of customers, household products, e.g. soap powder, that are bought by most of the population.
Radio	Cheaper than television. Usually reaches a large audience and often uses a memorable song or tune so that the advert will be remembered.	Cannot put across a visual message. Quite expensive relative to other methods of advertising. The advert needs to be remembered, the customer cannot look back at a hard copy of the advert. Not as wide an audience as television.	Local services or events are often advertised on the radio on local channels, e.g. local shops, car showrooms.

Activity 21.5 continues on page 380

Advertising media	Advantages	Disadvantages	Examples of suitable products/services to advertise using this method
Newspapers	National newspapers are often bought by particular customers and therefore the newspaper in which the advertisement is placed can be selected to target a particular group of people. A large number of people will purchase and read national newspapers. Local newspapers are relatively cheap to place adverts in and are a cost effective way to advertise. Adverts are permanent and can be cut out and kept. A lot of information can be put in the advert.	Newspaper adverts are usually only in black and white and are therefore not very eye-catching. Not as attention grabbing as television adverts and may not be noticed by the reader, especially if the advert is small.	Local products, local events in local newspapers Cars, banks in national newspapers.
Magazines	Magazines are read by a specific type of person, e.g. bicycle enthusiast reads bicycle magazines – very effective way to reach the target population if there are specialist magazines which cover a particular activity. Magazine adverts are in colour and therefore can look more attractive.	Magazines are often only published once a month or once a week. Advertising in magazines is relatively more expensive than newspapers.	Perfume in specialist magazines for women. Golf equipment in golf magazines.
Posters/billboards	They are permanent. Relatively cheap.	Can easily be missed as people go past them. No detailed information can be included in the advert.	Local events. Products purchased by a large section of the population as posters are seen by everyone passing the advertisement.
Cinemas	Can give visual image of the product and show the product in a positive way. Relatively low cost. Can be very effective if your target audience go to see particular films.	Seen by only a limited number of people who go to watch the film.	*Coca-Cola* when a film for teenagers is showing.
Leaflets	Cheap method of advertising. Given out in the street to a wide range of people. They could be delivered door to door or mailed to a large number of people. Sometimes contain a money-off voucher to encourage the reader to keep the advert. The adverts are permanent and can be kept for future reference.	May not be read.	Leaflets are often used to advertise local events. Could be given out to promote retail outlets and may contain a money-off voucher on the leaflet.

Activity 21.5 continues on page 381

Advertising media	Advantages	Disadvantages	Examples of suitable products/services to advertise using this method
Internet	A large amount of information can be placed on a website, which can be seen by a vast number of people at home and abroad. Orders can be made instantly via the website.	Internet searches may not highlight the website and it could be missed. In some countries internet access is limited. There is a lot of competition from other websites. Security issues may discourage customers from buying on-line.	Products that customers are already familiar with, e.g. CDs, electrical goods, books. Services such as train information and ticketing, and insurance, are also suitable.
Others	Very cheap form of advertising, e.g. on delivery vehicles and on the sides of bags from shops.	May not be seen by everyone.	Shops use the bags given out with purchases to advertise their name. *Coca-Cola* uses neon signs to advertise its name.

Activity 21.6

Student's own answers

Activity 21.7

a) A new magazine aimed at teenage boys: price reductions, free gifts with the magazine, competitions.

b) A new type of pen which is very comfortable to use and does not smudge: point-of-sale displays and demonstrations.

c) A company making a famous brand of football boots wants to expand sales: competitions, free gifts.

d) A new fast food takeaway opens in a small town: money-off coupons, price reductions, competitions.

e) A soft toy has been invented that changes colour when hugged and can be dressed in different clothes which change colour when warmed: point-of-sale displays and demonstrations.

Activity 21.8

Student's own answers

Unit 22

Activity 22.1

Student's own answers

Activity 22.2

Student's own answer in the form of a letter which details the advantages of a wholesaler, giving examples.

Activity 22.3

a) Farm tractor: channel of distribution 1 or possibly 2 would be used. The product is not something bought very often, it is expensive and expert advice should be given about the product. A personal sales adviser may well be sent out by the manufacturer to the potential customer to discuss the product and explain its qualities. A retailer specialising in agricultural equipment may be used instead and they would also be able to give expert advice about the product.

b) Children's clothes for export: because the product is going to be exported and will be sold in many retail outlets then channel of distribution 4 would probably be used. This will allow the use of an agent in the export market who will be familiar with local customs and practices. Whether a wholesaler is also used will depend on the particular country and how many retail outlets will sell the clothes. If only a few large outlets are going to be used then the wholesale stage may be missed out, but if the clothes are sold to many smaller outlets then a wholesaler will be used to enable a wider distribution and possibly lower distribution costs.

c) Tins of peas: channel of distribution 3 will probably be used because the tins of peas will be sold to many food retailers and it would not be cost effective to sell straight to the retailer. However, if the retailer was very large, the wholesaler would be omitted for these customers because large quantities would be purchased.

d) Made-to-measure suit: channel of distribution 1 will almost certainly be used as direct customer contact is needed by the manufacturer. You cannot sell made-to-measure suits from racks of clothes in clothes shops!

Activity 22.4

a) Tins of vegetables from the cannery to the wholesalers: road transport is most likely because the cannery and the wholesaler would probably not be situated on a river or near to a railway station.

b) Cocoa beans from the plantation to the chocolate factory in another country: sea freight will be used to get the beans to the other country (unless the countries are near to each other by land). This will be the most cost effective method as time is not of crucial importance. Road (maybe rail if the track is close by) transport will probably then be used to get the beans to the factory.

c) Fresh cut flowers from the farm to the retailer in another country: air freight will most probably be used because getting the product quickly to the shops will be very important or it will be ruined. The relative value of the product is quite high and it is not a heavy product which will make it suitable for air transport.

d) Crude oil from the oil field to the refinery: an oil pipeline, if it is available, will be the most economic way of transporting the product. Road or rail is more expensive and if the oil fields are in remote areas then the roads/rail system may not be very developed.

e) Cars from the factory to the car showrooms: assuming the showrooms are in the same country as the factory, then rail transport may be used for part of the journey and then road will be used for the final part of the journey as it is unlikely that the showroom will be situated next to a railway station. Road transport may be used for the whole journey.

f) Coal from the coal mine to the steel mill: rail transport, if a line is available, will be the cheapest way to transport the coal. If a rail link is not available then it may be worthwhile, in the long run, to build one. If this is not available then road transport may be used but it would probably be more expensive.

g) Logs from the forests to the saw mills: if possible, because of the weight of the logs, rivers would be the best form of transport. The logs are very heavy and would be expensive to transport by road/rail. The logs float in the water and there will be no hurry for the logs to reach the saw mill. Where rivers or canals are not available then road or rail transport may have to be used.

h) Soft toys from the factory to the retailer in the same country: the products are relatively light weight and the retailer is not likely to be situated near to a railway station therefore road transport is the most suitable form of transport.

Activity 22.5
Student's own answer

Unit 23
Activity 23.1
a) ABC: flow production, as the chocolate bars are mass produced and each type of chocolate bar is the same.
Alexander: job production, as each customer wants individual attention. Each hair style is different to meet each customer's needs.

b) Batch production is the most suitable method, given that the components are standardised for use in several engines. The production of engines will not be large enough to make flow production viable.

Activity 23.2
Changes identified should include – reduced space needed for production; work-in-progress is reduced; less stock of raw materials; finished product not stored; more of a flow through the factory; some machines are grouped together.

Activity 23.3

Student's own answers

Activity 23.4

Student's own answers

Activity 23.5

Student's own answers

Unit 24

Activity 24.1

a) Factors: market, availability of water, raw materials, transport and communication, availability of skilled labour, power.

b) Raw materials or availability of water are likely to be the most important to the location decision.

Activity 24.2

a) Student's own answer

b) The additional information might be rent of the shops, taxes to pay, male/female ratio, competition.

Activity 24.3

Student's own answer in correct report format.

Activity 24.4

a) and b) Electrician, discussion of: needs to be near to local customers; personal preference of owner; rent/taxes on premises; possibly availability of labour; competition from other electricians.

Computer software firm, discussion of: personal preference of owners; customers do not need direct contact; availability of labour; rent/taxes on premises; possibly technology.

Scuba training centre, discussion of: needs direct contact with customers; needs to be sited near suitable dive sites where the customers will go; near to other businesses such as in holiday resorts; climate; rent/taxes on premises; personal preference of owners.

Unit 25

Activity 25.1

a) 10,000¥

b) 6,000¥

Activity 25.2

a) £250

b) £200

Activity 25.3

a) Consumers

b) Clothes are traded freely throughout the world with few trade restrictions. Businesses are able to buy supplies of clothing from the lowest-cost producers in other countries.

c) Student's own answer

Activity 25.4

Student's own answer

Activity 25.5

a) Unemployed: may be offered a job; government: tax revenue from profits tax could rise; businesses: which could supply goods to the new factory.

b) Competitors of the new factory; workers employed by competitors of the factory; people who live near the site where the factory might be built.

c) Student's own answer

Answers to revision questions

Unit 1

1 a) Needs are: shelter, clean water, clothing. Wants are: luxury house, *Coca-Cola*, car, designer jeans.
   b) Needs are necessary for life, but wants are not. Our wants are limitless and contain many luxury items. Our needs are necessary items.
2 Scarcity means that there are limited resources available to satisfy human wants. This creates the economic problem of scarcity.
3 Land – a building or area of land will be needed for making a good or providing a service. Also, raw materials are natural products that come from the land.
   Labour – workers will be needed to produce, pack and deliver the product. Even fully automated factories require some maintenance staff or drivers.
   Capital – equipment, machinery and vehicles will be needed for production or supply of a product or a service. Even a window cleaner needs ladders, buckets and a sponge.
   Enterprise – someone will be needed to *show enterprise* by having the original product idea and bringing the other resources together to produce the product.
4 Opportunity cost is the benefits given up from the next most preferred item when another good is chosen. So, assume that a consumer had £40 to spend. She wanted to buy both a pair of shoes and a radio, but as she could not afford both she decided to buy the radio. The benefit that she would have gained from the pair of shoes becomes the opportunity cost of the radio.
5 Governments experience opportunity cost when they spend money on projects, e.g. giving up building a new motorway in order to pay for the purchase of new army tanks.
   Businesses experience opportunity cost, e.g. when deciding to purchase a new machine rather than replacing a delivery truck – the truck becomes the opportunity cost.
6 Division of labour is when an activity is split up into separate tasks and each worker then specialises on a particular task.
7 Division of labour allows workers to become experts in particular tasks, enabling them to work faster. Also, less time is wasted as workers stay at one work station without having to move from one machine to the next.
8 Fetching the ingredients from the store; making the cake mixture; pouring the mixture into cake tins; controlling the baking of the cakes; decorating the cakes; testing the quality; packing them – any four of these, or similar, tasks.
9 Any three of the following: provision of goods and services; research into new products; employment of workers and the payment of incomes; paying taxes to the government.
10 Business objectives are the aims and targets of a business, set by the owners and managers.
11 Any three of the following: profits, growth, good public image, increasing value added, providing a service, survival (for new firms in particular), responding to changing consumer needs.
12 Added value is the difference between the selling price of a product and the cost of the materials and components purchased by the firm to make it.
13 Attempt to establish a quality and upmarket image that would allow higher prices to be charged; find a cheaper source of materials and components needed.
14 To reduce the chances of being taken over; to satisfy the managers' aims of controlling a larger business to achieve greater status and pay; to maintain or increase market share if the overall market is expanding. Any two of these.
15 Owners, workers, managers, consumers, government, local community – any group with a direct interest in the performance and decisions of the business. Any three of these.
16 Owners may want short-term profits, but consumers want lower prices; the local community might want jobs to be kept, but managers might prefer cost-cutting measures that would reduce the number of jobs. Other examples are possible.
17 a) Likely to lose their jobs, unless they can find work in the shopping centre – this could involve retraining and lower pay or a period of unemployment benefit.
   b) Profits give returns to the owners and the risk takers and can be used to reinvest back into the business for expansion. But profits may be at the expense of workers' jobs (lower costs), long-term customer loyalty (higher prices) and the support of the local community (low cost method of production that might pollute the surrounding area).

Unit 2

1 Primary sector activity extracts natural products from the land while secondary sector activity uses and processes raw materials in the manufacturing of finished goods. The tertiary sector provides services, e.g. retailing, leisure and banking.

2 Tertiary sector – as people's incomes rise so their demand for consumer services grows, e.g. for financial services and holidays.

3 Answers could include: all resources such as property are privately owned; decisions on what goods and services to produce are made by private firms; no government involvement in the economy; business decisions taken on the basis of profit; supply is led by demand in the free market.

4 a) Benefits of free market economies to firms: can choose which method of production to use; can work towards making a profit; can purchase the resources they need for production; new businesses can be set up easily.

   b) Benefits to consumers: freedom of choice on how income is spent; ranges of products to choose from; competition between firms should assist in keeping prices down; producers respond to changing tastes.

5 Command economies have no private sector. In mixed economies some resources are controlled by the state (government) and some are controlled by private individuals.

6 They will be operated with a profit motive as opposed to a public service motive; jobs may be lost as cost cuts are looked for to increase profits; loss making services may be closed down; they may end up as monopolies, keeping prices high.

7 Any three of the following:
   Investors (shareholders) – before deciding which business to invest in
   Banks – before lending money
   Workers – to see how many fellow workers there will be
   Competitors – to compare with own business
   Government – different tax rates may apply.

8 a) Owner of printing firm: capital employed
      Owner of fruit farm: number of employees.
   b) Student's own answer.

9 A take-over means that one firm buys control of the assets of another business. A merger is an agreed joining together of two businesses to create one larger one.

10 Internal growth (organic growth) is achieved when a firm increases its sales, its number of branches and its range of products by *not* taking over or merging with another business. External growth is achieved by a merger with, or a take-over of, another business.

11 A bus company merging with another bus company. A bicycle manufacturer taking over another bicycle manufacturing firm. Any example where one firm takes over or merges with another firm providing the same good or service.

12 A soft drinks manufacturer takes over a chain of cafés. A diamond mining firm takes over a chain of high class jewellers. Any example where one firm takes over another firm providing the next stage of production.

13 This type of integration should ensure a market for the firm's products. The manufacturing firm is now able to control the retailing and marketing of its products.

14 A petrol retailing business takes over an oil exploration business. A steel making firm merges with an iron ore mining business. Any example where one firm takes over or merges with another firm providing it with parts or materials.

15 a) Internal, as no other business is being taken over or merged with.
   b) Advantages: lower average costs; bigger market share; better known business; may be more profitable and earn the owner higher returns. Disadvantages: bigger business to control; contact with customers may be lost; riskier – more capital may have to be put into the business.

16 The owners of a small business may want to avoid the risks and pressures of expanding their business. The market the firm operates in may be very specialised and small and this may prevent the business from growing.

Unit 3

1 a) Workers' co-operative – because all of the workers will own the business, there will be no *external* shareholders and they will be able to take business decisions themselves.
   b) Public limited company – as the expansion will require a great deal of capital this might be difficult to raise unless the firm can sell shares to the public. Specialist managers will have to be employed and they may prefer the status of working for a plc.

c) Sole trader – little capital is required; no other owners will be brought in to the business; little risk of losing large sums of money invested in the business, therefore limited liability may be considered unnecessary.

d) Public corporation – as the main aim is to provide a public service and not to make profits, state ownership in the form of a public corporation would seem to be the best option.

e) Partnership – as several of the solicitors wish to own the business jointly, a sole trader is not appropriate. They are not allowed to create a limited company. They would be advised to draw up a Deed of Partnership.

f) Private limited company – the current owner wants to pass the business on to his son, therefore the business must be a separate legal unit and have *continuity* – a sole trader firm would not offer these benefits.

2 Decisions may take longer than in a sole trader business; unlimited liability; cannot sell shares; need to reform the partnership if a partner dies.

3 Limited liability (owners can only lose their original investment if the company fails); can sell shares to family, friends, workers to raise extra finance; higher status with customers; legal unit that has continuity if one of the owners dies.

4 Accounts of the company have to be made public; there could be a split or *divorce* between ownership and control; shares are available for purchase on the open market and there is therefore a risk of take-over.

5 The public sector of industry refers to those organisations owned and controlled by the state, such as nationalised industries. Public limited companies are in the *private sector* of industry as they are owned by private shareholders.

6 Sharing of risks, sharing of costs, different companies may have different skills or experiences to contribute to the joint venture, e.g. one firm could have a successful product but the other could already have offices in the country where they both intend to set up their joint venture.

7 and 8 The conflict of objectives between owners and managers in a plc results from the *divorce between ownership and control* in such companies. While the owners – the shareholders – may prefer high dividends in the short term, the managers may prefer to put more profits back into the business to finance expansion.

9 Franchise: the giving of the rights by one business (the franchisor) to another business (the franchisee) to use its name and to supply its products.

10 a) Advantages: independence; can sell any products he chooses; can keep all of the profits. Student to provide an explanation for any one of these.
Disadvantages: limited sources of capital; no one to discuss decisions with; no continuity of business; unlimited liability. Student to provide an explanation for any one of these.

b) Advantages for Tom: well established brand name; management, staff training and marketing support; ready-made business idea. Student to give an explanation for any one of these.
Advantages for franchisor: expansion paid for by franchisee; sale of licences is a source of revenue; management problems are borne by franchisee.

11 Public service is the main aim, not profit; programmes may be made for minority groups even though they may not be financially profitable; programmes are not influenced by commercial considerations; there may not be any advertising on the channel.

Unit 4

1 Dangerous products could be produced and sold; firms could damage the environment during production as there would be no controls to prevent this; monopolies could be created and this could lead to high prices; workers might be exploited by being paid very low wages and given poor working conditions; unregulated advertising may lead to misleading claims being made about products.

2 Low inflation, low unemployment, economic growth, balance of payments.

3 Any two of the following: industrial conflict as workers may press for wage increases to keep up with inflation; job losses in industries where cheaper products from abroad may be substituted; reluctance of businesses to expand because of uncertainty about the future; balance of payments problems or depreciation of country's currency.

4 To increase economic growth; to increase people's incomes; to reduce inequality in society;

to discourage discontent and unrest caused by unemployment.

5   Economic growth is an increase in the real value of a country's GDP.

6   GDP is the total value of all goods and services produced in a country in one year.

7   Trade cycle:

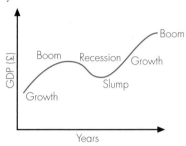

Boom: when demand for goods and services continues to rise, causing inflation to increase. Firms have little if any spare capacity to increase output.
Recession: real GDP falls as output declines, leading to higher unemployment.

8   When the value of imports exceeds the value of exports.

9   Direct taxes are taken out of income and profit. Indirect taxes are added on to the prices of goods and services.

10 Less spending by consumers will reduce demand for hotels. This will lead to lower output and unemployment; higher exchange rate will make holidays in this country less competitive; businesses will be less likely to borrow money to invest in expansion.

11 It would be likely to increase the demand for luxury foreign holidays as mortage-payers and people with credit commitments would have more disposable income.

12 Both firms will be badly affected but Firm A is likely to be more affected because: as higher interest rates could lead to a higher exchange rate, export prices will have to rise; they sell luxury goods that are often bought on loans, so the consumer will now be less likely to purchase these goods. But higher tariffs will hit the flour importer and Firm A as imports will be more expensive. A higher exchange rate could, however, make imports cheaper and this could cancel out the effect of tariffs.

13 Answers need to have some *local* reference: legal protection against dangerous goods or goods

which do not do the job for which they were intended; banning of misleading adverts; making illegal, unfair claims about a product or a price reduction during a sale; obscure or misleading credit/HP agreements.

14 A monopoly is a single firm that controls the sales of a good in a market.

15 Consumers will have less choice than if the market had several firms operating in it. Prices charged by a monopolist might be much higher without competition. Less chance of new firms joining the industry with new products/ideas.

16 Choosing *not* to employ or promote people because of their colour, race, religion or sex.

17 Protection around dangerous machinery; clean and hygienic working conditions and washing facilities; limits on number of hours worked; controls over dangerous materials or production methods; reasonable workplace temperature; provision of safety equipment and clothing.

18 Helps to prevent exploitation of workers by firms through the payment of very low wages. Low paid workers will have more money to spend and this will increase demand for certain products. People will be encouraged to look for work now that it is better paid. Employers may be encouraged to train workers in new skills.

19 Small firms offer important advantages: employment for many people; wider choice of goods and services for consumers; more competition; they can grow to become important large businesses in the future; they may operate in areas where unemployment would otherwise be high.

20 Organising trade fairs and exhibitions in other countries; information and advice about the markets in other countries; sometimes governments will guarantee payment if the firm in the other country does not pay; encouraging banks to lend at lower interest rates to exporters; introducing tax incentives and subsidies.

Unit 5

1   A constraint limits or prevents a business from taking a certain decision or behaving in a particular way. There may be economic, legal, technological and environmental constraints on business activity.

2 Student's own answers as the list is very long indeed!

3 Student's own answer, but might include robots, computer controlled equipment.

4 He *might* continue to be successful if he can sell to sufficient consumers who want traditional clothing made in the traditional way. If the firm operates in a low cost, competitive market it is unlikely to survive.

5 Similar answer to above. In a competitive *mass* market such an approach is unlikely to lead to business success.

6 Fear of losing jobs; fear of not understanding new technology; fear of not being able to pass new qualifications and training programmes; fear of loss of job status as other experts are recruited.

7 As with Question 6, but also fear of not being able to understand the new technological skills of new workers that the managers are responsible for; possible danger of excess power and influence of IT experts.

8 Consult with workers; tell workers why change is needed and how they will be affected; inform and persuade them of the benefits; offer job security and retraining programmes to update skills.

9 Air pollution and noise pollution – but also waste products dumped in rivers and sea.

10 Firms do not pay directly for pollution that they cause, unless they are fined or have to purchase permits. On the other hand, they would have to pay for more up-to-date and *cleaner* machines and methods of production.

11 A group of people with common interests or demands who act together to try to get their demands met.

12 Direct action such as boycotts, demonstrations, action to stop other oil tankers sailing. Indirect action such as organising a publicity campaign against the business or putting pressure on government to change the law and force greater safety measures on oil companies.

13 Fear of bad publicity and negative consumer reaction – these could damage sales and profits.

14 Too expensive to take the action demanded; perhaps consumer resistance is only short term; pressure group might be quite weak and have little influence; firm may not deal directly with public, but with other firms.

15 Social costs are those paid for by society unlike private costs that are paid for by the firm itself. So a decision to close a factory will reduce business costs but put costs on society in the form of higher unemployment and benefits to be paid to the unemployed.

16 Cost-benefit analysis attempts to measure all of the social costs and social benefits of a business or government decision before taking action – such as deciding to build a new airport. Businesses will, generally, consider only the private costs and benefits.

17 a) More jobs; higher incomes; other firms might be attracted to the area; higher tax payments by the business.

   b) Rubbish from the restaurant and take-away food; packaging materials might be used that are harmful to the environment; smells and fumes from the kitchen might be bad for local residents.

18 A complete ban on certain business activity, e.g. closing all nuclear power stations; legal limits on pollution levels; sale of permits to force firms to *pay* for pollution.

Unit 6

1 Any two from the following: calculating price; calculating whether a profit or loss is being made; comparing with other products or past cost data.

2 Rent on the factory will be a fixed cost as it will not vary with the output of carpets. Management salaries, advertising, heating and lighting are other examples that could have been used.

3 Carpet manufacturers need wool as one of their raw materials. The greater the number of carpets made, the greater the need for wool. Therefore, the cost of wool will vary with the output of carpets.

4 Line from origin (0) is sales revenue. Line from fixed costs (F) is total cost. Vertical axis is £(costs/revenue) and horizontal axis is units of output.

5 a) 6000 units
  b) 1500 units.

6 Contribution = £13 − £5 = £8

$$\frac{£40,000}{£8} = 5,000 \text{ units.}$$

7 It could try to reduce variable costs per unit, lower fixed costs or increase revenue, e.g. by raising the selling price.

8 By reducing the break-even level of output the firm will increase the safety margin and the profits being made.

9 Any two from the following: shows the level of output needed to break even; shows the safety margin and the range of profitable output; allows comparisons to be made between different price and cost levels; can be used to assess the effect of other decisions, e.g. selecting most profitable location.

10 Any two from the following: assumes no stocks held; lines used are assumed to be straight; costs are not necessarily constant, e.g. if the firm expands the scale of operation.

11 Direct costs can be identified as being caused by a particular product or department – they can be allocated directly to that product or department. Indirect costs cannot be identified as being caused by one product or department – they cannot be directly allocated. These are also known as overhead costs.

12 This is the total arrived at by the addition of variable cost and fixed cost.

13 This is arrived at by dividing total cost by the current level of output – it is also known as the cost per unit.

14 Economies of scale are the benefits received by firms when they expand the scale of operation. These lead to a reduction in average costs or costs per unit.

15 Marketing economies – costs of advertising can be *spread* over more stores.
Purchasing economies – buying larger quantities from suppliers should give lower costs per unit.
Technical economies – benefiting from the purchase of the latest stock control and supermarket check-out computer equipment. Managerial and financial economies should also be possible.

16 Communication problems between branches and between head office and branches – these could reduce efficiency. Low morale or poor motivation from staff if they feel unimportant as part of a much larger, more impersonal organisation.

17 A prediction of sales for a future time period, based on past results and known future market changes.

18 A financial plan for the future containing financial and/or numerical targets.

19 Any two from the following: budgets can provide targets and a sense of direction; they can bring about a more efficient allocation of resources; they can be used to compare with actual results to measure performance; setting budgets and targets with staff can provide motivation.

20 A variance is the difference between a budgeted figure and an actual result.

Unit 7

1 Any two of the following: calculate profit/loss; see which product or department of the business is doing best/worst; assist in setting prices; ensure that bills are paid on time and customers pay for goods received; compare performance with other businesses; ensure that the business does not pay out so much at one time that it is without money to pay creditors.

2 Any three of the following: shareholders/investors in the business, employees, local community, governments, suppliers and competitors.

3 Gross profit – sales revenue less variable costs. Net profit – sales revenue less all costs. The difference is, therefore, fixed costs or expenses which are deducted before arriving at net profit, but not gross profit.

4 This part of the profit and loss account shows how much profit after tax is paid out in dividends, and how much is retained in the business.

5 Depreciation is the loss in the value of a firm's fixed assets over a period of time.

6 It tells a manager the total value of the firm's assets (what it owns) and the total value of its debts (liabilities). It sets out the ways a business has raised its capital and the uses to which it has been put.

7 Assets are items owned by a business. A liability is money owed by the business to other firms and individuals.

8 Capital employed is the sum of all of the capital invested in a business.

9 Ratios make comparisons between two pieces of accounting data and these comparisons are more useful than just looking at one total value and they give a better idea of how well the company has performed.

10 The return on capital employed ratio compares the operating profits of the business with capital employed. A return of 20 per cent means that the operating profits of that year were equal to 20 per cent of the firm's capital employed.

11 The current ratio compares current assets with current liabilities. A result of less than one means that the business could not easily pay off its short-term debts from short-term assets – a result of 0.75 would be considered too low for most businesses because it shows that the firm's short-term assets only cover 75% of its short-term debts.

12 Net profit can be calculated: 2004 = €9,000
2005 = €7,000

Return on capital employed:
2004 = 9/70 = 12.9%
2005 = 7/80 = 8.75%
Gross profit margin:
2004 = 15/100 = 15%
2005 = 16/120 = 13.3%
Net profit margin: 2004 = 9/100 = 9%
2005 = 7/120 = 5.8%

In 2005 this business recorded a poorer performance than in 2004. All three ratios reported a lower per cent. The firm increased its sales turnover, but at the expense of profitability. Perhaps the firm lowered its prices or costs of materials rose and the firm did not increase its prices. Either of these factors would explain the lower gross profit margin. The net profit margin fell due to both a lower gross profit margin and business expenses rising faster than sales turnover. Corrective action will be needed if this firm is to avoid a further weaker performance in 2006.

13 Ratios ignore factors such as the quality of management and the state of the economy. When making comparisons with other companies, accounting values may have been calculated in different ways. Ratios are based on past performance and may not be a good guide for the future.

14 They would provide details of: the company's profitability and dividend payments; how these had changed over recent years; the current position and wealth of the business; whether it was able to pay its debts; the share price; how it had recently changed. Further analysis could give an idea of the company's performance and liquidity.

15 a) Gross profit = Sales revenue less cost of goods sold
   b) £60,000
   Total cost = £40,000 + £8,000 + £12,000
                     = £60,000
   c) Cleaning costs, heating costs, linen costs, hot water costs.
   d) £10,080 − £6,000 = £4,080

16 $2004 = \dfrac{17,000}{15,000} = 1.1$ $2005 = \dfrac{12,000}{18,000} = 0.67$

The liquidity of company X has worsened considerably in 12 months.

Unit 8

1 Cash that is received by a business.
2 Cash sales, payments by debtors, loans, sale of shares, investors, sale of assets (e.g. buildings).
3 Cash paid out by a business.
4 Payments for goods and materials, payment of wages, paying back loans, purchasing fixed assets, repaying loans, paying creditors.
5 Cash flow cycle: the stages between paying out for materials and labour and receiving cash from the sale of goods.
6 Student's own answer.
7 The longer the time period between making cash payments and the receipt of cash from customers, the greater the need to finance this gap with working capital.
8 a) £800; b) £800; c) £1,200; d) £3,700
9 Despite good profits the cash balance has fallen, possibly because: more fixed assets have been bought; goods have been sold on credit; suppliers have asked for quicker payment; a bank loan has been repaid.
10 a) Student's own answer – sufficient examples exist in the text to provide the necessary structure.
   b) Points made could include: reduce monthly expenses; ask debtors to pay more quickly; sell some fixed assets to raise cash; delay paying for purchases from suppliers; arrange an overdraft with bank to cover negative cash flow period.

Unit 9

1 Finance is needed to purchase buildings and equipment and to buy in stocks. As the business

is new it will not have made any profits, so the owners will need other sources of finance, such as loans or their own capital.

2 Revenue expenditure is purchase of day-to-day items that will be used up in a short time. Capital expenditure is the purchase of fixed assets such as buildings and vehicles.

3 Internal finance is obtained from the firm's own resources. External finance is in the form of loans, grants or sales of shares. This is finance obtained from individuals and institutions outside of the business.

4 Selling off stocks to reduce the value of stocks held – this reduces the amount of capital 'tied up' in stocks. Using retained profits – will not lead to any interest charges. A sole proprietor may use personal savings – available quickly and no interest payments.

5 Short-term finance is needed for up to three years, for example, the finance needed to pay for a seasonal increase in stocks. Long-term finance is needed for time periods over ten years, for example, the finance needed for the purchase of buildings.

6 Overdraft – a flexible form of finance that is only taken as and when the firm needs it. Debt factoring – provides cash quickly as there is no wait for debtors (the firm's customers) to pay.

7 A bank loan is for a certain amount for a fixed time period. An overdraft can vary with the needs of the business, to a certain degree, and so the firm pays interest only on what is needed. Loans have to be paid back in regular instalments.

8 Share capital is said to be permanent because it never has to be repaid.

9 Loans can be arranged quickly – a share issue cannot. Loans do not change the ownership of the company – issuing more shares might do this. Loans do not reduce the share price – selling a large number of new shares could do this. Interest on loans is paid before tax – dividends are paid after tax.

10 Leasing – the computers will never be owned, but the firm will have the use of them. Leasing charges will be quite high and will have to be paid regularly.

Long-term loan – interest will have to be paid and the capital sum repaid after an agreed time period.

Shares – permanent capital that will not have

to be repaid, but the computers will depreciate quickly leaving the business with assets of very low value. Dividends will be expected by the shareholders. High cost of new share issue.

Computers are often leased as firms do not want to own rapidly depreciating assets. Maintenance costs are usually paid for by the leasing company.

11 Limited companies are able to sell shares to family, friends of owners etc. – not possible for a sole trader. Companies may have retained profits after dividends have been paid, but the sole trader may have a trading surplus that belongs to the owner. If this is put back into the business then the owner is, in effect, using his own savings. These are the two main differences.

12 A document completed by a business, often when it is first formed, giving details of aims, expected activities and forecasted income and expenditure.

13 Benefits of a business plan: gives managers a direction to follow; helps managers to assess whether the business is on 'track' once it is operating, by comparing with the business plan; used by lenders such as banks to test the viability of the business scheme. Any two of these answers.

14 Any relevant details possible such as: qualifications and experience of managers/owners – to see if they are well equipped to run the business; marketing plan – to see if the business has planned which market it is aiming for and how it intends to sell the products; cash flow forecast – to see if the owners have thought about the financing needs of the business; location of business – to establish the equipment needed.

15 Any two points including: current profits – is the business likely to make a profit and pay dividends? Recent profits – to see if the company is becoming more or less profitable. Recent movements in the share price – if it is a plc. Performance and liquidity ratios.

Unit 10

1 This refers to the levels of management and division of responsibilities within an organisation.

2 The structure will probably show more levels of hierarchy as more managers are needed to deal with a larger business. The need to delegate

more will create more levels in the organisation, thus widening the spans of control.

3 It shows who should report to which manager, the formal chain of command and the formal communication channels – all useful for a new recruit.

4 Delegation means passing down authority to workers to perform tasks.

5 To give the manager more time to concentrate on more important 'strategic' issues. To help train people to accept authority and prepare to be managers themselves.

6 More interesting and rewarding work; employee feels more important; good way of seeing if staff can accept authority and undertake tasks themselves.

7 Advantages: more time for important strategic work; managers can measure success of staff more easily; managers are less likely to make mistakes. Disadvantage: may be loss of control.

8 a) The number of people that a manager is directly responsible for.
   b) 7.
   c) Greater job satisfaction for the workers as there is less management control – this could improve the quality of the work that they do. Managers are likely to delegate more.
   d) Less direct control over the work of subordinates. If poorly trained the workers may make more mistakes as the manager cannot control them all, all of the time.

9 a) Staff managers are specialists who provide support to all sections of the business. Line managers are part of the chain of command carrying out the primary purpose of the business, e.g. production.
   b) Any one of the following: all employees are aware of where they fit into the organisation; communication channels are clear; responsibility is clear.

10 a) A section of the business with responsibility for a particular area of operations, e.g. marketing or finance.
   b) Any two of the following: major investment projects; decisions to take over or merge with another firm; long-term growth strategy; overall objectives; new organisational proposals.

11 Student's own answer referring to the chain of command from the headteacher or principal to the staff of the school/college.

12 Many decisions are not taken by head office, but are delegated to lower level managers.

13 Quicker decision-making as each decision does not have to go through head office. Decisions are taken by managers who are closer to the action, e.g. marketing decisions for selling a product in Germany might be better taken in Germany than in the head office in the US.

Unit 11

1 Any three from the following: planning, organising, co-ordinating, commanding, controlling.

2 Students need to explain why several of the following qualities would be important in a manager who replaces Sabrina: intelligence – to cope with new ideas; initiative – to take command; self-confidence – to be able to set an example; determination – to be able to lead others and push ideas through; communication skills – to be able to put ideas across; energy – to set high standards of effort.

3 Which clothes to buy, the prices to sell them at, the number and location of the stores, the number of staff in each store, etc.

4 Strategic decisions are important, long-term decisions such as where to locate a new store or whether to take over another business. Tactical decisions are likely to be made more frequently and be of less importance, such as when to have a 'sale' of goods, the layout of the store, the closing time of the store.

5 Marketing, Finance, Human Resources, Production, Administration.

6 Marketing – researching consumer demand (market research) and setting the prices for the products.
Finance – managing cash flow and keeping accurate accounting records.
Human Resources – recruiting new staff and organising training programmes.
Production – ordering stocks of materials and checking quality of production.
Students may think of other tasks too.

7 a) and b) for each plan:
New range of shoes: market research of consumers' tastes; sales of existing ranges; competitors' ranges of shoes; competitors' prices. This information will help managers to decide

which shoes are likely to be most popular and which ranges competitors already sell.

- Lower prices for existing shoes: sales of existing shoes; what happened to sales the last time prices were changed; competitors' prices; the cost of making the shoes. This information should help the managers decide whether a price reduction will increase sales by very much and whether it will lead to higher profits.
- Replace workers with machines: cost of machines; wage costs of workers to be replaced; reliability of machines; how long they are expected to last. The managers need to know whether the cost of the machines will, over their lifetime, be greater or less than the cost of paying the workers that they replace.

8 a) There is risk involved with this decision as the future is always uncertain: demand could fall perhaps because the country's economy goes into recession; one machine might be more reliable than the other; the cost of borrowing money could rise (the rate of interest); competitors might purchase an even more efficient machine.

b) The decision-making process – students should explain this – will not eliminate risk but it might reduce it. It will force managers to: think about objectives; discuss the problem; collect data to aid the decision; look back to review the decision to see whether it was successful or not.

Unit 12

1 Communication is the passing of information between sender and receiver. To be effective, communication should include *feedback* to ensure that the message has been received and understood.

2 There must be a sender, receiver, a channel of communication or medium, and feedback.

3 One-way communication does not allow for feedback from the receiver of a message, but two-way communication does.

4 In a situation where the receivers of the message have to understand it and react appropriately, e.g. new safety regulations, changes in working practice, hours, holiday arrangements. Two-way communication allows the sender to check that receivers have understood what is required.

5 Internal communication is between staff working for the same business or organisation. External communication is between the business and other organisations or people who do not work in the business, such as customers or suppliers.

6 Letters, noticeboards, memos.

7 When giving details of new shift or holiday arrangements; when disciplining a member of staff for lateness; when the manager wants to discuss new working conditions with staff.

8 and 9

a) Meeting or possibly a notice – but will everyone read it? The medium chosen must enable the manager to have contact with all of the staff concerned.

b) Meeting so that they can ask questions if they are unclear.

c) E-mail or telephone call, possibly a one-to-one conversation. A channel of communication that makes it easy to reply quickly.

d) Meeting or letter to all staff or possibly a notice, depending on how important it is.

e) Letter – these details will form part of the employee's employment contract so they should be in writing.

10 Student's own choice and selection – advantages explained in text.

11 See table on page 394.

12 a) Any factor that prevents a message being received or understood.

b) Message unclear; wrong channel used; technical breakdown; message passes through too many people and gets distorted; poor attitude of receiver.

c) The answer will depend on the barriers selected by the student. Some examples include: use the shortest chain of command possible; make sure there is feedback so that checks can be made to ensure the message has been understood; send by more than one channel to make sure it is received, e.g. a letter following up a telephone call; improve attitude of staff to communication by consultation and discussion; improve clarity of messages.

(Table for Unit 12, Question 11)

	Advantages	**Disadvantages**
Letters	Can be referred to more than once Can contain plans or drawings etc. Hard evidence	Not immediate Content may not be understood No immediate feedback
Memorandum	Direct to the relevant people Can be referred to more than once	Formal – unlike conversations etc. No immediate feedback
Meeting	Direct and immediate feedback possible Good for discussions. Enables communication between a group of people at once.	Time consuming No guarantee that all those present have understood.
One-to-one conversation	Direct and immediate feedback	Time consuming if a number of people need to be contacted No written evidence
E-mail	Quick Able to send to a large number of people immediately Possible to circulate large documents more quickly and cheaply than as hard copy	All must have access to computers May not be read – might be too many e-mails being received
Telephone	Direct feedback possible Quick	Assumes the receiver can be contacted. No hard evidence

Unit 13

1 They are more productive, i.e. they produce more output and the quality is better.
2 A – ii)
   B – i)
   C – iii).
3 Money, security, job satisfaction, esteem needs, social needs.
4 Monetary rewards, non-monetary rewards, introducing ways to give job satisfaction.
5 Joe is paid a salary and Kiran is paid a wage.
6 For example: income tax; pension contributions; trade union subscriptions.
7 €250.
8 Sarah is paid by time rate and Selina is paid by piece rate.
9 An advantage of using time rate is that it is easy to calculate an employee's pay. A disadvantage of using time rate is that good and bad workers get paid the same, there is no additional reward to an employee for working harder.
10 For bus drivers, hotel receptionists, bar staff, swimming pool attendants.
11 An advantage of using piece rate is that it is an incentive for the workers to work harder. A disadvantage of using piece rate is that the workers may concentrate on producing a lot of products and not worry about the quality of the products.
12 On a production line or in any situation where the output can be measured.
13 For example, commission, profit sharing, bonus, performance-related pay.
14 Appraisal is a method of assessing the effectiveness of an employee.
15 Rewards given to employees that are not cash payments.
16 For example: discounts on the company's products; company vehicle; free accommodation; expense accounts; share options; free trips abroad; health care; subsidised meals; housing; children's education; 'prizes' for good performance (e.g. paid holiday).
17 For example: pay; opportunities for promotion; fringe benefits; colleagues; the nature of the work itself; level of responsibility; recognition of good work; chance for training.
18 a) job enlargement – to give workers a greater variety of tasks e.g. arranging displays, serving customers.
    b) job enrichment – to add more responsibility to the job, e.g. making up the menu, ordering the ingredients, being responsible for hiring new staff.

c) job rotation – to move between jobs to give workers greater variety..

19 Autocratic, laissez-faire, democratic.

20 a) formal   b) informal
    c) informal   d) formal.

Unit 14

1 Recruitment and selection; wages and salaries; industrial relations; training programmes; health and safety; redundancy.

2 When an employee leaves a job, when a new business is starting up and when a business is successful and wants to expand.

3 To study the tasks and activities that the job involves so that they know what the new employee will need to do.

4 It lists the desirable and essential requirements for the job.

5 a) The post is filled from within the organisation.
    b) External recruitment.
    c) Advantage – saves time and money; the person is already known to the business. Disadvantage – there will be no new ideas introduced; there may be jealousy and rivalry amongst existing employees.

6 For example, local newspapers, national newspapers, specialist magazines and journals, recruitment agencies, centres run by the government.

7 For example, name, address, date of birth, nationality, education and qualifications, work experience. Each should be justified as to why it needs to be included. (One mark for each example and two marks for explanation.)

8 For example, duties involved, qualifications required, salary, where to send the application.

9 High marks would be awarded for including a good range of factors and explaining why they are important. Examples of factors include: experience; prior training and qualifications; personal qualities such as self-motivation and ambition; organisational skills; leadership ability.

10 So that they can assess the suitability of the person for the job and see what they are like.

11 Skills tests to test out the ability of the applicant; aptitude tests to show the candidate's potential to gain additional skills; personality tests where a particular type of personality is required; group

tests to assess competitive strengths and team-work.

12 Induction training, on-the-job training, off-the-job training.

13 To introduce the employee to the company and its way of doing things. This is so that the employee can quickly settle into the new job.

14 The employee gets away from the place of work and can concentrate on the training. A broad range of skills can be taught.

15 Dismissal is when the employee is told to leave the job because they are not carrying it out efficiently or because of misconduct, whereas redundancy is when the employee is no longer needed through no fault of their own.

Unit 15

1 A trade union is a group of workers who have joined together to ensure their work interests are protected.

2 Craft union, general union, industrial union, white-collar union.

3 To receive a number of benefits such as protection from unfair dismissal, representation, improved conditions of employment.

4 This is where a firm will only deal with one particular trade union and no others.

5 a) Employees: will have greater strength because there is only one union; there are no disagreements between different unions; there will be a better working relationship between management and the union.
    b) Employers: only one union; to negotiate with; there will be a better working relationship between management and the union; disputes will probably be solved more quickly; it is easier to agree changes.

6 They represent employers and negotiate with trade unions, they give advice, they act as a pressure group.

7 To keep everyone happy – it is easier to negotiate with a group of workers rather than each worker individually. Collective agreements may help to ensure stability. Negotiation may 'define' potential conflicts.

8 This is where workers and management agree an increase in benefits, in return for an increase in productivity.

9 Discussion of, for example – strike, picketing, work to rule, go slow, non-cooperation,

overtime ban. (One mark for the example and two marks for explanation.)

10 For example, there may be disagreements over pay and conditions or the way particular workers are treated by the business. Redundancies, re-organisation or new work schedules may also cause conflict.

11 Establish formal grievance and dispute procedures and improve communication between management and workers.

12 a) (One mark per point and a second for explaining why it would be a problem.) For example: redundancies might occur and this would cause ill-feeling amongst the employees; need to retrain staff to handle new machines and this can be expensive; disputes may occur over new methods of pay.

    b) Answer depends on the examples given in (a) but an appreciation should be shown of how management can handle industrial relations problems. For example, discussion of how redundancy can be handled, such as redundancy pay, voluntary redundancy, last in first out, early retirement, retraining schemes, importance of good communication.

Unit 16

1 No, a market is simply where buyers and sellers come together.

2 For example: the Stock Market, market for computers, market for potatoes.

3 A product-orientated business is one where the main focus of activity is on the product itself, whilst a market-orientated business is where market research is carried out to find out what the customer wants.

4 If a business is entirely product-orientated then it may not be responding to consumer needs. It may be producing a product that is out of date or one that no longer meets the needs of customers. Market-orientated companies will probably take the customers away from the product-orientated companies and they will lose their markets.

5 Responds to customer needs; likely to increase sales because the customer is getting what they want; identifies gaps in the market and can produce the products to fill these gaps.

6 So that it can plan how to use the money most effectively – it must not waste money or spend money the business cannot afford.

7 To increase sales revenue and profitability; to increase or maintain market share; to maintain or improve the image of the product or a business; to target a new market or market segment; to develop new products or improve existing products.

8 To take a general look at the market before launching a new product; to assess the strengths and weaknesses of the product to see what needs to be improved or emphasised in the advertising; to assess the potential markets and the competition.

9

Strengths	Weaknesses
■ new product – first on the market ■ healthy drink – added vitamins	■ new production techniques
Opportunities	**Threats**
■ increasing trend for people to purchase healthy drinks ■ economy booming – more disposable income	■ competitors launch their own version of the health drink

10 Market segmentation is where the market has been divided up into groups of consumers who have similar needs. Student's examples should be discussed.

11 a) Segmented by income group – expensive furniture, cheaper furniture, etc. Or by age group if younger people in the market buy more fashionable furniture whilst older people buy more traditional furniture. Or by lifestyle as single flat-dwellers may require functional, modern furniture. Own examples of furniture to illustrate this.

    b) Breakfast cereals could be split up by age – children or adults, sex – male or female, lifestyle – health conscious, weight conscious. Student's examples of breakfast cereals to illustrate this.

12 Some customers in a market are not having their needs satisfied.

Unit 17

1 Research to find out about a particular market, for example, size, customer wants, competition. It includes primary and secondary research.

2 To find out about a market when launching or developing new products; to find out why sales are falling or not rising; to improve existing products; to remain competitive; to increase market share; to find out what kind of people buy their product; to find out which forms of promotion are most effective; to find out what price people are prepared to pay.

3 Qualitative information gathers opinions or judgements whereas quantitative information finds out about the quantity of something.

4 Primary research is original information carried out for a particular purpose whereas secondary research is second-hand information and was gathered by someone else for some purpose other than your own.

5 Questionnaires, interviews, consumer panels, observation.

6 Describe in detail how different types of primary research could be carried out, for example, a detailed description of how to carry out a questionnaire. More than one type of research can be credited.

7 Original information; relevant to needs; quality of information under the control of the company; information not available to the competition.

8 Examples might include:
   External sources – government statistics, information provided by trade associations, specialist journals, research reports, newspapers, government reports, media reports, market research agencies' reports – all related to the sports people play.
   Internal sources – Customer records from existing sports centres, Finance department.

9 For the highest marks it should be indicated how the example is of value to the company. For example, trade association statistics might provide information about the size of the market and the underlying trends. This would be of benefit to a company in determining its market share and therefore its relative performance. It may also help it to develop strategies for the future.

10 Reasons might include – the information being out of date; an unrepresentative sample filled in the questionnaire or were interviewed; too small a sample was questioned; badly designed questionnaire gave a misleading impression; newspaper articles may be biased.

11 To ensure that there is a market for the product in the other country; to find out what competition exists; to make sure the investment will yield a good return.

12 Discussion of factors such as: whether the questions should be closed or open; which questions need to be included; the questions should not be misleading – the phrasing needs to be considered; not too many questions should be included.

Unit 19

1 Consumer goods, consumer services, producer goods, producer services.

2 For example, the product should satisfy consumer needs, have a good design, have something very distinctive compared with the competition, and be not too expensive to produce.

3 Generate ideas about the new product – further research of best idea – decide if there will be a big enough market for the new product – develop a prototype – test launch in one part of the market – full launch.

4 This is a unique name for a product that makes it different to other brands.

5 a) Student's own examples, such as *Coca-Cola*.
   b) Student's own development of the examples in a).

6 That it will not be successful and the business will lose money.

7 a) Discussion of such things as: safety, eye-catching, carries information about the product.
   b) Discussion of such things as: protects the product, promotes the brand image, eye-catching, carries information about the product, pleasing shape, easy to handle.

8 The stages should be identified and axes labelled correctly.

9 The answer should include discussion of factors such as: nature of the product (e.g. fashion good); speed of innovation of new ideas; durability of the product leading to early saturation of the market. Suitable examples should also be included for maximum marks.

10 Product A has a typical product life cycle whereas product B appears to have had extension

strategies successfully applied. There should be a description of the changes in sales of the two products to go along with this explanation.

11 There should be discussion of factors such as: the nature of the product (e.g. fashion good); speed of innovation of new ideas; durability of the product leading to early saturation of the market; the extension strategies that have, or could, be used.

12 Introduction: price skimming as few/no competitors.
Growth: penetration pricing by competitors as a few competing products are introduced, small reduction in your prices to compete with these products.
Maturity: competitive pricing/promotional pricing as competition becomes intense.
Saturation: competitive pricing/prices are reduced to compete with existing competitors, no new competitors in the market.
Decline: price reductions to encourage sales as sales are falling. Some competitors stop making the product.

Unit 20

1 Where a product is wanted by the consumer but they must also be able to pay for the product.

2 Diagram

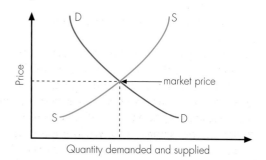

3 Rise in the price of substitute products; increase in demand due to effective advertising; the product becomes more fashionable; increase in consumers' income.

4 Market price falls and sales fall.

5 Elastic demand measures the sensitivity of changes in price – if demand is elastic then consumers are price sensitive, so if prices rise the quantity demanded will fall by a greater percentage than the increase in price. If demand

is inelastic then consumers are not price sensitive, so if prices rise the quantity demanded will fall by a smaller percentage than the increase in price.

6 Increase in taxes; increase in wage rates; increase in the price of raw materials.

7 Market price falls and sales increase.

8 Because it is difficult to increase the quantity supplied to the market very quickly.

9 Any two pricing methods from the following: price skimming, penetration pricing, cost-plus pricing, promotional pricing, competitive pricing, psychological pricing.

10 Answers should focus on either costs or the market, ideally indicating the part pricing decisions play in the overall marketing strategy of the business. Factors might include: product image; competitors' prices; costs of production; the stage of the product life cycle; entry into new markets.

11 a) £20
   b) about £22/23
   c) less than £20
   d) more than £25.

12 a) Skimming or psychological pricing – as it is a new and luxurious product, a high price can be charged.
   b) Cost-plus pricing – to make sure the profit is made.
   c) Yes, it should use promotional pricing to try to boost sales.

13 Explanation of points, such as: seasonal nature of some products (seasonal demand); cash flow problems; to stimulate spending at quiet times of the year.

Unit 21

1 Promotion gives consumers information about the rest of the marketing mix – without it consumers would not know about the product, the price it sells for and where it is sold. It is essential for the creation of a brand image.

2 Advertisements, promotion, personal selling, public relations.

3 To inform people about particular issues; to introduce new products into the market; to compete with competitor's products; to improve the company image; to increase sales, to create a brand image.

4 Set objectives; decide the advertising budget; create an advertising campaign; select the media to use; evaluate the effectiveness of the campaign applied to the new breakfast cereal.

5 a) Informative advertising is where the emphasis of advertising or sales promotion is to give full information about the product. Persuasive advertising is trying to persuade the consumer that they really need the product and should buy it.

  b) Student's own answer – most probably informative advertising.

6 The target audience is the people who are potential buyers of the product or service.

7 Radio, newspapers (local or national), magazines, television, internet, leaflets, direct mail, posters/billboards.

8 Student's own explanation.

9 a) The graph shows that sales and advertising expenditure are positively correlated in this case, i.e. if one increases then so does the other. However, there is a time lag between the advertising expenditure and its impact on sales. Thus, the rise in advertising expenditure in January is followed by an increase in sales in February.

  b) Advertising in this example does have an impact on sales. This does not mean that it is cost effective. The increased advertising costs may be higher than the increased revenue from more sales.

10 Advertising: raises product awareness; persuades people to try it; needs to persuade customers away from competitors' products, to which they may feel some loyalty.

11 Costs of advertising and packaging; competitors' brands; the nature of the product itself; market research on the impact of packaging and advertising.

12 Because products are different; the products are at different stages of their life cycle; the target market might be different. Student's own examples should be included.

13 When the exact nature of the product itself can change; when customers need advice on how their requirements may be met.

14 PR helps to promote a good image for the business. Student's own example should be included.

15 Could include: cut prices; special promotional offers; advertise more; change the menu.

Unit 22

1 Probably: Producer – agent – wholesaler – retailer – consumer.

2 Probably: Manufacturer – consumer, or Manufacturer – retailer – consumer.

3 For example, because they do not want to buy in large quantities; credit is given; advice on products is supplied; retailer is given a lot of choice of products to buy; to save storage space; wholesaler can buy cheaper in bulk from producer. (Two marks for each example that is explained.)

4 Advantages to the manufacturer: bulk buys; storage; reduced administration; reduced transport costs as fewer journeys; reduced promotional costs.

5 Advantages might include: wider market; potential for growth; new market segment; cuts out the middleman, creating the possibility of lower prices and therefore increased sales; not dependent on the retailer any more. Disadvantages might include: high transportation costs; not a high enough market demand; high marketing costs; loss of a regular market; competition.

6 Factors to consider: what is the type of product? Is the product very technical? How often is the product purchased? How expensive is the product? How perishable is the product? Where are the customers located? Where do competitors sell their product?

7 Roads, railways, canals and rivers, sea, air, pipelines.

8 How quickly the product needs to get to the customer – will the product go rotten quickly, e.g. bread needs to get to customers quickly or it will go stale. How expensive it is to transport – some products are very heavy and will be expensive to transport, for example, you would not use air freight to send coal to another country as it is heavy in relation to its price, whereas it may be suitable to use air freight for diamonds.

9 Possible disadvantages: cannot guarantee fast delivery; products may not arrive in a good condition; may not be able to advertise on the sides of vehicles. Possible advantage: no need to pay for upkeep and service of lorries, which is especially useful as they are not continually being used. Overall, it may be a cheaper option.

10 Student's own example, such as: sea to deliver to another country and then road once the goods have arrived in that country.

Unit 23

1 The difference between the final selling price and the cost of raw materials/components.
2 Output per head has increased by 50 units per day (150–100).
3 Increase in profits.
4 A single product is made at a time specifically to a customer's order.
5 A larger quantity is made at one time and is therefore cheaper to produce. It becomes easier to plan raw material requirements.
6 The workers would find their jobs more monotonous; investment needs are greater and so finance might be difficult; the product will have to be standardised; if one machine breaks down the whole production process must stop.
7 The size of the market; the type of product demanded; technological aspects of the product – can it be produced using flow production methods?
8 Advantages: sudden increases in demand can be met immediately; supply can be maintained when there are problems with production.
Disadvantages: cash flow problems; cash is tied up in stock; storage costs; stock might go out of date.
9 Advantages: reduced storage costs (less space is needed in warehouse); reduced expiry dates (stock will not go out of date and be of no use); less cash tied up in materials.
Disadvantages: raw materials/components need to be available on the production line when they are needed or production will cease; communication needs to be efficient to ensure orders arrive on time; if there are problems with delivery then production will stop.
10 Before minimum stock levels are reached (allowing time for delivery), so that there will be no hold up in production.
11 Lean production means the use of continuous improvement and the elimination of waste and delay to achieve greater efficiency.
12 For a certain amount of resources (employees, machinery, etc.) output has increased, for example, workers have been trained and they can now produce more goods in a day.
13 Discussion of, for example, employees having increased wages or increased job security, and owners of the business (shareholders in a Ltd/plc) having increased profits.

14 The Production department will have a changed production process, probably less staff will be needed and different skills will be required. The Human Resources department will possibly need to make some workers redundant, retrain some or recruit new employees with different skills.
15 To ensure that products are not sold which have faults, otherwise the business will get a bad reputation and sales will fall.

Unit 24

1 a) Advantages: more control over manufacture; raw materials and components may have to be exported as well, thus increasing costs; no need to recruit and/or train new employees; there may be strict planning regulations to comply with in the other market.
   b) Customer demand may be different; different climate; competition; cultural or religious differences.
2 To encourage/discourage foreign investment. To stop/encourage businesses locating in certain areas, for example, it would encourage businesses to locate in areas of high unemployment. To regulate pollution.
3 Any two from the following: closeness to the market or raw materials; availability of power and water; availability of government grants; transport links; availability of skilled labour; personal preference. (The importance of each factor needs to be discussed to gain extra marks.)
4 Whether the finished product is bulky to transport or whether the raw materials/components are more expensive to transport needs to be considered in determining where the cheapest place to locate the factory would be.
5 Explanation of the importance of any six of the following: market, raw materials/components, availability of labour, government influence, transport and communications, power, water supply, personal preference of the owners, climate.
6 Discussion of factors such as: will customers come specifically to the shop or do they want passing trade; rent paid on the shop; availability of vacant premises.
7 Discussion of factors such as: where the business customers are located; available vacant premises; personal preference of owners; availability of skilled employees; rent/taxes on the property; technology available.

8 Discussion of factors such as: primary sector businesses do not need to be near customers whereas service sector businesses may need to provide a personal service and have direct access to customers; primary sector will be governed by nature – suitable farming land or where the minerals are found; service sector will need to consider its customer needs much more and possibly where other businesses are located.

Unit 25

1 The price of one currency in terms of another.
2 Currency appreciation is when a currency buys more of another currency than before: e.g. €1:$2 changes to €1:$3.
  Currency depreciation is when one currency buys less of another currency than before: e.g. €1:$2.5 changes to €1:$2.
3 Currency appreciation will make the price of exports higher and therefore less competitive. But if the exporter imports materials and components they might benefit from lower prices for these goods.
4 Currency depreciation will make imports more expensive so the importing firm will lose competitiveness.
5 The EU single market creates a large market for all EU businesses with no barriers to trade at all.
6 The firm can import materials and components from other EU countries without any import tariffs. It can export to a much larger market with no trade barriers – this should give economies of scale.
7 A common currency exists when more than one country agrees to use the same currency for all transactions.
8 No exchange rate risks, e.g. if the firm exports to EU countries there is no risk of a currency appreciation making exports more expensive. No costs of converting one EU currency into another. Able to compare prices of supplies easily from any EU country.

9 Do not want the greater competition that the euro might bring. They want interest rates to be controlled by the Bank of England not by the European Central Bank. Do not want consumers to compare their prices easily with competitors from EU.
10 EU Social Charter – a series of measures which force all EU countries to give the same employment rights to workers. Designed to prevent firms in any EU country exploiting workers.
11 Students need to consider both sets of arguments before stating their views.
  For globalisation: cheaper goods, wider choice, more competition.
  Against globalisation: some firms/countries less able to compete, leads to unemployment and social problems.
12 Student's own example, but reasons given might include: obtain cheap raw materials; take advantage of cheap labour; enter new market; to avoid trade barriers; to produce goods closer to the market; to spread risks by operating in many different markets.
13 More competition for local fast food restaurants which may put some out of business. Might lead to local firms being forced to become more efficient. Multinational may buy supplies and services from local businesses.
14 a) Tariffs are taxes on imported goods and quotas are limits on the quantities of goods that may be imported.
  b) Students should give both sides of the argument before stating their views.
    For controls: limits imports and makes local firms more competitive; may protect local jobs; tariffs raise finance for the government.
    Against controls: raises prices; limits choice; reduces competition – may lead to local firms being less efficient; other countries may retaliate.

Glossary

accountant a professionally qualified person who has responsibility for keeping accurate accounts and for producing the final accounts

accounts the financial records of a firm's transactions

acquisition see **take-over**

added value the difference between the selling price of a product or service and the cost of inputs such as materials and components

agent an independent person or business that is appointed to deal with the sales and distribution of a product or range of products

AIDA model a simple way of planning an advert's design: it stands for attention, interest, desire, action

annual general meeting (AGM) a legal requirement for all companies; all shareholders may attend. They vote on who they want to be on the board of directors for the coming year and on other issues raised by the board or themselves

appraisal method of assessing the effectiveness of an employee, usually involving an interview with a senior member of staff

appropriation account the part of the profit and loss account which shows how the profit after tax is distributed – either as dividends or kept in the company as retained profits

arbitrator a person who listens to both sides in an industrial dispute (**trade union** and management) and then gives a ruling on what the arbitrator thinks is fair to both sides

assets the items of value which are owned by the business, e.g. land, buildings, equipment and vehicles

autocratic leadership instructions and strategies are issued from above with little opportunity for contributions to decision-making from less senior employees

average cost per unit the total cost of production divided by total output

balance of payments the record of the difference between a country's exports and imports

balance sheet shows the value of a firm's **assets** and **liabilities** at a particular time

batch production products are made in batches of a certain quantity, usually as orders come in

best fit see **line of best fit**

bonus an additional amount of payment above normal pay as a reward for good work

brand image where a product is given an image or identity to distinguish it from its competitors' brands

brand loyalty when consumers keep buying the same brand again and again instead of choosing a competitor's brand

brand name the unique name of a product that distinguishes it from other brands

break-even charts graphs showing how costs and revenues of a business change with sales; they show the level of sales the business must make in order to break even

break-even point the level of sales at which total costs equal total revenue

budgets plans for the future containing numerical or financial targets

business decisions these include **strategic decisions** (very important ones which can affect the overall success of the business), **tactical decisions** (those which are taken more frequently and which are less important) and **operational decisions** (day-to-day decisions which will be taken by lower-level managers)

capital the money invested into a business by the owners

capital expenditure money spent on **fixed assets** which will last for more than one year

cash flow the **cash inflows** and **outflows** over a period of time

cash flow cycle a means of showing the stages between paying out cash for labour, materials, etc. and receiving cash from the sale of goods

cash flow forecast an estimate of future **cash inflows** and **outflows** of a business, usually on a monthly basis

cash inflows the sums of money received by a business during a period of time

cash outflows the sums of money paid out by a business during a period of time

centralised a management structure in which most decisions are taken at the centre, or at higher levels of management

chain of command a structure within an organisation which allows instructions to be passed down from senior management to the lower levels of management

channel of distribution the means by which a product is passed from the place of production to the customer or retailer

closed shop all employees must be a member of the same trade union

closing cash (or bank) balance the amount of cash held by the business at the end of each month. This becomes next month's **opening cash balance**

collective bargaining negotiation between one or more trade unions and one or more employers (or **employers' associations**) on pay and conditions of employment

commission payment relating to the number of sales made

common currency an agreement between countries to use the same currency for all business and other transactions, such as the euro in the European Union

communication the transferring of a message from the sender to the receiver, who understands the message

communication nets the ways in which members of a group communicate with each other

competitive pricing a pricing strategy where the product is priced in line with, or just below, competitors' prices to try to capture more of the market

conglomerate integration a firm merges with or takes over another firm in a completely different industry. Also known as **diversification**

consumer panels groups of people who agree to provide information about a specific product or general spending patterns over a period of time

contract of employment a legal agreement between employer and employee listing the rights and responsibilities of workers

contribution the selling price of a product less its variable cost

corporation tax the tax paid by limited companies on their profits

cost-benefit analysis the valuation by a government agency of all social and private costs and benefits resulting from a decision

cost of goods sold the cost of the goods actually sold by the business during a time period

cost-plus pricing the cost of manufacturing the product plus a profit mark-up

craft union a trade union which represents a particular type of skilled worker

currency appreciation occurs when the value of a currency rises – it buys more of another currency than before

currency depreciation occurs when the value of a currency falls – it buys less of another currency than before

current assets the **assets** such as cash, stocks and **debtors** which are held for only short periods of time

current liabilities see **liabilities**

debtors customers who owe money to the business

decentralised a management structure in which many decisions are not taken at the centre of the business but are delegated to lower levels of management

de-industrialisation occurs when there is a decline in the importance of the **secondary** (or manufacturing) **sector** of industry in a country

delegation giving a subordinate the authority to perform particular tasks (NB it is the authority to perform a task which is being delegated – not the final responsibility)

democratic leadership senior employees consult with junior ones in policy-making

depreciation the fall in the value of a **fixed asset** over time

desk research see **secondary research**

development area a region of a country where businesses will receive financial support to establish themselves (often regions of high unemployment)

direct costs costs that can be directly related to or identified with a particular product or department

direct taxes taxes paid directly from incomes, such as income tax or profits tax

diseconomies of scale the factors that lead to an increase in average costs as a business grows beyond a certain size

disposable income the level of income a taxpayer has after paying income tax

diversification see **conglomerate integration**

dividends payments made to shareholders from the profits of a company after it has paid corporation tax

division of labour when the production process is split up into different tasks and each worker performs one of these tasks. Also known as **specialisation**

e-commerce the use of the internet and electronic communications to carry out business transactions

economic growth when a country's **gross domestic product** increases – more goods and services are produced than in the previous year

economic problem the fact that there are unlimited **wants** but limited resources to produce the goods and services to satisfy those wants. This creates **scarcity**

economies of scale the factors that lead to a reduction in average costs as a business increases in size

employer federation see **employers' association**

employers' association a group of employers join together to give benefits to their members. Also called **employer federations** and **trade associations**

ethical decision a decision taken by a manager or company because of the moral code observed in that firm

exchange rate appreciation when the value of a country's currency rises compared to other currencies

exchange rate depreciation when the value of a country's currency falls compared with other currencies

exchange rates the price of one currency in terms of another, e.g. £1:$1.5

exports goods and services sold from one country to other countries

external benefits see **social benefits**

external communication messages between one organisation and another organisation or individuals not employed in the business

external costs see **social costs**

external growth occurs when a business takes over or merges with another business. Often called **integration** (see **vertical integration** and **horizontal integration**) as one firm is integrated into another one

external recruitment the vacancy is filled by someone who is not an existing employee and will be new to the business

external sources sources of information outside the company used to compile market research as a basis for marketing decisions

factors of production resources needed to produce goods or services

feedback the response from the receiver of a message which shows whether the message has been understood and, if necessary, acted upon

field research see **primary research**

final accounts accounts produced at the end of the year giving details of the profit or loss made over the year and the worth of the business

fixed assets the **assets** which are likely to be kept by the business for more than one year. Most fixed assets, apart from land, **depreciate** over time so the value of these will fall on the balance sheet from one year to the next

fixed costs costs which do not vary with the number of items sold or produced in the short term

flow production large quantities of a product are produced in a continuous process. Also called **mass production** because of the large quantity of a standardised product that is produced

forecasts predictions of the future, e.g. likely future changes in the size of the market

formal group a group designated to carry out specific tasks within a business

freight a term used to describe bulk goods or products while they are being transported

fringe benefits non-monetary rewards given to employees

general union a trade union which represents workers (often unskilled but also including semi-skilled) from a variety of trades

globalisation increase in worldwide competition between businesses

go slow a form of **industrial action** when the employees do their normal tasks but more slowly than usual

gross domestic product (GDP) the total value of output of goods and services in a country in one year

gross profit profit made when **sales revenue** is greater than the cost of goods sold

haulage the transport of bulk goods or products; usually refers to road transport but can also refer to rail transport

horizontal integration one firm merges with or takes over another one in the same industry at the same stage of production

imports goods and services bought in by one country from other countries

indirect costs costs which cannot be directly related to a particular product. Often called **overheads** or **overhead costs**

indirect taxes taxes added to the prices of goods. Tax payers pay the tax as they purchase the goods, e.g. value added tax (VAT)

induction training introduction given to a new employee, explaining the firm's **organisational structure**, activities and procedures

industrial action steps taken by **trade unions** to decrease or halt production

industrial tribunal a legal meeting which considers workers' complaints of unfair dismissal or discrimination at work

industrial union a **trade union** which represents all types of workers in a particular industry

inflation the increase in the average price level of goods and services over time

informal group group of people who form independently of any official groups because they have interests or aims in common

informative advertising advertising where the emphasis of advertising or sales promotion is to give full information about the product

integration see **vertical**, **horizontal** and **conglomerate integration**

internal communication messages between people working in the same organisation

internal growth occurs when a business expands its existing operations

internal recruitment the vacancy is filled by someone who is an existing employee of the business

internal sources sources of information within the company, used to compile market research as a basis for marketing decisions

job analysis the responsibilities and tasks relating to a job are identified and recorded

job description document which outlines the responsibilities and duties expected to be carried out by someone employed to do a specific job

job enlargement where extra tasks of a similar level of work are added to a worker's **job description**

job enrichment involves looking at jobs and adding tasks that require more skill and/or responsibility

job production a single product is made at a time, usually to the customer's exact specifications

job rotation involves the workers doing each specific task for only a limited time and then changing round on a regular basis

job satisfaction enjoyment derived from feeling that you have done a good job

job specification document which outlines the requirements, qualifications and expertise required from a person to do a specific job

just-in-time (JIT) a production method that involves reducing or virtually eliminating the need to hold stocks of raw materials or unsold stocks of the finished product

Kaizen production Kaizen is a Japanese term meaning *continuous improvement*, through the elimination of waste

laissez-faire **leadership** employees are left to make many of the decisions rather than receiving clear instructions from their seniors

lead time the margin of time between the date when stock is obtained and the date when it is sold on

leadership styles approaches to dealing with people when in a position of authority. See also **autocratic**, *laissez-faire* and **democratic**

lean production techniques used by business to cut down on any waste and therefore increase efficiency, for example, by reducing the time it takes for the product to be developed and made available for sale

liabilities items owed by the business. **Long-term liabilities** are long-term borrowings which do not have to be repaid within one year. **Current liabilities** are amounts owed by the business which must be repaid within one year

limited liability where the owners of a company cannot be held responsible for the debts of the company they own

line managers managers with direct authority over subordinates in their department; they are able to take decisions in their departmental area

line of best fit a line drawn through a series of points, e.g. sales data, which best shows the trend of that data

liquidity the ability of a business to pay back its short-term debts

lock-out employees are locked out of their workplace

long-term liabilities see **liabilities**

marginal costs extra costs a business will incur by producing one more unit of output

market where buyers and sellers come together to exchange products for money; this will not usually be a single location

marketing the management process which identifies customer **wants** and anticipates their future wants

marketing budget a financial plan for the marketing of a product or product range for a specified period of time

market-orientated a description applied to a business in which **market research** is carried out to find out consumer wants before a product is developed and produced

market research finds out consumer **wants** before a product is developed and produced

market segmentation the market is divided up into groups of consumers who have similar **needs**

mass production see **flow production**

medium of communication the method used to send a message

merger when the owners of two businesses agree to join their firms together to make one business

message the information or instructions being passed by the **sender** to the **receiver**

monopoly a business which controls all of the market for a product

motivation why employees want to work effectively for the business

multinational businesses those with factories, production or service operations in more than one country. Also known as **transnational businesses**

needs goods or services essential for living

negotiation another name for **collective bargaining** – joint decision-making involving bargaining between representatives of the management and of the workforce within a firm

net cash flow the difference, each month, between **cash inflows** and **outflows**

net profit profit made by a business after all costs have been deducted from **sales revenue**; it is calculated by subtracting **overhead costs** from **gross profits**

non-cooperation a form of **industrial action** when employees refuse to comply with new working practices

no-strike agreements when **trade unions** and management agree to have pay disputes settled by an independent **arbitrator** instead of taking **strike action**

off-the-job training being trained away from the workplace, usually by specialist trainers

one-way communication transmission of a message which does not call for or require a response

on-the-job training watching a more experienced worker doing the job and learning skills under their supervision

opening cash (or bank) balance the amount of cash held by the business at the start of the month

operational decisions see **business decisions**

opportunity cost the next best alternative given up by choosing another item

organisational structure the levels of management and division of responsibilities within an organisation

overheads/overhead costs see **indirect costs**

overtime ban a form of **industrial action** when employees refuse to work longer than their normal working hours

packaging the physical container or wrapping for a product, also used for promotional purposes

partnership agreement the written and legal agreement between business partners

penetration pricing a pricing strategy where price is set lower than the competitors' prices in order to be able to enter a new market

performance-related pay pay related to the effectiveness of the employee

persuasive advertising advertising or promotion which is trying to persuade the consumer that they really need the product and should buy it

picketing a form of industrial action; employees who are taking action stand outside their workplace to prevent or protest at the delivery of goods, arrival and departure of other employees, etc.

pictogram a means of showing data, in which pictorial symbols are used to represent fixed numbers of items

pie chart a circular graph used to show what proportion of the collected data comes into each of the chosen categories

planning permission when a government body allows a business to build a factory or office in a particular location

point of sale the place where the product is being sold, usually a shop

pressure groups groups formed by people who share a common interest and who will take action to achieve the changes they are seeking

price skimming a pricing strategy where a high price is set for a new product on the market

primary research the collection and collation of original data via direct contact with potential or existing customers. Also called **field research**

primary sector industry which extracts the natural resources of the earth

private benefits the financial gains made by a business as a result of a business decision

private costs the costs of a business decision actually paid for by the business

production is the provision of a product or a service to satisfy consumer **wants** and **needs**

productivity the output measured against the inputs used to create it

productivity agreement workers and management agree an increase in benefits, in return for an increase in productivity

product life cycle the stages a product will pass through from its introduction, through its growth until it is mature and then finally its decline

product-orientated a description applied to a business whose main focus of activity is on the product itself. See also **market-orientated**

profit and loss account account showing how the **net profit** of a business and the **retained profit** of a company are calculated

profit-sharing a proportion of the profits is paid out to employees

promotional pricing a pricing strategy where the product is sold at a very low price for a short period of time

prospectus a detailed document issued by the directors of a company when they are converting it to public limited company status. It is an invitation to the general public to buy shares in the newly formed plc

psychological pricing a pricing strategy where particular attention is paid to the effect that the price of a product will have upon consumers' perceptions of the product

public relations policies, strategies or measures taken to promote a good image for a company and/or its products

questionnaires a set of questions to be answered as a means of collecting data for **market research**

quota sample people selected on the basis of certain characteristics (e.g. age, gender, income) as a source of information for **market research**

random sample people selected at random as a source of information for **market research**

real income the value of income in the context of current price levels

receiver in communication, the person who receives a **message**

redundancy when an employee loses their job because they are no longer needed, rather than due to any aspect of their work being unsatisfactory. Also called **retrenchment**

representative (union) person with responsibility to communicate **trade union** information between members and regional offices and to represent the union members to management

retailer a retailer is an outlet selling goods direct to the customer (see also **wholesaler**). Some producers are also retailers, having their own retail branches as well as their own production sites

retrenchment see **redundancy**

revenue the income during a period of time from the sale of goods and services

revenue expenditure money spent on day to day expenses which do not involve the purchase of a long-term **asset**, e.g. **wages** and rent

salary payment for work, usually paid monthly. See also **wage**

sales revenue the income to a business during a period of time from the sale of goods or services

scarcity the lack of sufficient products to fulfil the total **wants** of the population

secondary research the use of information that has already been collected and is available for use by others. Also called **desk research**

secondary sector industry which manufactures goods using the raw materials provided by the **primary sector**

segment a specific group of customers or potential customers. See **market segmentation**

sender see **transmitter**

shareholders the owners of a limited company; they have bought **shares** which represent part ownership of a company

shop steward an unpaid representative of a **trade union** at factory/office level

single-union agreement a firm will deal only with one particular **trade union** and no others

social benefits the gains to society resulting from a business decision. Also known as **external benefits**

social costs the costs paid by the rest of society, rather than the business, as a result of a business decision. Also known as **external costs** because they are costs paid for by the rest of society 'outside' the business

span of control the number of subordinates working directly under a manager

specialisation see **division of labour**

staff managers specialist advisers who provide support to line managers and to the board of directors

stakeholders groups in society who have a direct interest in the performance and activities of business

start-up capital the finance needed by a new business to pay for essential **fixed** and **current assets** before it can begin trading

strategic decisions see **business decisions**

strike a form of industrial action where employees refuse to work

tactical decisions see **business decisions**

take-over when one business buys out the owners of another business which then becomes part of the 'predator' business, i.e. the firm which has taken it over. Also called **acquisition**

target audience people who are potential buyers of a product or service

target market the group of people for whom a particular product is designed

tertiary sector industry which provides services to consumers and the other sectors of industry

total costs the combined total of **fixed costs** and **variable costs**

total quality management (TQM) the continuous improvement of products and processes by focusing on quality at each stage of production

trade association see **employers' association**

trade union a group of workers join together to ensure their interests are protected

trading account shows how the **gross profit** of a business is calculated

transmitter the **sender** of a **message**, the person starting off the process by sending the message

transnational businesses see **multinational businesses**

trend the underlying movement or direction of data over time

two-way communication when a **receiver** gives a response to a **message** and there is a discussion about it

unemployment when people who are willing and able to work cannot find a job

unincorporated business one which does not have a separate legal identity. See also **sole traders** and **partnerships**

unit cost the cost of producing one item, i.e. total costs of production divided by total output

variable costs costs which vary with the number of items sold or produced. They are often called **direct costs** as they can be directly related to or identified with a particular product

vertical integration when one firm merges with or takes over another one in the same industry but at a different stage of production. Vertical integration can be *forward* (a firm integrates with another firm which is at a later stage of production, i.e. closer to the consumer) or *backward* (a firm integrates with another firm at an earlier stage of production, i.e. closer to the raw material supplies)

wage payment for work, usually paid weekly. See also **salary**

wants goods or services which people would like to have but which are not essential for living

white-collar union a **trade union** which represents non-manual workers (office workers, management and professional staff)

wholesaler a wholesaler buys in bulk (large quantities) from the manufacturer and sells on smaller quantities either to **retailers** or, occasionally, direct to customers

worker participation the employees contribute to decision-making in the business. See also **works councils** and **democratic leadership**

works councils committees, made up of workers, who are consulted or informed on matters that affect employees

work to rule a form of **industrial action** when rules are strictly obeyed so that work is slowed down

Index